# SAT® Subject Test:

## LITERATURE

## 2015–2016

# OTHER KAPLAN BOOKS FOR COLLEGE-BOUND STUDENTS

AP Biology
AP Calculus AB & BC
AP Chemistry
AP English Language & Composition
AP English Literature & Composition
AP Environmental Science
AP European History
AP Human Geography
AP Macroeconomics/Microeconomics
AP Physics B & C
AP Psychology
AP Statistics
AP U.S. Government & Politics
AP U.S. History
AP World History

ACT Strategies, Practice, and Personalized Feedback
ACT 6 Practice Tests with 12 Expert Video Tutorials

SAT Strategies, Practice, and Review
SAT Premier
12 Practice Tests for the SAT
SAT Critical Reading Workbook
SAT Math Workbook
SAT Writing Workbook

Frankenstein: A Kaplan Score-Raising Classic
The Tales of Edgar Allan Poe: A Kaplan Score-Raising Classic
Dr. Jekyll and Mr. Hyde: A Kaplan Score-Raising Classic
The Scarlet Letter: A Kaplan Score-Raising Classic
The War of the Worlds: A Kaplan Score-Raising Classic
Wuthering Heights: A Kaplan Score-Raising Classic

SAT Subject Test: Biology E/M
SAT Subject Test: Chemistry
SAT Subject Test: Mathematics Level 1
SAT Subject Test: Mathematics Level 2
SAT Subject Test: Physics
SAT Subject Test: U.S. History

# SAT® Subject Test:

## LITERATURE

### 2013–2014

**Tony Armstrong**

PUBLISHING

New York

© 2015 by Kaplan, Inc.

Published by Kaplan Publishing, a division of Kaplan, Inc.
395 Hudson Street
New York, NY 10014

Stress Management chapter by Dr. Ed Newman and Bob Verini. © 1996, Kaplan, Inc.

Excerpt from AMADEUS: A PLAY BY PETER SHAFFER. © 1981, 2001 by Peter Shaffer. Reprinted by permission of HarperCollins Publishers.

Excerpt from THE REMAINS OF THE DAY by Kazuo Ishiguro. © 1989 Kazuo Ishiguro. Reprinted by permission of Alfred A. Knopf, a division of Random House, Inc.

"I and Your Eyes" from THE ESSENTIAL ETHERIDGE KNIGHT by Etheridge Knight. © 1986. Reprinted by permission of the University of Pittsburgh Press.

"The Boarder" from A DREAM OF GOVERNORS by Louis Simpson. © 1959 by Louis Simpson. Reprinted by permission of Wesleyan University Press.

"Merritt Parkway" from COLLECTED EARLIER POEMS 1940–1960 by Denise Levertov. © 1958 by Denise Levertov. Reprinted by permission of New Directions Publishing Corp.

"The Train from Rhodesia" from SELECTED STORIES by Nadine Gordimer. © 1950 by Nadine Gordimer, renewed in 1978 by Nadine Gordimer. Reprinted by permission of Russell & Volkening as agents for the author.

Printed in the United States of America

10 9 8 7 6 5 4 3 2 1

ISBN-13: 978-1-61865-849-4

Kaplan Publishing books are available at special quantity discounts to use for sales promotions, employee premiums, or educational purposes. For more information or to purchase books, please call the Simon & Schuster special sales department at 866-506-1949.

# Table of Contents

# ABOUT THE AUTHOR

**Tony Armstrong** has been teaching American and British literature and humanities courses at North Central High School in Indianapolis, Indiana, since 1990. He is finishing up his MA in English at Indiana University, from which he also has his English BA. Since the mid-1990s, he has performed various tasks for ETS/College Board, including emending current versions and writing test items for future editions of the SAT Subject Test: Literature, as well as writing items for the PRAXIS exams.

Tony would like to thank Grace Freedson, Don Reis, Jan Guffin, Anne Connell, Kathy Allison, Jocelyn Sisson, Kellard Townsend, Becca Bucalos, Elizabeth Newkirk, Susan Weatherly, Max, Lucy, the longsuffering Tiffany, and J.C.

# AVAILABLE ONLINE

## FOR ANY TEST CHANGES OR LATE-BREAKING DEVELOPMENTS
kaptest.com/publishing

The material in this book is up-to-date at the time of publication. However, the College Board and Educational Testing Service (ETS) may have instituted changes in the test after this book was published. Be sure to read the materials you receive when you register for the test.

If there are any important late-breaking developments—or any changes or corrections to the Kaplan test preparation materials in this book—we will post that information online at **kaptest.com/publishing**.

For customer service, please contact us at **booksupport@kaplan.com**.

Part One

# The Basics

# Chapter 1: **About the SAT Subject Tests**

- Frequently Asked Questions
- SAT Subject Test Mastery

You're serious about going to the college of your choice. You wouldn't have opened this book otherwise. You've made a wise decision, because this book can help you to achieve your college admissions goal. It'll show you how to score your best on the SAT Subject Test: Literature. But before you begin to prepare for the Literature Test, you need some general information about the SAT Subject Tests and how this book will help you prep.

## FREQUENTLY ASKED QUESTIONS

Before you dive into the specifics of the content of the SAT Subject Test: Literature, check out the following FAQs (frequently asked questions) about SAT Subject Tests in general. The information here is accurate at the time of publication, but it's a good idea to check the test information at the College Board website at collegeboard.com.

### What Are the SAT Subject Tests?

Known until recently as the College Board Achievement Tests, the SAT Subject Tests focus on specific disciplines such as English, U.S. history, world history, mathematics, physical sciences, and foreign languages. Each Subject Test lasts one hour and consists almost entirely of multiple-choice questions.

### How Do the SAT Subject Tests Differ from the SAT?

The SAT is largely a test of verbal and math skills. True, you need to know some vocabulary and some formulas for the SAT, but it's designed to measure how well you read and think rather than what you know. SAT Subject Tests are very different. They're designed to measure what you know about specific disciplines. Sure, critical reading and thinking skills play a part on these tests, but their main purpose is to determine exactly what you know about writing, math, history, chemistry, and so on.

The Literature Test is designed to measure your abilities in *close* reading of texts by asking questions about narrative elements, rhetorical devices, contextual meaning, and the like.

## How Do Colleges Use the SAT Subject Tests?

Many people will tell you that the SATs measure only your ability to perform on standardized exams—that they measure neither your reading and thinking skills nor your level of knowledge. Maybe they're right. But these people don't work for colleges. Those schools that require SATs feel that they are an important indicator of your ability to succeed in college. Specifically, they use your scores in one or both of two ways:

1. To help them make admissions decisions
2. To help them make placement decisions

Like the SAT, the SAT Subject Tests provide schools with a standard measure of academic performance, which they use to compare you to applicants from different high schools and different educational backgrounds. This information helps them to decide whether you're ready to handle their curriculum.

SAT Subject Test scores may also be used to decide what course of study is appropriate for you once you've been admitted. A low score on the English Language Test, for example, may mean that you have to take a remedial English course. Conversely, a high score on the Mathematics Level 2 Test may mean that you'll be exempted from an introductory math course.

## What SAT Subject Tests Should I Take?

The simple answer is: take the ones that you'll do well on. High scores, after all, can only help your chances for admission. Unfortunately, many colleges demand that you take particular tests, usually one of the Math Tests. Some schools will give you some choice in the matter, especially if they want you to take a total of three Subject Tests. So before you register to take any tests, check with colleges to find out exactly which tests they require. Don't rely on high school guidance counselors or admissions handbooks for this information. They might not give you accurate details.

## When Can I Take the SAT Subject Tests?

Most of the SAT Subject Tests are administered six times a year: in October, November, December, January, May, and June. A few of the Subject Tests are offered less frequently. Due to admissions deadlines, many colleges insist that you take SAT Subject Tests no later than December or January of your senior year in high school. You may even have to take them sooner if you're interested in applying for "early admission" to a school. Those schools that use scores only for placement decisions may allow you to take the Subject Tests as late as May or June of your senior year. You should check with colleges to find out which test dates are most appropriate for you.

You can take up to three Subject Tests on the same day.

## How Do I Register for the SAT Subject Tests?

The College Board administers the SAT Subject Tests, so you must sign up for the tests with them. The easiest way to register is online. Visit the College Board's website at collegeboard.com and click on "Register for the SAT" for registration information. If you register online, you immediately get to choose your test date and test center, and you have 24-hour access to print your admission ticket. You'll need access to a credit card to complete online registration.

If you would prefer to register by mail, you must obtain a copy of the *SAT Paper Registration Guide*. This publication contains all of the necessary information, including current test dates and fees. It can be obtained at any high school guidance office or directly from the College Board.

> **DO THE LEGWORK**
>
> Want to register for an SAT Subject Test or get more info? Ask your school counselor's office for the *SAT Paper Registration Guide*, which contains a Registration Form, test dates, fees, and instructions.
>
> **By mail:** Mail in the Registration Form to the College Board.
>
> **Online:** If you have a credit card, you can register online at collegeboard.com.

## How Are the SAT Subject Tests Scored?

Like the SAT, SAT Subject Tests are scored on a 200–800 scale. If you just sign your name and leave, you get 200 points. Get everything right, or miss just a few questions, and you get a perfect score of 800 in most cases. There are always variables to consider, but this is a general explanation of the scoring.

## What's a "Good" Score?

That's tricky. The obvious answer is: the score that the college of your choice demands. Keep in mind, though, that SAT Subject Test scores are just one piece of information that colleges will use to evaluate you. The decision to accept or reject you will be based on many criteria, including your high school transcript, your SAT score, your recommendations, your personal statement, your interview (where applicable), your extracurricular activities, and the like. So failure to achieve the necessary score doesn't automatically mean that your chances of getting in have been damaged. For those who want a numerical benchmark, a score of 600 is considered very solid.

### What Should I Bring to the SAT Subject Tests?

It's a good idea to get your test materials together the day before the tests. You'll need an admission ticket, a form of identification (check the *Registration Guide or* College Board's website to find out what is and what is not permissible), a few sharpened No. 2 pencils, a good eraser, and a calculator (for Math Levels 1 and 2). If you'll be registering as a standby, collect the appropriate forms beforehand. Also, make sure that you have good directions to the test center. (We even recommend that you do a dry run getting to the site prior to test day—it can save you the grief of getting lost!)

## SAT SUBJECT TEST MASTERY

Now that you know a little about the SAT Subject Tests, it's time to let you in on a few basic test-taking skills and strategies that can improve your scoring performance. You should practice these skills and strategies as you prepare for your SAT Subject Tests.

### Use the Test Structure to Your Advantage

The SAT Subject Tests are different from the tests that you're used to taking. On your high school exams, you probably go through the questions in order. You probably spend more time on hard questions than on easy ones, since hard questions are generally worth more points. And you often show your work, since your teachers tell you that how you approach questions is as important as getting the right answers.

Well, forget all that! None of this applies to the SAT Subject Tests. You can benefit from moving around within the tests, hard questions are worth the same points as easy ones, and it doesn't matter how you answer the questions or what work you did to get there—only what your answers are.

**The SAT Subject Tests are highly predictable**. Because the format and directions of the SAT Subject Tests remain unchanged from test to test, you can learn how the tests are set up in advance. On test day, the various question types on the tests shouldn't be new to you.

One of the easiest things you can do to help your performance on the SAT Subject Tests is to understand the directions before taking the test. Since the instructions are always the same, there's no reason to waste a lot of time on test day reading them. Learn them beforehand, as you work through this book and study the College Board publications.

**Many SAT Subject Test questions are arranged by order of difficulty**. Not all of the questions on the SAT Subject Tests are equally difficult. The questions often get harder as you work through different parts of the test. This pattern can work to your benefit. As you work, you should always be aware of where you are in the test.

---

**NOT LIKE HIGH SCHOOL**

The SAT Subject Tests are very different from test you've taken in high school. All questions are worth the same number of points, and you don't get any credit for showing your work.

**DON'T GET LOST**

Learn SAT Subject Test directions as you prepare for the tests. You'll have more time to spend answering the questions on test day.

**LOOK FOR CLUES**

Where a question appears on an SAT Subject Test can tell you something about how to approach it. Many questions on the Subject Tests are arranged in order of difficulty—easier questions first, harder questions last.

When working on more basic problems, you can generally trust your first impulse—the obvious answer is likely to be correct. As you get to the end of a test section, you need to be a bit more suspicious. Now the answers probably won't come as quickly and easily—if they do, look again because the obvious answers may be wrong. Watch out for answers that just "look right." They may be distracters—wrong answer choices deliberately meant to entice you.

**You don't need to answer the questions in order**. You're allowed to skip around on the SAT Subject Tests. High scorers know this fact. They move through the tests efficiently. They don't dwell on any one question, even a hard one, until they've tried every question at least once.

When you run into questions that look tough, circle them in your test booklet and skip them for the time being. Go back and try again after you've answered the more basic ones—if you've got time. On a second look, troublesome questions can turn out to be remarkably simple.

If you've started to answer a question but get confused, quit and go on to the next question. Persistence may pay off in high school, but it usually hurts your SAT Subject Test scores. Don't spend so much time answering one hard question that you use up three or four questions' worth of time. That'll cost you points, especially if you don't even get the hard question right.

**The SAT Subject Tests have a "guessing penalty" that can actually work in your favor**. The College Board likes to talk about the guessing penalty on the SAT Subject Tests. That's a misnomer. It's really a wrong answer penalty. If you guess wrong, you get penalized. If you guess right, you're in great shape.

The fact is, if you can eliminate one or more answer choices as definitely wrong, you'll turn the odds in your favor and actually come out ahead by guessing. The fractional points that you lose are meant to offset the points you might get "accidentally" by guessing the correct answer. With practice, however, you'll see that it's often easy to eliminate several answer choices on some of the questions.

**The SAT Subject Test answer grid has no heart**. It sounds simple, but it's extremely important: Don't make mistakes filling out your answer grid. When time is short, it's easy to get confused going back and forth between your test booklet and your grid. If you know the answers, but misgrid, you won't get the points. Here's how to avoid mistakes.

*Always circle the questions you skip*. Put a big circle in your test booklet around any question numbers that you skip. When you go back, these questions will be easy to relocate. Also, if you accidentally skip a box on the grid, you can check your grid against your booklet to see where you went wrong.

---

### SKIPPING ALLOWED

You should do the questions in the order that's best for you. Don't pass up the chance to score easy points by wasting time on hard questions. Skip hard questions until you've gone through every question once. Come back to them later, time permitting.

---

### GUESSING RULE

Don't guess, unless you can eliminate at least one answer choice. Don't leave a question blank, unless you have absolutely no idea about it.

---

### HIT THE SPOT

A common cause of major SAT Subject Test disasters is filling in all of the questions with the right answers—in the wrong spots. Every time you skip a question, circle it in your test booklet and be double sure that you skip it on the answer grid as well.

| **THINK FIRST** |

---

**THINK FIRST**

Always try to think of the answer to a question before you shop among the answer choices. If you've got some idea of what you're looking for, you're less likely to be fooled by "trap" choices.

---

**SPEED LIMIT**

Work quickly on easier questions to leave more time for harder questions—but not so quickly that you lose points by making careless errors. And it's okay to leave some questions blank if you have to—even if you leave a few blank, you can still get a high score.

---

*Always circle the answers you choose*. Circling your answers in the test booklet makes it easier to check your grid against your booklet.

*Grid five or more answers at once*. Don't transfer your answers to the grid after every question. Transfer them after every five questions. That way, you won't keep breaking your concentration to mark the grid. You'll save time and gain accuracy.

## A Strategic Approach to SAT Subject Test Questions

Apart from knowing the setup of the SAT Subject Tests that you'll be taking, you've got to have a system for attacking the questions. You wouldn't travel around an unfamiliar city without a map, and you shouldn't approach the SAT Subject Tests without a plan. What follows is the best method for approaching SAT Subject Test questions systematically.

**Think about the questions before you look at the answers**. The College Board loves to put distracters among the answer choices. Distracters are answers that look like they're correct but aren't. If you jump right into the answer choices without thinking first about what you're looking for, you're much more likely to fall for one of these traps.

**Guess—when you can eliminate at least one answer choice.** You already know that the "guessing penalty" can work in your favor. Don't simply skip questions that you can't answer. Spend some time with them to see whether you can eliminate any of the answer choices. If you can, it pays for you to guess.

**Pace yourself**. The SAT Subject Tests give you a lot of questions in a short time. To get through the tests, you can't spend too much time on any single question. Keep moving through the tests at a good speed. If you run into a hard question, circle it in your test booklet, skip it, and come back to it later if you have time.

You don't have to spend the same amount of time on every question. Ideally, you should be able to work through the more basic questions at a brisk, steady clip and use a little more time on the harder questions. One caution: Don't rush through easier questions just to save time for the harder ones. The basic questions are points in your pocket, and you're better off not getting to some harder questions if doing so would mean losing easy points because of careless mistakes. Remember, you don't get extra credit for answering hard questions.

**Locate quick points if you're running out of time**. Some questions can be done more quickly than others because they require less work or because choices can be eliminated more easily. If you start to run out of time, locate and answer any of the quick points that remain.

# Chapter 2: **Getting Ready for the SAT Subject Test: Literature**

- Time
- Test Layout
- Types of Passages
- Types of Questions
- Test-Taking Do's
- Test-Taking Don'ts
- Stress Management
- Tips for Just Before the Test

## TIME

You will have 60 minutes to complete the exam. Keep in mind that the test will contain 6 to 8 literary passages and you will have to answer anywhere from 4 to 12 multiple-choice questions about each. If you give yourself an average of 2 minutes to read each passage, you will have almost $\frac{3}{4}$ of a minute to answer each question.

## TEST LAYOUT

A passage will appear on the first page of the test. Only occasionally will a title appear above a poetry selection. Otherwise, you can expect that a literary piece will remain *unidentified* by either title or author. However, the year of publication will almost always appear in parentheses after the passage.

Anywhere from 4 to 12 questions with 5 possible multiple-choice answers apiece will follow the literary passages; the number of questions will depend on the length and complexity of the piece. After you answer these questions, you will move on to the next passage, which will have its own set of questions, and so on.

# TYPES OF PASSAGES

## Genre

You may expect almost any literary genre to appear on the test. There might be epic, dramatic, lyric, expository, narrative, or imagistic poetry; closed or open form poetry; complete poems or poetic excerpts; excerpts from short stories, novels, novellas, or novelettes; excerpted essays, biographies, autobiographies, diaries, journals, or histories; and although they do not appear as often, you might even see play excerpts.

## Time Period

One distinctive feature about the SAT Subject Test: Literature is that it examines the way literature uses the English language. Therefore, you will never see a passage on the test taken from any time period earlier than the Renaissance—the Middle English of Medieval times and the Old English of the Anglo-Saxon period are too foreign to be considered English anymore. Nor will you see a contemporary translation of any pre-Renaissance work. A translation removes us from the original words intended by the primary author; we can't closely examine a literary work's original language if it is in translation. So don't worry about seeing any version of *Beowulf*, "The Wanderer," "The Seafarer," *The Canterbury Tales*, *Sir Gawain and the Green Knight*, or the like.

You will, however, more than likely see the following on the test:

- At least one work from the Renaissance or the 17th century
- At least one work from the 18th century
- At least two works from the 19th century
- Representative works from the 20th century

Any mixture of prose and poetry could appear from these eras.

## Author

As long as he or she is writing in English and has written during or after the Renaissance, any published author's work may be used for the test. Again, since the SAT Subject Test wants to study English language, no non-English works or their translations will be used. Therefore, if you were planning on reviewing material written by Dante, Sappho, Tolstoy, Flaubert, Goethe, or some other author who does not write in English, don't bother.

The test makers for the Literature Test are also careful to include works from women writers and authors of color. Dead white males may have dominated Western literature for the past several centuries, but they don't have to reign absolute on the SAT Subject Test: Literature.

## Content

The usual topics can be found in the content of the test's passages: love, life, death, nature, society, family, tradition, human foibles. Once in a while, a less serious idea may slip in as well: social embarrassment, sibling rivalry, or a walk down the street. As long as the passage contains literary merit and can inspire a variety of questions, it can be used for the test.

However, the test creators do want to remain mindful of what they call "sensitivity issues." Any passage that might be viewed as socially, politically, or sexually volatile will not be included. Some of the poetry of Anne Sexton or Sylvia Plath, for instance, would be off-limits because it deals too frankly with suicide. Furthermore, if a work comes from a cultural perspective with which not all English speakers would be familiar, excerpts from it would never appear on the test. For example, if a passage from a Kate Chopin story relies too heavily on the reader's knowledge of the Creole culture in Louisiana, the passage could not be used; similarly, if a C. S. Lewis essay requires that a reader be well-versed in Christian theology, that work would also be inadmissible.

## Length

Keeping in mind the time limit for the exam, the test creators cannot use too many lengthy passages. Also, the test will usually be constructed in such a way that, if a particularly long passage with several questions appears on the test, the next passage will usually be shorter with fewer questions. A poem is probably too short to use if it has fewer than eight lines; therefore, a haiku would almost never make its way to the test. On the other hand, something such as Gray's "Elegy Written in a Country Churchyard," which contains 128 lines, is too long to consider as a single exam item. Prose passages will probably have a minimum of 12–15 lines. However, ten consecutive paragraphs in a Dickens novel would be too big a chunk for the test taker. Since dialogue tends to read more quickly than do other types of literature, modern play excerpts have the luxury of being a little lengthier on the test.

# TYPES OF QUESTIONS

## Introductory and Concluding Questions

The questions at the beginning and end of a passage's "set" usually deal with the passage as a whole. They tend to deal with items such as the speaker's tone, the purpose of the passage, the manner of the passage's development, and so on. Look for the first test item in a set to be both broad and only mildly difficult, so as to reduce exam stress. Expect the last questions not only to be general but also to try to incorporate much of what has already been questioned; the effect is a well-rounded conclusion.

### EXAMPLE:

> In May, when sea-winds pierced our solitudes,
> I found the fresh Rhodora in the woods,
> Spreading its leafless blooms in a damp nook,
> *Line* To please the desert and the sluggish brook.
> *(5)* The purple petals, fallen in the pool,
> Made the black water with their beauty gay;
> Here might the red-bird come his plumes to cool,
> And court the flower that cheapens his array.
> Rhodora! if the sages ask thee why
> *(10)* This charm is wasted on the earth and sky,
> Tell them, dear, that if eyes were made for seeing,
> Then Beauty is its own excuse for being:

Why thou wert there, O rival of the rose!
I never thought to ask, I never knew:
(15)    But, in my simple ignorance, suppose
The self-same Power that brought me there brought you.

(1839)

The poem can best be explained as

(A)    a sonnet to an object of beauty.

**(B)    an ode to a flower.**

(C)    a comparison between flora and fauna.

(D)    a polemic for conserving Nature.

(E)    a conversation with Beauty.

## Line-Specific Questions

The bulk of the questions in a set will refer specifically to certain lines in the passage. These questions chronologically guide you through the work and even help to "teach" the passage to you, if you pay attention.

### EXAMPLE:

In the Spring of the Year, when [the snakes] first creep out of
their Holes, they are feeble, heavy, slow, and easily taken; and if
a small Bounty were allowed *per* Head, some Thousands might

*Line*    be collected annually, and *transported* to Britain. There I would
(5)    propose to have them carefully distributed in *St. James Park*, in
the *Spring-Gardens*, and other Places of Pleasure about London;
in the Gardens of all the Nobility and Gentry throughout the
Nation; but particularly in the Gardens of the *Prime Ministers*,
the *Lords of Trade* and *Members of Parliament*; for to them we are
(10)    *most particularly* obliged.

(1751)

In lines 2–4, how does the narrator make the gathering of snakes sound agreeable?

**(A)    It could be both easy and profitable.**

(B)    The event could become an annual holiday.

(C)    It would be a chance to regain contact with Britain.

(D)    It would be pleasurable and sporting.

(E)    The result would gain America favor with Britain.

## "EXCEPT" Questions

Sometimes, a question has more than one right answer. In this case, the test will use an EXCEPT question. Here, four of the answers are right, but one is wrong. You are thus directed by the question to choose the answer that is incorrect.

EXAMPLE:

> Fly envious time, till thou run out thy race,
> Call on the lazy leaden-stepping hours,
> Whose speed is but the heavy plummet's pace;        *plummet* pendulum
> Line    And glut thyself with what thy womb devours,
> (5)     Which is no more than what is false and vain,
> And merely mortal dross;        *dross* debris, garbage
> So little is our loss,
> So little is thy gain.

(1633)

All the following could be said of lines 7–8 EXCEPT that

   (A)   their parallel structure reinforces the vanity of earthly things.

   (B)   their brevity represents time's lack of power.

   (C)   their antithesis stresses the unimportance of time's acquisitions.

   **(D)   their metrical shift imitates the chaos of eternity.**

   (E)   their matter-of-fact tone causes the speaker to sound assured.

## Roman Numeral Questions

These questions abide by the same principle as the *EXCEPT* questions: there may be more than one right answer to a question. In this format, the student is given a series of items listed with Roman numerals. She is then asked which items apply to the question. The setup is deceptively simple; this type of question can be very time consuming as the student runs through different possible combinations of correct answers.

EXAMPLE:

> O, why was I born a man, of whom to make a brute! The glad ship
> is gone; she hides in the dim distance. I am left in the hottest hell of
> unending slavery. O God, save me! God, deliver me! Let me be free!
> Is there any God? Why am I a slave? I will run away.

(1845)

Which of the following do lines 1–4 feature?

   I.   Rhetorical questions

   II.   A desperate tone

   III.   A philosophical and theological scope

   IV.   A new resolution

   (A)   I and II only

   (B)   I, II, and III only

   (C)   I, II, and IV only

   (D)   II, III, and IV only

   **(E)   I, II, III, and IV**

## Definition Questions

As the SAT Subject Test: Literature is an examination of language, once in a while there must be a question asking about the definition of a word in its context. These questions will usually deal with a common word used in an unusual way.

### EXAMPLE:

> Virtue how frail it is!
> Friendship how rare!
> Love how it sells poor bliss
> For proud despair!
> But we, though soon they fall,
> Survive their joy, and all
> Which ours we call.

*Line*
*(5)*

(1821)

The word "survive" in line 6 is closest in meaning to

(A) **outlast.**

(B) endure.

(C) exist.

(D) thrive.

(E) experience.

## Term Questions

To test what you have achieved as a student of literature, the SAT Subject Test will occasionally ask about literary terms.

### EXAMPLE:

> When, in disgrace with Fortune and men's eyes,
> I all alone beweep my outcast state,
> And trouble deaf heaven with my bootless cries,
> And look upon myself and curse my fate,
> Wishing me like to one more rich in hope,
> Featured like him, like him with friends possessed,
> Desiring this man's art, and that man's scope,
> With what I most enjoy contented least;
> Yet in these thoughts myself almost despising,
> Haply I think on thee, and then my state,
> Like to the lark at break of day arising
> From sullen earth, sings hymns at heaven's gate;
> For thy sweet love remembered such wealth brings
> That then I scorn to change my state with kings.

*Line*
*(5)*

*(10)*

(1609)

The poem can be categorized as

(A) **a sonnet.**
(B) a pastoral.
(C) heroic couplets.
(D) blank verse.
(E) a villanelle.

## Language Questions

The test also likes to cover the use of rhetoric, since rhetorical devices are a means for manipulating language.

### EXAMPLE:

> Though *Winter* frowns to Fancy's raptur'd eyes
> The fields may flourish, and gay scenes arise;
> The frozen deeps may break their iron bands,
> Line And bid the waters murmur o'er the sands.
> (5) Fair *Flora* may resume her fragrant reign,        *Flora*  Roman goddess of flowers
> And with her flow'ry riches deck the plain;
> *Sylvanus* may diffuse his honors round        *Sylvanus*  Roman forest deity
> And all the forest may with leaves be crown'd:
> Show'rs may descend, and dews their gems disclose,
> (10) And nectar sparkle on the blooming rose.

(1773)

Lines 5 and 9 both feature

(A) assonance.
(B) **alliteration.**
(C) paradox.
(D) antithesis.
(E) rhetorical questions.

## Grammar and Mechanics Questions

Once in a while, a question will deal with pronoun reference, dependent clauses, modifying phrases, and the like. Be patient; these questions are designed to clarify the passage for you. For instance, in a poem, there may be a complex or slightly ambiguous sentence that could block your full understanding of the work. Let a grammar question analyze for you the internal workings of that sentence.

### EXAMPLE:

> When our two souls stand up erect and strong,
> Face to face, silent, drawing nigh and nigher,
> Until the lengthening wings break into fire
> At either curvéd point,—what bitter wrong

*Line*
(5)      Can the earth do to us, that we should not long
         Be here contented? Think. In mounting higher,
         The angels would press on us and aspire
         To drop some golden orb of perfect song
         Into our deep, dear silence. Let us stay
(10)     Rather on earth, Belovéd,—where the unfit
         Contrarious moods of men recoil away
         And isolate pure spirits, and permit
         A place to stand and love in for a day,
         With darkness and the death-hour rounding it.

                         (1850)

A verb in imperative mood can be found in line

    (A)    2.
    (B)    4.
    (C)    **6.**
    (D)    7.
    (E)    12.

There are other types of questions, but the ones listed above are some of the most common.

Now that we have discussed the various components of the test, let's look at some test-taking tips.

## TEST-TAKING DO'S

You're sitting at your desk and following the second hand around the clock face. The proctor says "Begin." Now, what do you do?

- **DO** *check to see how many questions are on the test.* There will be anywhere from 61–63—not a big margin of difference ... until you get down to the last few minutes of the test. Knowing exactly how many questions there are will help you pace yourself better.

- **DO** *scan a passage's questions before reading the passage itself.* This method may seem time consuming, but it will give you a context by which to read the passage. Being familiar with the questions will educate you on what to look for.

- **DO** *read the passage briskly.* If you read too slowly, you will not just cost yourself valuable test time, you could also get so bogged down in the passage that you will lose its meaning. Don't worry about stumbling over an unknown word here or there; the questions will probably help you over those hurdles, anyway. The idea the first time through is simply to get a feel for the passage, a general overview.

- **DO** *mark it up! Annotate!* Neatness does *not* count. As you read through the passage, make little notes; they will jog your short-term memory when you go back through the passage with the questions. Furthermore, in a poem like the one below, *mark where the sentences begin and end.* Knowing a poem's sentences—if the poem is constructed in sentences—will help you understand it much better.

If Shelley's "Ozymandias" were to appear as a text for the SAT Subject Test: Literature, one might make some notes to the right in this way:

| | | |
|---|---|---|
| | I met a traveler from an antique land | (why is it "antique"?) |
| | Who said— "Two vast and trunkless legs of stone | (what's "trunkless"?) |
| | Stand in the desert. Near them, on the sand, | ("desert"…end of sentence) |
| Line | Half sunk a shattered visage lies, whose frown | (statue in the desert) |
| (5) | And wrinkled lip, and sneer of cold command | (bad guy…sneers)  (sonnet! this is a sonnet!) |
| | Tell that its sculptor well those passions read | |
| | Which yet survive, stamped on these lifeless things, | |
| | The hand that mocked them, and the heart that fed; | (who's mocking?) (synecdoche at l. 8) |
| | And on the pedestal, these words appear: | (semi-colon ends sentence in l. 9) |
| (10) | "My name is Ozymandias,* King of Kings; | (footnote, ancient king) |
| | Look on my Works, ye Mighty, and Despair!" | (Despair, end of sentence) |
| | Nothing beside remains. Round the decay | (nothing remains—irony in |
| | Of that colossal Wreck, boundless and bare | (inscription, short sentence—why?) |
| | The lone and level sands stretch far away." | (sounds lonely) |

(1818)

*Ozymandias: Greek name for Ramses II of Egypt, who ruled in the 13th century BCE.

Notice that many of the notes on the right are just questions. It's okay not to have all the answers in the first reading. It's NOT okay to try to have them all the first time. You will slow yourself down. The questions you ask can be revisited later; they may actually help you.

- **DO** *watch for question cues.* Does the "stem" or the introduction of the question include an EXCEPT? Am I restricted to certain line numbers when I look for answers in the text? Pay close attention to the way the question is worded.

Also, think about where the question appears on the test. Remember that the first and last questions for the passage will tend to be of a general nature. Let them guide your overall view of the work. The first question for this poem appears below:

1.  The poem appears to be

    (A)   elegiac verse.

    (B)   a Romantic ballad.

    (C)   a fragment from an epic poem.

    (D)   an ode to Ozymandias.

    (E)   a Petrarchan sonnet.

Of course, (E) is the right answer, because this is a 14-line iambic pentameter poem with a specific rhyme scheme (See chapter 3 under "Poetic Styles and Genres"). But how will this help you get a general feeling for the work? You know that a sonnet is discursive; that is, it discusses a topic rather than tells a story. So you need to be looking for some point, some strongly insinuated idea.

**KAPLAN)**

- **DO** *narrow your field.* As you read the questions, you will find that many of the answers are *obviously* wrong. Eliminate as many of these "distracters" as you can so that you can concentrate on the more appealing answers. So then, *this question...*

2. The "traveler" character in line 1 is describing

    (A)   a partially toppled statue.

    (B)   a recently disentombed mummy.

    (C)   an obnoxiously drunk Egyptian.

    (D)   a somewhat confused pharaoh.

    (E)   a highly eroded palace.

becomes *this...*

The "traveler" character in line 1 is describing

    (A)   a partially toppled statue.

    (B)   ~~a recently disentombed mummy.~~

    (C)   ~~an obnoxiously drunk Egyptian.~~

    (D)   ~~a somewhat confused pharaoh.~~

    (E)   a highly eroded palace.

for *these reasons...*

The "traveler" character in line 1 is describing

    (A)   a partially toppled statue.

    (B)   ~~a recently disentombed mummy.~~    (legs are "vast"—mummy is human size)

    (C)   ~~an obnoxiously drunk Egyptian.~~    (obviously statue; (C) worded too strongly, anyway)

    (D)   ~~a somewhat confused pharaoh.~~    (ditto on statue)

    (E)   a highly eroded palace.

Later on, you rightly assume that since the "traveler" concentrates on the relationship between the sculptor and his subject, these "trunkless legs" are probably just part of a statue, so (E) can be eliminated, too.

## TEST-TAKING DON'TS

- **DON'T** *succumb to fallacies.* It is very important for you to remember that if you select an answer for a question and you don't have *text to back it up*, then the answer may be doomed. Since you are not expected to know any biographical, social, or political information connected to the literary work, and you are expected to know only a very little history, you have nothing but the *work itself* and your knowledge of literary terms to aid you.

For the question below, you will see thoughts from some test takers indicating why they chose the answers they did. Focus on the fallacies of those who did not choose (E).

The "lone and level sands" (line 14) indicate which of the following themes?

(A)   Politics is the only discipline worth pursuing.

(B)   Absolute power corrupts absolutely.

(C)   Life is pointless without love.

(D)   The common people should be vigilant against tyranny.

(E)   The natural outlasts the mortal.

*Partial Reading Fallacy:* "I chose (A) because, well, I remember it was about a king..." (*Remember*? Go back to the text! Revisit it often!)

*English Class Fallacy:* "I chose (B) because we just talked about this theme in class, so I know it's a good idea." (One theme does not apply to all works!)

*Personal Fallacy:* "I chose (C) because it's like, so true—in my life." (What about in Ozymandias's life? or the traveler's? or the speaker's? They're in the poem; you're not.)

*Forced Meaning Fallacy:* "I chose (D) because, even if it's not true, it *should* be, man. Tyranny is everywhere!" (Don't go "everywhere." Just stay here.)

*Textual Support:* "Well, since 'the lone and level sands stretch far away,' Nature is still there. But where is Ozymandias? Nowhere. The mortal is gone. So that's the theme. Plus, that makes the inscription ironic, because the king thought he was super powerful, but there's only this broken statue left of him." (Thank you.)

- **DON'T** *stress*. This book will provide all the review you need to ace the SAT Subject Test: Literature.

# STRESS MANAGEMENT

The countdown has begun. Your date with THE TEST is looming on the horizon. Anxiety is on the rise. The butterflies in your stomach have gone ballistic. Perhaps you feel as if the last thing you ate has turned into a lead ball. Your thinking is getting cloudy. Maybe you think you won't be ready. Maybe you already know your stuff, but you're going into panic mode anyway. Worst of all, you're not sure of what to do about it.

Don't freak! It is possible to tame that anxiety and stress—before and during the test. We'll show you how. You won't believe how quickly and easily you can deal with that killer anxiety.

## Make the Most of Your Prep Time

Lack of control is one of the prime causes of stress. A ton of research shows that if you don't have a sense of control over what's happening in your life, you can easily end up feeling helpless and hopeless. So just having concrete things to do and to think about—taking control—will help reduce your stress. This section shows you how to take control during the days leading up to taking the test.

## Identify Sources of Stress

In the space provided, jot down anything you identify as a source of your test-related stress. The idea is to pin down that free-floating anxiety so that you can take control of it. Here are some common examples to get you started:

- I always freeze up on tests.
- I'm nervous about the term questions (or the Roman numeral questions, etc.).
- I need a good/great score to go to Acme College.
- My older brother/sister/best friend/girlfriend or boyfriend did really well. I must match their scores or do better.
- My parents, who are paying for school, will be really disappointed if I don't test well.
- I'm afraid of losing my focus and concentration.
- I'm afraid I'm not spending enough time preparing.
- I study like crazy, but nothing seems to stick in my mind.
- I always run out of time and get panicky.
- I feel as though thinking is becoming like wading through thick mud.

## Sources of Stress

_____    _____

_____    _____

_____    _____

_____    _____

Take a few minutes to think about the things you've just written down. Then rewrite them in some sort of order. List the statements you most associate with your stress and anxiety first and put the least disturbing items last. Chances are, the top of the list is a fairly accurate description of exactly how you react to test anxiety, both physically and mentally. The later items usually describe your fears (disappointing Mom and Dad, looking bad, etc.). As you write the list, you're forming a hierarchy of items so you can deal first with the anxiety provokers that bug you most. Very often, taking care of the major items from the top of the list goes a long way toward relieving overall testing anxiety. You probably won't have to bother with the stuff you placed last.

## Use Your Strengths and Weaknesses

Take one minute to list the areas of the test that you are good at. They can be general ("poetry") or specific (EXCEPT questions). Put down as many as you can think of, and if possible, time yourself. Write for the entire time; don't stop writing until you've reached the one-minute stopping point.

## Strong Test Subjects

_____     _____

_____     _____

_____     _____

_____     _____

Next, take one minute to list areas of the test you're not so good at, just plain bad at, have failed at, or keep failing at. Again, keep it to one minute and continue writing until you reach the cutoff. Don't be afraid to identify and write down your weak spots! In all probability, as you do both lists, you'll find you are strong in some areas and not so strong in others. Taking stock of your assets and liabilities lets you know the areas you don't have to worry about and the ones that will demand extra attention and effort.

## Weak Test Subjects

_____     _____

_____     _____

_____     _____

_____     _____

Facing your weak spots gives you some distinct advantages. It helps a lot to find out where you need to spend extra effort. Increased exposure to tough material makes it more familiar and less intimidating. (After all, we mostly fear what we don't know and are probably afraid to face.) You'll feel better about yourself because you're dealing directly with areas of the test that bring on your anxiety. You can't help feeling more confident when you know you're actively strengthening your chances of earning a higher overall test score.

Now, go back to the "good" list and expand it for two minutes. Take the general items on that first list and make them more specific; take the specific items and expand them into more general conclusions. Naturally, if anything new comes to mind, jot it down. Focus all of your attention and effort on your strengths. Don't underestimate yourself or your abilities. Give yourself full credit. At the same time, don't list strengths you don't really have; you'll only be fooling yourself.

Expanding from general to specific might go as follows. If you listed "poetry" as a broad topic you feel strong in, you would then narrow your focus to include areas of this subject about which you are particularly knowledgeable. Your areas of strength might include a good understanding of imagery, a strong sense of metrical construction, etc.

Whatever you know comfortably goes on your "good" list. Okay. You've got the picture. Now, get ready, check your starting time, and start writing down items on your expanded "good" list.

## Strong Test Subjects: An Expanded List

_____    _____

_____    _____

_____    _____

_____    _____

After you've stopped, check your time. Did you find yourself going beyond the two minutes allotted? Did you write down more things than you thought you knew? Is it possible you know more than you've given yourself credit for? Could that mean you've found a number of areas in which you feel strong?

You just took an active step toward helping yourself. Notice any increased feelings of confidence? Enjoy them.

Here's another way to think about your writing exercise. Every area of strength and confidence you can identify is much like having a reserve of solid gold at Fort Knox. You'll be able to draw on your reserves as you need them. You can use your reserves to solve difficult questions, maintain confidence, and keep test stress and anxiety at a distance. The encouraging thing is that every time you recognize another area of strength, succeed at coming up with a solution, or get a good score on a test, you increase your reserves. And there is absolutely no limit to how much self-confidence you can have or how good you can feel about yourself.

## Imagine Yourself Succeeding

This next little group of exercises is both physical and mental. It's a natural follow-up to what you've just accomplished with your lists.

First, get yourself into a comfortable sitting position in a quiet setting. Wear loose clothes. If you wear glasses, take them off. Then, close your eyes and breathe in a deep, satisfying breath of air. Really fill your lungs until your rib cage is fully expanded and you can't take in any more. Then, exhale the air completely. Imagine you're blowing out a candle with your last little puff of air. Do this two or three more times, filling your lungs to their maximum and emptying them totally. Keep your eyes closed, comfortably but not tightly. Let your body sink deeper into the chair as you become even more comfortable.

With your eyes shut you can notice something very interesting. You're no longer dealing with the worrisome stuff going on in the world outside of you. Now you can concentrate on what happens inside you. The more you recognize your own physical reactions to stress and anxiety, the more you can do about them. You might not realize it, but you've begun to regain a sense of being in control.

Let images begin to form on the "viewing screens" on the back of your eyelids. You're experiencing visualizations from the place in your mind that makes pictures. Allow the images to come easily and naturally; don't force them. Imagine yourself in a relaxing situation. It might be in a special place you've visited before or one you've read about. It can be a fictional location that you create in your imagination, but a real-life memory of a place or situation you know is usually better. Make it as detailed as possible and notice as much as you can.

Stay focused on the images as you sink farther back into your chair. Breathe easily and naturally. You might have the sensations of any stress or tension draining from your muscles and flowing downward, out your feet and away from you.

Take a moment to check how you're feeling. Notice how comfortable you've become. Imagine how much easier it would be if you could take the test feeling this relaxed and in this state of ease. You've coupled the images of your special place with sensations of comfort and relaxation. You've also found a way to become relaxed simply by visualizing your own safe, special place.

Now, close your eyes and start remembering a real-life situation in which you did well on a test. If you can't come up with one, remember a situation in which you did something (academic or otherwise) that you were really proud of—a genuine accomplishment. Make the memory as detailed as possible. Think about the sights, the sounds, the smells, even the tastes associated with this remembered experience. Remember how confident you felt as you accomplished your goal. Now start thinking about the upcoming test. Keep your thoughts and feelings in line with that successful experience. Don't make comparisons between them. Just imagine taking the upcoming test with the same feelings of confidence and relaxed control.

This exercise is a great way to bring the test down to earth. You should practice this exercise often, especially when the prospect of taking the exam starts to bum you out. The more you practice it, the more effective the exercise will be for you.

## Exercise Your Frustrations Away

Whether it is jogging, walking, biking, mild aerobics, pushups, or a pickup basketball game, physical exercise is a very effective way to stimulate both your mind and body and to improve your ability to think and concentrate. A surprising number of students get out of the habit of regular exercise, ironically because they're spending so much time prepping for exams. Also, sedentary people—this is a medical fact—get less oxygen to the blood and hence to the head than active people. You can live fine with a little less oxygen; you just can't think as well.

Any big test is a bit like a race. Thinking clearly at the end is just as important as having a quick mind early on. If you can't sustain your energy level in the last sections of the exam, there's too good a chance you could blow it. You need a fit body that can weather the demands any big exam puts on you. Along with a good diet and adequate sleep, exercise is an important part of keeping yourself in fighting shape and thinking clearly for the long haul.

Another thing happens when students don't make exercise an integral part of their test preparation. Like any organism in nature, you operate best if all your "energy systems" are in balance. Studying uses a lot of energy, but it's all mental. When you take a study break, do something active instead of raiding the fridge or vegging out in front of the TV. Take a 5- to 10-minute activity break for every 50 or 60 minutes that you study. The physical exertion gets your body into the act, which helps to keep your mind and body in sync. Then, when you finish studying for the night and hit the sack, you won't lie there, tense and unable to sleep because your head is overtired and your body wants to pump iron or run a marathon.

One warning about exercise, however: It's not a good idea to exercise vigorously right before you go to bed. This could easily cause sleep-onset problems. For the same reason, it's also not a good idea to study right up to bedtime. Make time for a "buffer period" before you go to bed: For 30 to 60 minutes, just take a hot shower, meditate, simply veg out.

## The Dangers of Drugs

Using drugs (prescription or recreational) specifically to prepare for and take a big test is definitely self-defeating. (And if they're illegal drugs, you can end up with a bigger problem than the SAT Subject Test: Literature on your hands.) Except for the drugs that occur naturally in your brain, every drug has major drawbacks—and a false sense of security is only one of them.

You may have heard that popping uppers helps you study by keeping you alert. If they're illegal, definitely forget about it. They wouldn't really work anyway, since amphetamines make it hard to retain information. Mild stimulants, such as coffee, cola, energy drinks, or over-the-counter caffeine pills can sometimes help as you study, since they keep you alert. On the down side, they can also lead to agitation, restlessness, and insomnia. Some people can drink a pot of high-octane coffee and sleep like a baby. Others have one cup and start to vibrate. It all depends on your tolerance for caffeine. Remember, a little anxiety is a good thing. The adrenaline that gets pumped into your bloodstream helps you stay alert and think more clearly. But too much anxiety, and you can't think straight at all.

Instead, go for endorphins—the "natural morphine." Endorphins have no side effects and they're free—you've already got them in your brain. It just takes some exercise to release them. Running around on the basketball court, bicycling, swimming, aerobics, power walking—these activities cause endorphins to occupy certain spots in your brain's neural synapses. In addition, exercise develops staying power and increases the oxygen transfer to your brain. Go into the test naturally.

## Take a Deep Breath . . .

Here's another natural route to relaxation and invigoration. It's a classic isometric exercise that you can do whenever you get stressed out—just before the test begins, even during the test. It's very simple and takes just a few minutes.

Close your eyes. Starting with your eyes and—without holding your breath—gradually tighten every muscle in your body (but not to the point of pain) in the following sequence:

1) Close your eyes tightly.
2) Squeeze your nose and mouth together so that your whole face is scrunched up. (If it makes you self-conscious to do this in the test room, skip the face-scrunching part.)
3) Pull your chin into your chest and pull your shoulders together.
4) Tighten your arms to your body, then clench your hands into tight fists.
5) Pull in your stomach.
6) Squeeze your thighs and buttocks together and tighten your calves.
7) Stretch your feet, then curl your toes (watch out for cramping in this part).

At this point, every muscle should be tightened. Now, relax your body, one part at a time, in reverse order, starting with your toes. Let the tension drop out of each muscle. The entire process might take five minutes from start to finish (maybe a couple of minutes during the test). This clenching and unclenching exercise should help you to feel very relaxed.

## And Keep Breathing

Conscious attention to breathing is an excellent way of managing test stress (or any stress, for that matter). The majority of people who get into trouble during tests take shallow breaths. They breathe using only their upper chests and shoulder muscles, and they may even hold their breath for long periods of time. Conversely, the test taker who, by accident or design, keeps breathing normally and rhythmically is likely to be more relaxed and in better control during the entire test experience.

So, now is the time to get into the habit of relaxed breathing. Do the next exercise to learn to breathe in a natural, easy rhythm. By the way, this is another technique you can use during the test to collect your thoughts and ward off excess stress. The entire exercise should take no more than three to five minutes.

With your eyes still closed, breathe in slowly and deeply through your nose. Hold the breath for a bit, then release it through your mouth. The key is to breathe slowly and deeply by using your diaphragm (the big band of muscle that spans your body just above your waist) to draw air in and out naturally and effortlessly. Breathing with your diaphragm encourages relaxation and helps minimize tension. Try it and notice how relaxed and comfortable you feel.

## Handling Stress During the Test

The biggest stress monster will be the test itself. Fear not; there are methods of quelling your stress during the test.

- Keep moving forward instead of getting bogged down in a difficult question. You don't have to get everything right to achieve a fine score. The best test takers skip difficult material temporarily in search of the easier stuff. They mark the questions that require extra time and thought. This strategy buys time and builds confidence so you can handle the tough stuff later.

- Don't be thrown if other test takers seem to be working more furiously than you are. Continue to spend your time patiently thinking through your answers; it's going to lead to better results. Don't mistake other people's sheer activity as a sign of progress and higher scores.

- Keep breathing! Weak test takers tend to forget to breathe properly as the test proceeds. They start holding their breath without realizing it, or they breathe erratically or arrhythmically. Improper breathing interferes with clear thinking.

- Some quick isometrics during the test—especially if concentration is wandering or energy is waning—can help. Try this: Put your palms together and press intensely for a few seconds. Concentrate on the tension you feel through your palms, wrists, forearms, and up into your biceps and shoulders. Then, quickly release the pressure. Feel the difference as you let go. Focus on the warm relaxation that floods through the muscles. Now you're ready to return to the task.

- Here's another isometric that will relieve tension in both your neck and eye muscles. Slowly rotate your head from side to side, turning your head and eyes to look as far back over each shoulder as you can. Feel the muscles stretch on one side of your neck as they contract on the other. Repeat five times in each direction.

# TIPS FOR JUST BEFORE THE TEST

- The best test takers do less and less as the test approaches. Taper off your study schedule and take it easy on yourself. You want to be relaxed and ready on the day of the test. Give yourself time off, especially the evening before the exam. By then, if you've studied well, everything you need to know is firmly stored in your memory banks.

- Positive self-talk can be extremely liberating and invigorating, especially as the test looms closer. Tell yourself things such as, "I choose to take this test," rather than, "I have to"; "I will do well," rather than "I hope things go well"; "I can," rather than "I cannot." Be aware of negative, self-defeating thoughts and images and immediately counter any you become aware of. Replace them with affirming statements that encourage your self-esteem and confidence. Create and practice visualizations that build on your positive statements.

- Get your act together sooner rather than later. Have everything (including choice of clothing) laid out days in advance. Most important, know where the test will be held and the easiest, quickest way to get there. You will gain great peace of mind if you know that all the little details—gas in the car, directions, etc.—are firmly in your control before the day of the test.

- Experience the test site a few days in advance. This is very helpful if you are especially anxious. If at all possible, find out what room your part of the alphabet is assigned to and try to sit there (by yourself) for a while. Better yet, bring some practice material and do at least a section or two, if not an entire practice test, in that room. In this situation, familiarity doesn't breed contempt; it generates comfort and confidence.

- Forego any practice on the day before the test. It's in your best interest to marshal your physical and psychological resources for 24 hours or so. Even racehorses are kept in the paddock and treated like royalty the day before a race. Keep the upcoming test out of your consciousness; go to a movie, take a pleasant hike, or just relax. Don't eat junk food or tons of sugar. And—of course—get plenty of rest the night before. Just don't go to bed too early. It's hard to fall asleep earlier than you're used to, and you don't want to lie there thinking about the test.

With what you've just learned here, you're armed and ready to do battle with the test. This book and your studies will give you the information you'll need to answer the questions. It's all firmly planted in your mind. You also know how to deal with any excess tension that might come along, both when you're studying for and taking the exam. You've experienced everything you need to tame your test anxiety and stress. You're going to get a great score.

Part Two

# Diagnostic Test

# HOW TO TAKE THE DIAGNOSTIC TEST

Before taking this diagnostic test, find a quiet room where you can work uninterrupted for one hour. Make sure you have several No. 2 pencils with erasers.

Use the answer grid provided to record your answers. Guidelines for scoring your test appear on the following page. Time yourself. Spend no more than one hour on the exam. Once you start the diagnostic test, don't stop until you've reached the one-hour time limit. You'll find an answer key and complete answer explanations following the test. Be sure to read the explanations for all questions, even those you answered correctly. Finally, you'll learn how the diagnostic test can help you in your review of literature.

Good luck!

# HOW TO CALCULATE YOUR SCORE

**Step 1: Figure out your raw score.** Use the answer key to count the number of questions you answered correctly and the number of questions you answered incorrectly. (Do not count any questions you left blank.) Multiply the number wrong by 0.25 and subtract the result from the number correct. Round the result to the nearest whole number. This is your raw score.

## SAT Subject Test: Literature Diagnostic Test

| Number right | Number wrong | Raw score |
| --- | --- | --- |

$$\boxed{\phantom{0}} - \left(0.25 \times \boxed{\phantom{0}}\right) = \boxed{\phantom{0}}$$

**Step 2: Find your scaled score.** In the Score Conversion Table below, find your raw score (rounded to the nearest whole number) in one of the columns to the left. The score directly to the right of that number will be your scaled score.

A note on your diagnostic test scores: Don't take these scores too literally. Practice test conditions cannot precisely mirror real test conditions. Your actual SAT Subject Test: Literature score will almost certainly vary from your diagnostic test scores. However, your score on the diagnostic test will give you a rough idea of your range on the actual exam.

## Conversion Table

| Raw | Scaled | Raw | Scaled | Raw | Scaled | Raw | Scaled |
| --- | --- | --- | --- | --- | --- | --- | --- |
| 63 | 800 | 43 | 700 | 23 | 510 | 3 | 330 |
| 62 | 800 | 42 | 690 | 22 | 500 | 2 | 320 |
| 61 | 800 | 41 | 680 | 21 | 500 | 1 | 310 |
| 60 | 800 | 40 | 670 | 20 | 490 | 0 | 300 |
| 59 | 800 | 39 | 660 | 19 | 480 | -1 | 290 |
| 58 | 800 | 38 | 650 | 18 | 470 | -2 | 280 |
| 57 | 800 | 37 | 640 | 17 | 460 | -3 | 280 |
| 56 | 790 | 36 | 630 | 16 | 450 | -4 | 270 |
| 55 | 790 | 35 | 620 | 15 | 440 | -5 | 260 |
| 54 | 780 | 34 | 610 | 14 | 430 | -6 | 250 |
| 53 | 780 | 33 | 610 | 13 | 420 | -7 | 250 |
| 52 | 780 | 32 | 600 | 12 | 410 | -8 | 240 |
| 51 | 770 | 31 | 590 | 11 | 410 | -9 | 230 |
| 50 | 760 | 30 | 580 | 10 | 400 | -10 | 220 |
| 49 | 750 | 29 | 570 | 9 | 390 | -11 | 210 |
| 48 | 740 | 28 | 560 | 8 | 380 | -12 | 200 |
| 47 | 730 | 27 | 550 | 7 | 370 | -13 | 200 |
| 46 | 720 | 26 | 540 | 6 | 360 | -14 | 200 |
| 45 | 710 | 25 | 530 | 5 | 350 | | |
| 44 | 710 | 24 | 520 | 4 | 340 | | |

# Diagnostic Test
# Answer Grid

1. Ⓐ Ⓑ Ⓒ Ⓓ Ⓔ
2. Ⓐ Ⓑ Ⓒ Ⓓ Ⓔ
3. Ⓐ Ⓑ Ⓒ Ⓓ Ⓔ
4. Ⓐ Ⓑ Ⓒ Ⓓ Ⓔ
5. Ⓐ Ⓑ Ⓒ Ⓓ Ⓔ
6. Ⓐ Ⓑ Ⓒ Ⓓ Ⓔ
7. Ⓐ Ⓑ Ⓒ Ⓓ Ⓔ
8. Ⓐ Ⓑ Ⓒ Ⓓ Ⓔ
9. Ⓐ Ⓑ Ⓒ Ⓓ Ⓔ
10. Ⓐ Ⓑ Ⓒ Ⓓ Ⓔ
11. Ⓐ Ⓑ Ⓒ Ⓓ Ⓔ
12. Ⓐ Ⓑ Ⓒ Ⓓ Ⓔ
13. Ⓐ Ⓑ Ⓒ Ⓓ Ⓔ
14. Ⓐ Ⓑ Ⓒ Ⓓ Ⓔ
15. Ⓐ Ⓑ Ⓒ Ⓓ Ⓔ
16. Ⓐ Ⓑ Ⓒ Ⓓ Ⓔ
17. Ⓐ Ⓑ Ⓒ Ⓓ Ⓔ
18. Ⓐ Ⓑ Ⓒ Ⓓ Ⓔ
19. Ⓐ Ⓑ Ⓒ Ⓓ Ⓔ
20. Ⓐ Ⓑ Ⓒ Ⓓ Ⓔ
21. Ⓐ Ⓑ Ⓒ Ⓓ Ⓔ

22. Ⓐ Ⓑ Ⓒ Ⓓ Ⓔ
23. Ⓐ Ⓑ Ⓒ Ⓓ Ⓔ
24. Ⓐ Ⓑ Ⓒ Ⓓ Ⓔ
25. Ⓐ Ⓑ Ⓒ Ⓓ Ⓔ
26. Ⓐ Ⓑ Ⓒ Ⓓ Ⓔ
27. Ⓐ Ⓑ Ⓒ Ⓓ Ⓔ
28. Ⓐ Ⓑ Ⓒ Ⓓ Ⓔ
29. Ⓐ Ⓑ Ⓒ Ⓓ Ⓔ
30. Ⓐ Ⓑ Ⓒ Ⓓ Ⓔ
31. Ⓐ Ⓑ Ⓒ Ⓓ Ⓔ
32. Ⓐ Ⓑ Ⓒ Ⓓ Ⓔ
33. Ⓐ Ⓑ Ⓒ Ⓓ Ⓔ
34. Ⓐ Ⓑ Ⓒ Ⓓ Ⓔ
35. Ⓐ Ⓑ Ⓒ Ⓓ Ⓔ
36. Ⓐ Ⓑ Ⓒ Ⓓ Ⓔ
37. Ⓐ Ⓑ Ⓒ Ⓓ Ⓔ
38. Ⓐ Ⓑ Ⓒ Ⓓ Ⓔ
39. Ⓐ Ⓑ Ⓒ Ⓓ Ⓔ
40. Ⓐ Ⓑ Ⓒ Ⓓ Ⓔ
41. Ⓐ Ⓑ Ⓒ Ⓓ Ⓔ
42. Ⓐ Ⓑ Ⓒ Ⓓ Ⓔ

43. Ⓐ Ⓑ Ⓒ Ⓓ Ⓔ
44. Ⓐ Ⓑ Ⓒ Ⓓ Ⓔ
45. Ⓐ Ⓑ Ⓒ Ⓓ Ⓔ
46. Ⓐ Ⓑ Ⓒ Ⓓ Ⓔ
47. Ⓐ Ⓑ Ⓒ Ⓓ Ⓔ
48. Ⓐ Ⓑ Ⓒ Ⓓ Ⓔ
49. Ⓐ Ⓑ Ⓒ Ⓓ Ⓔ
50. Ⓐ Ⓑ Ⓒ Ⓓ Ⓔ
51. Ⓐ Ⓑ Ⓒ Ⓓ Ⓔ
52. Ⓐ Ⓑ Ⓒ Ⓓ Ⓔ
53. Ⓐ Ⓑ Ⓒ Ⓓ Ⓔ
54. Ⓐ Ⓑ Ⓒ Ⓓ Ⓔ
55. Ⓐ Ⓑ Ⓒ Ⓓ Ⓔ
56. Ⓐ Ⓑ Ⓒ Ⓓ Ⓔ
57. Ⓐ Ⓑ Ⓒ Ⓓ Ⓔ
58. Ⓐ Ⓑ Ⓒ Ⓓ Ⓔ
59. Ⓐ Ⓑ Ⓒ Ⓓ Ⓔ
60. Ⓐ Ⓑ Ⓒ Ⓓ Ⓔ
61. Ⓐ Ⓑ Ⓒ Ⓓ Ⓔ
62. Ⓐ Ⓑ Ⓒ Ⓓ Ⓔ
63. Ⓐ Ⓑ Ⓒ Ⓓ Ⓔ

# Diagnostic Test

*Questions 1–13 refer to the following poem. After reading the poem, choose the best answer to each question.*

The people I love the best
jump into work head first
without dallying in the shallows
*Line* and swim off with sure strokes almost out of
*(5)*     sight.
They seem to become natives of that element
the black sleek heads of seals
bouncing like half-submerged balls.

I love people who harness themselves, an ox to a
*(10)*     heavy cart,
Who pull like water buffalo, with massive patience,
Who strain in the mud and the muck to move
    things forward,
Who do what has to be done, again and again.

*(15)* I want to be with people who submerge
in the task, who go into the fields to harvest
and work in a row and pass the bags along,
who are not parlor generals and field deserters
but move in common rhythm
*(20)* when the food must come in or the fire be put out.

The work of the world is common as mud.
Botched it smears the hands, crumbles to dust.
But the thing worth doing well done
has a shape that satisfies, clean and evident.
*(25)* Greek amphoras for wine or oil,
Hopi vases that held corn, are put in museums
but you know they were made to be used.
The pitcher cries for water to carry
and the person for work that is real.

               (1973)

1. The animal references in stanzas one and two could best be identified as
   - (A) personification.
   - (B) a fable.
   - (C) understatement.
   - (D) extended metaphor.
   - (E) verisimilitude.

2. Which of the following is NOT present in the first stanza?
   - (A) Metaphor
   - (B) Third-person limited narrator
   - (C) Assonance
   - (D) Simple sentences
   - (E) Alliteration

3. The narrator's attitude toward parlor generals and field deserters can best be described as one of
   - (A) derision.
   - (B) tolerance.
   - (C) admiration.
   - (D) impatience.
   - (E) compassion.

4. This poem can best be characterized as an example of
   - (A) a lyrical ballad.
   - (B) a fable.
   - (C) free verse.
   - (D) mock heroic.
   - (E) iambic pentameter.

**GO ON TO THE NEXT PAGE**

5. The speaker perceives work chiefly in terms of

    (A) bestial toil.
    (B) generals and followers.
    (C) a harvest worth gathering.
    (D) satisfaction and worthwhileness.
    (E) forbearance and endurance.

6. "The pitcher cries for water" (line 28) is most simply a reference to its

    (A) thirst and longing.
    (B) appropriateness as a museum treasure.
    (C) sentimentality.
    (D) yearning and despair.
    (E) pragmatic purpose.

7. The tone of this poem is one of

    (A) condescension and contempt.
    (B) respect and admiration.
    (C) jealousy and envy.
    (D) deference and humility.
    (E) wistfulness and nostalgia.

8. The narrator references the amphora and Hopi vases because they are

    (A) costly.
    (B) valuable.
    (C) practical.
    (D) beautiful.
    (E) unusual.

9. Many lines within this poem, such as those in stanza three, are not end stopped, but they demonstrate

    (A) run-on structures.
    (B) enjambment.
    (C) heroic couplets.
    (D) Petrarchan rhyme.
    (E) juxtaposition.

10. The theme of the poem is best expressed by the lines

    (A) "...but move in a common rhythm/when the food must come in or the fire be put out" (lines 19–20).
    (B) "I love people who harness themselves..." (line 9).
    (C) "I want to be with people who submerge/in the task" (lines 15–16).
    (D) "The people I love the best/jump into work head first..." (lines 1–2).
    (E) "The pitcher cries for water to carry/and the person for work that is real" (lines 29–30).

11. The best example of irony in this poem can be found in the following phrase:

    (A) "The people I love the best/jump into work head first" (lines 1–2).
    (B) "I want to be with people who submerge/in the task" (lines 15–16).
    (C) "Botched it smears the hands, crumbles to dust" (line 22).
    (D) "Hopi vases that held corn, are put in museums/but you know they were made to be used" (lines 26–27).
    (E) "The pitcher cries for water to carry/and the person for work that is real" (lines 29–30).

12. In line 6, the word "element" can best be understood to represent

    (A) swimming seals.
    (B) bouncing balls.
    (C) patient water buffalo.
    (D) toiling oxen.
    (E) meaningful work.

13. The repeated phraseology used in the third stanza can be identified as

    (A) alliteration.
    (B) anaphora.
    (C) apposition.
    (D) apostrophe.
    (E) assonance.

**GO ON TO THE NEXT PAGE**

*Questions 14–23 refer to the following passage. After reading the passage, choose the best answer to each question.*

There is a canal two rods wide along the northerly and westerly sides of the pond, and wider still at the east end. A great field of ice has
*Line* cracked off from the main body. I hear a song
(5) sparrow singing from the bushes on the shore. He too is helping to crack it. How handsome the great sweeping curves in the edge of the ice, answering somewhat to those of the shore, but more regular! It is unusually hard, owing to the recent severe
(10) but transient cold, and all watered or waved like a palace floor. But the wind slides eastward over its opaque surface in vain, till it reaches the living surface beyond. It is glorious to behold this ribbon of water sparkling in the sun, the bare face of
(15) the pond full of glee and youth, as if it spoke the joy of the fishes within it, and of the sands on its shore.

The change from storm and winter to serene and mild weather, from dark and sluggish hours
(20) to bright and elastic ones, is a memorable crisis which all things proclaim. It is seemingly instantaneous at last. Suddenly an influx of light filled my house, though the evening was at hand, and the clouds of winter still overhung it, and the eaves
(25) were dripping with sleety rain. I looked out the window, and lo! where yesterday was cold gray ice there lay the transparent pond already calm and full of hope as in a summer evening reflecting a summer evening sky in its bosom, though none
(30) was visible overhead. The pitch pines and shrub oaks about my house, which had so long drooped, suddenly resumed their several characters, looked brighter, greener, and more erect and alive, as if effectually cleansed and restored by the rain. I
(35) knew that it would not rain any more. You may tell by looking at any twig of the forest, aye, at your very woodpile, whether its winter is past or not. As it grew darker, I was startled by the honking of geese flying low over the woods, like weary
(40) travelers getting in late from southern lakes, and indulging at last in unrestrained complaint and mutual consolation. Standing at my door, I could hear the rush of their wings; when, driving toward my house, they suddenly spied my light, and with
(45) hushed clamor wheeled and settled in the pond.

In the morning I watched the geese from the door through the mist, sailing in the middle of the pond, fifty rods off, large and tumultuous. But when I stood on the shore they at once rose up
(50) with great flapping of wings at the signal of their commander, and when they had got into rank circled about over my head, twenty-nine of them, and then steered straight to Canada, with a regular honk from the leader at intervals. A plump of
(55) ducks rose at the same time and took the route to the north in the wake of their noisier cousins.

For a week I heard the circling groping clangor of some solitary goose in the foggy mornings, seeking its companion, and still peopling the
(60) woods with the sound of a larger life than they could sustain. In April the pigeons were seen again flying express in small flocks, and in due time I heard the martins twittering over my clearing, though it had not seemed that the township con-
(65) tained so many that it could afford me any, and I fancied that they were peculiarly of the ancient race that dwelt in hollow trees ere white men came. In almost all climes the tortoise and the frog are among the precursors and herald of this season,
(70) and birds fly with song and glancing plumage, and plants spring and bloom, and winds blow to correct this slight oscillation of the poles and preserve the equilibrium of Nature.

As every season seems best to us in its turn, so
(75) the coming in of spring is like creation of Cosmos out of Chaos and the realization of the Golden Age.

(1854)

14. From the passage, one can infer that the

(A) geese are back.
(B) pond is melting.
(C) woodpile is well stocked.
(D) martins are singing.
(E) mornings are foggy.

**GO ON TO THE NEXT PAGE**

15. The overall purpose of this passage seems to be the narrator's

    (A) desire to sound poetic.
    (B) need to explain the unexpected sunshine in his house.
    (C) description of the bird life around him.
    (D) celebration of the oncoming season.
    (E) delight to see the pond water.

16. What is the predominant literary device used throughout this passage?

    (A) Restrained description
    (B) Personification
    (C) Bombastic narration
    (D) Hyperbole
    (E) Rhetorical question

17. The tone of this passage can best be described as

    (A) colloquial.
    (B) informative.
    (C) unrestrained.
    (D) audacious.
    (E) poetic.

18. The narrator describes the water as all of the following EXCEPT

    (A) a canal two rods wide.
    (B) a ribbon.
    (C) a transparent pond.
    (D) a reflection of the sky.
    (E) a mirror of his soul.

19. The geese are best characterized through a series of

    (A) similes and metaphors.
    (B) comic descriptors.
    (C) emotional reflections.
    (D) unrelated impressions.
    (E) aural and visual images.

20. The geese are described as all of the following EXCEPT

    (A) weary travelers.
    (B) the last to arrive.
    (C) regimental in action.
    (D) cranky and commiserating.
    (E) raucous relatives.

21. Which is a subject not treated in this passage?

    (A) The connectedness of people to nature
    (B) The innocence of mankind
    (C) The cyclical certainty of nature
    (D) The glory of a long-awaited event
    (E) The animals heralding a change

22. One thing that is syntactically consistent within this passage is the

    (A) use of periodic sentences.
    (B) scarcity of prepositional phrases.
    (C) artful handling of a rhetorical question.
    (D) lack of simple sentences.
    (E) overuse of parallelism.

23. The word "plump" in line 54 most closely compares to the term

    (A) chubby.
    (B) fat.
    (C) full.
    (D) clutch.
    (E) club.

**GO ON TO THE NEXT PAGE**

*Questions 24–33 refer to the following passage. After reading the passage, choose the best answer to each question.*

Very gradually, in tiny slivers, day began to break through the fog, and from my position in the brush I could see ten or fifteen meters up the
*Line* trail. The mosquitoes were fierce. I remember
(5) slapping at them…then looking up and seeing the young man come out of the fog. He wore black clothing and rubber sandals and a gray ammunition belt. His shoulders were slightly stooped, his head cocked to the side listening to something.
(10) He seemed at ease. He carried his weapon in one hand, muzzle down, moving without any hurry up the center of the trail. There was no sound at all— none that I can remember. In a way, it seemed, he was part of the morning fog, or my own imagina-
(15) tion, but there was also the reality of what was happening in my stomach. I had already pulled the pin on a grenade. I had come up to a crouch. It was entirely automatic. I did not hate the young man; I did not see him as the enemy; I did not
(20) ponder issues of morality or politics or military duty. I crouched and kept my head low. I tried to swallow whatever was rising from my stomach, which tasted like lemonade, something fruity and sour. I was terrified. There were no thoughts
(25) about killing. The grenade was to make him go away—just evaporate—and I leaned back and felt my mind go empty and then fill up again. I had already thrown the grenade before telling myself to throw it. The brush was thick and I had to lob
(30) it high, not aiming, and I remember the grenade seeming to freeze above me for an instant, as if a camera had clicked and I remember ducking down and holding my breath and seeing little wisps of fog rise from the earth. The grenade
(35) bounced once and rolled across the trail. I did not hear it, but there must've been a sound, because the young man dropped his weapon and began to run, just two or three quick steps, then he hesitated, swiveling to his right, and he glanced
(40) down at the grenade and tried to cover his head but never did. It occurred to me then that he was about to die. I wanted to warn him. The grenade made a popping noise—not soft but not loud either—not what I'd expected—and there was

(45) a puff of dust and smoke—a small white puff— and the young man seemed to jerk upward as if pulled by invisible wires. He fell on his back. His rubber sandals had been blown off. There was no wind. He lay at the center of the trail, his right leg
(50) bent beneath him, his one eye shut, his other eye a huge star-shaped blue.
All I could do was gape at the fact of the young man's body. Even now, I haven't finished sorting it out. Sometimes I forgive myself, other times
(55) I don't. In the ordinary hours of life I try not to dwell on it, but now and then, when I'm reading a newspaper or just sitting alone in a room, I'll look up and see the young man coming out of the morning fog. I'll watch him walk toward me, his
(60) shoulders slightly stooped, his head cocked to the side, and he'll pass within a few yards of me and suddenly smile at some secret thought and then continue up the trail to where it bends back into the fog.

(1990)

24. The narrator responds to his difficult situation by

   (A) becoming paralyzed by fear.
   (B) continuing up the trail into the fog.
   (C) shooting his rifle.
   (D) throwing a grenade.
   (E) screaming while attacking.

25. The narrator experiences all the following sensations EXCEPT

   (A) a desire to warn the enemy of his danger.
   (B) difficulty in his ability to swallow.
   (C) extreme anger upon seeing his enemy.
   (D) an upset stomach.
   (E) a lack of real hatred.

**GO ON TO THE NEXT PAGE**

26. The syntactical variance of sentence lengths in the first paragraph best accomplishes which of the following?

    (A) Confuses the reader because of the irregular rhythm
    (B) Lulls the reader into a sense of security
    (C) Punctuates the tenseness of the situation
    (D) Demonstrates the writer's ability to vary his style
    (E) Reflects the writing style of the era

27. This passage could be said to begin

    (A) in a sinister manner.
    (B) *in medias res.*
    (C) melodramatically.
    (D) passively.
    (E) ironically.

28. The narrator's actions can best be described as

    (A) planned and deliberate.
    (B) arbitrary and random.
    (C) reactionary and pragmatic.
    (D) reflective and subjective.
    (E) heroic and laudable.

29. The narrator's attitude toward the dead enemy can best be described as

    (A) fear and anger.
    (B) regret and rationalization.
    (C) fraternity and humanity.
    (D) courage and patriotism.
    (E) satisfaction and pride.

30. All of the following are present in the passage EXCEPT

    (A) onomatopoeia.
    (B) foreshadowing.
    (C) idiomatic expression.
    (D) metaphor.
    (E) rationalization.

31. The theme of this passage can best be summed up with which of the following statements?

    (A) "Do unto others as you would want them to do to you."
    (B) "War makes man do things he would not do otherwise."
    (C) "Act first; regret later."
    (D) "Look out for yourself; no one else will."
    (E) "All is just in love and war."

32. The last sentence of the first paragraph describes the dead man using all of the following literary devices EXCEPT

    (A) parallelism.
    (B) anaphora.
    (C) metaphor.
    (D) simile.
    (E) imagery.

33. The most likely reason for the use of dashes in lines 43–45 is to

    (A) demonstrate the writer's syntactical skills.
    (B) reveal the narrator's emotional horror.
    (C) eliminate the need for conjunctions.
    (D) reveal the writer's lack of control.
    (E) provide structural variety to the paragraph.

**GO ON TO THE NEXT PAGE**

Questions 34–43 refer to the following passage. After reading the passage, choose the best answer to each question.

Act II, Scene I
Enter CLEOPATRA, IRAS, and ALEXAS

CLEOPATRA.  What shall I do, or whither shall
Line  I turn?
(5)  Ventidius has o'ercome, and he will go.

ALEXAS.  He goes to fight for you.

CLEOPATRA.  Then he would see me, ere he
went to fight:
Flatter me not:  If once he goes, he's lost,
(10)  And all my hopes destroyed.

ALEXAS.  Does this weak passion
Become a mighty queen?

CLEOPATRA.  I am no queen:
Is this to be a queen, to be besieged
(15)  By yon insulting Roman, and to wait
Each hour the victor's chain?  These ills are small:
For Antony is lost, and I can mourn
For nothing else but him.  Now come, Octavius,
I have no more to lose! prepare thy bands;
(20)  I'm fit to be a captive:  Antony
Has taught my mind the fortune of a slave.

IRAS.  Call reason to assist you.

CLEOPATRA.  I have none,
And none would have:  My love's a noble madness,
(25)  Which shows the cause deserved it.  Moderate
sorrow
Fits vulgar love, and for a vulgar man:
But I have loved with such transcendent passion,
I soared, at first, quite out of reason's view,
(30)  And now am lost above it.  No, I'm proud
'Tis thus:  Would Antony could see me now
Think you he would not sigh, though he must
leave me?
Sure he would sigh; for he is noble-natured,
(35)  And bears a tender heart:  I know him well.
Ah, no, I know him not; I knew him once,
But now 'tis past.

IRAS. Let it be past with you:
Forget him, madam.

(40)  CLEOPATRA. Never, never, Iras.
He once was mine; and once, though now
'tis gone,
Leaves a faint image of possession still.

ALEXAS. Think him inconstant, cruel, and
(45)  ungrateful.

CLEOPATRA. I cannot: If I could, those thoughts
were vain.
Faithless, ungrateful, cruel, though he be,
I still must love him.

(1678)

34.  Which of the following statements most
accurately describes Cleopatra?

(A)  She is not a queen.
(B)  In her grief, she is angry at Antony for dying.
(C)  She is jealous that Antony has run off with
another woman.
(D)  She disdains "vulgar" people who fall crazily
in love.
(E)  She realizes her love for Antony is
unreasonable, but she cannot bear to forget
him.

35.  Which of the following best summarizes the
main idea of Cleopatra's speech in lines 13-21?

(A)  It's not fitting for a powerful queen to be
conquered by a Roman.
(B)  No trial is as difficult for Cleopatra as
mourning Antony's absence.
(C)  Cleopatra is not afraid to be captured
because Antony already treated her like a
slave.
(D)  Cleopatra is humbled in the face of the loss
of her kingdom.
(E)  Cleopatra feels she isn't living up to her
station.

**GO ON TO THE NEXT PAGE**

36. In line 15, who is the "insulting Roman"?

    (A) Octavius
    (B) Iras
    (C) Antony
    (D) Ventidius
    (E) Aeneas

37. In line 24, Cleopatra calls her love a "noble madness" for all of the following reasons EXCEPT

    (A) her love is a "transcendent passion."
    (B) her sorrow for Antony's loss is total.
    (C) since she is a queen, her emotions must be noble.
    (D) her grief surpasses the "moderate sorrow" of "vulgar" lovers.
    (E) she rejects reason to keep loving Antony.

38. "Noble-natured" in line 34 is an example of

    (A) assonance.
    (B) an oxymoron.
    (C) alliteration.
    (D) onomatopoeia.
    (E) an Epithalamion.

39. The tone of Cleopatra's speech in lines 23–37 can best be described as

    (A) hysterical.
    (B) maudlin.
    (C) saccharine.
    (D) sarcastic.
    (E) tremulous.

40. In what poetic meter is this play written?

    (A) Iambic tetrameter
    (B) Iambic pentameter
    (C) Anapestic pentameter
    (D) Anapestic hexameter
    (E) None of the above

41. Which line contains a trochee?

    (A) 1
    (B) 12
    (C) 28
    (D) 15
    (E) 34

42. Judging by the year it was completed, this selection was written in what period of English history?

    (A) Edwardian era
    (B) Elizabethan era
    (C) Victorian era
    (D) Cromwellian era
    (E) Georgian era

43. Which of the following lines contains a neologism?

    (A) 2
    (B) 26
    (C) 35
    (D) All of the above
    (E) None of the above

**GO ON TO THE NEXT PAGE**

*Questions 44–58 refer to the following poem. After reading the poem, choose the best answer to each question.*

Cold in the earth—and the deep snow piled
    above thee.
Far, far removed, cold in the dreary grave!
*Line* Have I forgot, my Only Love, to love thee
(5) Severed at last by Time's all-severing wave?

Now, when alone, do my thoughts no longer
    hover
Over the mountains, on that northern shore,
Resting their wings where heath and fern leaves
(10)     cover
Thy noble heart forever, ever more?

Cold in the earth—and fifteen wild Decembers,
From those brown hills, have melted into spring;
Faithful indeed is the spirit that remembers
(15) After such years of change and suffering!

Sweet Love of youth, forgive, if I forget thee,
While the World's tide is bearing me along;
Other desires and other hopes beset me,
Hopes which obscure but cannot do thee
(20)     wrong!

No later light has lightened up my heaven,
No second morn has ever shone for me;
All my life's bliss from thee dear life has given,
All my life's bliss is in the grave with thee.

(25) But, when the days of golden dreams had
    perished,
And even Despair was powerless to destroy,
Then did I learn how existence could be
    cherished,
(30) Strengthened, and fed without the aid of joy.

Then did I check the tears of useless passion—
Weaned my young soul from yearning after
    thine;
Sternly denied its burning wish to hasten
(35) Down to that tomb already more than mine.

And even yet, I dare not let it languish,
Dare not indulge in Memory's rapturous pain;
Once drinking deep of that divinest anguish,
How could I seek the empty world again?

(1845)

44. This poem is best identified as

(A) a ballad.
(B) an apostrophe.
(C) an elegy.
(D) a lyric.
(E) a sonnet.

45. This poem's structure is specifically that of

(A) *aabb* rhyme scheme throughout.
(B) blank verse.
(C) free verse.
(D) alternating rhymed couplets.
(E) alternating rhymed lines within quatrains.

46. The metaphor present in the second stanza concerns

(A) northern mountains.
(B) noble heart.
(C) heath and fern.
(D) winged thoughts.
(E) hovering birds.

47. Which stanza contains examples of ALL of the following: alliteration, assonance, anaphora, and consonance?

(A) One
(B) Four
(C) Five
(D) Six
(E) Eight

48. The reader can infer from this passage that the narrator has

(A) continued to weep for a loved one.
(B) found new joy to live for.
(C) never stopped yearning.
(D) lamented a death for 15 years.
(E) been unfaithful to the departed.

**GO ON TO THE NEXT PAGE**

49. The narrator's diction within the last two stanzas is that of

    (A) a sorrowful child.
    (B) a desperate mourner.
    (C) an ominous portender.
    (D) a passionate young woman.
    (E) a struggling disciplinarian.

50. The narrator's tone in stanzas four and five can best be described as

    (A) apology and acquittal.
    (B) lamentation and sorrow.
    (C) resignation and determination.
    (D) reminiscence and nostalgia.
    (E) desperation and despair.

51. In line 36, the word "it" refers to

    (A) "tears of useless passion" (line 31).
    (B) "my life's bliss" (line 24).
    (C) "days of golden dreams" (line 25).
    (D) "my young soul" (line 32).
    (E) "Memory's rapturous pain" (line 37).

52. The narrator's present attitude toward what might have been is one of

    (A) wistful regret.
    (B) despair and anguish.
    (C) passionate remorse.
    (D) blissful reminiscence.
    (E) change and suffering.

53. The underlying theme of this poem can best be summarized as

    (A) "Time heals all wounds."
    (B) "Absence makes the heart grow fonder."
    (C) "Out of sight, out of mind."
    (D) "Out of sight, but not out of mind."
    (E) "Faith heals all wounds."

54. Stanzas one and eight can best be said to

    (A) capture the message of the poem.
    (B) bring the poem full circle.
    (C) imply blissful, unrequited passion within the narrator.
    (D) demonstrate the narrator's therapeutic healing.
    (E) remonstrate with the narrator's suicidal notion.

55. The final stanza of this poem has at least two examples of

    (A) metaphor.
    (B) oxymoron.
    (C) synecdoche.
    (D) onomatopoeia.
    (E) conceit.

56. The reader can infer from stanza four that

    (A) a new love has entered the narrator's life.
    (B) the narrator has worse things to cope with than another's death.
    (C) one's existence can only be strengthened by feeding it with joy.
    (D) life, even after great loss, can and should continue.
    (E) the narrator was destroyed by Despair.

**GO ON TO THE NEXT PAGE**

57. The narrator makes reference to all of the following EXCEPT
    (A) the passing of fifteen years.
    (B) new hopes and desires that obscure memory.
    (C) memories like winged spirits.
    (D) the inability to live without the departed.
    (E) fear of the soul's indulgence in rapturous pain.

58. The reader can infer from the last stanza that the narrator
    (A) has conquered the urge to remember.
    (B) cannot control the urge to indulge in self-pity.
    (C) refuses to be kept down by melancholy.
    (D) has weaned his or her soul from useless, passionless yearning.
    (E) dare not allow his or her soul to drink too deeply of anguished memories for fear of not being able to function in the world.

GO ON TO THE NEXT PAGE

*Questions 59–63 refer to the following passage. After reading the passage, choose the best answer to each question.*

I love the land and the buffalo and will not part with it. I want you to understand well what I say. Write it down on paper…I hear a great deal of
Line talk from the gentlemen whom the Great Father*
(5) sends us, but they never do what they say. I don't want any of the medicine lodges† within the country. I want the children raised as I was….

I have heard that you intend to settle us on a reservation near the mountains. I don't want to
(10) settle. I love to roam over the prairies. There I feel free and happy, but when we settle down, we grow pale and die. I have laid aside my lance, bow, and shield, and yet I feel safe in your presence. I have told you the truth. I have no little lies hid about
(15) me, but I don't know how it is with the commissioners. Are they as clear as I am? A long time ago this land belonged to our fathers; but when I go to the river, I see camps of soldiers on its banks. These soldiers cut down my timber; they kill my
(20) buffalo; and when I see that, my heart feels like bursting. I have spoken.

(1867)

* *Great Father*: President Andrew Jackson
† *medicine lodges*: schools and churches

59. The probable reason why the passage opens with "I love the land and buffalo and will not part with it," is to

(A) establish the speaker's purpose and bold tone immediately.
(B) refute charges that the speaker values possessions more than nature.
(C) coerce the speaker's audience into agreeing to his demands.
(D) set the narrative that follows in context.
(E) present a logical concession to this argument.

60. One message the speaker in this passage makes clear is that he

(A) embraces the notion of settling with his people on a reservation near the mountains.
(B) wants his children raised as he was.
(C) needs to feel safe in the presence of his audience.
(D) insists on being told the truth and not the usual pack of falsehoods.
(E) demands that the schools and churches of the white settlers allow his people access as well.

61. The speaker does NOT want any of the following things EXCEPT

(A) the white men to hunt buffalo any more.
(B) to negotiate with the commissioners who seem to have betrayed him in the past.
(C) that the soldiers remain to help him protect his land.
(D) his people to be left alone to their own devices.
(E) the opportunities to share customs and culture of the white settlers.

62. It can be inferred from this passage that if the speaker's people are forced to relocate to a reservation, they will probably

(A) adapt.
(B) perish.
(C) disappear.
(D) be resentful.
(E) lose their cultural identity.

**GO ON TO THE NEXT PAGE**

63. According to the speaker, what has happened to the forests and buffalo?

(A) They have been used up by tribes of Native Americans.

(B) They have been seized by the commissioners and allocated only sporadically to the tribes.

(C) They have been forbidden to the Native Americans.

(D) They have been destroyed by the soldiers.

(E) They have been deeded to the speaker's father, but the treaties are ignored.

## STOP!

**If you finish before time is up, you may check your work.**

# Diagnostic Test:
# Answer Key

| | | | |
|---|---|---|---|
| 1. D | 21. B | 41. E | 61. D |
| 2. B | 22. D | 42. B | 62. B |
| 3. A | 23. D | 43. E | 63. D |
| 4. C | 24. D | 44. C | |
| 5. D | 25. C | 45. E | |
| 6. E | 26. C | 46. D | |
| 7. B | 27. B | 47. C | |
| 8. C | 28. C | 48. D | |
| 9. B | 29. B | 49. E | |
| 10. E | 30. C | 50. A | |
| 11. D | 31. C | 51. D | |
| 12. E | 32. D | 52. A | |
| 13. B | 33. B | 53. D | |
| 14. B | 34. E | 54. B | |
| 15. D | 35. B | 55. B | |
| 16. B | 36. A | 56. D | |
| 17. E | 37. C | 57. D | |
| 18. E | 38. C | 58. E | |
| 19. E | 39. A | 59. A | |
| 20. B | 40. B | 60. B | |

# ANSWERS AND EXPLANATIONS

## Questions 1–13

The people I love the best
jump into work head first
without dallying in the shallows
*Line*   and swim off with sure strokes almost out of
(5)      sight.
They seem to become natives of that element
the black sleek heads of seals
bouncing like half-submerged balls.

I love people who harness themselves, an ox to a
(10)      heavy cart,
Who pull like water buffalo, with massive patience,
Who strain in the mud and the muck to move
     things forward,
Who do what has to be done, again and again.

(15)  I want to be with people who submerge
in the task, who go into the fields to harvest
and work in a row and pass the bags along,
who are not parlor generals and field deserters
but move in common rhythm
(20)  when the food must come in or the fire be put out.

The work of the world is common as mud.
Botched it smears the hands, crumbles to dust.
But the thing worth doing well done
has a shape that satisfies, clean and evident.
(25)  Greek amphoras for wine or oil,
Hopi vases that held corn, are put in museums
but you know they were made to be used.
The pitcher cries for water to carry
and the person for work that is real

## 1. D

The use of the seals, oxen, and buffalo is a purposeful comparison between these performing and working creatures and people who perform meaningful labor, an *extended metaphor* of the first two stanzas. *Personification* (A) gives human characteristics or qualities to an inanimate object or animal. You might be tempted by this answer choice, but note that the animals here are not given human characteristics; just the opposite. Although *fables* (B) often contain animals as allegorical characters, in this poem, animals are referred to in their normal sense. *Understatement* (C)—the deliberate attenuation of meaning sometimes designed to produce the opposite effect—doesn't occur in these stanzas. *Verisimilitude* (E) is the quality or characteristic of being true or real. It is not relevant to this question.

## 2. B

Please note: you are asked to identify something that is NOT found in stanza one. The narrator is indicated as first person from line 1 on; the second and third stanzas begin with *I*. Lines 7–8 actually contain a double *metaphor* (A): people to seals, seals to bouncing balls. Although several lines show evidence of *assonance* (C), the repetition of vowel sounds in a sequence of words with different endings, lines 6–7 have the best examples of assonance in the first stanza: "*seem…/sleek…seals.*" Despite the length of the two sentences that comprise the first stanza, each sentence is actually a *simple sentence* in its creation—(D), with multiple prepositional phrases. *Alliteration*—the repetition of initial consonant sounds—(E), is clearly present.

## 3. A

The narrator clearly has little tolerance for anyone who is not fully engaged in his or her work and has no respect for armchair generals or anyone who might desert the field of battle. *Derision* therefore conveys the narrator's contempt. In light of the correct answer, the narrator feels no *charity* towards either the general or the deserter ((B) and (C)). Although one might argue that the author's no-tolerance tone shows *impatience* (D), the question asks for the BEST response, which is derisiveness—note the scornful phrases "parlor general" and "deserters." No indication whatsoever of narrator *compassion* (E) for these types is evident.

## 4. C

*Free verse* is characterized by varying line lengths, lack of traditional meter, and nonrhyming lines, which certainly describe this poem. A *ballad* (A) is a common stanza form, which usually consists of quatrains that alternate four-beat and three-beat lines with a specific rhyme scheme. Despite the mention of animals in this poem, they are not used allegorically, ruling out *fable* (B). This poem is not a satire or spoof of anything serious and thus not *mock heroic* (D). One may find a few regular meters here and there within this poem, but no meter dominates the lines; the poem is not in *iambic pentameter* (E).

## 5. D

The narrator lauds labor that she perceives as worthwhile and beneficial to all. Although animals are mentioned in the first half of the poem (A), the poet is really talking about human toil. The poet has nothing but disdain for the general in the parlor (B). Although a *harvest* is mentioned (C), it is only one example of labor. A suggestion of endurance and patience can be found in this poem, but the chief idea is "the thing worth doing well done."

## 6. E

The pitcher's purpose is to hold water. It "cries" to do the job for which it was intended. Water is referred to metaphorically in line 28; (A) is off the mark. The pitcher is a museum piece, but the quotation is not a reference to a *museum treasure* (B). The tone of the quotation is not *sentimental* (C). One might think the "cry" is *yearning* (D), but the water reference is metaphorical.

## 7. B

The poet demonstrates *respect* and *admiration* for those who perform common labor for the common good. The only tone of *contempt* is for those like the general and the deserter; no *condescension* is present (A). Neither *jealousy* nor *envy* (C) is present in the tone of this poem. Although the poet defers to those who labor honestly, *humility* (D) is not evident, nor are *wistfulness* or *nostalgia* (E).

## 8. C

It is because these items have a useful purpose that the poet has chosen to feature them in this poem. The poet is not concerned with the *value* of these antiquities ((A) and (B)). The *beauty* of these items lies in their practicality, not necessarily their physical beauty (D). The only thing *unusual* about these antiquities is that they are kept from performing the task for which they were created (E).

## 9. B

When a sentence continues on to the next line of a poem, without a natural pause or stop, that is *enjambment*. Although the sentence may seem to *run on* (A), this response is not relevant to the question of end stopping. This poem does not contain rhyming pairs of iambic pentameter lines (C). *Petrarchan rhyme* (D) refers to a particular type of sonnet rhyme scheme. *Juxtaposition* (E) is the purposeful placement of one idea with another; this is not a relevant response to this question.

## 10. E

The poet's underlying meaning lies in the vessels that were created to serve a practical purpose and the humans who perform worthwhile labor—all else is meaningless. The other responses are, indeed, feelings of the narrator, but none of the other choices is as broad as (E), which BEST states the theme.

## 11. D

Irony refers to a contradiction between what something really is and how it is perceived. In this case, the poet is commenting on the difference between how the Hopi vases were intended to be used (to hold corn) and how they are seen today (as displayed objects in museums).

## 12. E

The word *element* in line 6 is a reference to line 2, "jump into *work* headfirst."

## 13. B

*Anaphora* is the repetition of the same word or phrase at the beginning of successive phrases or clauses, as in the repetition of *who* in this stanza. *Alliteration* (A) is the repetition of initial consonant sounds. *Apposition* (C) is a renaming of a noun or pronoun, not a repetitive structure. *Apostrophe* (D) is an address to an inanimate object, such as the wind or an ocean. *Assonance* (E) is the repetition of vowel sounds in a sequence of words with different endings, such as in "I will *sign* the papers, *wind* the clock, and *find* my way to bed."

## Questions 14–23

There is a canal two rods wide along the
northerly and westerly sides of the pond, and
wider still at the east end. A great field of ice has
Line cracked off from the main body. I hear a song
(5) sparrow singing from the bushes on the shore. He
too is helping to crack it. How handsome the great
sweeping curves in the edge of the ice, answering
somewhat to those of the shore, but more regular!
It is unusually hard, owing to the recent severe
(10) but transient cold, and all watered or waved like
a palace floor. But the wind slides eastward over
its opaque surface in vain, till it reaches the living
surface beyond. It is glorious to behold this ribbon of water sparkling in the sun, the bare face of
(15) the pond full of glee and youth, as if it spoke the
joy of the fishes within it, and of the sands on its
shore.

The change from storm and winter to serene
and mild weather, from dark and sluggish hours
(20) to bright and elastic ones, is a memorable crisis
which all things proclaim. It is seemingly instantaneous at last. Suddenly an influx of light filled my
house, though the evening was at hand, and the
clouds of winter still overhung it, and the eaves
(25) were dripping with sleety rain. I looked out the
window, and lo! where yesterday was cold gray ice
there lay the transparent pond already calm and
full of hope as in a summer evening reflecting a
summer evening sky in its bosom, though none
(30) was visible overhead. The pitch pines and shrub
oaks about my house, which had so long drooped,
suddenly resumed their several characters, looked
brighter, greener, and more erect and alive, as if
effectually cleansed and restored by the rain. I
(35) knew that it would not rain any more. You may
tell by looking at any twig of the forest, aye, at
your very woodpile, whether its winter is past or
not. As it grew darker, I was startled by the honking of geese flying low over the woods, like weary
(40) travelers getting in late from southern lakes, and
indulging at last in unrestrained complaint and
mutual consolation. Standing at my door, I could
hear the rush of their wings; when, driving toward
my house, they suddenly spied my light, and with
(45) hushed clamor wheeled and settled in the pond.

In the morning I watched the geese from the
door through the mist, sailing in the middle of
the pond, fifty rods off, large and tumultuous. But
when I stood on the shore they at once rose up
(50) with great flapping of wings at the signal of their
commander, and when they had got into rank
circled about over my head, twenty-nine of them,
and then steered straight to Canada, with a regular honk from the leader at intervals. A plump of
(55) ducks rose at the same time and took the route to
the north in the wake of their noisier cousins.

For a week I heard the circling groping clangor
of some solitary goose in the foggy mornings,
seeking its companion, and still peopling the
(60) woods with the sound of a larger life than they
could sustain. In April the pigeons were seen again
flying express in small flocks, and in due time I
heard the martins twittering over my clearing,
though it had not seemed that the township con-
(65) tained so many that it could afford me any, and
I fancied that they were peculiarly of the ancient
race that dwelt in hollow trees ere white men
came. In almost all climes the tortoise and the frog
are among the precursors and herald of this sea-
(70) son, and birds fly with song and glancing plumage,
and plants spring and bloom, and winds blow to
correct this slight oscillation of the poles and preserve the equilibrium of Nature.

As every season seems best to us in its turn, so
(75) the coming in of spring is like creation of Cosmos
out of Chaos and the realization of the Golden
Age.

(1854)

## 14. B

The correct response must be inferred. (C) contradicts
the passage, since the narrator says (lines 35–38) that
looking at the woodpile can tell you winter is over—that
is, the wood that was stocked up before winter has been
used up. (A), (D), and (E) are actually statements of fact,
which do not have to be inferred at all. They do, however
add up to the overall, not-too-subtle inference that the
*pond is melting*, (B).

## 15. D

The narrator is so excited, so taken by the changes he sees, he can only praise the coming of the spring. There is no proof for (A) and no basis for this judgment. (B) and (C) are too straightforward and are too specific to be correct; neither describes the passage's overall purpose. Although there is truth to (E), the melting pond is but one detail within the bigger picture.

## 16. B

*Personification* certainly prevails. For example, the geese are tired, squabbling travelers, seeking refuge for the night, wheeling around (as if in a car), falling into rank as ordered by their commander, etc. The description within this passage is anything but *restrained* (A). *Bombast* (C) has connotations of being affected. This narrator is not putting on any act within this writing. Although one may see the narrator's description as occasionally overdone, *hyperbole* (D) is not as predominant as personification. A *rhetorical question* (E), or a question meant to be answered by the writer, is not in evidence within this passage.

## 17. E

The narrator's clever use of figurative language, multiple levels of sensory images, and manipulation of sentence rhythms create a *poetic* tone to this passage. This passage uses too much figurative language to be just *colloquial* (A). Although the narrator shares *information* with the reader, (B) would not be the best description of the narrator's tone. Some may feel that the celebratory nature of this poem is out of control (C), but *unrestrained* is not the BEST response. *Audacious*—bold and impudent—(D) is not appropriate to describe the tone of this passage.

## 18. E

A *mirror of his soul* is not a comparison found in this passage. The other references can be found in the passage: (A), *a canal two rods wide* (line 1); (B), *a ribbon* (lines 13–14); (C), *a transparent pond* (line 27); (D), *a reflection of the sky* (lines 28–29).

## 19. E

Lines 38–56 are loaded with sounds and visual images that bring the geese alive within this passage. Although the passage does contain both *similes and metaphors* (A), they do not dominate the description of the geese. Perhaps some might be amused by the narrator's descriptions (B), but *comic descriptors* is not the BEST description of the geese. The narrator does not *reflect emotionally* (C) in the description of the geese. The writer has tight control of the description; the images are related (D).

## 20. B

Lines 68–70 state that in almost all regions, the tortoise and the frogs, not the geese, appear first in the spring. The simile of geese like *weary travelers* (A) can be found in lines 39–40. Lines 50–54 describe the *regimental force* of geese led by the honking commander (C). Lines 41–42 mention the unrestrained complaint and mutual consolation (D) among the geese. Lines 54–56 talk about the ducks who are following their noisier cousins, the geese (E). Nowhere does it say or imply the geese are the *last to arrive* (B). Be careful with EXCEPT questions: you are asked to identify what is NOT present.

## 21. B

*The innocence of mankind* is NOT discussed within this passage. The passage itself reveals how very connected at least one person is to the world of nature (A). The narrator makes it clear that what is going on has happened before and will happen again (C). Obviously, the narrator has been *awaiting* the passing of winter and has been looking forward to a new season (D). The geese and ducks' return, the tortoise, frogs, and other creatures are all announcing an imminent *change* (E).

## 22. D

Actually, there are very few *simple sentences* within this passage, making this the correct response. Some *periodic sentences* (A) are used in this passage, but so are many other sentence structures. Many *prepositional phrases* (B) are used in this passage. No *rhetorical questions* are evident within this passage (C). Although some *parallelism* exists in this piece, it is certainly not overused (E).

## 23. D

*Plump* in this case is most like the word *clutch*, which is a term meaning a brood of chicks. This is similar to other collective descriptors, such as a *pride* of lions or a *pod* of whales.

**Questions 24–33**

Very gradually, in tiny slivers, day began to break through the fog, and from my position in the brush I could see ten or fifteen meters up the

Line trail. The mosquitoes were fierce. I remember
(5) slapping at them…then looking up and seeing the young man come out of the fog. He wore black clothing and rubber sandals and a gray ammunition belt. His shoulders were slightly stooped, his head cocked to the side listening to something.
(10) He seemed at ease. He carried his weapon in one hand, muzzle down, moving without any hurry up the center of the trail. There was no sound at all— none that I can remember. In a way, it seemed, he was part of the morning fog, or my own imagina-
(15) tion, but there was also the reality of what was happening in my stomach. I had already pulled the pin on a grenade. I had come up to a crouch. It was entirely automatic. I did not hate the young man; I did not see him as the enemy; I did not
(20) ponder issues of morality or politics or military duty. I crouched and kept my head low. I tried to swallow whatever was rising from my stomach, which tasted like lemonade, something fruity and sour. I was terrified. There were no thoughts
(25) about killing. The grenade was to make him go away—just evaporate—and I leaned back and felt my mind go empty and then fill up again. I had already thrown the grenade before telling myself to throw it. The brush was thick and I had to lob
(30) it high, not aiming, and I remember the grenade seeming to freeze above me for an instant, as if a camera had clicked and I remember ducking down and holding my breath and seeing little wisps of fog rise from the earth. The grenade
(35) bounced once and rolled across the trail. I did not hear it, but there must've been a sound, because the young man dropped his weapon and began to run, just two or three quick steps, then he hesitated, swiveling to his right, and he glanced
(40) down at the grenade and tried to cover his head but never did. It occurred to me then that he was about to die. I wanted to warn him. The grenade made a popping noise—not soft but not loud either—not what I'd expected—and there was a puff of dust and smoke—a small white puff— and the young man seemed to jerk upward as if

(45) pulled by invisible wires. He fell on his back. His rubber sandals had been blown off. There was no wind. He lay at the center of the trail, his right leg bent beneath him, his one eye shut, his other eye a
(50) huge star-shaped blue.

All I could do was gape at the fact of the young man's body. Even now, I haven't finished sorting it out. Sometimes I forgive myself, other times I don't. In the ordinary hours of life I try not to
(55) dwell on it, but now and then, when I'm reading a newspaper or just sitting alone in a room, I'll look up and see the young man coming out of the morning fog. I'll watch him walk toward me, his shoulders slightly stooped, his head cocked to the
(60) side, and he'll pass within a few yards of me and suddenly smile at some secret thought and then continue up the trail to where it bends back into the fog.

(1990)

## 24. D

The narrator responds to the enemy's presence by lobbing a grenade at him. The narrator is moved to action; he's not too scared to act (A). The passage ends as the narrator envisions the *enemy* continuing along the path without interruption; the *narrator* does not continue up the trail (B). The narrator does not *shoot his rifle* (C), and the passage gives no indication that the narrator makes much sound (E).

## 25. C

"I did not hate the young man; I did not see him as the enemy," lines 18–20, indicate that this is the correct response. The narrator does not feel *anger* toward the enemy. The narrator does say that "I wanted to warn him," line 42 (A). In lines 21–22, the narrator says that "I tried to swallow whatever was rising from my stomach" (B) and (D). The same reason that (C) is the correct answer makes (E) incorrect. The narrator feels *no hatred* toward his enemy.

## 26. C

Short, staccato sentences juxtaposed with longer ones build *tension* within this paragraph. The variance may *confuse* some readers (A), but this is not the correct response. Sentence variation keeps the reader more, not less alert (B). (D) may be true, but the writer's sentence writing skill is not the BEST response to this question. We do not have the necessary information to determine the validity of (E).

## 27. B

*In medias res* is the correct response since the passage opens in the middle of the action, without any information building up to this scene. The opening may seem a bit mysterious, but there is no indication of a *sinister* mood (A). The passage is more matter-of-fact at the start than *melodramatic* (C). Although the narrator does not act until he sees the enemy, he is still actively attentive to his surroundings (D). There is no *irony* in the straightforward opening of this piece (E).

## 28. C

The narrator states that his mind went empty and that he "had already thrown the grenade before telling [himself] to throw it" (lines 28–29). In other words, he sees the enemy and throws the grenade at him—kill or be killed. He is reacting in a practical (*pragmatic*) manner to his situation. This difficult question is a good example of how process of elimination can get you to the right answer choice. In line 18, the narrator admits that his actions were "entirely automatic," ruling out (A). He reacts to his situation—seeing danger. It is practical for him to throw his "weapon" at the danger; it is not an *arbitrary* move, discounting (B). *Reflective and subjective* (D) are not how the narrator reacts until later. The narrator's actions are too controversial to make *heroic and laudable* (E) the appropriate adjectives to describe them.

## 29. B

*Regret and rationalization* are the essence of the piece—this can be seen particularly in the last paragraph of the passage. The narrator admits fear, but he never talks about being *angry* (A). The narrator's *humanity* is mainly evidenced by his occasional regret at killing his "enemy"; while there is a hint of *fraternity* in the narrator's attitude toward his adversary, (C) is not the BEST choice. (D) and (E) are not found anywhere in this passage.

## 30. C

The passage contains no *idiomatic expressions*; that is, particular phrases or word combinations that are peculiar to a certain language or region of a country and that usually can't be translated literally, such as "It's raining cats and dogs." *Onomatopoeia* can be located in this passage in "there was a puff of dust and smoke" (lines 44–45) and in lines 42–43, "the grenade made a popping noise" (A). *Foreshadowing* (B) is present at the opening of the passage as soon as the narrator describes his hiding in the jungle and the appearance of the enemy with a gun. One of them is bound to be killed. Perhaps the most outstanding *metaphor* (D) can be found in the last sentence of the first paragraph in the "huge star-shaped blue" (lines 50–51) eye. The narrator refers to rationalizing (E)—"sorting it out" and "sometimes I forgive myself" (lines 53–54)—in the last paragraph.

## 31. C

This is the best statement to summarize the theme of this particular passage. (A) may need to be read twice to see that it is incorrect. (B), (D), and (E) are trite responses that often describe the thematic undertones of war literature.

## 32. D

No *simile* is present in the last sentence of paragraph 1. *Parallel structure* (A) is found in the series of phrases describing the dead enemy (his right leg bent, his one eye shut…(lines 49–51). *Anaphora* (B) is present because phrases in the series repeat "his." The eye as a star-shaped hole is certainly a vivid *metaphor* (C). The *imagery* of this sentence is vivid and disturbing (E).

## 33. B

Reminiscent of Marlow in Conrad's *Heart of Darkness*, it is the horror, the unbelievability of what is happening, that the narrator is having difficulties with. The dash implies hesitation, speechlessness, as if the narrator cannot quite grasp that his survival instinct has caused this ghastly action and its result. The use of the dash does not generally qualify anyone as *syntactically skillful* (A). The conjunction "and" is used directly after the dashes (C). (D) is an opposite: The dashes are used for a specific effect in the piece. While the dashes do provide *variety* (E), the most likely reason for their use is to communicate the narrator's mood.

**Questions 34–43**

Act II, Scene I
Enter CLEOPATRA, IRAS, and ALEXAS

CLEOPATRA.  What shall I do, or whither shall
Line  I turn?
(5)  Ventidius has o'ercome, and he will go.

ALEXAS.  He goes to fight for you.

CLEOPATRA.  Then he would see me, ere he
went to fight:
Flatter me not:  If once he goes, he's lost,
(10)  And all my hopes destroyed.

ALEXAS.  Does this weak passion
Become a mighty queen?

CLEOPATRA.  I am no queen:
Is this to be a queen, to be besieged
(15)  By yon insulting Roman, and to wait
Each hour the victor's chain?  These ills are small:
For Antony is lost, and I can mourn
For nothing else but him.  Now come, Octavius,
I have no more to lose! prepare thy bands;
(20)  I'm fit to be a captive:  Antony
Has taught my mind the fortune of a slave.

IRAS.  Call reason to assist you.

CLEOPATRA.  I have none,
And none would have:  My love's a noble madness,
(25)  Which shows the cause deserved it.  Moderate
sorrow
Fits vulgar love, and for a vulgar man:
But I have loved with such transcendent passion,
I soared, at first, quite out of reason's view,
(30)  And now am lost above it.  No, I'm proud
'Tis thus:  Would Antony could see me now
Think you he would not sigh, though he must
leave me?
Sure he would sigh; for he is noble-natured,
(35)  And bears a tender heart:  I know him well.
Ah, no, I know him not; I knew him once,
But now 'tis past.

IRAS. Let it be past with you:
Forget him, madam.

(40)  CLEOPATRA. Never, never, Iras.
He once was mine; and once, though now 'tis
gone,
Leaves a faint image of possession still.

ALEXAS. Think him inconstant, cruel, and
(45)  ungrateful.

CLEOPATRA. I cannot: If I could, those thoughts
were vain.
Faithless, ungrateful, cruel, though he be,
I still must love him.

(1678)

**34. E**

The only statement that summarizes Cleopatra's characteristics from the information in the passage is (E). In line 13, Cleopatra says, "I am no queen" (A), but it's clear she means it ironically. Even if one misses the irony, Alexas's question immediately before provides proof that Cleopatra is indeed royalty. Though Cleopatra grieves over Antony's absence (B), and one may argue she's angry with him, there's no evidence that he died. She says he is "lost," and she mourns him, but that doesn't mean he was killed. Likewise, there's no evidence he ran off with another woman (C). Cleopatra disdains "vulgar" lovers for their "moderate sorrow," which implies a tepid love, as opposed to the "transcendent passion" she has for Antony, which she calls a "noble madness" (D).

**35. B**

Though four of the five answers are true, (B) captures the MAIN IDEA of the speech. Cleopatra dismisses the battle against the Roman (A) as a small problem next to her grief over Antony. Likewise, her mention of possible capture (C) and feeling less than a queen (E) are "small ills" in comparison with losing her lover. Cleopatra shows no humility at the prospect of losing her kingdom (D); rather, she "can mourn for nothing else" but Antony.

**36. A**

It's clear Octavius is the "insulting Roman" (line 15) who is laying siege to Cleopatra's kingdom by her exclamation in lines 18–19, "Now come, Octavius, I have no more to lose!"

## 37. C

Only (C) is unsupported by the text. Cleopatra and her questioners never suggest she or her feelings are noble simply because of her royalty.

## 38. C

Alliteration (C) is a repetition of two or more consonants in adjacent words or syllables. Assonance (A) is a repetition of two or more vowel sounds in adjacent words or syllables. An oxymoron (B) is a combination of words that seem to be opposite in meaning, as in "hellish ecstasy." Onomatopoeia (D) is a word or words identify something by imitating the sound associated with it, as in "sizzle" or "purr." An epithalamion (E) is a poem written to honor a wedding.

## 39. A

Hysterical (A) comes closest to describing the tone of Cleopatra's speech, as it deals with madness and love beyond reason. Maudlin (B) connotes a treacly, sentimental feeling that lacks the vigor of Cleopatra's passion. Saccharine (C) is a synonym of maudlin. To be sarcastic (D) is to be cutting and abrasive toward someone else. Cleopatra writhes in pain and grief, but she does not lash out at Antony. Tremulous (E) implies timidity and shyness, far different from Cleopatra's unbridled agony.

## 40. B

The play was written in iambic pentameter (B), in which each line contains five iambic feet. An iambic foot consists of two syllables, a soft one followed by a stressed one, as in "the queen." Therefore, each line contains ten syllables. In some cases, the lines are shorter because one person's dialogue ends and the next speaker finishes the meter, as in lines 10–13. Iambic tetrameter (A) consists of four iambic feet, for a total of eight syllables per line. Poems written in anapestic pentameter (C) feature lines of five anapestic feet. Each anapestic foot contains two soft syllables followed by one stressed syllable, as in "choo-choo train." Anapestic hexameter (D) refers to lines of six anapestic feet, for a total of 18 syllables. It's easy to remember the number of feet per line when you've memorized the Greek prefixes "mono-" (one), "di-" (two), "tri-" (three), and so on, and add "meter" to the end: monometer, dimeter, trimeter, etc.

## 41. E

A trochee is a metrical foot of two syllables where the first is stressed and the second unstressed, as in "knocking." The only line containing a trochee is 34 (E), which begins with "Sure he," where "sure" is stressed and "he" isn't.

## 42. B

Though the SAT Literature test will not have many questions pertaining to history, students should be familiar with major literary eras. The Elizabethan era (B), in which Dryden wrote Antony and Cleopatra, was also the age of Shakespeare. It ran from 1558–1603, the years of Elizabeth I's reign. The Edwardian era, which covered the reign of King Edward VII, ran from 1901–1910. This followed the Victorian era (C), 1837–1901, spanning the reign of Queen Victoria. Oliver Cromwell (D) ruled from 1653–1658, but his influence spanned several years before and after he served as Lord Protector of England. The Georgian era (E), 1714–1830, included the reigns of kings George I, II, III, and IV.

## 43. E

A neologism is a new word that might at first seem nonsensical, such as Lewis Carroll's "jabberwocky." None of the lines have neologisms, so the correct answer is (E).

**Questions 44–58**

Cold in the earth—and the deep snow piled
   above thee.
Far, far removed, cold in the dreary grave!
Have I forgot, my only Love, to love thee
Line  Severed at last by Time's all-severing wave?
(5)   Now, when alone, do my thoughts no longer
   hover
Over the mountains, on that northern shore,
Resting their wings where heath and fern leaves
   cover
(10)  Thy noble heart forever, ever more?

Cold in the earth—and fifteen wild Decembers,
From those brown hills, have melted into spring;
Faithful indeed is the spirit that remembers
After such years of change and suffering!

(15)  Sweet Love of youth, forgive, if I forget thee,
While the world's tide is bearing me along;
Other desires and other hopes beset me,
Hopes which obscure, but cannot do thee
   wrong!

(20)  No later light has lightened up my heaven,
No second morn has ever shone for me;
All my life's bliss from thee dear life has given,
All my life's bliss is in the grave with thee.

But, when the days of golden dreams had
(25)   perished,
And even Despair was powerless to destroy,
Then did I learn how existence could be
   cherished,
Strengthened, and fed without the aid of joy.

(30)  Then did I check the tears of useless passion—
Weaned my young soul from yearning after
   thine;
Sternly denied its burning wish to hasten
Down to that tomb already more than mine.

(35)  And even yet, I dare not let it languish,
Dare not indulge in memory's rapturous pain;
Once drinking deep of that divinest anguish,
How could I seek the empty world again?

**44. C**

This poem is an *elegy*, a lament over someone's death. Reject (A), *ballad*, based on the poem's meter and lack of refrain. An *apostrophe* (B) is an address to an inanimate object. While the poem has the intense emotion of a *lyric* (D), *elegy* (C) fits the poem perfectly. The poem lacks the fourteen-line structure of a *sonnet* (E).

**45. E**

This poem *alternates its rhyming lines* within each four-line stanza, or quatrain. The incorrect rhyme scheme in (A) is designed to catch a careless test taker. *Blank verse* (B) consists of unrhymed lines in iambic pentameter. *Free verse* (C) is characterized by varying line lengths, lack of traditional meter, and nonrhyming lines. The rhyme scheme here is *abab*, eliminating (D).

**46. D**

All of stanza two concerns the narrator's thoughts. (A), (B), and (C) provide the background for the narrator's thoughts about her lover's gravesite, whereas (E) is a distracter: the narrator's thoughts, and not birds, "hover."

**47. C**

Stanza five contains *alliteration* and *assonance* when it says "later light has lightened…"; *anaphora* is present in the "No" and "all my…" repetitions; *consonance* is present in line 21 as well ("*later light*").

**48. D**

The narrator makes it clear that she *no longer weeps* (A), that her life may be cherished *without joy* (B), that she has trained herself *not to yearn* (C), and that she has, indeed, remained *faithful to the departed* (E). She does continue to remember her dead lover, however.

**49. E**

Look at the words *check*, *weaned*, *yearning*, *sternly denied*, and *dare not indulge* to see that the narrator has been working hard to keep her anguished soul from dwelling too long with rapturous but painful memories of the deceased.

## 50. A

*Apology* and *acquittal* dominate these two stanzas. Although many of the other feelings are present throughout the poem and within these stanzas, the dominant tone is that of the narrator's sorrowful begging for forgiveness and exoneration from the departed spirit because she, the narrator, has picked up the pieces of her shattered life.

## 51. D

This response takes the reader back to stanza seven, lines 32–33, where the narrator says "Weaned my young soul from yearning after thine." This "young soul" is the antecedent to the word *it* in line 36.

## 52. A

The narrator has stated her resolve to avoid the strong emotions of grief and has decided no longer to suffer. Her present attitude can best be described as *wistful regret*.

## 53. D

Although all of the sentiments offered in these responses may have a bit of credence, the BEST response for this poem is (D). Although someone has been departed for fifteen years and life has had to continue for the living, thoughts of the departed are never far from the narrator's mind.

## 54. B

Some may think that these two stanzas hold the key to the poem's meaning (A), but the narrator's description of her life after her loss in the other stanzas is critical to *the message of the poem*. If the reader looks closely, he or she will find these stanzas have a redundancy about them that BEST suggests the cyclical or looping characteristic of the poem's structure.

## 55. B

The final stanza of Emily Brontë's poem has much to offer, including a rhetorical question. The middle two lines, which include "rapturous pain" and "divinest anguish," certainly offer two fine examples of *oxymoron*.

## 56. D

Stanza four assures the reader that life continues, despite losses. No matter how much the loss is felt, life must go on; it is worth living.

## 57. D

Nowhere does it say that the narrator is actually incapable of living without the departed. Stanza three mentions *fifteen* Decembers that have subsequently melted into spring (A); stanza four talks about other *hopes*, which beset the narrator (B); stanza two sets up the metaphor of thoughts as *winged spirits* (C). The final stanza mentions that the narrator fears for the soul that might linger in the memories of *rapturous pain* (E).

## 58. E

Although you might be tempted to choose several of these responses, the most accurate response, in light of the final stanza, is that the narrator must be careful NOT to let her soul linger too long in anguished memory or the world and day-to-day life will seem "empty."

## Questions 59–63

I love the land and the buffalo and will not part with it. I want you to understand well what I say. Write it down on paper…I hear a great deal of
*Line* talk from the gentlemen whom the Great Father*
(5) sends us, but they never do what they say. I don't want any of the medicine lodges† within the country. I want the children raised as I was….

I have heard that you intend to settle us on a reservation near the mountains. I don't want to
(10) settle. I love to roam over the prairies. There I feel free and happy, but when we settle down, we grow pale and die. I have laid aside my lance, bow, and shield, and yet I feel safe in your presence. I have told you the truth. I have no little lies hid about
(15) me, but I don't know how it is with the commissioners. Are they as clear as I am? A long time ago this land belonged to our fathers; but when I go to the river, I see camps of soldiers on its banks. These soldiers cut down my timber; they kill my
(20) buffalo; and when I see that, my heart feels like bursting. I have spoken.

(1867)

\* *Great Father*: President Andrew Jackson
† *medicine lodges*: schools and churches

## 59. A

The passage opens with a discussion of the land and the buffalo to *establish the speaker's purpose and bold tone immediately*. This speaker has a very definite point to make, and he is not going to make the telling a soft one. He wants to be heard, and he jumps right in with his strong tone and states his purpose. There really is no argument, so he is not *refuting charges* (B), nor is he offering any *concession* (E). He is not *coercing* anyone (C); he simply tells how he feels and hopes the right people are listening. These opening lines about the buffalo and land relate to the succeeding narrative (D) but don't provide a context or setting for it. The speaker has a purpose, and these opening lines declare his intentions from the very start.

## 60. B

This passage makes clear that the speaker *wants his children raised as he was*. The last sentence of the first paragraph states this message: "I want the children raised as I was…." Right after that, he says, "I don't want

to *settle*" (lines 9–10) (A). The speaker says he *feels safe* with his audience, but this is more a declaration of his courage than a need to be protected (C). He says, "I have told you the truth….[but] I don't know how it is with the commissioners" (lines 13–16), which suggests he may not have been told the *truth*, but this is not strong enough to support (D) an a response, because it uses the more fervent phrase, "usual pack of falsehoods;" nor is the speaker "insisting" on the honesty of his hearers. Finally, he makes no mention of Indians being allowed access to *schools and churches of the white settlers* (E).

## 61. D

The speaker wants *his people to be left alone to their own devices*. This is potentially a confusing question because it presents you with negatives (what he does *not* want) and the one thing he *does* want is what you must decide. If you read through the passage, you will see that he does *not* want white men to hunt his buffalo (A); he prefers *not* to negotiate with suspect commissioners (B); he does *not* want the soldiers on his land (C); and he does *not* want the white man's culture (E). The only thing he truly desires is that they just be left alone, making (D) the only possible response.

## 62. B

If the speaker's people are forced to relocate to a reservation, they will probably *perish*. The speaker seems to be strongly suggesting this. He tells his audience that he does not want to settle but to be left to roam the prairies. He assures his listeners that "when we settle down, we grow pale and die" (lines 11–12). Despite any prior knowledge you may possess, you must look only to this passage to answer this question. The question reminds you with "It can be inferred from this passage…," and that is all you must consider when you choose the correct response.

## 63. D

The forests and the buffalo *have been destroyed by the soldiers*. There is no indication that the land or the buffalo have been *used up by Native American tribes* (A). From what we read in this passage, we do not know if the *commissioner has allocated* the lands or animals to anyone (B) or *forbidden* them to anyone (C). And, although *treaties* had most likely been broken (E), this is not part of this passage. The speaker says, "I see camps of soldiers on its banks. These soldiers cut down my timber [forests]; they kill my buffalo; and when I see that, my heart feels like bursting" (lines 18–21).

## HOW TO USE THE RESULTS OF YOUR DIAGNOSTIC TEST IN YOUR REVIEW

After taking the diagnostic test, you should have an idea of what subjects you are strong in and what topics you need to study more. You can use this information to tailor your approach to the following review chapters. If your time to prepare for the test is limited, skip right to the chapters that you need to review most.

Part Three

# Literature Review

# Chapter 3: **Terms You Need to Know for the SAT Subject Test: Literature**

- Narrative Elements
- Literary Elements
- Literary Devices
- Rhetorical Devices
- Sound Devices
- Poetic Styles and Genres
- Prose Terms
- Voice

In this chapter, we will review literary terms associated with the SAT Subject Test's various genres and types of questions.

The literary terms discussed herein are the ones most frequently found on the test. This chapter arranges the terms according to certain categories, so if you are familiar with a certain group of terms, you may go on to another section.

## NARRATIVE ELEMENTS

These elements form the familiar "witch's hat" diagram and trace the course of a story's progress:

climax

rising action

falling action

exposition

denouement

## Exposition

Also known as the *introduction*, this part of a story gives basic background on characters, plot, and setting. Exposition "sets the scene." Any device or description that helps to introduce a narrative may be referred to as an *expository element*. Dickens's "It was the best of times, it was the worst of times," is a famous bit of exposition that helps to set the social background for *A Tale of Two Cities*.

## Rising Action

Also known as *complication*, this part of the story develops *conflict*, a necessity for any narrative: if there is no conflict, then there is no story. Generally, the main types of conflict include the following: human versus environment ("Joe lost his job because of the recession."), human versus human ("Joe punched his boss in the gut."), and human versus self ("Joe felt guilt-ridden for punching his boss in the gut.").

## Climax

The climax of a story is sometimes called its "high point" or "point of no return." Here, something occurs to alter forever the story's main progression. In Shakespeare's *Romeo and Juliet*, the tomb scene—where the misguided lovers kill themselves—is a classic example of climax.

## Falling Action

Also known as *reversal*, falling action speeds the story to its end. As the term implies, falling action is a descent, a result of the climax's forceful influence. ("After Joe died [climax!] from the grief of punching his boss, everyone in the office assembled at Joe's desk to remember him fondly.")

## Denouement

Also known as the *conclusion*, the denouement gives the story closure ("The office workers erected a statue in Joe's name.").

# LITERARY ELEMENTS

If narrative elements are the *movement* of a story, then literary elements are the things being *moved*. An author manipulates plot, characterization, setting, theme, tone, and mood to *create* the story.

> STORY SAMPLE: Under an impolite sun, Regina impatiently stood on the street corner waiting for the "Don't Walk" sign to stop flashing. Fifth and Main was a wasteland of transportation: not one car, not one truck adulterated either street. And still, the "Don't Walk" sign winked mockingly at her. Checking her watch one last time, and craning her neck for a glimpse of any oncoming Subaru, she briskly pattered into Main. Out of nowhere, a moped rounded Fifth and flattened her.

Now, here are the story's literary elements.

## Plot

Plot is the action of the story, the sequence of events that creates a cause/effect pattern. In the story sample, the plot is as follows: a woman is impatiently waiting to cross a street; she finally does so, against the light; an errant moped knocks her down.

## Characterization

This element is not just a list of people in a story. Characterization is also about personality and how personality develops throughout the narrative, if at all. A character may be either "static" (remaining unchanged in a story) or "dynamic" (undergoing some kind of personality alteration). Additionally, a character can either have "roundness," with a fully developed and complex personality, or "flatness," having little development at all. Regina is obviously static, as the incident with the moped gives her no time in the story to alter her personality.

## Other character terms you may encounter on the test

*Protagonist:* This is the main character of the story; Regina is the protagonist here.

*Antagonist:* This is an opponent of the protagonist; although we do not see an actual character in this role, we may assume that the moped rider is Regina's antagonist.

*Foil:* This is a character whose function it is to emphasize the personality traits of some other character. In a way, the moped rider stresses Regina's impatience or her rebelliousness against the "Don't Walk" sign.

*Tragic hero:* This is the protagonist of a tragedy. Traditionally, it is a person of noble birth who suffers a downfall because of a tragic flaw in his or her personality. Again, Regina would not be in the running here, but Hamlet and Macbeth fit the bill.

*Antihero:* This is a protagonist with villainous qualities; Regina wouldn't work, but Satan from Milton's *Paradise Lost* makes a good antihero.

## Setting

This element refers to the time and place in which the literary work occurs. Our story above takes place in a daytime, contemporary, urban setting.

## Theme

*Theme*'s definition is harder to pin down. For our purposes, we will say that theme is an idea or an observation set forth by the story as a universal truth. To oversimplify the concept, one could say that a moral is one type of theme, but it is not the only type. A theme in Regina's situation might be that impatience can blind us to our surroundings. A more pessimistic theme could also be that no matter how we prepare, life will always find a way to crush us.

## Tone

A story's tone displays the attitude of its narrator, his or her opinion of the characters and events in the story. This particular narrator seems at first sympathetic with Regina, calling the sun "impolite," perhaps maltreating Regina with its heat. The narrator also calls the streets a "wasteland of transportation," apparently supporting Regina's upcoming decision to cross the street. However, the narrator suddenly and matter-of-factly describes the moped running into Regina. Here, he no longer seems sympathetic to her—almost as if he has abandoned her in her moment of rashness. Thus, tone does not have to stay consistent throughout a work.

Tone is determined by diction and syntax, elements that will be discussed in "Rhetorical Devices" later.

## Mood

Mood is the emotional atmosphere of a story, perhaps what the reader feels while reading the narrative. We might call this story's mood darkly comic, as Regina is suddenly cut down by a fast but nonlethal vehicle. The suddenness of the event might be comic, but smiling at someone's pain is a little dark.

# LITERARY DEVICES

Literary *elements* provide the basic makeup of the work; literary *devices* supply color, uniqueness, or dynamism to a work.

## Imagery

Imagery is the most basic of literary devices. It is any description that appeals to the senses. An *image* may be composed simply of colorful language, or it may be categorized by any of the terms that follow in this section on "Literary Devices."

> ACCURATE EXAMPLE: Decked out in a powder-blue tuxedo that was two sizes too tight, a gasping Clarence stumbled light-headed into the gymnasium's sweat-soaked multitude. (The language here appeals to various senses.)
>
> INACCURATE EXAMPLE: In his tuxedo, Clarence entered the gymnasium. (The language in this example is direct; it lacks imagery.)

## Metaphor

A metaphor presents two things that seem very different as if they are the same.

> EXAMPLES:  The sun is a pizza in the sky. (The sun is directly compared to a pizza.)
>
> The sun is a disc of crust with rays of melted cheese. (This is called an *indirect metaphor*; a comparison is still being made between the sun and a pizza, but the pizza is not mentioned by name.)

The sun is a pizza, whose pepperoni sunspots adorn its cheesy face. It rises from the oven of the East, to sate the hunger of the morning's inhabitants. (This is called an extended metaphor or a *conceit*, whose initial comparison is developed more fully in the text.)

## Simile

A simile uses *like* or *as* to make a comparison.

*LIKE* EXAMPLE: Eating Zack's oatmeal was like slathering wet cardboard on your tongue. (Oatmeal is compared to wet cardboard using *like*.)

*AS* EXAMPLE: Grandma's tiptoeing was as subtle as an elephant's. (Using *as*, Grandma's movement is compared to a big animal's.)

## Personification

This device makes an inanimate object sound as if it is human.

ACCURATE EXAMPLE: As Reginald stared at the diamonds, greed whispered sweet nothings in his ear. (*Greed* is personified, because whispering is a human action.)

INACCURATE EXAMPLE: The Cadillac's horn howled at the moon. (The car sounds like a living thing, but *howling* is usually associated with wolves and dogs—not humans.)

## Apostrophe

Related to personification, apostrophe is a speaker's direct address to either a) a nonhuman entity or b) an absent human.

NONHUMAN EXAMPLE:    Embarrassment! Why do you come to me today?

I wish that you would go away!

I cannot stand your cheeks ablush!

You make my much-shamed blood to rush! (Embarrassment is spoken to as if it were human.)

ABSENT HUMAN EXAMPLE: Little Oscar clambered into his school bus seat and opened up his brown bag. Wrapped in blue cellophane was yet another anchovy and mint jelly sandwich. "Mom, you did it again!" he cried. (Since Mom is not on the bus, Oscar is apostrophizing to her.)

## Hyperbole (hi-PUR-bul-ee)

This term is a fancy way of saying "exaggeration."

EXAMPLE: If you have ever heard a teacher say, "I've told you a million times to put a heading on your paper!" she is obviously exaggerating. Thus, she is using hyperbole.

## Metonymy

In metonymy, a larger whole—usually an abstract—is represented by one of its parts.

> EXAMPLE: The tin star was the one thing the honest people of Carson City revered. (It would be pretty silly to take this image literally; you imagine a lot of boom town characters tipping their hats and curtsying to a badge in the street. What the narrator means is that these people respected the *law*, and the law is metonymically represented by the tin star worn by a sheriff.)

## Synecdoche

Related to metonymy, synecdoche (si NECK duh KEY) *usually* occurs when a part represents a specific, tangible whole, rather than an abstract.

> EXAMPLE: "Who is ready for recess?" asked Mrs. Grimble. Hands flew in the air. (What a frightening image this would be if taken literally. Of course, the hands don't fly by themselves; they are attached to students. Yet, because the hands *represent* the students, we have an example of synecdoche.)

## Allusion

An allusion is a reference to something outside the written work. Most allusions refer either to general literature, classical mythology, or the Bible.

> GENERAL LITERARY EXAMPLE: He told me that if I paid him, he'd give me the privilege of cleaning his garage. I told the little Tom Sawyer to forget it. (Twain's Tom Sawyer tricked other boys into thinking that whitewashing his Aunt Polly's fence was fun. They paid him for the privilege of painting. Thus, the speaker is *alluding* to a general work of literature.)

> CLASSICAL EXAMPLE: Larry nearly collapsed in a drunken heap. He looked—and smelled—like Bacchus on a binge. (Bacchus is the Roman god of wine. He appears in several literary works, so he is more accurately defined as an allusion from *classical* mythology. The SAT Subject Test: Literature expects you to know some basics of mythology, but you don't have to memorize the whole pantheon. Zeus, Apollo, and a few others might be considered common knowledge, but don't worry about minor characters such as Tithonus or King Minos.)

> BIBLICAL EXAMPLE: Mack was so happy to have rinsed off the grime and soot of the day that when he emerged from the shower, he felt like Adam himself. (Mack feels like a "new man" when he's done showering. In fact, he feels like the *first* man: Adam in the Garden of Eden. The SAT Subject Test: Literature does not expect anyone to be a biblical scholar; it will try to respect people of all backgrounds. However, the story of Adam and Eve goes beyond its religious significance: Like David and Goliath, the story of Eden is alluded to in a great deal of Western literature, secular or religious. So you may find an allusion to one of these Bible stories in an SAT Subject Test: Literature passage.)

## Symbolism

One of the most significant of literary devices, symbolism occurs when one thing in a literary work stands for another. Many times, some item will represent a person or an abstract concept.

> EXAMPLE: Outside the house, the garden was wilted and browned. Inside the house, Sarah lay dying in her bed. (Thus, the garden is a symbol for Sarah, or for death itself.)

## Irony

One of the most common of literary devices, irony falls into three categories: verbal, situational, and dramatic. In every case, there is some unexpected but fitting twist to be discovered.

> VERBAL EXAMPLE: Mowing the lawn had taken its toll on Beauregard: His shirt was stained, the sweat dribbled down his face, and grass clippings had pasted themselves to his bare legs. Margaret eyed him up and down: "Ooooh, baby, you look *good.*" (Of course, he does not, so Margaret is being verbally ironic.)

> SITUATIONAL EXAMPLE: In Guy de Maupassant's "The Necklace," a woman borrows an expensive necklace from an acquaintance and then loses it. She buys an identical necklace to replace it but does not tell the acquaintance about the loss. For the next ten years, the woman and her husband work diligently to pull themselves out of the debt the new necklace has created. When they emerge debt-free and greatly careworn, the woman runs into the acquaintance again and reveals the whole story. The acquaintance then tells the woman that the borrowed necklace was only a fake. (The twist in this situational irony is unexpected but somehow fitting: If the woman had only been honest about the loss, she could have saved herself ten years of hard labor.)

> DRAMATIC EXAMPLE: Brian sat in front of the television, oblivious to the world. Behind him, Adelaide hefted a coconut cream pie. "This time," she whispered to herself, "this time you will pay, and you will pay dearly." (Brian doesn't know what is about to happen, but the narrator has clued the audience in to the details. In this case, we have dramatic irony.)

## Paradox

A paradox is a seeming contradiction with a greater truth. Wordsworth, for instance, tells us that "the child is the father of the Man." Ordinarily, the man would be the father of the child, so we seem to have a contradiction. The deeper truth could be expressed this way: Who we are as children influences our identities as adults.

# RHETORICAL DEVICES

Whereas literary devices create pictures for our minds and appeal to our senses, rhetorical devices manipulate the language on the page.

## Diction

*Diction* is a term relating to *word choice*. The words that a writer chooses determine how the narrator relates a story and how a reader views a situation, idea, or character. Consider the following sentences:

The teacher *talked*. We *sat* at our desks.

*Talked* and *sat* are two very common, basic verbs. Therefore, the diction in the sentences is straightforward. However, the sentences lack detail or color. What do the following variations indicate about the situation in the classroom?

The teacher *droned*. We *slouched* at our desks.
The teacher *spat facts*. We *scribbled notes* at our desks.
The teacher *rambled*. We *fidgeted* at our desks.
The *educator expostulated* while we *gazed in awe* at our desks.

## Syntax

This term relates to phrasing, the way words are put together in a sentence or series of sentences. Consider the familiar sentence patterns below:

Dick and Jane play. They play in the yard. They play all day. They play
with a ball. Dick gives Jane the ball. Jane gives Dick the ball. Dick grins.
Jane grins. Dick and Jane grin. They grin and play with the ball.

Dick and Jane are driving us nuts. The simplistic syntax—that is, the pattern of short and repetitious sentences—cannot interest anyone except a novice reader. For the experienced audience, a more varied and fluid style becomes necessary:

All day long, Dick and Jane played ball in the yard. They took turns
tossing it to one another, a pastime that amused and delighted them both.

The above isn't great literature, but its syntax is more complex than the first grade's version.

Notice how both *diction* and *syntax* help to create *tone* and *mood* (see "Literary Elements" earlier in this chapter).

## Balance

Balance can appear in a sentence, a paragraph or stanza, or a whole work. Balance indicates harmony and implies the integration of smaller ideas into a larger idea. It can also demonstrate duality or point out opposites. The most commonly used "balancing acts" are repetition, parallelism, and antithesis.

## Repetition

To repeat a word, phrase, sentence, stanza, symbol, image, or idea—at the very least—places emphasis on that item. Sometimes, repetition can also create sensations associated with recurrence, such as unity or routine.

> EXAMPLE: Then the housekeeper peered into the distance, saying, "And I will wipe the grime from the floors and from the cabinets and from the surfaces of counters, and I will wipe it from walls and from tables and, yea, from the rooftops; I will wipe the grime from the back roads and byways of this great nation. Lo, the planet itself shall feel my wipe." (Not only is the word *wipe* repeated, but prepositional phrases featuring *from* also make several appearances.)

## Parallelism

This term indicates that two or more items share a similar construction or treatment in a literary work. Two of the most basic types of parallelism are *grammatical* and *thematic*.

> GOOD GRAMMATICAL PARALLEL: My favorite activities are tying shoes, licking stamps, and courting danger. (The three activities are all expressed the same way: as gerund phrases.)

> BAD GRAMMATICAL PARALLEL: To whittle, to churn butter, and chewing tobacco seemed to be the only things occupying the folks on the porch. (The activities are expressed as infinitive phrases and a gerund phrase. Thus, the parallel structure is ruined; the list does not "match up" grammatically.)

In athematic parallelism, what is paralleled is a pair of similar situations or ideas (themes).

> EXAMPLE: Delia couldn't bring herself to admit to Gerald that she had burned his baby-blue leisure suit. Outside on the playset, their daughter was wondering if she should tell her brother about flushing his turtle down the toilet. (A parallel theme relating to secrets and betrayal is emerging in this scene.)

## Antithesis

A common literary device found on the SAT Subject Test: Literature, antithesis is a pairing of opposites to make a point. Alexander Pope tells us that man is "In doubt to deem himself a god, or beast/In doubt his mind or body to prefer/Born but to die, and reasoning but to err." These lines are rife with antithesis: "god" as a being high in creation is paired with "beast," one of the lowest; "mind" as a governor of logic is matched with "body," governor of passion. Furthermore, "born" is paired with "die" and "reasoning" with "err." The point of all these opposites is that man is a creature caught in the middle of creation, a blend of opposites and contradictions.

## Rhetorical Question

A narrator uses this type of question to emphasize a point. The question requires no response, simply the audience's consideration of an idea. During a test, a teacher might have noticed a student copying from you. If the teacher addresses the person with the question, "Just what do you think you're doing?" she doesn't really need an answer. She is simply drawing the student's attention to his misconduct.

# SOUND DEVICES

Sounds can have great impact on a passage of literature. They can guide the way we feel about a situation, a character, or an idea. Sounds are the poetry of a prose work and the heart of a poem.

## Rhyme

Rhyme occurs when two or more words sound the same except for their initial letter(s). Rhyme connotes a harmony of ideas; that is why it is used sometimes in poetry: to keep its theme unified.

> EXAMPLE: Pope describes a social setting in which people have a range of conversational topics: "One speaks the glory of the British Queen/And one describes a charming Indian screen." The rhyme of *Queen* and *screen* displays the disparity of the topics: The first is lofty, the second is mundane.

## Rhythm

This sound device refers to the cadence that a phrase or series of phrases develops. Mixed rhythms help keep the reader's attention. Repeated rhythms can help unify certain ideas in a passage.

> What rhythms would be appropriate for a description of waves
> welling up on a beach?  (long, fluid, but repetitive rhythms?)

> What rhythms would work best to describe paramedics trying
> to revive a car accident victim? (short, clipped dialogue and description?)

## Alliteration

Alliteration is the repetition of a sound at the beginning of words in a phrase.

> EXAMPLE: Coleridge describes a river that goes "meandering in a mazy motion."
> The point here is not just to choose a repeated sound for emphasis but to choose an
> *appropriate* sound. The *m* prolongs the description, since *m* can be a continuous sound.
> So the course of the river sounds slow, almost hypnotic.

## Assonance

Assonance is the repetition of vowel sounds within words.

> EXAMPLE: The petite clerk meekly ate the bee. (The long *e* sound in the line emphasizes the smallness of the subject and the action. The sound of long *e* moves the tongue close to the roof of the mouth, minimizing the opening. Perhaps, then, a repetition of a more open vowel—the *a* in *father*, for instance—would not stress smallness as well here.)

## Consonance

This device refers to the repetition of consonant sounds within words.

> EXAMPLE: Tony's fingertips typed at the computer until dawn. (The repeated *t* in the line mimics the contact between Tony's fingers and the keys.)

## Onomatopoeia

This device uses words that imitate the sound they represent.

> EXAMPLES: Anita bonked Jared on the head when he tried to zip past her. (*Bonked* is an action that sounds comically clunky. The sound of *zip* implies some kind of speedy action, like wind whizzing past you.)

# POETIC STYLES AND GENRES

Following is a list of terms associated exclusively with poetry.

## Rhyme Scheme

This is the pattern of a poem's rhyme. In analyzing a poem, the reader marks the rhyme scheme by using capital letters; each identical set of letters represents a rhyme. Look at the following limerick:

> There once was a very small teacher,
> Diminutive, minuscule creature,
> Who stood every day
> At the board and would say
> "Had a date once, but I couldn't reach 'er."

The rhyme scheme is expressed as AABBA; the first, second and fifth lines rhyme ("A"), then the third and fourth rhyme ("B"). Were this poem to continue in limerick stanzas, then the rhyme scheme would look like this: AABBACCDDCEEFFE, and so on.

## Meter

Meter is the set rhythm of a poem. For the SAT Subject Test: Literature, you probably have to know only one type of meter by name: *iambic pentameter*. An iamb is a metrical foot of two syllables, with the accent on the second syllable. The similar sounding words *Mary* and *Marie* both have two syllables, but *Marie* is the iamb: Its accent is on the second syllable. *Pentameter* has a Greek root *penta*, meaning "five." Thus, in iambic pentameter, there are five iambs to a line.

> EXAMPLE: "But *soft*! What *light* through *yon*der *win*dow *breaks*?/ It *is* the *East* and *Jul*iet *is* the *sun*!" (The italicized syllables represent the accents of the iambs. Iambic pentameter is one of the most common meters in English language poetry.)

## Couplets and Heroic Couplets

A couplet is two consecutive rhyming lines in a poem; the rhyme scheme looks like this: AABBCCDD, etc. Heroic couplets also rhyme this way but follow an iambic pentameter rhythm. Heroic couplets are so named because they try to emulate the loftiness of epic poetry.

COUPLETS EXAMPLE:

> There is a bird
> I've often heard
> Who likes to drink
> Out of a sink.

HEROIC COUPLETS EXAMPLE:

> There is a grand, majestic bird, I think
> Who sucks the living waters from the sink,
> And then with pinions through the azure skies,
> He pauses—dabs his beak—and on he flies.

## Sonnet

A sonnet has 14 lines of iambic pentameter and features a specific rhyme scheme. It is a serious, usually discursive poem that compacts a unified idea into a small space. The SAT Subject Test: Literature *often* features one sonnet among its passages. You will see several in the practice tests at the end of this book. The following is Shakespeare's Sonnet #64:

|  |  |  |
|---|---|---|
| | When I have seen by Time's fell hand defaced | |
| | The rich proud cost of outworn buried age, | *cost* outlay |
| | When sometime lofty towers I see down-rased | *sometime* formerly |
| Line | And brass eternal slave to mortal rage; | *brass eternal* everlasting brass |
| (5) | When I have seen the hungry ocean gain | *mortal rage* ravages of mortality |
| | Advantage on the kingdom of the shore, | |
| | And the firm soil win of the wat'ry main, | |
| | Increasing store with loss and loss with store; | |
| | When I have seen such interchange of state, | |
| (10) | Or state itself confounded to decay, | *confounded* reduced |
| | Ruin hath taught me thus to ruminate, | |

> That Time will come and take my love away.
> This thought is as a death, which cannot choose
> But weep to have that which it fears to lose.

## Blank Verse

This type of poetry features unrhymed iambic pentameter. It is often used by Renaissance playwrights, such as Shakespeare, and survives all the way up into the 20th century, where poets like Robert Frost dabbled in it. See "Meter" earlier in this chapter for the *Romeo and Juliet* example of blank verse.

## Sprung Rhythm

This type of poetry features a variety of set meters and a complex rhyme scheme. Gerard Manley Hopkins developed this lively style in the 19th century. The following are sprung rhythm lines taken from his poem "God's Grandeur"; the italicized words display the uneven stresses of sprung rhythm's meter:

> The *world* is *charged* with the *grand*eur of *God*.
> It will *flame out*, like *shi*ning from *shook foil*;
> It *gath*ers to a *great*ness, like the *ooze* of *oil*
> *Crushed*. Why do *men* then *now* not *reck* his *rod*?

Each line has different places of accentuation. Compare this unevenness with the regular rhythm of the *Romeo and Juliet* lines in the earlier "Iambic Pentameter" example.

## Free Verse

This type of poetry has no regular rhyme scheme or meter.

> EXAMPLE:

> This lady I know
> Delightful
> In the        light
> She soothes my
> Soul
> Marks everything
> Half        off.

## Ode

An ode praises someone or something still in existence. Keats's "Ode on a Grecian Urn" praises the beauty of an historical artifact: "Thou still unravished bride of quietness/Thou foster child of silence and slow time/Sylvan historian...."

## Elegy

An elegy honors someone dead. Gray's "Elegy Written in a Country Churchyard" is an example: "Let not Ambition mock their useful toil/Their homely joys, and destiny obscure/Nor Grandeur hear with a disdainful smile/The short and simple annals of the poor."

## Ballad

A ballad is a narrative poem, usually with a tragicomic tone. Its stanzas tend to be four lines long, with an ABCBDEFE rhyme scheme. You can hear a ballad's meter in this:

> Sir Horsbreth held his sword up high;
> It glistened like uranium.
> But heavy was it also, as
> It dropped upon his cranium.

## Concrete Poetry

This genre, sometimes called emblematic poetry, forms its words into pictures on the page, which have something to do with the poem's theme.

```
EXAMPLE:                 This is how
         her mouth     looked as
    I told       A      her that my
    mouth        A      had been on
    every        U      carton, and
    jug of       G      juice and
     every       H      jelly jar
      I found    !   inside our
     brand new refrigerator.
```

# PROSE TERMS

Since prose genres (novels, short stories, etc.) tend to be too long to include in their entirety on the SAT Subject Test: Literature, we need not worry about defining them here. However, prose items will be excerpted for use on the test. What follows are terms that tend to be associated with prose.

## Point of View

This term refers to the perspective and possible limitations the narrator has in a short story, novel, or other narrative. Different kinds of narrators and narrative techniques have different effects on literary works.

*First Person (Major Character):* This point of view has a narrator who is usually the main character of the narrative. For example, Huck tells his own story in Twain's novel *The Adventures of Huckleberry Finn.*

*First Person (Minor Character):* Here, a character who is not the main focus of the narrative tells the story. This may be the most limited point of view. One example is in Fitzgerald's *The Great Gatsby:* Gatsby himself is the central focus of the novel, but his neighbor Nick relates Gatsby's adventures. Likewise, Captain Ahab is the focus of *Moby-Dick*, but one of the captain's sailors, Ishmael, is the storyteller who opens the novel with the very simple line, "Call me Ishmael."

*Third Person (Observer):* Here, the narrator is not a character in the story, nor does he know the thoughts and feelings of the story's characters. In Hemingway's "Hills Like White Elephants," the narrator describes a couple having a tense conversation. However, we are never allowed inside the minds of these characters and must discover through their words and body language what they really feel.

*Third Person (Limited Omniscient):* "The Story of an Hour" by Kate Chopin is a good example of this point of view. The narrator, who is not a character in the story, knows only of Mrs. Mallard's thoughts and feelings—no one else's. Because of this limitation, we miss out on a crucial piece of information that allows for a surprise ending in the story.

*Third Person (Omniscient):* In many of Thomas Hardy's novels, we find this point of view. Here, the narrator can know all of the thoughts and feelings of every character, can "see" any location at any time in the novel and have almost a God's eye view. The practice tests in this book feature a few passages from Hardy that demonstrate this omniscience.

## Narrative Distance

Narrative distance refers to the narrator's proximity in relation to the other characters. A narrator can be physically close (usually first-person narrators) or physically distant (usually third person omniscient), psychologically close (sympathetic with characters) or psychologically distant (cold).

## Exercise

What is the narrative distance? *Match the best answer with the examples below:*

___1.  Agnes wanted desperately to tell Herbert that her heart was his. She knew, though, that such an admission might compromise him. So she heroically kept her love closed off and let him be.

(A) Physically close
(B) Physically distant
(C) Psychologically close
(D) Psychologically distant

___2.  I managed to overhear somethin' growlin' in Zeke's overalls. Coulda been he's hungry, coulda been somethin' else. I wasn't stickin' around to find out.

___3.  A long time ago, in a land miles away …

___4.  Eldon bade his wife good-bye, picked up his briefcase, walked out the door, and got into his car. He reached into the glove compartment. Underneath the maps and batteries, he found what he needed. The divorce papers were a little crimped but ready to sign.

    1 = C, 2 = A, 3 = B, 4 = D

## Narrative Shift

This term refers to a significant change in the way the author is telling the story. This device usually manifests itself as a change in verb tense. Most narratives are told in past tense, but occasionally, a narrator shifts to present for a greater sense of immediacy.

# VOICE

When you put them all together—from narrative elements to prose terms—or at least when you mix and match an assortment of these devices, you come up with *voice*. An author considers three things that go into a work's voice: The author's own style of writing, the work's audience, and the author's writing purpose. Voice is the dominant element in a written work, because it is all-encompassing.

# Chapter 4: **Working with Poetry**

- Modes
- Types of Verse

Of all the genres that appear on the SAT Subject Test: Literature, poetry is the most prevalent. On any given version of the test, there will be a maximum of one play excerpt, perhaps one or two nonfiction pieces, and two or three fictional works; the exam may, however, include as many as three or four poems.

Poetry's predominance on the test may be attributed to its ability to be presented completely: The test's prose works can almost never be seen in their entirety, but many poems are brief enough to fit on one page. Thus, the opportunity to offer whole works for analysis makes the SAT Subject Test: Literature seem less fragmented.

Poetry also has the most economical use of language among all written genres. Its dense imagery and compact phrasing force the closest kind of analysis from the reader; it is then perhaps the type of literature best suited for the test.

Another plus about poetry is its many modes, devices, and forms. The variety offered by the genre prevents the test from becoming stale or redundant. Following is a review of modes into which the reader can categorize any poem.

## MODES

- *Narrative*—Occasionally, as with a piece of fiction, a poem simply tells a story. Epics such as Milton's *Paradise Lost* (an excerpt of which is presented as a "practice" poem in this chapter) or ballads like "Sir Patrick Spens" fall into this category.

- *Discursive*—Many times the SAT Subject Test: Literature will feature this type of poem, because the discursive mode expounds on a topic; it is an "idea" poem. Several questions about theme and the way structure develops theme can be derived from this kind of work. Bryant's "Thanatopsis" and Whitman's "Song of Myself," both discussed later, are examples.

- *Imagistic*—Almost all poems feature imagery, but sometimes a poem is pure image, wishing neither to tell a tale nor to formulate a theme. The genre of haiku or brief poems such as Pound's "L'Art 1910" and "In a Station of the Metro" are simple images without plot or moral.

- *Lyric*—Often a poem's meter and rhyme give it a songlike quality. In fact, the music created for Jonson's "Song: to Celia" and the medieval ballad "Barbara Allan" still exists. Dickinson's "Because I Could Not Stop for Death," a work found in this chapter, comes from a body of 1,776 lyric poems; some English teachers joke derisively that any of these verses can be set to the tune of "Camptown Races" (doo-da, doo-da).

Of course, as with most works of literature, any kind of categorization will have gray areas. Many poems feature more than one mode, and some poems contain all of them.

In addition to these modes, there are numerous devices that all together help to develop ideas in a poetic work. You just reviewed them in chapter 3; be sure to review them again before the exam.

# TYPES OF VERSE

Now, we move on to the three basic verse forms of poetry. Just about any poem will exhibit one of these patterns of rhyme and meter.

## Rhyming Verse

This is the oldest type of poetry, featuring not only lines with end rhyme but also certain kinds of set rhythms known as meters. In the days of oral tradition, poets like Homer did not write down their verse but instead memorized it completely. Both rhyme and meter were mnemonic devices that could help to imprint the verse on the poet's mind. Hundreds of years after the oral tradition, poets were still formulating poetry using meter and rhyme. It wasn't until the Renaissance that nonrhyming forms of poetry were developed in the Western world, and not until the 19th century that Gerard Manley Hopkins and Walt Whitman would experiment with multimetrical and nonmetrical verse. Because rhyming poems have such a long history, you can expect to see more than one on the SAT Subject Test: Literature.

When the test presents you with such verse, keep in mind that rhyming lines will help to unify an idea. In fact, you could say that the harmony of the rhyme symbolizes the completion of an idea. Look at the way the rhyming stanzas in "Because I Could Not stop for Death" present distinct ideas that still flow into each other:

> Because I could not stop for Death
> He kindly stopped for me—
> The carriage held but just Ourselves—
> And Immortality.
>
> *Line*
> (5)     We slowly drove—He knew no haste
> And I had put away—
> My labor and my leisure too,
> For His Civility.
>
> We passed the School, where Children strove
> (10)     At Recess—in the Ring—

We passed the Fields of Gazing Grain—
We passed the Setting Sun—

Or rather—He passed us—
The Dews drew quivering and chill—
(15)  For only Gossamer, my Gown—
My Tippet, only Tulle—                    *Tippet … Tulle*   a light shawl made of fine netting

We paused before a House that seemed
A Swelling of the Ground—
The Roof was scarcely visible—
(20)  The Cornice—in the Ground—

Since then—'tis Centuries—and yet
Feels shorter than the Day
I first surmised the Horses' Heads
Were toward Eternity.

(1890)

## Analysis

*Stanza 1:* Death arrives in a carriage for the speaker. They begin their ride through eternity together.

*Stanza 2:* Death's pace is slow, and his demeanor is polite. This behavior encourages the speaker to relax. The rhyme here is described as "slant," a kind of "almost rhyme." Perhaps the speaker is still becoming accustomed to the newness of the carriage journey.

*Stanza 3:* The carriage journey is described. They pass wheat fields and schoolchildren. Although the meter is steady here, the rhyme is lost, but then, the speaker is out of joint with what she sees. She is in a relaxed state, while the children are not merely playing at recess but "striving." The nonrhyme makes sense.

*Stanza 4:* Actually, the idea of passing the sun continues from Stanza 3 into this verse. The break between the stanzas provides a slight pause that makes line 13 something of a surprise, and the deliberate slowness of the carriage is thus emphasized. Then, the chill but unburdened feelings associated with death are demonstrated by the dew and the speaker's "clothes," respectively. The slant rhyme appears again, perhaps indicating the contrast between the quivering dews and the speaker's light apparel.

*Stanza 5:* Death's carriage reaches the speaker's grave. Rhyme returns, but only because the same word is repeated at the end of lines 18 and 20. This repetition may foreshadow the continued comfort she feels throughout the centuries in her death.

*Stanza 6:* The speaker talks about the seeming brevity but actual longevity of death here. The slant rhyme could indicate this contrast, or it might be something more: The rhyme is nearly identical to that of Stanza 2, and in Stanza 6 the speaker is recalling the events of Stanza 2.

Of course, since poetry is so packed with meaning, rhyme is not the only thing to which one should pay attention. Consider the following items: With what characteristics do they imbue the death experience in Dickinson's work?

- The personification of Death on a carriage
- The alliterated *l* sound in line 7
- The personification of grain (line 11) and the sun (line 13)
- The house metaphor describing the grave in Stanza 5
- Death's politeness throughout the poem
- The total lack of exertion associated with the speaker's death

The poem above helps to discuss the various stages that rhyme can go through in a poem. However, the next two forms of poetry consistently feature no rhyme.

## Blank Verse

Popularized in the plays of Christopher Marlowe, then adopted by Shakespeare and later nondramatic poets, blank verse is a type of poetry featuring iambic pentameter with no rhyme scheme. The iamb is a two-syllable metrical "foot" with an accent on the second syllable; there will be five of these iambs in a line of pentameter:

> I *want* to *ride* my *bike* a*long* the *road*
> Un*less* your *Cadil*lac is *run*ning *well.*

"I want" is the first iamb, with an accent on the second syllable; "to ride" is the second iamb; and so on. "Road" and "well" do not rhyme; they create a "blank" at the end of the lines. Thus, we have two lines of blank verse.

Marlowe and Shakespeare recognized that this verse form mimics the normal rhythms of English and is more conversational and more natural without the rhyme.

## Anastrophe

One problem that occurs in both rhyming verse and blank verse, however, is the use of anastrophe, or the inversion of a sentence to suit rhyme scheme and metrical rhythm. If you see a poem on the SAT Subject Test: Literature whose words are understandable but whose meaning is lost on you, you may be fighting against the anastrophe of the poem's sentences. As an example, an excerpt from Bryant's blank verse "Thanatopsis" is presented below:

> Go forth, under the open sky, and list              *list* listen
> To Nature's teachings, while from all around—
> Earth and her waters, and the depths of air—
> Comes a still voice.—
*Line*
*(5)*                          Yet a few days, and thee              *Yet...thee* Here, Nature's voice starts
> The all-beholding sun shall see no more
> In all his course; nor yet in the cold ground,
> Where thy pale form was laid, with many tears,

(10)    Nor in the embrace of ocean, shall exist
Thy image. Earth, that nourished thee, shall claim
Thy growth, to be resolved to earth again,
And, lost each human trace, surrendering up
Thine individual being, shalt thou go
To mix forever with the elements,
(15)    To be brother to the insensible rock
And to the sluggish clod, which the rude swain
Turns with his share, and treads upon. The oak
Shall send his roots abroad, and pierce thy mould.

    Yet not to thine eternal resting-place
(20)    Shalt thou retire alone, nor couldst thou wish
Couch more magnificent. Thou shalt lie down
With patriarchs of the infant world—with kings,
The powerful of the earth—the wise, the good,
Fair forms, and hoary seers of ages past,
(25)    All in one mighty sepulcher.

*rude swain* uneducated country boy
*share* plow blade

(1821)

## Analysis

As you read the work, you want to locate where sentences begin and end; this process will help you break the poem down into discrete units of meaning. However, you will also want to "de-anastrophize" the sentences, or convert them into regularly patterned grammar. Take the following lines as an example:

> Yet a few days, and thee
> The all-beholding sun shall see no more
> In all his course; nor yet in the cold ground,
> Where thy pale form was laid, with many tears,
> Nor in the embrace of ocean, shall exist
> Thy image.

Notice that this blank verse sentence ends in the middle of line 10; sentences do not have to wait until the end of a line to finish, nor should a reader pause at the end of a line if it lacks punctuation. Keep going until a comma, period, or some other punctuation stops you.

Now that you have located the sentence, you can understand it better by mentally rearranging it into a more standard type of grammar:

> Yet a few days, and the all-beholding sun shall no more see thee in all his course; nor yet shall thy image exist in the cold ground, where thy pale form was laid with many tears, nor in the embrace of ocean.

Replace the *thee*'s and *thy*'s with *you*'s and *your*'s, and the grammar will sound even more familiar.

Just as we examine the individual stanzas to locate meaning in a rhyming poem, so we take a blank verse poem apart sentence by sentence:

*Sentence 1* (lines 1–4): Listen to Nature, and her voice will speak to you.

*Sentence 2* (lines 5–10): After only a brief time on earth, you will no longer be seen by the sun. Mourners will have placed you in the earth, but your image will not exist either in the ground or in the sea.

*Sentence 3* (lines 10–17): Your image—your essence—will have dissolved into Nature and become one with it, so much so that you will be related to the earth itself. Ironically, the living will plow the dirt that you have joined and walk on you.

*Sentence 4* (lines 17–18): The oak tree's roots will grow through your remains.

*Sentence 5* (lines 19–21): But you will not be alone in death, and, in fact, your resting place will be quite luxurious.

*Sentence 6* (lines 21–25): You will be in great company. Famous and important people will share the earth with you in a kind of collective tomb.

Because of its discursive nature, this excerpt is almost like an essay. It introduces a thesis, then goes on to provide and explain examples of its main idea. Furthermore, look at the word choices that create the passage's comforting tone: *still voice*, (line 4); *Earth, that nourished thee, shall claim/Thy growth* (lines 10–11); *brother* (line 15); *eternal resting place* (line 19); *Couch … magnificent* (line 21); *lie down* (line 21); *Fair forms* (line 24). The conversational use of blank verse and the comforting tone combine in "Thanatopsis" to create a single idea: we need not fear the natural course of death; it is a communal experience with both Nature and our fellow humans, high and low.

Now we have one more verse form to cover before we go on to our practice passage.

## Free Verse

This form of poetry contains no meter and no rhyme. It represents the most recent development in poetic literature, breaking with the more traditional forms of the genre. Canto 52 from Whitman's "Song of Myself" provides the discussion:

> The spotted hawk swoops by and accuses me, he complains of my gab and my loitering.
>
> I too am not a bit tamed, I too am untranslatable,
> I sound my barbaric yawp over the roofs of the world.
>
> *Line*      The last scud* of day holds back for me,
> *(5)*       It flings my likeness after the rest and true as any on the shadow'd wilds,
>             It coaxes me to the vapor and the dusk.

I depart as air, I shake my white locks at the runaway sun,
I effuse my flesh in eddies, and drift it in lacy jags.

I bequeath myself to the dirt to grow from the grass I love,
*(10)* If you want me again look for me under your boot-soles.

You will hardly know who I am or what I mean,
But I shall be good health to you nevertheless,
And filter and fiber your blood.

Failing to fetch me at first keep encouraged,
*(15)* Missing me one place search another,
I stop somewhere waiting for you.

(1891)

*scud* clouds or mist driven by wind

Whitman's exuberance in this poem would be inappropriately expressed in a rhyming, metered poem. He is celebrating his individuality in phrases such as "I too am not a bit tamed, I too am untranslatable" (line 2), "I sound my barbaric yawp" (line 3), and "You will hardly know who I am or what I mean" (line 11). His energy and uniqueness would be too restricted by rhyme and meter, so free verse provides a more fitting voice for him.

## Comparing the Three Forms

If you consider the three poetic passages presented so far, you might see that they share a common theme. This is the idea that death is not something to be feared—it is a comforting experience that continues and deepens our association with the earth. Nevertheless, the various verse forms of the passages place a different twist on this theme. Dickinson's fairly consistent meter but differing rhymes might be mimicking the carriage's rhythm as she travels to her new "house" in the ground. Bryant's lack of rhyme creates a more conversational explanation of death, but the meter of blank verse still keeps the tone formal. The gloss note in line 5 tells us that Nature herself is speaking; her soothing but still precise language makes her our teacher and guide through the experience of death. Whitman also "bequeaths" himself to the earth, but his unmetered language makes him less formal. He is not our teacher, but our brother, "waiting" for us "somewhere" when we are ready to join him in the "dirt to grow from the grass."

## THINGS TO REMEMBER

- Poetry is the most prevalent genre on the exam.
- To tackle poetry,
    - know your modes: narrative, discursive, imagistic, lyric;
    - know your verse types: rhyming, blank, free; and
    - know by heart the poetic terms and the literary, rhetorical, and sound devices in chapter 3 so you won't waste valuable time trying to define unfamiliar words.

## SAMPLE QUESTIONS

"And now
Through all restraint broke loose he wings his way          *he* Satan
Not far off Heaven, in the precincts of light,

*Line*      Directly towards the new-created world,

(5)        And man there placed, with purpose to assay
If him by force he can destroy, or worse,
By some false guile pervert: and shall pervert;
For man will hearken to his glozing lies,                    *glozing* flattering
And easily transgress the sole command,

(10)       Sole pledge of his obedience; so will fall
He and his faithless progeny. Whose fault?
Whose but his own? Ingrate, he had of me
All he could have; I made him just and right,
Sufficient to have stood, though free to fall.

(15)       Such I created all th'ethereal powers
And spirits, both them who stood and them who failed:
Freely they stood who stood, and fell who fell.
Not free, what proof could they have given sincere
Of true allegiance, constant faith, or love,

(20)       Where only what they needs must do appeared,
Not what they would? What praise could they receive,
What pleasure I, from such obediences paid,
When Will and Reason (Reason also is Choice),
Useless and vain, of freedom both despoiled,

(25)       Made passive both, had served Necessity,
Not me? they therefore as to right belonged,
So were created, nor can justly accuse
Their Maker or their making or their fate,
As if predestination overruled

(30)       Their will, disposed by absolute decree
Or high foreknowledge. They themselves decreed
Their own revolt, not I. If I foreknew,
Foreknowledge had no influence on their fault,
Which had no less proved certain unforeknown.           *had ... unforeknown* "if I had not foreknown it"

(35)       So without least impulse of shadow of fate,
Or aught by me immutably foreseen,
They tresspass, authors to themselves in all,
Both what they judge and what they choose; for so
I formed them free, and free they must remain

(40)       Till they enthrall themselves: I else must change
Their nature, and revoke the high decree
Unchangeable, eternal, which ordained
Their freedom; they themselves ordained their fall.

The first sort by their own suggestion fell,

(45)    Self-tempted, self-depraved; man falls, deceived

By the other first: man therefore shall find grace;

The other, none. In mercy and justice both,

Through Heaven and Earth, so shall my glory excel;

But mercy, first and last, shall brightness shine."

*first sort*   Satan, etc.

1.  The speaker in this passage seems to be

    (A)   Satan.

    (B)   God.

    (C)   Adam.

    (D)   a third-person limited omniscient narrator.

    (E)   a fallen angel, one of Satan's troops.

2.  The speaker's view of creation (line 4) is best seen in the phrase

    (A)   "all restraint broke loose" (line 2).

    (B)   "in the precincts of light" (line 3).

    (C)   "and shall pervert" (line 7).

    (D)   "glozing lies" (line 8).

    (E)   "faithless progeny" (line 11).

3.  The speaker's view of "man" (line 5) is best illustrated in the phrase

    (A)   "glozing lies" (line 8).

    (B)   "Sole pledge of his obedience" (line 10).

    (C)   "Ingrate" (line 12).

    (D)   "all th'ethereal powers/And spirits" (lines 15–16).

    (E)   "Not free" (line 18).

4.  In lines 11–34, the speaker addresses all of the following topics EXCEPT

    (A)   the inevitability of humankind's downfall.

    (B)   the concept that humans have qualities of higher beings.

    (C)   the need for free will in humankind's creation.

    (D)   the pointlessness of forced servitude.

    (E)   the idea that foreknowledge precludes free will.

5.  Who is responsible for man's downfall, according to the speaker in lines 26–46?

    I.    Man

    II.   Satan

    III.  God

    IV.   Fate

    (A)   II only

    (B)   I and II only

    (C)   II and III only

    (D)   I, II, and IV only

    (E)   I, II, III, and IV

6.  The speaker sees himself in lines 40–43 as a/an

    (A)   ruler.

    (B)   architect.

    (C)   scientist.

    (D)   judge.

    (E)   victim.

7. The "other" in lines 46 and 47 must be

   (A)  Eve.

   (B)  Adam.

   (C)  God and his angels.

   (D)  Satan and his demon horde.

   (E)  the world.

8. Lines 44–49 of the passage are a/an

   (A)  solitary grieving for God, but small comfort to Satan.

   (B)  hopeful outcome for Adam, but a disappointment for Eve.

   (C)  optimistic outlook for humankind, but pessimistic for Satan.

   (D)  altered view of Satan, but a consistent view of Eve.

   (E)  demonstration of Satan's great power, but a warning of God's wrath.

9. The passage as a whole seems to emphasize all of the following EXCEPT

   (A)  God's power, mercy, and justice.

   (B)  man's ability to reason freely.

   (C)  man's responsibility in his own downfall.

   (D)  the certainty of man's fall.

   (E)  Satan's role as God's instrument.

# ANSWERS AND EXPLANATIONS

**1. (B)**

The speaker in this passage says, "he had of me/All he could have; I made him just and right," (lines 12–13). The *he* is man—more specifically Adam, the first man—and God is traditionally viewed as man's maker, especially if Satan is seen as an agent of man's downfall.

**2. (B)**

(A), (C), (D), and (E) either relate to Satan's fall from heaven or man's fall from God's grace. The phrase in (B) modifies heaven and can even be compared to the later phrase "new-created world." God has a high opinion of His creation but a low opinion of his creatures.

**3. (C)**

After the word "Ingrate," God goes on to describe the disloyalty of man. God therefore surmises that the reason man has disobeyed and broken from God is that he was not sufficiently grateful for being created.

**4. (E)**

God says, "I made him just and right/Sufficient to have stood, though free to fall/Such I created all th'ethereal powers/And spirits" (lines 13–16). Thus, man is made with free will and with enough power to support himself, just as God has created the beings of heaven; (B) cannot work. (C) and (D) are insufficient because in lines 18–21, God explains the need for free will. If man is "Not free, what proof could they have given sincere/Of true allegiance, constant faith, or love/Where only what they needs must do appeared/Not what they would?" It is with free will that man demonstrates genuine, unforced love and obedience. The following quote from lines 26–30 proves (A) untrue: "they therefore as to right belonged/So were created, nor can justly accuse/Their Maker or their making or their fate/As if predestination overruled/Their will." Man cannot blame fate for his downfall, even if fate has determined that the fall will happen. Free will, according to Milton's God, exists within the confines of predestination. Lines 32–34 at once continue this idea and prove (E) correct: "If I foreknew/Foreknowledge had no influence on their fault/Which had no less proved certain unforeknown." Milton's God equates foreknowledge with fate. God says that predestination or foreknowledge does not cause man's fall but merely predicts it.

**5. (B)**

The idea that man is responsible for his fall is first acknowledged in lines 31–32: "They themselves decreed/Their own revolt." The idea continues in lines 43–46, which also blame Satan: "...they themselves ordained their fall./The first sort by their own suggestion fell/Self-tempted, self-depraved; man falls, deceived/By the other first." As the gloss note indicates, the "first sort" are Satan and his ilk. Man falls by his own decree, but also because "the other[s]"—the "first sort"—have "deceived" him.

**6. (A)**

Because God is making a "high decree" in these lines, which is something a king or queen has the power to do, he sounds most like a ruler.

**7. (D)**

"Other" refers to line 44's "first sort," or (as the gloss note indicates) Satan and his demon horde.

**8. (C)**

Lines 46–47 says that "man therefore shall find grace" but the other—Satan—shall have none. Later on, God refers to his own mercy, which, according to line 46, must be reserved for man. The reason for this difference is that Satan has deceived man, voluntarily helping to bring about man's downfall (lines 45–46).

**9. (E)**

See the following explanations: Question #8 for (A); Question #4 for (B), (C), and (D). Although God makes reference to fate, he does not connect predestination to Satan's power. Satan has free will and is therefore not a tool or puppet of God.

# Chapter 5: **Working with Nonfiction**

- Nonfiction and the Test
- Understanding Nonfiction on the SAT Subject Test: Literature
- Reading Nonfiction

## NONFICTION AND THE TEST

Nonfiction is becoming increasingly popular among writers of standardized tests. The AP English Literature and Composition Exam, the AP English Language and Composition Exam, and the SAT Subject Test: Literature all seem to be developing a greater fondness for essay excerpts, autobiographical and biographical prose, speeches, sermons, and treatises. The reason for this increase may have something to do with the lack of nonfiction literature in high school curricula. Many English teachers would rather discuss a poem that is full of imagery or a short story that is crammed with dialogue; nonfiction works are sometimes incorrectly perceived as a little drier and, hence, a little less inviting than works of verse or fictional prose. So standardized tests have begun a recent campaign to capitalize on the dearth of nonfiction works studied in the high school classroom. The idea is that since most high school students have been exposed to dozens of poems and fictional works, but relatively few nonfiction pieces, a greater amount of nonfiction on the test will reward those students who have a more well-rounded reading background.

Another reason nonfiction pieces are more frequently seen in literature tests is that they can present themes in different ways than other kinds of works. An essay, for instance, is a direct treatment of an idea; many essays, because they are not narrative, lack dialogue, characterization, and plot. The reader can then better focus on the way diction, syntax, and style present an idea.

The bottom line is that you should expect to see nonfiction passages on the SAT Subject Test: Literature, whether you have a lot of experience with these kinds of works or not. As you move through the exam, you should therefore be aware of the probable presence of nonfiction and plan to deal with its particular problems.

# UNDERSTANDING NONFICTION ON THE SAT SUBJECT TEST: LITERATURE

We suggest first that when you encounter a nonfiction work on the test, you determine what its *unifying idea* is. A quick scan of the passage can help you figure out an excerpt's overall theme. Perhaps repetitive wording or an obvious topic sentence will aid you in this step.

Next, identifying the passage's *mode* or *purpose* can guide you in better understanding the work. Any piece of nonfiction will have at least one of four purposes:

1. *Persuasive*: Here, the writer wants to change the reader's mind or convince the audience to take action. Frequently, to fulfill this purpose, the writer will use certain appeals: *logos*, *pathos*, and *ethos*. With *logos*, the writer wants to speak to one's logical mind. Employing verifiable evidence, rational analogies, and common sense anecdotes, the writer wants to convince his audience that there is no error in his thought. Next, *pathos* is the emotional appeal. Using stories that tug at our sympathies or language that is particularly moving, the writer tries to stir our feelings so that we will side with her argument. Finally, *ethos* is an appeal to ethics; that is, to the rightness or morality of a concept. The writer wants us to believe that his ideas are part of a higher cause. An easily noted example of the persuasive mode is Martin Luther King Jr.'s "I Have a Dream" speech, in which the activist uses logical reasoning, emotionally charged imagery, and outcries against unethical behavior to dissuade the audience from the evils of racial prejudice.

2. *Expository*: Less complex than the persuasive piece, an expository work simply gives the audience information. It might explain a process or reveal previously unknown facts about an already familiar topic. For instance, esteemed nonfiction writer James McPhee has written an essay about the Loch Ness monster that recounts the latest developments in the search for the Scottish legend. The essay does not try to convince the reader one way or the other about the monster's supposed existence, nor does it tell the story of the monster's supposed origins. It merely offers information about the most recent efforts to track down the beast.

3. *Descriptive*: Most often, this mode is the most difficult to sustain in an entire essay, much less a longer work. If a piece only describes a landscape, a city scene, or a crowd of people, it may seem to lack the importance of a persuasive or an expository work. For that reason, the descriptive mode is usually joined to other modes in nonfiction. Still, the travel essays of Anne Morrow Lindbergh are examples of works that thrive merely on describing a scene.

4. *Narrative*: This purpose appears in nonfiction works such as biographies and histories. This mode most closely resembles fictional prose in that it tells a story. Plot, characterization, and dialogue may all be present in this type of nonfiction, except that the tales are supposed to be based on fact. Jon Krakauer's autobiographical *Into Thin Air*, about his experiences climbing Mt. Everest, is a recent example of this mode.

Of course, most nonfictional works do not fit neatly into these categories; most will be hybrids of more than one mode. Thoreau's classic *Walden* is a good example: It is a book-length narrative of his two-year experiment living in a cabin in the woods. In the work, he often describes various natural settings found in the New England area. He offers information about flora and fauna that he has studied during the experiment and even exposes the pasts and personalities of his neighbors. Furthermore, he is constantly trying to convince the reader of certain transcendental philosophies. Thus, *Walden* is a work that encompasses all four nonfiction modes. Still, a particular nonfiction passage on the SAT Subject Test: Literature will probably have one dominant mode; if you can determine the passage's purpose, you can make answering the questions easier.

# READING NONFICTION

To figure out an excerpt's unifying idea and its purpose, you should scan the passage, then annotate as you read through it more thoroughly. A sample passage follows for practice. We have underlined helpful phrases for discovering the main ideas as you read.

<u>My loving people</u>, we have been persuaded by some, that are careful of our safety, to take heed how we commit

*Line* ourselves to armed multitudes, for fear
(5) of treachery; <u>but</u> <u>I assure you</u>, I do not desire to live to distrust <u>my faithful and loving people</u>. Let tyrants fear; I have always so behaved myself that, under God, I have placed my chiefest strength

(10) and safeguard in <u>the loyal hearts and good will of my subjects</u>. And therefore, I am come amongst you at this time, not as for my recreation or sport, <u>but being resolved</u>, in the midst

(15) and heat of the battle, to live or die amongst you all; to lay down, for my God, and for my kingdom, and for <u>my people</u>, my honor and my blood, even the dust. <u>I know I have but the body of</u>

(20) <u>a weak and feeble woman; but</u> I have the heart of a king, and of a king of England, too; and think foul scorn that Parma* or Spain, or any prince of Europe, should dare to invade

(25) the borders of my realms: to which, <u>rather than any dishonor should grow</u> <u>by me</u>, I myself will take up arms, I myself will be your general, judge, and rewarder of every one of your virtues in

(30) the field. I know already, by your forwardness, that you have deserved rewards and crowns; <u>and we do assure</u> <u>you,</u> on the word of a prince, they shall be duly paid you. In the mean my

(35) lieutenant general shall be in my stead, than whom never prince commanded a more noble and worthy subject; not doubting by your obedience to my

**KAPLAN**

(40)      general, by your concord in the camp,
          and by your valor in the field, we shall
          shortly have a victory over the enemies
          of my God, of my kingdom, and <u>of my</u>
          <u>people</u>.

                        (1588)

*Parma:* the duke of Parma, in Italy, who at the time of this speech is
     preparing to invade England under the King of Spain's command

From the underlined portions of the passage above, one can tell what the unifying idea and mode are because of certain repetitions. The speaker is constantly referring to her audience as her "people," her "loving people," or her loyal "subjects." We know then that she is a ruler addressing the people of her country. From the repeated phrase "I/we assure you," we can also assume that her mode is persuasive; she has to convince her "people" of something. If one also sees the contrasts—evident by the repeated conjunction *but* and the phrase *rather than*—in her speech, one can conclude that her mission is possibly to debunk previous misconceptions about her and instill in her people's minds a new image of their queen.

The next step after determining these broader concepts is to annotate the text for its smaller images, the ones that feed into the passage's unifying idea. Look at the notes to the side of the same passage:

|  |  |
|---|---|
| My loving people, we have been | assuming her people love her |
| persuaded by some, that are careful of | |
| our safety, to take heed how we commit | she's in danger? |
| *Line* ourselves to armed multitudes, for fear | |
| (5) of treachery; but I assure you, I do not | traitors, that's the danger |
| desire to live to distrust my faithful and | |
| loving people. Let tyrants fear; I have | going against advisor's wishes |
| always so behaved myself that, under | |
| God, I have placed my chiefest strength | "under God"—emotional appeal |
| (10) and safeguard in the loyal hearts and | |
| good will of my subjects. And | "others may not trust you; I do" |
| therefore, I am come amongst you at | |
| this time, not as for my recreation or | |
| sport, but being resolved, in the midst | she's a serious ruler, not a nominal monarch |
| (15) and heat of the battle, to live or die | |
| amongst you all; to lay down, for my | |
| God, and for my kingdom, and for my | |
| people, my honor and my blood, even | |
| the dust. I know I have but the body of | her honor and her people are foremost |
| (20) a weak and feeble woman; but I have | |
| the heart of a king, and of a king of | |
| England, too; and think foul scorn that | |
| Parma* or Spain, or any prince of | |
| Europe, should dare to invade | |

(25) the borders of my realms: to which,
rather than any dishonor should grow
by me, I myself will take up arms, I
myself will be your general, judge, and
rewarder of every one of your virtues in
(30) the field. I know already, by your
forwardness, that you have deserved
rewards and crowns; and we do assure
you, on the word of a prince, they shall
be duly paid you. In the mean my
(35) lieutenant general shall be in my stead,
than whom never prince commanded a
more noble and worthy subject; not
doubting by your obedience to my
general, by your concord in the camp,
(40) and by your valor in the field, we shall
shortly have a victory over the enemies
of my God, of my kingdom, and of my
people.

this is war!

there's some question of payment

lieutenant general: her representative

persuading: we'll win; I'm fighting w/you

(1588)

*Parma*: the duke of Parma, in Italy, who at the
time of this speech is preparing to invade England
under the King of Spain's command

These notes will help you to put the text into your own words as you read and to remember the passage's main ideas. That way, you will have a better frame of reference for the upcoming questions. By making yourself familiar with the passage through close reading and note making, you have given yourself an advantage when you begin answering the test questions. Your notes will help point you in the right direction without your having to reread large portions of the passage over again for each question.

## THINGS TO REMEMBER

- Nonfiction is becoming an increasingly popular genre on the exam.
- To tackle a nonfiction passage,
    - underline helpful phrases and make notes;
    - determine the unifying idea; and
    - identify the passage's mode or purpose (persuasive, expository, descriptive, narrative).

# SAMPLE QUESTIONS

Let's now shift our focus to another passage of nonfiction. The following excerpt is taken from Thomas More's *Utopia*, and although this piece of literature concerns a fictional place of social perfection, More's work is still considered to be nonfiction because of its thinly disguised critique of the archbishop's society.

Determine on your own what the unifying idea and mode of the excerpt are, make notes as you read, and then use those discoveries to help you in answering questions about the passage.

The woman is not married before she is eighteen years old. The man is four years older before he marry. If either the man or the woman be proved to have actually offended, before their
*Line*
(5)     marriage, with another, the party that hath so trespassed is sharply punished, and both the offenders be forbidden ever after in all their life to marry, unless the fault be forgiven by the prince's pardon. But both the goodman and the
(10)    goodwife of the house where that offence was committed, as being slack and negligent in looking to their charge, be in danger of great reproach and infamy. That offence is so sharply punished because they perceive that unless they
(15)    be diligently kept from the liberty of the vice, few will join together in the love of marriage, wherein all the life must be led with one, and also all the griefs and displeasures coming therewith patiently be taken and borne.
(20)        Furthermore, in choosing wives and husbands they observe earnestly and straitly a custom which seemed to us very fond and foolish. For a sad and an honest matron sheweth the woman, be she maid or widow, naked to the wooer. And
(25)    likewise a sage and discreet man exhibiteth the wooer naked to the woman. At this custom we laughed, and disallowed it as foolish. But they, on the other part, do greatly wonder at the folly of all other nations which, in buying a colt, whereas
(30)    a little money is in hazard, be so chary and circumspect, that though he be almost all bare, yet they will not buy him unless the saddle and all the harness be taken off, lest under those coverings be hid some gall or sore. And yet in
(35)    choosing a wife, which shall be either pleasure or displeasure to them all their life after, they be so reckless, that all the residue of the woman's body being covered with clothes, they esteem her scarcely by one handbreadth (for they can see no
(40)    more but her face), and so to join her to them not without great jeopardy of evil agreeing together, if anything in her body afterward should chance to offend and mislike them. For all men be not so wise as to have respect to the
(45)    virtuous conditions of the party. And the endowments of the body cause the virtues of the mind more to be esteemed and regarded, yea, even in the marriages of wise men. Verily so foul deformity may be hid under those coverings, that
(50)    it may quite alienate and take away the man's mind from his wife, when it shall not be lawful for their bodies to be separate again. If such deformity happen by any chance after the marriage is consummate and finished, well, there
(55)    is no remedy but patience. Every man must take his fortune well a worth. But it were well done that a law were made whereby all such deceits might be eschewed and avoided beforehand.

(1516)

Although at times it describes customs and displays two cultures that are trying to persuade each other of the correctness of a premarital practice, the above passage seems mainly to be giving information about a certain cultural procedure, so its mode is expository. Furthermore, since ideas about marriage are often broached here, the philosophy of love, attraction, and marriage seems to be the unifying idea.

As usual, the first question will be of a general nature:

1. The entire passage seems to be
   (A)   a re-enactment of a medical procedure.
   (B)   a description of a cultural practice.
   (C)   a lecture on human anatomy.
   (D)   a rendezvous supervised by chaperones.
   (E)   a recounting of a civil trial.

2. The speaker's tone seems to be
   (A)   matter-of-fact, yet occasionally superior.
   (B)   melancholy, but ultimately resolved.
   (C)   annoyed, yet extremely amused.
   (D)   confused, yet quietly awed.
   (E)   tongue-in-cheek, yet fairly angry.

3. The "offence" referred to in line 13 must be
   (A)   slander.
   (B)   heresy.
   (C)   witchcraft.
   (D)   fornication.
   (E)   theft.

4. The prince's authority in this passage is best described as
   (A)   overriding.
   (B)   figurative.
   (C)   cumbersome.
   (D)   cruel.
   (E)   deferential.

5. The seriousness of the "offence" can be demonstrated by all of the following EXCEPT
   (A)   the offenders' prohibition from marriage forever.
   (B)   the subsequent degradation of the offender's parents.
   (C)   the offender's lack of desire for social inclusion.
   (D)   the fear that a social institution might dissipate.
   (E)   the punishment of the offender who is about to be married.

6. The word *sad* (line 23) in the context of the passage must mean
   (A)   unhappy.
   (B)   poor.
   (C)   pathetic.
   (D)   unlucky.
   (E)   serious.

7. The narrator sees the task of the "honest matron" (line 23) and the "discreet man" (line 25) as "foolish" (line 27) probably because
   (A)   the matron and the man cannot possibly be qualified for such serious business.
   (B)   the idea of naked people examining each other seems ridiculous.
   (C)   the matron and the man are obviously influenced by the power of the prince.
   (D)   the advanced age of the matron and the man could impair their judgment.
   (E)   the thought of discovering a secret blemish seems repulsive.

**KAPLAN**

8. The colt analogy in lines 27–34 is used to

   (A) defend the task of the matron and man.

   (B) advocate against the abuse of animals.

   (C) ridicule the society being observed by the narrator.

   (D) praise the wisdom of the narrator's insight.

   (E) show the superiority of beasts over humans.

9. The sentence that begins "And the endowments of the body …" (lines 45–48) is

   (A) an attempt to prove that physical features are superior to mental ones.

   (B) a chauvinistic idea praising the beauty of women, not their personalities.

   (C) a warning against the seductive powers of the female sex.

   (D) an axiom explaining why wise men make the best husbands.

   (E) an aphorism showing that physical features amplify mental qualities.

10. The sentence that begins "If such deformity happen…" (lines 52–55) demonstrates all of the following EXCEPT that the narrator

   (A) has become less formal in his tone.

   (B) is admitting an imperfection in the described procedure.

   (C) is reflecting on his own regrettable situation.

   (D) can see that chance may ruin careful planning.

   (E) believes that marriage is permanent once consummated.

11. By the end of the passage, the narrator

   (A) maintains a belief in his own society's superiority.

   (B) begins to see an improvement that his own society could make.

   (C) wants to advise the reader against observing foreign governments.

   (D) longs to be married to a woman who has been subjected to this procedure.

   (E) seems uncomfortable with choices made in his personal life.

12. The most obvious change in the passage occurs in

   (A) the narrator's attitude.

   (B) the treatment of the offenders.

   (C) the society being observed.

   (D) the verb tense between paragraphs.

   (E) the diction of the matron and man.

# ANSWERS AND EXPLANATIONS

**1.  (B)**

The narrator is describing this experience as something altogether unfamiliar to him and his party; they are watching a "custom" that they consider to be "foolish." Those being studied, however, wonder at the foolishness of other "nations" for not following the same premarital process. Thus, this procedure is something that belongs to a particular culture; it is not a universal experience. (A), (C), and (E) make the practice sound too technical; (D) makes it sound potentially fun, when a very serious kind of scrutiny is going on here.

**2.  (A)**

For most of the passage, the narrator seems mainly to be reporting on the procedure he is witnessing and recording his group's reactions to it. Occasionally, though, he betrays feelings of superiority when he describes the practice as "foolish."

**3.  (D)**

The offence is committed by more than one offender at a time; (A), (B), (C), and (E) can be committed by an individual, but (D) requires more than one person. Furthermore, (D) is appropriately named as an "offence," especially when it occurs before a marriage and does not involve both the betrothed parties.

**4.  (A)**

Lines 6–9 clearly indicate that the prince has overriding powers. Custom says that unmarried fornicating partners are forever forbidden to marry anyone but that a pardon from the prince can overturn that decision.

**5.  (C)**

Lines 3–19 contain the evidence to prove (A), (B), (D), and (E) true.

However, even though the offenders are chastised and prevented from marrying, they do not necessarily wish to be ostracized from their society. Their prohibition from marriage comes from an external power, not from their inner desires.

**6.  (E)**

The key here is that the word *sad* is combined with *honest*. If it is a matron's job to display the woman to the wooer, then the best matron for the task would be both serious about her work and honest about its results. Any of the other options makes her sound less than ideal for the position.

**7.  (B)**

According to the edicts of this culture, the woman and the wooer should not have had any kind of physical relations; furthermore, no other custom has been mentioned in which the couple's nakedness would have been required. So they probably would not have seen each other naked before this point. Certainly, then, their meeting now like this would be awkward. The addition of the serious matron and the wise man would be a further humiliating condition of this meeting. Thus, to someone unaccustomed to this scene, the whole process could seem ridiculous.

**8.  (A)**

The colt analogy does not merely call up another instance in which a living being is scrutinized for physical imperfections; a further point of the example is that a colt is of lesser value than a human being. If people will closely examine a young horse for its bodily flaws before they commit to owning it, how much more important is it to discover the blemishes on a human being, who is worth more than the colt and who will be committing to a longer and more important partnership with another human? (B) and (E) place too much emphasis on the animal itself, and (C) and (D) do not understand that the analogy's source is not the narrator but people speaking for the Utopian culture.

**9.  (E)**

The sentence in lines 45–48 does not disregard the importance of mental qualities, so neither (A) nor (B) can be right. Instead, the sentence seeks to explain a chronology and a cause-effect relationship. Physical features are noticed first, then the internal qualities. Furthermore, whatever internal attributes a person may have seem better when they are housed in a pleasing body.

**10.  (C)**

Not once in the sentence does the narrator offer any autobiographical information. However, the narrator's less formal tone—mentioned in answer (A)—can be seen in his interjected *well*. (B) and (D) are proven in the idea that the examination takes place only once, before the marriage; physical imperfections can occur soon after the marriage takes place. Finally, (E) is proven in the narrator's claim that patience is the only way to deal with these post-wedding physical imperfections. He does not offer divorce or annulment as options. One must either have the patience to tolerate the imperfection or to wait until death separates the couple.

**11.  (B)**

After formerly seeing this custom as "foolish," the narrator in his last sentence admits that a "law" by which couples could avoid physical deception would be valuable. He has begun to see some wisdom in the Utopian society.

**12.  (A)**

(B), (C), and (D) remain constant in the passage, so these answers cannot be counted as reasonable contenders. (E) makes no sense because the matron and man have no dialogue and their speech is not described. If one reviews question 11, however, then the truth of (A) becomes more apparent.

# Chapter 6: **Working with Fiction**

- Narration
- Tone
- Dialogue

A sizable percentage of passages on the SAT Subject Test: Literature will fall into the category of fiction. These passages will almost always come from short stories and novels; therefore, they will be incomplete excerpts. In addition, although the test writers will try to select literary items that would normally be unfamiliar to most high school students, you might occasionally recognize an excerpt. However, you need to focus solely on the passage at hand; by no means should you consider plot lines or character development beyond what you see in the presented text. For instance, if you see an excerpt from *The Adventures of Huckleberry Finn* in which Huck discusses the dilemma of whether or not to turn in Jim as an escaped slave, you might remember that the end of Twain's novel reveals Jim to be already set free. However, this fact is considered "inadmissible evidence" as you analyze the passage in front of you. The questions discussing the excerpt will assume that no reader is familiar with the details surrounding the text.

## NARRATION

You can recognize fictional passages because they will almost always appear in the narrative mode; that is, they will usually be telling a story. As you scan a passage of fiction, then, the first thing to look for is the identity of the storyteller: Who is the narrator, and what point of view does she have?

- A *first-person major character* point of view will feature a narrator who is the protagonist of the work. Although this kind of narrator can be highly personal and can draw readers more immediately into the text, he also has a very subjective viewpoint. As such, he can be an unreliable source of information. The aforementioned Huck is a good example: We know that his relationship with Jim demonstrates Huck's goodness and capacity for altruism, but Huck continually questions the morality of befriending a runaway slave. Thus, as Huck relates his tale, we have to remove ourselves from his limited perspective if we are to grasp the themes of Twain's work.

- Perhaps the most limited of narrators is the *first-person minor character*. Possessing all the subjectivity of the major character point of view, this narrator is further hampered by watching the action from the sidelines. Since he is not the protagonist of the work, the first-person minor character narrator must watch as those more important than himself act out the "drama" of the text. A common resident of a small town, for instance, stands back and observes more significant characters develop a scandalous story in Faulkner's "A Rose for Emily."

The next group of narrators is categorized in the third person. These points of view occur outside the story; the text unfolds through the narration of "someone" who is not a character in the work. This distance from the story helps the point of view to become more objective; third-person narrators offer more reliable information.

- A *third-person observer* sees what is physically occurring in the story but is unable to "read" the thoughts or feelings of the characters. This point of view presents a fictional work almost as if it were a play.

- A *third-person limited omniscient* narrator can follow the thoughts and feelings of one character in the work, but the inner workings of other characters remain unknown to her.

- Finally, a *third-person omniscient* point of view is privy to all characters' thoughts and feelings.

## Exercise

Below you will find a sampling of four separate texts, each with a different point of view. Try to determine which is which:

(A)    First-person major character

(B)    First-person minor character

(C)    Third-person observer

(D)    Third-person limited omniscient

(E)    Third-person omniscient

_____1. I sat in the corner and watched as Madame flung herself into the arms of any man silly enough to hold her. Countless tuxedos were tainted either by her perspiration or her tears. Madame herself was a blot on the night, blacking out the glimmer of ingenues whose radiance was absorbed by Madame's nebulous void.

_____2. Marvin played his favorite game. He entered the elevator after everyone else, but failed to turn around politely and face the doors, or the ceiling, as all the other occupants had. Rather, he stared at each person individually, waiting for someone to stare back, to stare him down, to accept his challenge. People coughed, they looked at jittery newspapers, or they adjusted clothing. "C'mon," thought Marvin, "just one of you. Just one before the 19th floor ...."

_____3. The Grunt had at least a 65" waist. He was more puff than flab, though; there was a near-explosive tightness to him, as if he could float in a Macy's parade and never lose altitude. Oscar, by contrast, was half the Grunt's mass but double his density. Oscar had a squishiness to his physique, like a bag of warm wax. The two of them stared at each other when, suddenly, Oscar shifted his great weight on his feet, cocked his head to the side, and craned it slowly to the left ... to the right. Oscar closed his mouth; his Adam's apple cranked down, then bobbed up; sweat beads visibly grew on his upper lip.

_____4. Harold Veederson was hoarding money and his wife Jill knew it. The problem was that Harold knew that Jill knew, but he never felt guilty enough to stop. So she ran a steamroller over him. Jill then left town and all the citizens of Macaffeyville felt relieved that that Veederson mess was now over.

## Answers

The first passage is an example of (B). The focus is on "Madame," but her story is related by a character uninvolved in the action. The second passage displays Marvin's thoughts but no one else's, so it is an example of (D). In the third passage, the physical characteristics of Oscar and the Grunt are described to the point that we can infer what they are thinking, but we never get to see their actual thoughts; (C), then, is the right choice here. Finally, (E) is correct for the last passage. We not only know Harold's thoughts and Jill's, but we also are in on the entire town's feelings about the incident; the townspeople are "relieved" that it is over.

The next passage, under "Tone," will display an example of first-person major character point of view.

## TONE

Once you have determined the excerpt's point of view, you can more readily discover the tone of the piece and its plot line.

*Tone* refers to the narrator's attitude toward the subject. It is not enough to read what is being reported to us, to know the plot of the story; we must also examine the diction and syntax that the narrator is using so that we understand his feelings about characters and events. Perhaps then, we can also understand how we ourselves are supposed to feel about what we are reading.

Look at the following excerpt taken from Dickens's *Great Expectations*. See how the first-person major character point of view develops its tone (certain words and phrases are underlined for your special attention):

"...the office is one thing, and private life is another. When I go into the office, I leave the castle behind me, and when I come into the

*Line*
(5)    castle, I leave the office behind me. If it's not in any way disagreeable to you, you'll oblige me by doing the same. I don't wish it professionally spoken about."

Of course <u>I felt my good faith involved in the observance of his request</u>. The punch being very

(10)   nice, we sat there drinking it and talking, until it was almost nine o'clock. "Getting near gun-fire," said Wemmick then, as he laid down his pipe; "it's the Aged's treat."

Proceeding into the castle again, we found the

(15)   Aged heating the poker, with expectant eyes, as a preliminary to the performance of his great nightly ceremony. Wemmick stood with his watch in his hand until the moment was come for him to take the red-hot poker from the Aged, and

(20)   repair to the battery. He took it, and went out, and

presently <u>the stinger went off with a bang that shook the crazy little box of a cottage as if it must fall to pieces, and made every glass and tea-cup in it ring</u>. Upon this the Aged—<u>who I believe would

(25)   have been blown out of his arm-chair but for holding on by his elbows</u>—cried out exultingly, "He's fired! I heerd him!" and <u>I nodded at the old gentleman until it is no figure of speech to declare that I absolutely could not see him</u>.

(30)   The interval between that time and supper Wemmick devoted to showing me his collection of curiosities. They were mostly of a <u>felonious</u> character; comprising the pen with which a celebrated forgery had been committed, a

(35)   distinguished razor or two, some locks of hair, and several manuscript confessions written under condemnation—upon which Mr. Wemmick set particular value as being, to his own words, "every one of 'em lies, sir." These were <u>agreeably

(40)   dispersed</u> among small specimens of china and

glass, various neat trifles made by <u>the proprietor of the museum</u>, and some tobacco-stoppers carved by the Aged. They were all displayed in that chamber of the castle into which I had been

(45) first inducted, and which served, not only as the general sitting-room, but as the kitchen, too, if I might judge from a saucepan on the hob, and a brazen bijou over the fire-place designed for the suspension of a roasting-jack.

(50)      There was <u>a neat little girl in attendance</u>, who looked after the Aged in the day. When she had laid the supper-cloth, the bridge was lowered <u>to give her the means of egress</u>, and she withdrew for the night. <u>The supper was excellent; and</u>

(55) <u>though the castle was rather subject to dry rot,</u> <u>insomuch that it tasted like a bad nut, and though</u> <u>the pig might have been farther off, I was heartily</u> <u>pleased by my whole entertainment. Nor was</u> <u>there any drawback</u> on my little turret bedroom,

(60) <u>beyond there being such a very thin ceiling</u> <u>between me and the flagstaff that, when I lay</u>

<u>down on my back in bed, it seemed as if I had to</u> <u>balance that pole on my forehead all night.</u>

Wemmick was up early in the morning, and <u>I</u>
(65) <u>am afraid I heard him cleaning my boots.</u> After that, he fell to gardening, and I saw him from my Gothic window pretending to employ the Aged, and nodding at him in a most devoted manner. Our breakfast was as good as the supper, and at
(70) half-past eight precisely we started for Little Britain. By degrees, Wemmick got dryer and harder as we went along, and his mouth tightened into a post office again. At last, when we got to his place of business and he pulled out his key from
(75) his coat-collar, <u>he looked as unconscious of his</u> <u>Walworth property as if the castle and the</u> <u>drawbridge and the arbour and the lake and the</u> <u>fountain and the Aged had all been blown into</u> <u>space</u> together by the last discharge of the stinger.

(1861)

From the underlined parts of the passage, we can determine at least three things about the narrator's tone:

- **Formality:** Single words, such as *felonious* (line 32) instead of *criminal* and *egress* (line 53) instead of *exit* or even *departure*, indicate a lack of casual utterance in the speaker. The long, complex sentences also betray the narrator's formality.

- **Amusement:** Explaining that the "felonious" artifacts are "agreeably dispersed" (lines 39–40) among more commonplace household items shows that the narrator is noticing a humorous contrast. Calling the servant a "neat little girl" (line 50) also amusingly juxtaposes Wemmick's eccentricities with a more ordinary person from the outside world. Furthermore, the exaggerations employed by the narrator in lines 21–26 and lines 41–42 add to his mirth.

- **Humility:** Perhaps most striking in this passage is the narrator's wish not to offend or denigrate his host. In lines 8–9, the narrator seems to reassure himself that he is complying with his host's wishes. Lines 54–63 find the narrator complimenting both room and board, though still slipping in mild and good-natured criticisms. Finally, he is "afraid" that his boots are being cleaned by Wemmick (lines 64–65), as if the narrator doesn't want his host to stoop to such a task.

When we put all these emotions together, we understand that the narrator sees Wemmick as a likeable character; his "hardening" as he approaches work seems all the sadder and stranger to us because of the passage's tone.

# DIALOGUE

After uncovering a fictional work's point of view, plot line, and tone, we must also see how the passage balances between narrative description and dialogue. Neither aspect can be ignored, as both are vital to fiction's narrative mode. In the Dickens excerpt above, we notice that all the dialogue is reserved for the passage's most eccentric characters: Wemmick and the Aged. When we compare their amusing observations, their descriptions of the "castle," and their lower-middle-class dialect with Pip's more formal language in the narration, the narrator seems a more rational and trustworthy storyteller: a straight man for Wemmick's comic antics. One might also note that Wemmick's opening dialogue in the passage sets up Pip's final commentary at the end; they are bookends that neatly store the theme of the excerpt. Therefore, in tandem, dialogue and narrative description reveal characterization, plot, setting, tone, and theme.

## THINGS TO REMEMBER

- Fiction comprises a sizable percentage of the exam.
- Fiction passages are incomplete excerpts; if you recognize the passage, do not consider general plot lines of the entire work as you answer questions.
- To tackle a fiction excerpt,
    - identify the narrator (first-person major character, first-person minor character, third-person observer, third-person limited omniscient, third-person omniscient);
    - use diction and syntax to help identify the tone of the passage; and
    - evaluate the balance between dialogue and narrative description.

## SAMPLE QUESTIONS

Now, for practice, take a look at the Hamlin Garland passage below. As usual, mark up the excerpt; note its point of view, its tone, and the way dialogue and narrative description reveal the basic elements of the story. Then, answer the questions that follow the passage.

"Dodd's Family Bitters," said the man, waking out of his abstraction with a start and resuming his working manner. "The best bitter in the market." He alluded to it in the singular. "Like to
Line
(5)  look at it? No trouble to show goods, as the fellah says," he went on hastily, seeing Uncle Ethan's hesitation.

He produced a large bottle of a triangular shape, like a bottle for pickled onions. It had a red
(10)  seal on top and a strenuous caution in red letters on the neck, "None genuine unless 'Dodd's Family Bitters' is blown in the bottom."

"Here's what it cures," pursued the agent, pointing at the side, where, in an inverted
(15)  pyramid, the names of several hundred diseases were arranged, running from "gout" to "pulmonary complaints," etc.

"I gol! She cuts a wide swath, don't she?" exclaimed Uncle Ethan, profoundly impressed
(20)  with the list. "They ain't no better bitter in the world," said the agent with a conclusive inflection.

"What's its speshy-*ality*? Most of 'em have some speshy-*ality*."

(25) "Well—summer complaints—an'—an'—spring an' fall troubles—tones ye up, sort of."

Uncle Ethan's forgotten pan was empty of his gathered bugs.* He was deeply interested in this man. There was something he liked about him.

"What does it sell fur?" he asked after a pause.

(30) "Same price as them cheap medicines—dollar a bottle—big bottles, too. Want one?"

"Wal, mother ain't to home, an' I don't know as she's like this kind. We ain't been sick f'r years. Still, they's no tellin'," he added, seeing the answer (35) to his objection in the agent's eyes.

"Times is purty close too, with us, y'see; we've just built that stable—"

"Say I'll tell yeh what I'll do," said the stranger, waking up and speaking in a warmly generous (40) tone. "I'll give you ten bottles of the bitter if you'll let me paint a sign on that barn. It won't hurt the barn a bit, and if you want'o you can paint it out a year from date. Come, what d'ye say?"

"I guess I hadn't better."

(45) The agent thought that Uncle Ethan was after more pay, but in reality he was thinking of what his little old wife would say.

"It simply puts a family bitter in your home that may save you fifty dollars this comin' fall. You (50) can't tell."

Just what the man said after that Uncle Ethan didn't follow. His voice had a confidential purring sound as he stretched across the wagon seat and talked on, eyes half shut. He straightened up at (55) last and concluded in the tone of one who has carried his point:

"So! If you didn't want to use the whole twenty-five bottles y'self, why! sell it to your neighbors. You can get twenty dollars out of it easy, and still (60) have five bottles of the best family bitter that ever went into a bottle."

It was the thought of the opportunity to get a buffalo-skin coat that consoled Uncle Ethan as he saw the hideous black letters appearing under (65) the agent's lazy brush.

It was the hot side of the barn, and painting was no light work. The agent was forced to mop his forehead with his sleeve.

(70) "Say, hain't got a cookie or anything, and a cup of milk handy?" he said at the end of the first enormous word, which ran the whole length of the barn.

Uncle Ethan got him the milk and cookie, which he ate with an exaggeratedly dainty action (75) of his fingers, seated meanwhile on the staging which Uncle Ripley had helped him to build.

This lunch infused new energy into him, and in a short time "DODD'S FAMILY BITTERS, Best in the Market," disfigured the (80) sweet-smelling pine boards.

(1891)

*forgotten pan...gathered bugs: Uncle Ethan has been removing bugs from his potato patch

1. The agent and Uncle Ethan's conversation is best likened to one occurring between

   (A) an artist and a potential patron.

   (B) a business representative and a reluctant client.

   (C) a doctor and an indecisive patient.

   (D) a sales manager and a hesitant employee.

   (E) a manufacturer and an inept distributor.

2. The product being discussed is best described as

   (A) a condiment.

   (B) an alcoholic beverage.

   (C) a soft drink.

   (D) a vitamin supplement.

   (E) a health tonic.

3. The narrator's description of the "caution" in lines 9–12 displays what kind of tone?

   (A) Fearful

   (B) Relieved

   (C) Ironic

   (D) Questioning

   (E) Confident

4. The description of the product in lines 13–17 contains all of the following EXCEPT

   (A) hyperbole that casts doubt on the product's characteristics.

   (B) a pairing of disparate ailments that seems unlikely.

   (C) an indication of the agent's doggedness about the product.

   (D) a grand claim contrasting with the modest simile in lines 8–9.

   (E) proof that the agent believes in the quality of the product.

5. In line 18, Uncle Ethan's exclamation is meant to

   (A) praise the product's wide-ranging abilities.

   (B) express doubt in the product's traits.

   (C) encourage the agent in his endeavors.

   (D) bolster the agent's flagging confidence.

   (E) comment on the sign painted on the barn.

6. The hesitancy in lines 24–25 indicates the agent's

   (A) embarrassment.

   (B) uncertainty.

   (C) forgetfulness.

   (D) dishonesty.

   (E) contempt.

7. The hesitancy in lines 32–33 indicates Ethan's

   (A) reluctance to commit to a transaction.

   (B) fear of the agent's reprisal.

   (C) plans to deceive his wife.

   (D) preoccupation with his potato patch.

   (E) senility in his twilight years.

8. The word "close" in line 36 is nearest in meaning to

   (A) emotionally intimate.

   (B) financially strained.

   (C) fast-paced.

   (D) spatially confining.

   (E) mortally draining.

9. Lines 45–47 make clear that the point of view in this passage is

   (A) first-person major character.

   (B) first-person minor character.

   (C) third-person observer.

   (D) third-person limited omniscient.

   (E) third-person omniscient.

10. As it is described in lines 52–56, the agent's voice moves from

   (A) sleepy to alert.

   (B) hopeful to desperate.

   (C) beguiling to decisive.

   (D) inviting to withdrawn.

   (E) calm to irritated.

11. All of the following demonstrate the agent's imposition on Uncle Ethan EXCEPT

   (A) the amount of time it takes to fulfill their agreement's terms.

   (B) the help the agent receives from Uncle Ethan in building the "staging."

   (C) the admiration that Uncle Ethan feels for the agent.

   (D) the product offered in return for the barn advertisement.

   (E) the refreshments that Uncle Ethan supplies for the agent.

12. The narrator's opinion of the agent and the barn painting is best described as

   (A) suspicious.

   (B) disdainful.

   (C) uncertain.

   (D) awestruck.

   (E) respectful.

13. The passage portrays Uncle Ethan as

   (A) sagacious, but victimized.

   (B) innocent, but demanding.

   (C) impoverished, but clever.

   (D) well-intentioned, but duped.

   (E) intuitive, but corruptible.

# ANSWERS AND EXPLANATIONS

**1. (B)**

Although the agent is cutting a deal to paint Ethan's barn, and the product he is promoting supposedly has some kind of medicinal power, the agent is not primarily an artist or a doctor. He is a representative of the company that bottles Dodd's Family Bitters. He is painting an advertisement, and he offers no medical expertise in his explanations of the product. Furthermore, he seeks Uncle Ethan as a client who will allow the advertisement to appear on his property; the 25 bottles of bitters are payment for the barn sign—the agent doesn't care what happens to the bitters once he hands the supply over to Ethan. At first, Ethan shows his reluctance toward this transaction by making excuses, but he later agrees to the agent's proposal.

**2. (E)**

On the bottle are listed all the diseases and ailments that the bitters can cure; furthermore, the agent explains to Uncle Ethan that the product "tones ye up, sort of" (line 25). Thus, the bitters function as a tonic.

**3. (C)**

The caution on the bottle is described as "strenuous," but the only thing it warns against is the lack of authenticity of similar products. Such a warning seems trivial, especially when one considers the dubious powers possessed by the bitters.

**4. (E)**

The narrator's description that "several hundred" ailments are listed on the bottle's label seems exaggerated; it is even more unlikely that the tonic could cure this many health problems—so (A) cannot be a possible choice. It is also hard to believe that problems such as gout—afflicting the joints—and "pulmonary complaints"—concentrating on the lungs—could be cured by the same medicine; thus (B) doesn't work. The agent is described as having "pursued" the issue of the tonic's qualities, so he does not give up on his pitch: (C) cannot be an option. (D) is not the best choice because the medicine claims to be a cure-all, but it is bottled in a container that the narrator compares to a pickled onion bottle. (E) is the best choice because even though the agent explains the tonic's healing qualities, he does not necessarily have to believe his own pitch.

**5. (A)**

When Uncle Ethan notes that "she cuts a wide swath," the "she" is the product. The image seems to compare the bitters to a scythe that mows down health problems. Its "swath" is "wide" because it claims to cure "several hundred" ailments.

**6. (D)**

The bottle's own exaggerated labeling has helped to disprove its powers. In the wake of this information, the hesitant claims made by the agent sound like impromptu prefabrication.

**7. (A)**

A simple recollection of the content of Uncle Ethan's response can clarify this choice. He offers excuses for not wanting a bottle of the bitters, his own uninterrupted health and his wife's possible disapproval of the tonic.

**8. (B)**

When the agent asks, "Want one?" Uncle Ethan replies that times are pretty "close"—an excuse that implies he cannot afford to buy the bitters. His support for this statement is that he and his wife have recently built a stable, certainly a costly endeavor that would have depleted their finances.

**9. (E)**

These lines make reference to the thoughts of both the agent and Uncle Ethan.

**10. (C)**

The agent's voice is described as "purring," and he is stretched out on the wagon with his eyes "half shut." This attitude has an effect on Uncle Ethan that he doesn't "follow" what is being said; he has become fairly hypnotized by the agent's tone. Then, the agent straightens himself, and speaks as if he has "carried his point," or spoken decisively.

**11. (C)**

Since the terms of their agreement last for one full year, the agent is costing Uncle Ethan not only barn space, but also time; thus (A) does not apply. The barn sign is imposition enough, but somehow the agent is able to talk Ethan into helping him build the scaffolding needed to complete the paint job; so (B) does not work. (D) seems unlikely because the agent doesn't even have the decency to offer cash for the barn space; he instead offers a quantity of his questionable product. (E) is not an option because during his paint job, the agent has the nerve to ask for milk and a cookie. Ironically, these items imbue him with the energy he needs to finish his task; he does not rely on his much-touted tonic. No doubt, Uncle Ethan takes a liking to the agent (lines 27–28), but this reaction should lighten the imposition with which the agent burdens Ethan.

**12. (B)**

Without uncertainty or mere suspicion, the narrator clearly indicates his disdain for the agent and his project. The painted black letters are "hideous" (line 64), and the agent's brush is "lazy" (line 65). His cookie eating is "exaggeratedly dainty" (line 74), as if even this simple action must be falsified. Finally, the finished barn sign has "disfigured the sweet-smelling pine boards" (lines 79–80). The narrator's contempt is open and unmitigated.

**13 (D)**

Uncle Ethan wants to disappoint no one. He initially rebuffs the agent, but then reconsiders when he sees "the answer to his objection in the agent's eyes" (lines 34–35). He also offers his wife's disapproval as a reason not to surrender to the agent's proposals. Thus, his intentions are good, but the agent still tricks Ethan into using the barn space for a "hideous," "enormous," and disfiguring advertisement.

Notice how these questions float between narrative description and dialogue. Note also how narration and dialogue develop plot and characterization in different ways; yet each blends with the other to unify the text.

# Chapter 7: **Working with Play Excerpts**

- Benefits and Drawbacks
- Examples

Perhaps the most scarcely seen genre on the SAT Subject Test: Literature is the play. Try though they may, the test creators have a difficult time finding theatrical pieces that are appropriate for their testing process. Without a doubt, a Shakespearean soliloquy will easily find its way onto the test, because a monologue is more like a speech or a narrative passage than a dramatic piece. But a theatrical excerpt that contains dialogue presents a few problems.

## BENEFITS AND DRAWBACKS

The first problem is that all the reader's information must come from the characters' conversation. Dialogue by itself as presented in a written play is quite restrictive in establishing setting and exposition. Characters in a play may talk about the distant past or a faraway galaxy, but they cannot instantly travel there the way a narrator can.

A related problem is that play excerpts rarely provide enough context to be understood. The reader usually has to see an entire scene in order to follow all the character and plot references that the speakers make.

Another difficulty is that play excerpts take up the most space of any other written genre. It is impractical to include play excerpts on the test when spacing occurs between every set of the speakers' lines.

Yet in spite of all the difficulties, there are good reasons to include play passages on the test. The first is that if a dramatic excerpt can fit on one version of the SAT Subject Test: Literature, then that test will have a complete range of literary works: poetry, nonfiction, fiction, and play. Another benefit is that a play excerpt, with its conversational style, is easy to read, perhaps the easiest of all passages. For that reason, play excerpts are often found at the end of a test: the "dessert" after all the other "courses."

From a literary standpoint, the restrictive nature of the play excerpt offers a unique challenge to the reader. For instance, unlike the fictional narrative whose storyteller can move instantaneously through time and space, the play excerpt almost always takes place in real time. In addition, one is forced when perusing the dialogue-based text not only to seek clues involving characterization and tone but also to discover ideas relating to plot, theme, and setting. We have to rely on the dialogue and just a few lines of stage direction to find out everything in the story line.

# EXAMPLES

## Example 1

Keeping this last point in mind, let's take a look at a play excerpt and try to discover as many ideas pertaining to plot, characterization, and theme as possible. This Congreve piece, from *The Way of the World*, has purposefully been chosen because it contains neither an editorial introduction nor any stage directions. We must use only the dialogue to do our analysis:

*Mrs. Fainall.* Ay, ay, dear Marwood, if we will be happy, we must find the means in ourselves, and among ourselves. Men are ever in extremes, either doting or averse. While they are lovers, if they have fire and sense, their jealousies are insupportable; and when they cease to love (we ought to think
(5)    at least) they loathe; they look upon us with horror and distaste; they meet us like the ghosts of what we were, and as from such, fly from us.

*Mrs. Marwood.* True, 'tis an unhappy circumstance of life, that love should ever die before' us; and that the man so often should outlive the lover. But say what you will, 'tis better to be left than never to have been loved. To pass our youth in dull
(10)    indifference, to refuse the sweets of life because they once must leave us, is as preposterous as to wish to have been born old, because we one day must be old. For my part, my youth may wear and waste, but it shall never rust in my possession.

*Mrs. Fain.* Then it seems you dissemble an aversion to mankind only in compliance to my mother's humour.*

(15)    *Mrs. Mar.* Certainly. To be free; I have no taste of those insipid dry discourses, with which our sex of force must entertain themselves, apart from men. We may affect endearments to each other, profess eternal friendships, and seem to dote like lovers; but 'tis not in our natures long to persevere. Love will resume his empire in our breasts, and every heart, or soon or late, receive and
(20)    readmit him as its lawful tyrant.

*Mrs. Fain.* Bless me, how have I been deceived! Why, you profess a libertine.

*Mrs. Mar.* You see my friendship by my freedom. Come, be as sincere, acknowledge that your sentiments agree with mine.

Line
(5)

*KAPLAN)*

*Mrs. Fain.* Never.

(25)    *Mrs. Mar.* You hate mankind?

*Mrs. Fain.* Heartily, inveterately.

*Mrs. Mar.* Your husband?

*Mrs. Fain.* Most transcendently; ay, though I say it, meritoriously.

*Mrs. Mar.* Give me your hand upon it.

(30)    *Mrs. Fain.* There.

*Mrs. Mar.* I join with you; what I have said has been to try you.

*Mrs. Fain.* Is it possible? Dost thou hate those vipers, men?

*Mrs. Mar.* I have done hating 'em, and am now come to despise 'em; the next
thing I have to do, is eternally to forget 'em

(35)    *Mrs. Fain.* There spoke the spirit of an Amazon, a Penthesilea.†

*Mrs. Mar.* And yet I am thinking sometimes to carry my aversion further.

*Mrs. Fain.* How?

*Mrs. Mar.* Faith, by marrying; if I could not but find one that loved me very
well, and would be thoroughly sensible of ill usage, I think I should do myself
(40)    the violence of undergoing the ceremony.

*Mrs. Fain.* You would not make him a cuckold?

*Mrs. Mar.* No; but I'd make him believe I did, and that's as bad.

*Mrs. Fain.* Why had not you as good do it?

*Mrs. Mar.* Oh, if he should ever discover it, he would then know the worst,
(45)    and be out of his pain; but I would have him ever to continue upon the rack
of fear and jealousy.

*Mrs. Fain.* Ingenious mischief!

(1700)

*\*my mother's humour*    Mrs. Fainall's mother has suffered a recent romantic disappointment and, as a
result, distrusts all men.

†*Penthesilea*    Queen of the Amazons, killed by Achilles in the Trojan War

## Analysis of Example 1

### Plot

You can see that these characters philosophize more than they narrate. Still, they do bring out a few plot points.

Lines 13–14: As the footnote helps to relate, Mrs. Marwood is accused of hating men only to please Mrs. Fainall's mother, who has experienced a romantic setback.

Line 31: Mrs. Marwood is attempting to test Mrs. Fainall's true beliefs about men. The entire excerpt revolves around this plot point.

Lines 38–40: Although this comment does not relate to an actual part of the story, the comments here may be foreshadowing a future complication with a male character.

Thus, in a small sense, dialogue in a play excerpt helps to move the plot along. Conversation fulfills the function usually given to a narrator.

### Characterization

In a play excerpt, one can quote every line and show how each helps to reveal something about character. Perhaps then, this is another quality of drama: that more than any other genre, a play will, line by line, either establish, contradict, or reinforce something about a character. Rather than explain how each line develops characterization in this excerpt, however, we will mercifully just examine some highlights.

Lines 1–6: Mrs. Fainall clearly indicates her disdain for men in these lines.

Lines 22–28: In these lines, we see Mrs. Fainall's adamant nature. No amount of coaxing will sway her from her original position: Men stink.

Lline 31: Mrs. Marwood betrays herself here as clever, manipulative, and misanthropic. She is clever enough to devise a way that divines Mrs. Fainall's true feelings, she is manipulative in that she would lie to bring about a desired effect, and she is as much a man-hater as Mrs. Fainall. She has totally reversed the false opinions she delivered in lines 7–12.

Lines 33–34: Here, Mrs. Marwood seems to show a greater degree of hatred for men even than Mrs. Fainall.

Lines 38–46: In these lines, Mrs. Marwood shows her ironic side. It seems paradoxical to marry if one hates men, but she resolves the paradox by explaining that marriage would allow her to abuse a spouse psychologically. Thus, her plan to marry ironically fits her personality.

### Theme

lines 1–6: In these lines, Mrs. Fainall establishes the misanthropic thread that runs throughout the excerpt. By the end of the passage, we will understand that men are no good and that they deserve to be psychologically tortured.

lines 7–12 and 15–20: Mrs. Marwood briefly sets up a counter-philosophy here in which she seems to yearn for male companionship, albeit precarious or temporary. She would have us believe that a brief and unfulfilling romance is better than no love at all. However, this stance is only a ruse; her false longing for men then re-emphasizes Mrs. Fainall's original position.

So there is much to be derived from a passage of dialogue, even when there is no editorial introduction to provide context for us.

## Example 2

Unlike the example above, an introduction usually precedes a dramatic excerpt. It helps to provide background and gives the reader a framework in which to analyze the passage. This time, let's see how the editor's comments help to introduce a passage taken from Wilde's *An Ideal Husband*. We will also add an analysis of tone, as the characters' word choices and syntax always give away their attitudes (look for underlined phrases to be discussed in the Tone section). Finally, a third character in the scene will be discussed as an expository device.

*(Sir Robert, Lady Markby, and Mrs. Chevely are all attending a London high society party. Many of the male guests are members of the British Parliament, either from the House of Commons or the House of Lords.)*

   *Sir Robert Chiltern*: Good evening, Lady Markby! I hope you have brought
   Sir John with you?

   *Lady Markby*: Oh! I have brought a much more charming person than Sir
Line  John. Sir John's temper since he has taken seriously to politics has become
(5)   quite unbearable. Really, <u>now that the House of Commons is trying to
   become useful, it does a great deal of harm.</u>

   *Sir Robert Chiltern*: I hope not, Lady Markby. At any rate we do our best to
   waste the public time, don't we? But who is this charming person you have
   been kind enough to bring to us?

(10)  *Lady Markby*: Her name is Mrs. Chevely. One of the Dorsetshire Chevelys, I
   suppose. But I really don't know. Families are so mixed nowadays. Indeed, as
   a rule, everybody turns out to be somebody else.

   *Sir Robert Chiltern*: Mrs. Chevely? I seem to know the name.

   *Lady Markby*: She has just arrived from Vienna.

(15)  *Sir Robert Chiltern*: Ah! yes. I think I know whom you mean.

   *Lady Markby*: Oh, she goes everywhere there, and has such <u>pleasant scandals</u>
   about all her friends. I really must go to Vienna next winter. I hope there is a
   good chef at the Embassy.

*Sir Robert Chiltern*: If there is not, the Ambassador will certainly have to be
(20)    recalled. Pray point out Mrs. Chevely to me. I should like to see her.

*Lady Markby*: Let me introduce you. [To Mrs. Chevely.] My dear, Sir Robert
Chiltern is <u>dying</u> to know you!

*Sir Robert Chiltern* [bowing]: <u>Every one is dying</u> to know the brilliant Mrs.
Chevely. Our attachés at Vienna write to us about nothing else.

(25)    *Mrs. Chevely*: Thank you, Sir Robert. An acquaintance that begins with a
compliment is sure to develop into a real friendship. It starts in the right
manner. And I find that I know Lady Chiltern already.

*Sir Robert Chiltern*: Really?

*Mrs. Chevely*: Yes. She has just reminded me that we were at school together.
(30)    I remember it perfectly now. She always got the good conduct prize. I have a
distinct recollection of Lady Chiltern always getting the good conduct prize!

*Sir Robert Chiltern* [smiling]: And what prizes did you get, Mrs. Chevely?

*Mrs. Chevely*: My prizes came a little later on in life. I don't think any of
them were for good conduct, I forget!

(35)    *Sir Robert Chiltern*: I am sure they were for something charming!

*Mrs. Chevely*: I don't know that women are always rewarded for being
charming. I think they are <u>unusually punished</u> for it! Certainly, more women
grow old nowadays through the faithfulness of their admirers than through
anything else! At least that is the only way I can account for the terribly
(40)    <u>haggard</u> look of most of your pretty women in London!

*Sir Robert Chiltern*: What an <u>appalling</u> philosophy that sounds! To attempt
to classify you, Mrs. Chevely, would be an impertinence. But may I ask, at
heart, are you an optimist or a pessimist? Those seem to be the only two
<u>fashionable religions</u> left to us nowadays.

(45)    *Mrs. Chevely*: Oh, I'm neither. Optimism begins in a broad grin, and Pessimism
ends with blue spectacles. Besides, they are both of them merely poses.

*Sir Robert Chiltern*: You prefer to be natural?

*Mrs. Chevely*: Sometimes. But it is such a very difficult pose to keep up.

*Sir Robert Chiltern*: What would those modern psychological novelists, of
(50)    whom we hear so much, say to such a theory as that?

*Mrs. Chevely*: Ah! The strength of women comes from the fact that psychology cannot explain us. Men can be analysed, women … merely adored.

*Sir Robert Chiltern*: You think science cannot grapple with the problem of
(55) women?

*Mrs. Chevely*: Science can never grapple with the irrational. That is why it has no future before it, in this world.

*Sir Robert Chiltern*: And women represent the irrational.

*Mrs. Chevely*: Well-dressed women do.

(60) *Sir Robert Chiltern* [with a polite bow]: I fear I could hardly agree with you there. But do sit down. And now tell me, what makes you leave your <u>brilliant</u> Vienna for our <u>gloomy</u> London—or perhaps the question is indiscreet?

*Mrs. Chevely*: Questions are never indiscreet. Answers sometimes are.

*Sir Robert Chiltern*: Well, at any rate, may I know if it is politics or pleasure?

(65) *Mrs. Chevely*: Politics are my only pleasure. You see nowadays it is not <u>fashionable</u> to flirt till one is forty, or to be romantic till one is forty-five, so we poor women who are under thirty, or say we are, have nothing open to us but politics or philanthropy. And philanthropy seems to me to have become simply the refuge of people who wish to annoy their fellow-creatures. I
(70) prefer politics, I think they are more … becoming!

*Sir Robert Chiltern*: A political life is a noble career!

*Mrs. Chevely*: Sometimes. And sometimes it is a clever game, Sir Robert. And sometimes it is a great nuisance.

*Sir Robert Chiltern*: Which do you find it?

(75) *Mrs. Chevely*: I? A combination of all three.

(1895)

## Analysis of Example 2

### The Editorial Introduction

The reader does not have to infer setting, because the introductory comments from the editor take some of the guesswork out of this passage. Never pass over these comments, as you might be missing some crucial information otherwise.

Lady Markby's remark in lines 5–6 about the House of Commons and Mrs. Chevely's discussion of politics with Sir Robert seem more appropriate because of the editor's previous notes. Some of the superficiality and overly nice behavior demonstrated by the characters also seems understandable, since the editor has indicated that the scene takes place at a high society party.

### Ironic Tone

Irony is dominant in this passage, as it is with most of Wilde's works. Again, because so many ironic comments are made, only a few will be discussed.

Lines 5–6: Lady Markby's contrast between *useful* and *harm* ironically points out the ineptitude she perceives in the House of Commons.

Line 16: The term *pleasant scandals* is ironic because it is nearly an oxymoron; one would not expect a scandal to be pleasant in the least. This tone might indicate Lady Markby's desire to escape her monotony.

Line 37: Mrs. Chevely notes that women are "unusually punished" for being charming. As one would not expect punishment for behaving in a pleasing way, her comment is ironic. Later in these lines, she seems to say that great charm attracts great attention, which then becomes burdensome to the woman who has been charming.

Lline 44: The phrase "fashionable religion" also approaches oxymoron status; religion is associated with spiritual depth, while fashion is part of society's superficiality. Mrs. Chevely seems to criticize a society that treats religion only as a trend.

### Flattering Tone

Much of the flattery in the passage is associated with Sir Robert, and most of it is achieved through hyberbole.

Lines 22 and 23: No one is truly "dying" to meet Mrs. Chevely, so this sentiment is an obvious exaggeration. Certainly, though, the comment is meant as a compliment to her.

Lines 61–62: Sir Robert contrasts "brilliant" Vienna with "gloomy" London, thus exaggeratedly complimenting Mrs. Chevely's adopted town.

## Mocking Tone

Line 40: Mrs. Chevely takes London women down a notch when she calls them "haggard." Coincidentally, she is also building herself up, since she is now residing in Vienna and does not include herself as a Londoner.

Line 66: By using the word "fashionable," Mrs. Chevely is mocking what has become accepted behavior in society.

These combined tones help to underscore the trivial atmosphere of the party. They also provide Wilde with a means to criticize, if lightly, the society in which he lives.

## The Third Character: Lady Markby

A play excerpt will often contain a character who serves a primarily expository purpose. It is a common device in plays for the Character Who Knows All to give background information to the Character Who Knows Nothing. In this case, Lady Markby is the knowledgeable character; she can provide a blend of gossip and facts that will familiarize us with Mrs. Chevely. The audience is in the shoes of Sir Robert, however, the know-nothing character; he pumps Lady Markby for information, and we find out along with him who our next character is.

## THINGS TO REMEMBER

- Play excerpts are rarely seen on the exam.
- To tackle a play excerpt,
  - read the editorial introduction carefully; and
  - decipher as much as you can about plot, characterization, tone, and theme.

## SAMPLE QUESTIONS

The next step will be for us to run through some typical SAT Subject Test: Literature questions concerning a play passage; Shaw's *Pygmalion* will provide the excerpt. Remember what to scan for: Read the editor's introduction before you begin the passage; mark dialogue clues about plot, characterization, theme, and tone; be certain also that you do not skip over the stage directions in italics—they will help you envision the action of the play.

*[In this passage, linguistics professor Henry Higgins is trying to convince his servant, Mrs. Pearce, and his associate, Colonel Pickering, that teaching lower-class Eliza to speak a more elegant and refined style of English would be a worthwhile and interesting experiment. Note: The playwright is using nonstandard punctuation rules in this passage.]*

*Mrs. Pearce*: Wheres your mother?

*Liza*: I aint got no mother. Her that turned me out was my sixth stepmother.
But I done without them. And I'm a good girl, I am.

*Line*
(5)

**Higgins**: Very well, then, what on earth is all this fuss about? The girl doesn't belong to anybody—is no use to anybody but me. [*He goes to* Mrs. Pearce *and begins coaxing.*] You can adopt her, Mrs. Pearce: I'm sure a daughter would be a great amusement to you. Now don't make any more fuss. Take her downstairs; and—

**Mrs. Pearce**: But whats to become of her? Is she to be paid anything? Do be

(10)

sensible, sir.

**Higgins**: Oh, pay her whatever is necessary: put it down in the housekeeping book. [*Impatiently*]

What on earth will she want with money? She'll have her food and her clothes. She'll only drink if you give her money.

(15)

**Liza**: [*Turning on him*] Oh you *are* a brute. It's a lie: nobody ever saw the sign of liquor on me.

[*She goes back to her chair and plants herself there defiantly.*]

**Pickering**: [*In good-humored remonstrance*] Does it occur to you, Higgins, that the girl has some feelings?

(20)

**Higgins**: [*Looking critically at her*] Oh no, I don't think so. Not any feelings that we need bother about. [*Cheerily*] Have you, Eliza?

**Liza**: I got my feelings same as anybody else.

**Higgins**: [*To* Pickering, *reflectively*] You see the difficulty?

**Pickering**: Eh? What difficulty?

(25)

**Higgins**: To get her to talk grammar. The mere pronunciation is easy enough.

**Liza**: I don't want to talk grammar. I want to talk like a lady.

**Mrs. Pearce**: Will you please keep to the point, Mr. Higgins? I want to know on what terms the girl is to be here. Is she to have any wages? And what is to

(30)

become of her when youve finished your teaching? You must look ahead a little.

**Higgins**: [*Impatiently*] Whats to become of her if I leave her in the gutter? Tell me that, Mrs. Pearce.

**Mrs. Pearce**: That's her own business, not yours, Mr. Higgins.

*Higgins*: Well, when Ive done with her, we can throw her back into the
(35)    gutter; and then it will be her own business again; so thats all right.

*Liza*: Oh, you've no feeling heart in you: you dont care for nothing but yourself.
[*She rises and takes the floor resolutely.*] Here! Ive had enough of this. I'm going.
[*Making for the door.*] You ought to be ashamed of yourself, you ought.

*Higgins*: [*Snatching a chocolate cream from the piano, his eyes suddenly
(40)    beginning to twinkle with mischief*] Have some chocolates, Eliza.

*Liza*: [*Halting, tempted*] How do I know what might be in them? Ive heard of
girls being drugged by the like of you.

[*Higgins whips out his penknife; cuts a chocolate in two; puts one half into his
mouth and bolts it; and offers her the other half.*]

(45)    *Higgins*: Pledge of good faith, Eliza. I eat one half: you eat the other. [*Liza
opens her mouth to retort: he pops the half chocolate into it.*] You shall have
boxes of them, barrels of them, every day. You shall live on them. Eh?

*Liza*: [*Who has disposed of the chocolate after being nearly choked by it*] I
wouldnt have ate it, only I'm too ladylike to take it out of my mouth.

(1912)

1.  Col. Pickering and Mrs. Pearce seem to
    care most about

    (A)   Higgins's feelings.
    (B)   their own public image.
    (C)   the inconvenience Eliza poses.
    (D)   Eliza's well-being.
    (E)   Higgins's finances.

2.  By contrast, Higgins's priorities are
    centered around

    (A)   seducing Eliza into a romantic affair.
    (B)   conducting a successful experiment.
    (C)   imparting knowledge to the
          underprivileged.
    (D)   proving Pickering and Mrs. Pearce
          wrong.
    (E)   confirming the superiority of the
          upper classes.

3.  Eliza's personality is best described as

    (A)   self-respecting.
    (B)   industrious.
    (C)   spiteful.
    (D)   hypercritical.
    (E)   playful.

4.  Lines 4–8 demonstrate which of the following?

    I.   Higgins's disregard for Eliza's background
    II.  Higgins's single-minded purpose
    III. Higgins's insecurities about the experiment
    IV.  Higgins's methods of persuasion

    (A)  II only
    (B)  I and II only
    (C)  I, III, and IV only
    (D)  I, II, and IV only
    (E)  I, II, III and IV

5.  In lines 13–14, Higgins reconsiders a previous decision because he

    (A)  feels the pressures of his experiment and cannot think straight.
    (B)  needs Mrs. Pearce to respect him and Pickering to stop carping.
    (C)  is torn between his educational obligation to Eliza and his attraction to her.
    (D)  is preoccupied with the experiment and has a low opinion of Eliza.
    (E)  cannot rest until the experiment is complete and is reaching his breaking point.

6.  Lines 22–26 illustrate that, according to Higgins, Eliza is

    (A)  a stubborn child.
    (B)  a maddening enigma.
    (C)  a potential colleague.
    (D)  an educational challenge.
    (E)  an alluring temptation.

7.  The stage directions in line 41 provide

    (A)  an indication of Eliza's attraction to Higgins.
    (B)  a parallel to Eliza's previous indecisiveness.
    (C)  a sign that Eliza wants to become Higgins's pupil.
    (D)  a hint that Eliza has been bluffing all along.
    (E)  a contrast to Eliza's subsequent lines and actions.

8.  The chocolates are a likely symbol of Higgins's and Eliza's future relationship for all of the following reasons EXCEPT that

    (A)  she is suspicious of the chocolate, just as she is suspicious of him.
    (B)  he places the chocolate in her mouth, just as he will teach her to speak grammatically correct English.
    (C)  he slices through the chocolate, just as he has split her identity.
    (D)  he "bolts" (line 44) his half of the chocolate, just as he is certain of this experiment.
    (E)  she chokes on her half of the chocolate, just as she is reluctant to try this experiment.

9.  Despite their antagonism, both Eliza and Higgins share a common trait of

    (A)  tenacity.
    (B)  persuasiveness.
    (C)  confusion.
    (D)  caprice.
    (E)  secretiveness.

# ANSWERS AND EXPLANATIONS

**1.   (D)**

Pickering asks if Higgins is aware of Eliza's feelings (lines 18–19). Mrs. Pearce wants to know what Eliza will be paid and what will become of the girl once Higgins is through with her (lines 9–10, 28–30). They seem to be looking out for Eliza.

**2.   (B)**

Lines 20–21 show that Higgins is uninterested in Eliza herself, so (A) and (C) do not work. His experiment deals with improving Eliza's speech, not with making a political point, so (E) is out. (D) is wrong because Mrs. Pearce and Pickering do not express any doubt about Higgins's abilities. Lines 23–26, though, show how interested he is in correcting Eliza's grammar; furthermore, he tries to persuade both Mrs. Pearce and Eliza into accepting the conditions of the experiment, so (B) is the best choice.

**3.   (A)**

Eliza insists that she is a "good girl" (line 3) and that she has "feelings same as anybody else" (line 22). Furthermore, when she perceives that Higgins is mistreating her she tries to leave (lines 37–38). In each case, she is standing up for herself.

**4.   (D)**

Item I seems right because Eliza has just related her pathetic history, but Higgins in no way responds to her plight; he simply wants to start the experiment. II and IV are obvious choices because his question shows his frustration with delays, and his offer to Mrs. Pearce demonstrates the uncommon suggestion she will make to get his way. III seems unlikely, however, because Higgins is confident, even arrogant, in his statements to the other characters.

**5.   (D)**

The fact that he would agree so quickly to a stipend for Eliza, then reconsider his decision so abruptly and "impatiently," demonstrates that he is not thinking carefully. Since in his previous lines, he is perpetually referring to the experiment, his mind must be preoccupied with it. Additionally, when Higgins asserts that Eliza would only spend the money he would give her on alcohol, he is expressing his low opinion of her.

**6.   (D)**

Higgins notes that changing her pronunciation would only be one step toward her linguistic improvement. Eliza's syntax and word choice must also be corrected if the experiment is to be a success. This "difficulty" is therefore an educational challenge.

**7.   (E)**

The stage directions say that Eliza stops because she is tempted by the chocolate. Yet her following lines are still resistant to accepting the chocolate or any other offer from Higgins. Furthermore, when she opens her mouth, she is not ready to receive the bonbon; rather she wants to offer a "retort" to Higgins's comments.

**8.   (C)**

Eliza is a proud woman from the beginning of the passage to the end. When she chokes down the chocolate, she insists that she has done so simply because she is too much of a lady. Her identity has remained intact, despite Higgins's efforts to make her succumb to his will.

**9.   (A)**

Despite the objections of Mrs. Pearce and Colonel Pickering, Higgins insists on continuing the experiment. Furthermore, Eliza will neither give up on her suspicions about Higgins nor on her image as a "good girl." Thus, they are both tenacious.

Part Four

# Practice Tests

## HOW TO TAKE THE PRACTICE TESTS

Before taking a practice test, find a quiet room where you can work uninterrupted for one hour. Make sure you have several No. 2 pencils with erasers.

Use the answer grids provided to record your answers. Guidelines for scoring your test appear before each answer grid. Time yourself. Spend no more than one hour on each test. Once you start the practice test, don't stop until you've reached the one-hour time limit. You'll find an answer key and complete answer explanations following each test. Be sure to read the explanations for all questions, even those you answered correctly.

Good luck!

# HOW TO CALCULATE YOUR SCORE

**Step 1: Figure out your raw score.** Use the answer key to count the number of questions you answered correctly and the number of questions you answered incorrectly. (Do not count any questions you left blank.) Multiply the number wrong by 0.25 and subtract the result from the number correct. Round the result to the nearest whole number. This is your raw score.

## SAT Subject Test: Literature Practice Test 1

| Number right | Number wrong | Raw score |
|---|---|---|

$$\boxed{\phantom{0}} - \left(0.25 \times \boxed{\phantom{0}}\right) = \boxed{\phantom{0}}$$

**Step 2: Find your scaled score.** In the Score Conversion Table below, find your raw score (rounded to the nearest whole number) in one of the columns to the left. The score directly to the right of that number will be your scaled score.

A note on your practice test scores: Don't take these scores too literally. Practice test conditions cannot precisely mirror real test conditions. Your actual SAT Subject Test: Literature score will almost certainly vary from your practice test scores. However, your scores on the practice tests will give you a rough idea of your range on the actual exam.

## Conversion Table

| Raw | Scaled | Raw | Scaled | Raw | Scaled | Raw | Scaled |
|---|---|---|---|---|---|---|---|
| 63 | 800 | 43 | 700 | 23 | 510 | 3 | 330 |
| 62 | 800 | 42 | 690 | 22 | 500 | 2 | 320 |
| 61 | 800 | 41 | 680 | 21 | 500 | 1 | 310 |
| 60 | 800 | 40 | 670 | 20 | 490 | 0 | 300 |
| 59 | 800 | 39 | 660 | 19 | 480 | -1 | 290 |
| 58 | 800 | 38 | 650 | 18 | 470 | -2 | 280 |
| 57 | 800 | 37 | 640 | 17 | 460 | -3 | 280 |
| 56 | 790 | 36 | 630 | 16 | 450 | -4 | 270 |
| 55 | 790 | 35 | 620 | 15 | 440 | -5 | 260 |
| 54 | 780 | 34 | 610 | 14 | 430 | -6 | 250 |
| 53 | 780 | 33 | 610 | 13 | 420 | -7 | 250 |
| 52 | 780 | 32 | 600 | 12 | 410 | -8 | 240 |
| 51 | 770 | 31 | 590 | 11 | 410 | -9 | 230 |
| 50 | 760 | 30 | 580 | 10 | 400 | -10 | 220 |
| 49 | 750 | 29 | 570 | 9 | 390 | -11 | 210 |
| 48 | 740 | 28 | 560 | 8 | 380 | -12 | 200 |
| 47 | 730 | 27 | 550 | 7 | 370 | -13 | 200 |
| 46 | 720 | 26 | 540 | 6 | 360 | -14 | 200 |
| 45 | 710 | 25 | 530 | 5 | 350 | | |
| 44 | 710 | 24 | 520 | 4 | 340 | | |

# Practice Test 1
# Answer Grid

1. Ⓐ Ⓑ Ⓒ Ⓓ Ⓔ
2. Ⓐ Ⓑ Ⓒ Ⓓ Ⓔ
3. Ⓐ Ⓑ Ⓒ Ⓓ Ⓔ
4. Ⓐ Ⓑ Ⓒ Ⓓ Ⓔ
5. Ⓐ Ⓑ Ⓒ Ⓓ Ⓔ
6. Ⓐ Ⓑ Ⓒ Ⓓ Ⓔ
7. Ⓐ Ⓑ Ⓒ Ⓓ Ⓔ
8. Ⓐ Ⓑ Ⓒ Ⓓ Ⓔ
9. Ⓐ Ⓑ Ⓒ Ⓓ Ⓔ
10. Ⓐ Ⓑ Ⓒ Ⓓ Ⓔ
11. Ⓐ Ⓑ Ⓒ Ⓓ Ⓔ
12. Ⓐ Ⓑ Ⓒ Ⓓ Ⓔ
13. Ⓐ Ⓑ Ⓒ Ⓓ Ⓔ
14. Ⓐ Ⓑ Ⓒ Ⓓ Ⓔ
15. Ⓐ Ⓑ Ⓒ Ⓓ Ⓔ
16. Ⓐ Ⓑ Ⓒ Ⓓ Ⓔ
17. Ⓐ Ⓑ Ⓒ Ⓓ Ⓔ
18. Ⓐ Ⓑ Ⓒ Ⓓ Ⓔ
19. Ⓐ Ⓑ Ⓒ Ⓓ Ⓔ
20. Ⓐ Ⓑ Ⓒ Ⓓ Ⓔ
21. Ⓐ Ⓑ Ⓒ Ⓓ Ⓔ

22. Ⓐ Ⓑ Ⓒ Ⓓ Ⓔ
23. Ⓐ Ⓑ Ⓒ Ⓓ Ⓔ
24. Ⓐ Ⓑ Ⓒ Ⓓ Ⓔ
25. Ⓐ Ⓑ Ⓒ Ⓓ Ⓔ
26. Ⓐ Ⓑ Ⓒ Ⓓ Ⓔ
27. Ⓐ Ⓑ Ⓒ Ⓓ Ⓔ
28. Ⓐ Ⓑ Ⓒ Ⓓ Ⓔ
29. Ⓐ Ⓑ Ⓒ Ⓓ Ⓔ
30. Ⓐ Ⓑ Ⓒ Ⓓ Ⓔ
31. Ⓐ Ⓑ Ⓒ Ⓓ Ⓔ
32. Ⓐ Ⓑ Ⓒ Ⓓ Ⓔ
33. Ⓐ Ⓑ Ⓒ Ⓓ Ⓔ
34. Ⓐ Ⓑ Ⓒ Ⓓ Ⓔ
35. Ⓐ Ⓑ Ⓒ Ⓓ Ⓔ
36. Ⓐ Ⓑ Ⓒ Ⓓ Ⓔ
37. Ⓐ Ⓑ Ⓒ Ⓓ Ⓔ
38. Ⓐ Ⓑ Ⓒ Ⓓ Ⓔ
39. Ⓐ Ⓑ Ⓒ Ⓓ Ⓔ
40. Ⓐ Ⓑ Ⓒ Ⓓ Ⓔ
41. Ⓐ Ⓑ Ⓒ Ⓓ Ⓔ
42. Ⓐ Ⓑ Ⓒ Ⓓ Ⓔ

43. Ⓐ Ⓑ Ⓒ Ⓓ Ⓔ
44. Ⓐ Ⓑ Ⓒ Ⓓ Ⓔ
45. Ⓐ Ⓑ Ⓒ Ⓓ Ⓔ
46. Ⓐ Ⓑ Ⓒ Ⓓ Ⓔ
47. Ⓐ Ⓑ Ⓒ Ⓓ Ⓔ
48. Ⓐ Ⓑ Ⓒ Ⓓ Ⓔ
49. Ⓐ Ⓑ Ⓒ Ⓓ Ⓔ
50. Ⓐ Ⓑ Ⓒ Ⓓ Ⓔ
51. Ⓐ Ⓑ Ⓒ Ⓓ Ⓔ
52. Ⓐ Ⓑ Ⓒ Ⓓ Ⓔ
53. Ⓐ Ⓑ Ⓒ Ⓓ Ⓔ
54. Ⓐ Ⓑ Ⓒ Ⓓ Ⓔ
55. Ⓐ Ⓑ Ⓒ Ⓓ Ⓔ
56. Ⓐ Ⓑ Ⓒ Ⓓ Ⓔ
57. Ⓐ Ⓑ Ⓒ Ⓓ Ⓔ
58. Ⓐ Ⓑ Ⓒ Ⓓ Ⓔ
59. Ⓐ Ⓑ Ⓒ Ⓓ Ⓔ
60. Ⓐ Ⓑ Ⓒ Ⓓ Ⓔ
61. Ⓐ Ⓑ Ⓒ Ⓓ Ⓔ
62. Ⓐ Ⓑ Ⓒ Ⓓ Ⓔ
63. Ⓐ Ⓑ Ⓒ Ⓓ Ⓔ

# Practice Test 1

*Questions 1–7 refer to the following poem. After reading the poem, choose the best answer to each question.*

"Hope" is the thing with feathers—
That perches in the soul—
And sings the tune without the words—
And never stops—at all—

Line
(5)    And sweetest—in the Gale—is heard
And sore must be the storm—
That could abash the little Bird
That kept so many warm—

I've heard it in the chillest land—
(10)  And on the strangest Sea—
Yet, never, in Extremity,        *Extremity*   the most extreme situation
It asked a crumb—of Me.

(1891)

GO ON TO THE NEXT PAGE

1. The speaker's view of hope in the poem can best be described as

   (A) logical and rational.

   (B) empty and hopeless.

   (C) childlike and naïve.

   (D) questioning and doubtful.

   (E) admiring and humbled.

2. In the first stanza, hope has feathers because

   (A) it should be tarred and feathered and run out of the "soul."

   (B) it has a light and airy effect on the one that feels hope.

   (C) it is a bird of prey that claws and pecks at the one who feels hope.

   (D) it is like a bird that offers a kind of musical comfort.

   (E) it needs to be caged in order to be experienced.

3. According to line 5, hope is most pleasant when

   (A) trouble is present.

   (B) the soul is calm.

   (C) one listens for it.

   (D) there is a sweetness to it.

   (E) a storm is about to occur.

4. In the context of line 6, the word "sore" must mean

   (A) "sensitive."

   (B) "resentful."

   (C) "grievous."

   (D) "hurt."

   (E) "swollen."

5. In the second stanza, which of the following is true about hope?

   I. It is present even in difficult times.

   II. Only the most dire situation could shake it.

   III. It requires conflict in order to exist.

   (A) I only

   (B) II only

   (C) I and II only

   (D) II and III only

   (E) I, II, and III

**GO ON TO THE NEXT PAGE**

6. In the third stanza, what is true about hope?

   (A) Although it appears in even the harshest conditions, hope is not demanding.

   (B) Although it appears whenever a person needs it, hope must be fed.

   (C) Although it will make appearances from time to time, hope is undependable.

   (D) Although it shows up on land or sea, hope must be coaxed to come in hard times.

   (E) Although it has a comforting nature, hope can remain aloof in certain conditions.

7. The dashes in the poem create various pauses, but the last dash's pause

   (A) makes the speaker sound forgetful.

   (B) elevates the speaker.

   (C) builds to an anticlimax.

   (D) deflates the speaker's hope.

   (E) leads to a poignant contrast.

**GO ON TO THE NEXT PAGE**

*Questions 8–18 refer to the following passage. After reading the passage, choose the best answer to each question.*

*Revenge* is a kind of Wild Justice; which the more Man's Nature runs to, the more ought Law to weed it out. For as for the first Wrong, it doth
Line but offend the law; but the *Revenge* of that wrong,
(5) putteth the Law out of Office. Certainly, in taking *Revenge*, A Man is but even with his Enemy; But in passing it over, he is Superior; For it is a Prince's part to Pardon. And Salomon,* I am sure, saith, *It is Glory of a man to passe by an offence.*
(10) That which is past, is gone, and Irrevocable; And wise Men have Enough to doe, with things present and to come: Therefore, they doe but trifle with themselves, that labor in past matters. There is no man, doth a wrong, for the wrong's sake; But
(15) thereby to Purchase himselfe, Profit, or Pleasure, or Honour, or the like. Therefore why should I be angry with a Man, for loving himselfe better then mee? And if any Man should do wrong, meerely out of ill nature, why? Yet it is but like
(20) the Thorn, or Bryar, which pryck, and scratch, because they can do no other. The most Tolerable sort of *Revenge*, is for those wrongs which there is no Law to remedy: But then, let a man take heed, the *Revenge* be such as there is no law to punish:
(25) Else, Man's Enemy, is still before hand, And it is two for one. Some, when they take *Revenge*, are desirous the party should know, whence it commeth: This is the more Generous. For the Delight seemeth to be, not so much in doing the
(30) Hurt, as in Making the Party repent: But Base and Crafty Cowards, are like the Arrow, that flyeth in the Darke. Cosmus, Duke of *Florence*, has a Desperate Saying, against Perfidious or Neglecting Friends, as if those wrongs were unpardonable:
(35) *You shall reade* (saith he) *that we are commanded to forgive our Enemies; But you never read, that we are commanded to Forgive our friends.* But yet the Spirit of Job† was in a better tune; *Shall we* (saith he) *take Good at God's Hands, and not be content*
(40) *to take evill also?* And so of Friends in proportion. This is certaine; That a man that studieth *Revenge* keeps his own wounds greene, which otherwise would heale, and doe well. Publique *Revenges*, are, for the most part, Fortunate; As that for the Death
(45) of *Caesar*; for the Death of *Pertinax*; for the Death of *Henry* the Third of France;‡ And many more. But in private *Revenges* it is not so. Nay rather, Vindicative Persons live the life of Witches; who as they are Mischievous, So end they Infortunate.

(1597)

---

* King Solomon, reputed to be the wisest of ancient Hebrew kings, here quoted from *Proverbs* 19:11.

† In the Bible, a godly man who endures incredible suffering while still maintaining his faith; the quotation is from *Job* 2:10.

‡ Their assassinations were avenged by men who would be competent rulers.

8. The passage's main purpose seems to be

(A) to determine, in minute detail, the motives behind revenge.

(B) to explain, with several examples, the biblical response to revenge.

(C) to warn, in a loving tone, against the use of revenge.

(D) to discuss, with few exceptions, the error of revenge.

(E) to distinguish, for clarity's sake, the difference between "good" and "bad" revenge.

GO ON TO THE NEXT PAGE

9. The speaker suggests in lines 1–3 that "Law" should respond to revenge in what way?

(A) Law should help revenge flourish.

(B) Law should seek alternatives to revenge.

(C) Law should hold dominion over revenge.

(D) Law should be subject to public revenge.

(E) Law should help eliminate revenge.

10. In lines 5–21, the speaker offers all of the following ways for thinking about revenge EXCEPT that

(A) excusing wrong is better than taking revenge against it.

(B) revenge should not be taken against those who do wrong, since those who do wrong do not intend evil.

(C) it is difficult for the wise to counteract the effects of revenge, since the wise are consumed with matters of the present and future.

(D) revenge should not be taken against those who do wrong, since those who do wrong are simply following their nature.

(E) Solomon, the wisest of biblical kings, speaks against revenge.

11. According to the speaker, what is the most "Tolerable sort of *Revenge*" (lines 21–22)?

(A) The sort that fills the void left by a non-existent law

(B) The sort that wrests control from the law

(C) The sort that the law could never punish

(D) The sort that is not acted out rashly

(E) The sort that acts as a reminder to the wrongdoer

12. According to the speaker, what is the "more Generous" (line 28) type of revenge?

I. Revenge requiring the wrongdoer's contrition

II. Revenge identifying the avenger

III. Revenge allowing the wrongdoer some retaliation

(A) II only

(B) I and III only

(C) II and III only

(D) I and II only

(E) I, II, and III

13. The image of the "Arrow" in line 31 is meant to do all of the following EXCEPT

(A) discuss a particular type of revenge.

(B) contrast with a more forthcoming type of revenge.

(C) represent the covert actions of "Crafty Cowards."

(D) illustrate the Law's swiftness in dealing with revenge.

(E) portray the damaging effects of revenge.

**GO ON TO THE NEXT PAGE**

14. The quotes from Duke Cosmus and Job (lines 35–40) are contrasted to

    (A) suggest our acceptance of friends' shortcomings, rather than our possible need for revenge against their wrongdoings.

    (B) imply that friends may seek revenge against us, even though we are undeserving of such action.

    (C) display the superiority of religion's attitudes about revenge over Renaissance royalty's opinions.

    (D) demonstrate the naivete of a biblical character as opposed to the worldliness of a Renaissance duke.

    (E) encourage avoiding revenge against friends but to show tolerance for revenge against enemies.

15. The word "greene" in line 42 is closest in meaning to the word

    (A) alien.

    (B) naïve.

    (C) lush.

    (D) fresh.

    (E) rotting.

16. Near the end of the passage, Caesar, Pertinax, and Henry III are all used as examples of

    (A) avengers.

    (B) positive examples of public revenge.

    (C) negative examples of private revenge.

    (D) negative examples of public revenge.

    (E) positive examples of private revenge.

17. In the last sentence of the passage, the purpose of comparing "Vindicative Persons" to witches is to

    (A) show the satanic link between revenge and the avenger.

    (B) reveal that avengers are forced into secret lives, as are witches.

    (C) demonstrate the cause/effect relationship between revenge and downfall.

    (D) imply that there is a supernatural impetus at work in those who get revenge.

    (E) lessen the effects of revenge, which can best be described as "Mischievous."

18. To develop its central theme, the passage seems to rely most heavily on

    (A) onomatopoeia and alliteration.

    (B) simile and hyperbole.

    (C) biblical allusions.

    (D) condescending tone and syntax.

    (E) contrast and antithesis.

**GO ON TO THE NEXT PAGE**

*Questions 19–26 refer to the following poem. After reading the poem, choose the best answer to each question.*

Blue! 'Tis the life of heaven,—the domain
Of Cynthia*,—the wide palace of the sun,—
The tent of Hesperus†, and all his train,—
The bosomer of clouds, gold, gray, and dun.
Line
(5)   Blue! 'Tis the life of waters—ocean
And all its vassal streams, pools numberless,
May rage, and foam, and fret, but never can
Subside, if not to dark blue nativeness.
Blue! Gentle cousin of the forest-green,
(10)   Married to green in all the sweetest flowers,—
Forget-me-not,—the blue bell,—and, that queen
Of secrecy, the violet: what strange powers
Hast thou, as a mere shadow! But how great,
When in an Eye thou art, alive with fate!

(1818)

* Cynthia is another name for Artemis, Goddess of the Moon.

† Hesperus is the name of the Evening Star.

19. The entire poem seems to be

  (A) praise for melancholy.

  (B) an elegy for a dead pet.

  (C) an ode to a color.

  (D) a celebration of the sky.

  (E) an explanation of fate.

20. The poem can be categorized as

  (A) a sonnet.

  (B) a pastoral.

  (C) heroic couplets.

  (D) blank verse.

  (E) a villanelle.

21. In the first four lines of the poem, the type of description moves from

  (A) realistic to surrealistic.

  (B) orderly to chaotic.

  (C) internal to external.

  (D) personal to social.

  (E) royal to maternal.

22. A synonym for the word "train" in line 3 is

  (A) locomotive.

  (B) drag.

  (C) preparation.

  (D) retinue.

  (E) equipment.

23. The subject for the verb phrase "May rage, and foam, and fret, but never can/Subside..." (lines 7–8) is

  I. "waters."

  II. "ocean."

  III. "streams."

  IV. "pools."

  (A) I and III only

  (B) I, II, and III only

  (C) II, III, and IV only

  (D) IV only

  (E) I, II, III, and IV

**GO ON TO THE NEXT PAGE**

24. The clause "if not to dark blue nativeness" completes what idea in lines 5–8?

    (A) The powerlessness of water to escape its hue

    (B) The frustration of Nature in dealing with change

    (C) The inner turmoil of those who try to conquer the ocean

    (D) The grief of the speaker during his personal loss

    (E) The unluckiness of those who would spoil Nature

25. The speaker ironically climaxes the poem by shifting from

    (A) a discussion of Nature to a discussion of "fate."

    (B) the grandeur of Nature to the smallness of "an Eye."

    (C) insults about Nature to praises of "a mere shadow."

    (D) some doubts about Nature to some certainty about "thou."

    (E) a description of the "life of heaven" to being "alive with fate."

26. The speaker gives the poem's subject all of the following characteristics EXCEPT

    (A) sheltering qualities.

    (B) enlivening energies.

    (C) control over emotion.

    (D) greatness and strangeness.

    (E) familial connection.

GO ON TO THE NEXT PAGE

*Questions 27–34 refer to the following passage. After reading the passage, choose the best answer to each question.*

The Amphitheatre was a huge circular enclosure, with a notch at opposite extremities of its diameter north and south. From its sloping
Line internal form it might have been called the
(5) spittoon of the Jötuns.* It was to Casterbridge what the ruined Coliseum is to modern Rome, and was nearly of the same magnitude. The dusk of evening was the proper hour at which a true impression of this suggestive place could be
(10) received. Standing in the middle of the arena at that time there by degrees became apparent its real vastness, which a cursory view from the summit at noon-day was apt to obscure. Melancholy, impressive, lonely, yet accessible from every part
(15) of the town, the historic circle was the frequent spot for appointments of a furtive kind. Intrigues were arranged there; tentative meetings were there experimented after divisions and feuds. But one kind of appointment—in itself the most common
(20) of any—seldom had place in the Amphitheatre: that of happy lovers.

Why, seeing that it was pre-eminently an airy, accessible, and sequestered spot for interviews, the cheerfullest form of those occurrences never took
(25) kindly to the soil of the ruin, would be a curious inquiry. Perhaps it was because its associations had about them something sinister. Its history proved that. Apart from the sanguinary nature of the games originally played therein, such incidents
(30) attached to its past as these: that for scores of years the town-gallows had stood at one corner; that in 1705 a woman who had murdered her husband was half-strangled and then burnt there in the presence of ten thousand spectators. Tradition
(35) reports that at a certain stage of the burning her heart burst and leapt out of her body, to the terror of them all, and that not one of those ten thousand people ever cared particularly for hot roast after that. In addition to these old tragedies,

(40) pugilistic encounters almost to the death had come off down to the recent dates in that secluded arena, entirely invisible to the outside world save by climbing to the top of the enclosure, which few townspeople in the daily round of their lives ever
(45) took the trouble to do. So that, though close to the turnpike-road, crimes might be perpetrated there unseen at mid-day.

Some boys had latterly tried to impart gaiety to the ruin by using the central arena as a cricket-
(50) ground. But the game usually languished for the aforesaid reason—the dismal privacy which the earthen circle enforced, shutting out every appreciative passer's vision, every commendatory remark from outsiders—everything except the sky;
(55) and to play at games in such circumstances was like acting to an empty house. Possibly, too, the boys were timid, for some old people said that at certain moments in the summer time, in broad daylight, persons sitting with a book or dozing in the arena
(60) had, on lifting their eyes, beheld the slopes lined with a gazing legion of Hadrian's† soldiery as if watching gladiatorial combat; and had heard the roar of their excited voices; that the scene would remain but a moment, like a lightning flash, and
(65) then disappear.

(1886)

| *Jötuns | frost giants in Norse mythology |
| †Hadrian | Roman general occupying England in ancient times |

**GO ON TO THE NEXT PAGE**

27. The main purpose of the passage is most likely that of

    (A) discussing Roman military and cultural history.

    (B) promoting a town's featured landmark.

    (C) offering profiles of various types of townspeople.

    (D) discouraging people from visiting a dangerous site.

    (E) describing the features, mood, and effect of a location.

28. The metaphor of the arena as the "spittoon of the Jötuns" (line 5) makes the landmark sound

    (A) mammoth, but vulgar.

    (B) fearful, but calming.

    (C) brassy, but discolored.

    (D) strange, but magnetic.

    (E) accessible, but lonely.

29. At the beginning of the second paragraph, the narrator supposes that one would question what about the arena?

    (A) Why it is so old

    (B) Why it is so huge

    (C) Why romantic meetings wouldn't occur there

    (D) Why the Romans would have built it

    (E) Why people would never come there anymore

30. The sentence that starts "Tradition reports..." (lines 34–35) ends with a tone best described as

    (A) deadly serious.

    (B) dreadfully cold.

    (C) desperately anxious.

    (D) darkly humorous.

    (E) divinely focused.

31. In the second paragraph, the knowledge of which of the following contributes to the mood of the arena?

    I. Ancient history

    II. 18th-century history

    III. Current events

    (A) II only

    (B) I and II only

    (C) II and III only

    (D) I and III only

    (E) I, II, and III

32. Which pair of reasons in the third paragraph discourages the boys from playing cricket?

    (A) Uneven ground and heat of the arena stones

    (B) Lightning and other distractions

    (C) Ghost stories and lack of spectator praise

    (D) The arena's noise and private enclosure

    (E) Old people and their need for quiet

**GO ON TO THE NEXT PAGE**

33. The simile in lines 55–56 seems appropriate because

    (A) the arena was formerly used as an amphitheatre.

    (B) no one pays attention to the boys.

    (C) the sky is being personified.

    (D) the arena seems like an abandoned home.

    (E) the link between the old and the young is circular, like the arena.

34. All of the following could accurately be said of light and dark in the passage EXCEPT that

    (A) light can be deceptive in this setting.

    (B) light can actually keep things concealed in this setting.

    (C) many people prefer darkness in this setting.

    (D) darkness can actually improve the perception of the setting.

    (E) light allows for a more playful mood in this setting.

**GO ON TO THE NEXT PAGE**

*Questions 35–46 refer to the following poem. After reading the poem, choose the best answer to each question.*

> *Imagination!* who can sing thy force?
> Or who describe the swiftness of thy course?
> Soaring through air to find the bright abode,
Line   Th'empyreal palace of the thund'ring God          *empyreal* heavenly
> (5)   We on thy pinions can surpass the wind,
> And leave the rolling universe behind:
> From star to star the mental optics rove,
> Measure the skies, and range the realms above.
> There in one view we grasp the mighty whole,
> (10)   Or with new worlds amaze th'unbounded soul.
>
>       Though *Winter* frowns to *Fancy's* raptur'd eyes
> The fields may flourish, and gay scenes arise;
> The frozen deeps may break their iron bands,
> And bid the waters murmur o'er the sands.
> (15)   Fair *Flora* may resume her fragrant reign,          *Flora* Roman goddess of flowers
> And with her flow'ry riches deck the plain;
> *Sylvanus* may diffuse his honors round          *Sylvanus* Roman forest deity
> And all the forest may with leaves be crown'd:
> Show'rs may descend, and dews their gems disclose,
> (20)   And nectar sparkle on the blooming rose.
>
>       Such is thy pow'r, nor are thine orders vain,
> O thou the leader of the mental train:
> In full perfection all thy works are wrought,
> And thine the sceptre o'er the realm of thought.
> (25)   Before thy throne the subject-passions bow,
> Of subject-passions sov'reign ruler Thou,
> At thy command joy rushes on the heart,
> And through the glowing veins the spirits dart.
>
>       *Fancy* might now her silken pinions try
> (30)   To rise from earth, and sweep th'expanse on high;
> From *Tithon's* bed now might *Aurora* rise          *Aurora* goddess of dawn, who loved the mortal Tithonus
> cheeks all glowing with celestial dies,
> While a pure stream of light o'erflows the skies.
> The monarch of the day I might behold,
> (35)   And all the mountains tipt with radiant gold,
> But I reluctant leave the pleasing views,
> Which *Fancy* dresses to delight the *Muse*;
> *Winter* austere forbids me to aspire,
> And northern tempests damp the rising fire;
> (40)   They chill the tides of *Fancy's* flowing sea,
> Cease then, my song, cease the unequal lay.          *lay* song

(1773)

→

**GO ON TO THE NEXT PAGE**

35. Imagination, or Fancy, plays all the following roles in the poem EXCEPT as

    (A) a powerful ruler.

    (B) a creator of perfection.

    (C) a loyal friend.

    (D) an inspirer of creativity.

    (E) a winged being.

36. The irony of the questions in lines 1–2 is that

    (A) they imply that Imagination's power is indescribable, yet the speaker attempts the description, anyway.

    (B) they lead the reader to believe that Imagination is powerful, yet the first stanza proves Imagination is helpless without God's assistance.

    (C) they suggest a rhetorical mode for the poem, yet the lyricism of the verse is antirhetorical.

    (D) they refer to epic poetry conventions, yet Imagination—an abstract—becomes the epic hero of this work.

    (E) they insinuate that Imagination has neither "force" nor "swiftness," yet the rest of the poem proves this notion untrue.

37. In the first stanza, Imagination can do all of the following EXCEPT

    (A) reach the heights of heaven.

    (B) challenge the power of God.

    (C) envision the entire universe.

    (D) fly improbable distances.

    (E) create a new universe.

38. In lines 11–14, Winter is Fancy's

    (A) opponent.

    (B) assistant.

    (C) conqueror.

    (D) teacher.

    (E) relative.

GO ON TO THE NEXT PAGE

39. In lines 15–20, Flora and Sylvanus are both a part of

    (A) an imagined recurrence of spring in the middle of winter.

    (B) spring's final triumph after winter's deadly reign.

    (C) winter's sparkling pageantry and spectacle.

    (D) the actual rejuvenation of the earth after winter.

    (E) a tribute to ancient Roman festivals of the seasons.

40. Lines 15 and 19 both feature

    (A) assonance.

    (B) alliteration.

    (C) paradox.

    (D) antithesis.

    (E) simile.

41. In lines 21–28, Imagination's domain is

    (A) nature.

    (B) winter.

    (C) spring.

    (D) the mind.

    (E) Fancy.

42. The Aurora allusion in lines 31–33 is used as

    (A) a reference to the speaker's own sleeping lover.

    (B) a parallel between reality and Imagination.

    (C) a symbol for God's relationship to Imagination.

    (D) an image of both quiet power and abject embarrassment.

    (E) an analogy between Imagination and dawn.

43. The "monarch of the day" in line 34 is

    (A) Fancy.

    (B) the sun.

    (C) God.

    (D) Tithon (Tithonus).

    (E) the speaker.

44. The speaker reluctantly leaves "the pleasing views" (line 36) because

    (A) the gaudy pageantry of Imagination has grown tiresome.

    (B) a colder climate beckons to her and she is impatient for change.

    (C) a new fictional setting is beginning to form itself in her mind.

    (D) the reality of winter is encroaching on Imagination's effects.

    (E) she wants to escape from reality for all eternity but cannot.

**GO ON TO THE NEXT PAGE**

45. In the final line, the speaker calls her song an "unequal lay" because the poem

    (A) seems insignificant compared to Imagination's perfection.

    (B) cannot withstand the power that winter possesses.

    (C) shifts from iambic pentameter to trochaic trimeter lines.

    (D) requires several more drafts before it can achieve greatness.

    (E) will not gain immortality as Imagination has done.

46. The poem develops through the use of all of the following EXCEPT

    (A) heroic couplets.

    (B) images of royalty.

    (C) personification.

    (D) classical allusion.

    (E) a persuasive tone.

**GO ON TO THE NEXT PAGE**

*Questions 47–53 refer to the following poem. After reading the poem, choose the best answer to each question.*

> The time is after dinner. Cigarettes
>    Glow on the lawn;
> Glasses begin to tinkle; TV sets
>    Have been turned on. ·
>
> *Line*
> (5)  The moon is brimming like a glass of beer
>    Above the town,
> And love keeps her appointments—"Harry's here!"
>    "I'll be right down."
>
> But the pale stranger in the furnished room
> (10)  Lies on his back
> Looking at the paper roses, how they bloom,
>    And ceilings crack.

(1959)

47. The poem presents the "pale stranger" (line 9) as

   (A) unloved.

   (B) mocking.

   (C) disturbed.

   (D) insightful.

   (E) isolated.

48. The dominating literary device in the first stanza is

   (A) simile.

   (B) antithesis.

   (C) onomatopoeia.

   (D) synecdoche.

   (E) personification.

49. The image in lines 5–6 does all of the following EXCEPT

   (A) exemplify simile.

   (B) create a festive mood.

   (C) confirm the time of day.

   (D) reflect the sense of fulfillment in lines 7–8.

   (E) predict the stranger's paleness.

50. The quotations in lines 7–8 serve to

   (A) support line 7's assertion about love.

   (B) announce the pale stranger's arrival.

   (C) contrast the stranger's speech with his actions.

   (D) create a mood of suspense in the stanza.

   (E) personify love further by having it speak.

**GO ON TO THE NEXT PAGE**

51. An ironic shift in the poem is that

(A) more action occurs with the incorporeal people in the previous stanzas than with the materialized pale stranger.

(B) the action of the first two stanzas occurs downstairs, while the last stanza's action takes place upstairs.

(C) the stranger is described as pale, while the rest of the outside world seems to be bathed in bright color.

(D) love is described as "keeping her appointments," but the stranger is obviously not so reliable.

(E) the announcement that "Harry's here!" (line 7) uses an actual name, yet the pale stranger has no name.

52. The "paper roses" in line 11 symbolize

(A) the gregarious but superficial atmosphere outside the furnished room.

(B) the hopes and aspirations to which the stranger desperately clings.

(C) the combined beauty of the night, of the moon, and of love.

(D) the pity that the narrator expresses for the stranger.

(E) the need for the stranger to make things grow in his life.

53. The final line of the poem emphasizes

(A) the anger and frustration welling within the stranger.

(B) the eccentricity that cuts the stranger off from the other people.

(C) the disparity between the stranger and the people outside his room.

(D) the eventual downfall of a society that harbors someone like the stranger.

(E) the imminent breakthrough that the stranger will make with those outside.

**GO ON TO THE NEXT PAGE**

*Questions 54–63 refer to the following passage. After reading the passage, choose the best answer to each question.*

[*Enter* Servant *with candles, showing in* Marlow *and* Hastings]

**Servant:** Welcome, gentlemen, very welcome! This way.

*Line*
(5)  **Hastings:** After the disappointments of the day, welcome once more, Charles, to the comforts of a clean room and a good fire. Upon my word, a very well-looking house; antique but creditable.

**Marlow:**  The usual fate of a large mansion.
(10)  Having first ruined the master by good housekeeping, it at last comes to levy contributions as an inn.

**Hastings:** As you say, we passengers are to be taxed to pay all these fineries. I have often seen
(15)  a good sideboard, or a marble chimney-piece, though not actually put in the bill, inflame a reckoning confoundedly.

**Marlow:**  Travellers, George, must pay in all places: the only difference is, that in good inns
(20)  you pay dearly for luxuries; in bad inns you are fleeced and starved.

**Hastings:** You have lived very much among them. In truth, I have been often surprised, that you who have seen so much of the world, with your natural
(25)  good sense, and your many opportunities, could never yet acquire a requisite share of assurance.

**Marlow:** The Englishman's malady. But tell me, George, where could I have learned that assurance that you talk of? My life has been chiefly spent
(30)  in a college or an inn, in seclusion from that lovely part of the creation that chiefly teach men confidence. I don't know that I was ever familiarly acquainted with a single modest woman, except

my mother—But among females of another class,
(35)  you know—

**Hastings:** Ay, among them you are impudent enough of all conscience.

**Marlow:** They are of *us*, you know.

**Hastings:** But in the company of women of
(40)  reputation I never saw such an idiot, such a trembler; you look for all the world as if you wanted an opportunity for stealing out of the room.

**Marlow:** Why, man, that's because I do want to
(45)  steal out of the room. Faith, I have often formed a resolution to break the ice, and rattle away at any rate. But I don't know how, a single glance from a pair of fine eyes has totally overset my resolution. An impudent fellow may counterfeit modesty;
(50)  but I'll be hanged if a modest man can ever counterfeit impudence.

**Hastings:** If you could but say half the fine things to them that I have heard you lavish upon the barmaid of an inn, or even a college bed-maker—

(55)  **Marlow:** Why, George, I can't say fine things to them; they freeze, they petrify me. They may talk of a comet, or a burning mountain, or some such bagatelle;* but, to me, a modest woman, drest out in all her finery, is the most tremendous object of
(60)  the whole creation.

**Hastings:** Ha! ha! ha! At this rate, man, how can you ever expect to marry?

**Marlow:** Never; unless, as among kings and princes, my bride were to be courted by proxy. If,
(65)  indeed, like an Eastern bridegroom, one were to

**GO ON TO THE NEXT PAGE**

be introduced to a wife he never saw before, it might be endured. But to go through all the terrors of a formal courtship, together with the
*Line* episode of aunts, grandmothers, and cousins, and
(70) at last to blurt out the broad staring question of, Madam, will you marry me? No, no, that's a strain much above me, I assure you.

**Hastings:** I pity you. But how do you intend behaving to the lady you are come down to visit at
(75) the request of your father?

**Marlow:** As I behave to all ladies. Bow very low, answer yes or no to all her demands. But for the rest, I don't think I shall venture to look in her face till I see my father's again.

(80) **Hastings:** I'm surprised that one who is so warm a friend can be so cool a lover.

(1773)

\* *bagatelle* trifle

54. Hastings's attitude toward Marlow can best be described as

(A) antagonistic but ultimately yielding.

(B) friendly but lightly critical.

(C) warm but somewhat mysterious.

(D) polite but constantly badgering.

(E) aloof but strangely soothing.

55. The characters talk about the setting as if it is

(A) Hastings's home.

(B) Marlow's home.

(C) a hostelry.

(D) a tavern.

(E) an apartment.

56. In lines 9–12, Marlow's opinion of the setting could be described as

(A) worldly and jaded.

(B) scientific and well proven.

(C) empathetic and sorrowful.

(D) harsh and cruel.

(E) inexperienced and foolish.

57. According to Hastings in lines 13–17, the setting's luxurious surroundings will

(A) cause a sizable increase in local taxes.

(B) create ill will among Marlow, Hastings, and their host.

(C) help Marlow and Hastings forget their recent troubles.

(D) account for the high cost of staying there.

(E) distract Marlow and Hastings from their true mission.

58. The conversation turns from inns to women with the introduction of what topic?

(A) Masculinity

(B) Luxury

(C) Love

(D) Money

(E) Self-confidence

**GO ON TO THE NEXT PAGE**

59. Marlow's relationships with women can be summed up in the following way:

 (A) He is comfortable with refined women, uncomfortable with unrefined women.

 (B) Unrefined women are uncomfortable around him, refined women comfortable.

 (C) He is comfortable with unrefined women, uncomfortable with refined women.

 (D) He treats all women in an unrefined and unconscionable manner.

 (E) He treats all women with grace, humility, respect, and even awe.

60. The word "tremendous" in line 59 is closest in meaning to

 (A) "wonderful."

 (B) "huge."

 (C) "fortunate."

 (D) "unbelievable."

 (E) "dreaded."

61. In lines 63–72, Marlow is against marriage because

 (A) the influence of Eastern custom has ruined Western marital practices.

 (B) the suitor's high expectations for marriage are too easily disappointed.

 (C) the rituals and procedures leading up to marriage are too arduous.

 (D) the relatives of the bride never understand the reasons for marrying.

 (E) the potential rejection after asking for engagement is too much to endure.

62. Hastings' final comment is an example of all of the following EXCEPT

 (A) an observation about Marlow's puzzling nature.

 (B) Hastings's gentle criticisms of his friend.

 (C) a reflection of the way Marlow's father has raised him.

 (D) an echo of Hastings's sentiments in lines 22–26.

 (E) antithesis revealing Marlow's duality.

63. The conversation can best be described as

 (A) a general critique that becomes a partial character study.

 (B) a farcical investigation that becomes a well-considered proposal.

 (C) a philosophical discussion that becomes a harsh scrutiny.

 (D) a satirical examination that becomes a wistful remembrance.

 (E) a routine inspection that becomes a lewd recommendation.

# STOP!

**If you finish before time is up, you may check your work.**

**Turn the page
for answers and explanations
to Practice Test 1.**

# Answer Key
# Practice Test 1

| | | |
|---|---|---|
| 1. E | 22. D | 43. B |
| 2. D | 23. C | 44. D |
| 3. A | 24. A | 45. B |
| 4. C | 25. B | 46. E |
| 5. C | 26. C | 47. E |
| 6. A | 27. E | 48. D |
| 7. E | 28. A | 49. E |
| 8. D | 29. C | 50. A |
| 9. E | 30. D | 51. A |
| 10. C | 31. E | 52. A |
| 11. A | 32. C | 53. C |
| 12. D | 33. A | 54. B |
| 13. D | 34. E | 55. C |
| 14. A | 35. C | 56. A |
| 15. D | 36. A | 57. D |
| 16. B | 37. B | 58. E |
| 17. C | 38. A | 59. C |
| 18. E | 39. A | 60. E |
| 19. C | 40. B | 61. C |
| 20. A | 41. D | 62. C |
| 21. E | 42. E | 63. A |

# ANSWERS AND EXPLANATIONS

**1. (E)** The speaker notes that hope's song "never stops—at all" (line 4) and that only the worst storm "could abash the little Bird" (line 7). Certainly, hope's longevity and perseverance are being admired by the speaker. At the end of the poem, she also remarks that hope has never "asked a crumb" of her; she is humbled that, although hope has been tenacious on her behalf, she has not been asked to do the same for it.

**2. (D)** Hope's perching in line 2 indicates that it is a bird. Line 3 makes it obvious that it is a singing bird. One may furthermore infer that hope would offer a song of comfort.

**3. (A)** The poem is already in a figurative or metaphorical mode when it compares hope to a bird. That figurative language continues with the description of the "Gale," a storm that must represent some kind of trouble. (E) would not be a good choice here, because it views the Gale literally.

**4. (C)** The word *sore* modifies the word *storm* somehow. The speaker notes that the storm would have to be "sore" to disconcert the "Bird," or hope. "Grievous" is the only definition that fits the stanza contextually.

**5. (C)** The "Gale" represents hard times or trouble, and hope's song is "sweetest" in these times; thus, I is validated. The storm that would shake hope would have to be "sore" or severe, so II now makes sense. However, in the first stanza, we see hope perching in the soul without a conflict being described; therefore, III lacks support.

**6. (A)** Hope appears in the "chillest" land and on the "strangest" sea; certainly the superlative forms of these adjectives indicate extremity. However, hope demands nothing of the speaker, not even a "crumb."

**7. (E)** Throughout the poem, the speaker has been focused on her perceptions of hope and the consistent comfort that it provides. Once we come to the last dash in the poem, though, the phrase "of Me" appears. The speaker has turned the focus of the poem on herself and is thus emphasizing a contrast: Hope provides despite everything, yet it requires nothing.

**8. (D)** Although responses (A) through (E) touch on some aspect of the passage, (D) is the most complete answer. The narrator explains the various wrongs of revenge—that it flies in the face of the law, that the avenger does not consider the wrongdoer's motivations, that it dwells too much on the past—but then he does offer one or two exceptions to his ideas (e.g., public revenge is tolerable under certain circumstances).

**9. (E)** The infinitive *to weed* or *to weed out* means "to eliminate." The narrator says, therefore, that the more people turn to revenge, the more the law should seek to eliminate revenge.

**10. (C)** The narrator remarks, "That which is past, is gone, and Irrevocable" (line 10). Therefore, whoever seeks revenge is foolishly focused on the past, which cannot be changed. It is not that wise men have difficulty in seeking revenge; rather, they are sensibly concerned with the present and the future.

**11. (A)** Lines 21–23 tell us that "The most Tolerable sort of *Revenge*, is for those wrongs which there is no Law to remedy." In other words, if a wrongdoing is not punishable by law, then revenge against the wrongdoer may be considered more acceptable. This idea is different from answer (C), which implies that no law could *ever* be legislated to take care of the wrongdoing—a highly improbable notion.

**12. (D)** In lines 26–28, the narrator says "Some, when they take *Revenge*, are desirous the party should know, whence it commeth: This is the more Generous." In other words, if a party (a wrongdoer) knows whence (from where) revenge will be taken against him, then the avenger is identifying himself; Item II is supported. Then, the narrator continues:

"For the Delight seemeth to be, not so much in doing the Hurt, as in Making the Party repent." So, as Item I points out, the avenger is giving the wrongdoer a chance to be contrite—not to retaliate, as Item III would have it.

**13. (D)** The "Arrow" image is illustrating a kind of fast and furtive revenge, a type that is contrasted with the more forthright revenge described previously. (D), therefore, has to be the right choice, because it incorrectly associates the Arrow image with the actions of the law.

**14. (A)** After quoting Cosmus, who implies that we do not have to forgive friends who do us wrong, the narrator says that "the Spirit of Job was in a better tune"; the narrator prefers Job's idea that we must accept both good and evil, even in our comrades: "And so of Friends in proportion."

**15. (D)** The idea here is that when a wrong is committed against us, we are figuratively wounded. If we choose to seek revenge for the wrongdoing, we are in essence keeping the past alive, keeping our wounds fresh, or "greene."

**16. (B)** Prior to mentioning the three rulers, the narrator states that "Publique *Revenges*, are, for the most part, Fortunate." The last footnote further confirms that each ruler's avenger became an able ruler. Thus, we are supplied with positive examples of public revenge.

**17. (C)** Lines 48–49 tell us that, as witches are "Mischievous, So end they Infortunate." In other words, the evil that witches do will lead to their downfall. Prior to this thought, the narrator has already equated "Vindicative" or vengeful people with witches; thus, vengeful people may also wind up "Infortunate."

**18. (E)** Although response (C) makes a couple of appearances in the text, (E) is the most complete answer. From beginning to end, the narrator makes several contrasts: unacceptable forms of revenge versus a few acceptable ones; the power of law versus the power of lawlessness; Duke Cosmus's ideas versus Job's. In addition, the narrator also uses antithesis, pairing opposites like "past" and "present" (lines 10–12), "Enemies" and "friends" (lines 36–37), and "Publique" and "private" (lines 43–47).

**19. (C)** An ode is a poem of praise, and this sonnet praises the color blue. The speaker calls blue "the life of heaven" (line 1) and wonders at "how great" (line 13) the color is; surely, these are expressions of admiration.

**20. (A)** The poem has 14 lines; it has a Shakespearean sonnet rhyme scheme (ABABCDCDEFEFGG); it is written in iambic pentameter. Conspicuously, it is a sonnet.

**21. (E)** In lines 1–2, the speaker refers to blue as a "domain" and a "wide palace"—images recalling royalty. In line 4, blue is called the "bosomer of clouds," a motherly metaphor.

**22. (D)** Line 3 continues the royal images of lines 1–2. Hesperus, a royal traveler of the sky, is depicted in his tent and is accompanied by his "train" of lesser stars, or his "retinue."

**23. (C)** The word "waters" is the object of the preposition "of" in line 5, so it already has a function. The dash after "waters" indicates that a new idea is coming up. Then, "*ocean*" ("May rage") and "all its vassal *streams*" ("May rage") and "*pools* numberless/May rage." Items II–IV comprise a compound subject.

**24. (A)** Lines 5–8 show us that ocean and streams and pools "May rage," but they can only "Subside" to their blue color. No matter what action they take, they cannot shake their blueness.

**25. (B)** The other responses either create false ironies or contrast items that are not ironic. However, (B) does notice a true irony. For much of this poem, the speaker concentrates on the grand designs of nature: the sky, the ocean and other bodies of water, the forest. In the final couplet, however, we shift to the blue found "in an Eye." After describing such areas of large scope, the speaker unexpectedly focuses on a small thing. Thus, an irony plays out in the last two lines.

**26. (C)** Anger and worry are indicated by the waters' actions ("rage" and "fret"), but these actions "Subside" on their own; blue is not regulating the emotions of the waters, merely controlling their blueness.

**27. (E)** There is a partial truth in the other options, but (E) is the most complete answer. The physical features of the Amphitheatre are found in phrases such as "huge circular enclosure" (lines 1–2), "real vastness" (lines 11–12), and "accessible, and sequestered spot" (line 23). The arena's mood is described as "something sinister" (line 27); later, it is described as having a "dismal privacy" (line 51). Its effect is summed up in lines 22–27, which tell us that the "soil of the ruin" discouraged romantic meetings, and in lines 52–56, which describe the arena's power of "shutting out every appreciative passer's vision."

**28. (A)** A spittoon is a kind of urn into which tobacco chewers spit their excess tobacco juice. To describe the arena in such a way assuredly makes it sound vulgar. But the arena looks like a spittoon for the Jötuns, frost giants, so here we have the mammoth size of the arena, as well.

**29. (C)** The previous paragraph ends with the following comment: "But one kind of appointment—in itself the most common of any—seldom had place in the Amphitheatre: that of happy lovers." So people in love rarely meet here. The beginning of the next paragraph continues that idea, noting that, even though the arena seems a likely spot for romantic rendezvous, there are aspects about it that actually discourage romance.

**30. (D)** The commonplace comment that no one cared for hot roast after seeing a woman's heart burst while she was burning in a fire seems to make

light of a highly dramatic scene. Furthermore, to compare her manner of death to a cooked entrée is an odd juxtaposition. There is humor going on here, but it is of a dark nature.

**31. (E)** The imposing atmosphere of the arena worsens if one knows about the "sanguinary nature of the games originally played therein" (lines 28–29), presumably ancient Roman gladiatorial combat. The arena is also more imposing if one is familiar with the 1705 burning of a female murderer. Then, there are "pugilistic encounters almost to the death" that have occurred "down to the recent dates" (lines 40–41). Thus, Items I–III have documented support.

**32. (C)** Lines 50–54 report that the boys' "game usually languished" because of a lack of "every commendatory remark from outsiders." The narrator further explains that "Possibly, too, the boys were timid," because old people relate stories of having seen ancient Roman soldiers along the arena's slopes (lines 56–65).

**33. (A)** An arena, in this case called an "Amphitheatre," is a place of performance, and the boys feel as if they are "playing to an empty house"—an unoccupied theater.

**34. (E)** The potential for a playful mood in this setting could be exhibited by either the "happy lovers" or the boys playing cricket. However, neither group is fully comfortable in the arena, and the lighting does not help to improve their attitudes.

**35. (C)** Imagination is primarily the powerful ruler by giving "orders" (line 21), being "the leader of the mental train" (line 22), holding "the sceptre o'er the realm of thought" (line 24), and so on. Since the speaker never places herself on the same level with Imagination, and in fact sounds as if she is an awestruck subject of this ruler, Imagination does not appear to be a friend. Furthermore, with the onset of winter in line 38, Fancy's (Imagination's) "sea" is chilled, and Imagination ceases to interact with the speaker. In a way, it therefore lacks loyalty.

**36. (A)** These stanzas do nothing except describe Imagination's power, but the rhetorical questions of the speaker in the first two lines make Imagination sound so forceful, so swift, that no one can achieve the right description.

**37. (B)** In line 3, Imagination soars until it can "find the bright abode," or heaven. Merely finding God's residence is not the same as challenging Him. Furthermore, Imagination may have creative powers similar to God's, but that does not put it in competition with God.

**38. (A)** In lines 11–14, Winter is merely frowning at Fancy, or Imagination. Winter is opposed to Fancy, but "fields may flourish," anyway. Imagination will not be conquered by Winter until line 38.

**39. (A)** If Winter is opposing Fancy, then Winter must be a part of reality; Fancy is that which conjures up ideas in "the realm of thought" (line 24). However, since Winter has not yet conquered Fancy, Imagination can still create an fantasy scene of spring. It is then appropriate for Flora and Sylvanus to take part in this scene, because they are deities associated with Nature.

**40. (B)** Line 15 features a repeated initial *f*, while line 19 has a repeated initial *d*.

**41. (D)** Even though Imagination may conjure up thoughts of springtime, it has no real control over nature. Line 24 also clearly indicates that the mind is Imagination's domain.

**42. (E)** Just as Aurora could rise from her bed at this moment, so Fancy could also "rise from earth" (line 30). Perhaps the analogy links the beginning of a new day to the beginning of a new idea.

**43. (B)** Aurora, or the dawn, has just risen and a "pure stream of light o'erflows the skies" (line 33). Thus, the monarch is the sun.

**44. (D)** Lines 38–40 describe Winter hampering the speaker and halting Fancy's flow.

**45. (B)** The speaker tells her song to "Cease then," as if it should stop in response to something else. In fact, she wants it to cease in response to Winter's actions. If the reality of Winter is going to take over her imagined spring, then her song is "unequal" to Winter's power.

**46. (E)** The speaker's mode in the poem is descriptive, or perhaps explanatory. However, she never attempts to change an opinion or incite action.

**47. (E)** The stranger is set apart from many things: He is not in the first two stanzas of the poem; he is not mentioned in, or a part of, any conversation; and he is lying still in a room when there is social activity occurring outside.

**48. (D)** In synecdoche, the part stands for the whole. The cigarettes are not glowing all by themselves, nor are the glasses tinkling autonomously. They are parts of an easeful setting: people casually intermingling.

**49. (E)** The image in lines 5–6 does not focus on the paleness of the moon. Rather, it emphasizes the moon's fullness ("brimming") and its celebratory aspect ("glass of beer").

**50. (A)** The assertion in line 7 is that "love keeps her appointments." Following the dash, it is announced that "Harry's here!" and the final quote of the stanza indicates that Harry is there to meet someone. Harry has shown up, and thus love is a reliable visitor.

**51. (A)** The people of the first two stanzas are indeed incorporeal. They are real enough but merely represented by cigarettes, tinkling glasses, functioning televisions, and clipped dialogue; not one facial feature or body part is described. Yet we imagine their actions of smoking, drinking, turning knobs, and conversing. On the other hand, the pale stranger who "Lies on his back" (line 10) is doing nothing but looking. He is given physical description but does not engage in action the way the others do.

**52. (A)** Because we see plurals being used ("cigarettes," "glasses"), we know that people are formed in groups outside the room, just as there is a group of roses on the wall. Perhaps the people are even desirable like roses; after all, Harry is here to meet someone—there is some kind of mutual connection or attraction there. But just as the interactions among the people lack depth, so too the roses are paper: Both the people and the roses have a "thinness" about them.

**53. (C)** Just as a crack is a division, so the stranger is divided from the rest of the people, both in behavior and in space. The rest of the options assume too much about the situation.

**54. (B)** Lines 22–26 give a good account of Hastings's tone. He begins with a compliment to Marlow, that the latter has "natural good sense," but then he notes that Marlow lacks a "share of assurance." Thus, Hastings is friendly enough to be complimentary but not so complimentary as to ignore a small shortcoming.

**55. (C)** The characters seem to be commenting on an inn, another name for a hostelry. The servant who ushers them in welcomes both of them, indicating that they are strangers to the place; therefore, the inn is probably not a home belonging to either of them.

**56. (A)** Marlow notes that the seeming inn has suffered "the usual fate"; thus, he has some knowledge in these matters and must be a traveler familiar with other inns. But there is also something cynical in his comment: He offhandedly notes that merely by maintaining a decent house, a family's finances can suffer, forcing them to convert the house into an inn. To remark on a hardship like that so casually seems a bit jaded.

**57. (D)** Hastings's idea is that an inn's "extras" have to be paid for somehow by the customers who stay there. Luxuries like "a good sideboard, or a marble chimney-piece" may not be listed in a final bill, but they can "inflame a reckoning confoundedly," or drive up the price of just staying at an inn.

**58. (E)** As soon as Hastings begins talking about Marlow's lack of "assurance" in line 26, the conversation shifts from the topic of inns to the ins and outs of courtship.

**59. (C)** In lines 34–35, Marlow implies that "among females of another class"—that is, of the lower or unrefined classes—he is comfortable, even shameless. However, "in the company of women of reputation" (lines 39–40)—in other words, upper-class or refined women—Hastings criticizes that Marlow is "an idiot" and "a trembler" (lines 40–41).

**60. (E)** Marlow's fear of refined women has already been established before this line. For instance, in line 56, he says that women "petrify" him. Thus, a woman "drest out in all her finery" is a scary thing to him.

**61. (C)** Marlow tells us in lines 67–72 that "formal courtship" is full of "terrors" and that relatives only add to the pressures of "blurting out" the marriage proposal. He admits that the whole process is a "strain." He has previously used the Eastern bridegroom example only as a contrast to the pressures of face-to-face courtship.

**62. (C)** This response assumes too much about Marlow's background. The rest of the options are viable.

**63. (A)** Marlow and Hastings begin criticizing inns in general, then converse about one aspect of Marlow's personality: the way he relates to women.

# HOW TO CALCULATE YOUR SCORE

**Step 1: Figure out your raw score.** Use the answer key to count the number of questions you answered correctly and the number of questions you answered incorrectly. (Do not count any questions you left blank.) Multiply the number wrong by 0.25 and subtract the result from the number correct. Round the result to the nearest whole number. This is your raw score.

## SAT Subject Test: Literature Practice Test 2

| Number right | | Number wrong | | Raw score |
|:---:|:---:|:---:|:---:|:---:|
| ☐ | − ( 0.25 × | ☐ | ) = | ☐ |

**Step 2: Find your scaled score.** In the Score Conversion Table below, find your raw score (rounded to the nearest whole number) in one of the columns to the left. The score directly to the right of that number will be your scaled score.

A note on your practice test scores: Don't take these scores too literally. Practice test conditions cannot precisely mirror real test conditions. Your actual SAT Subject Test: Literature score will almost certainly vary from your practice test scores. However, your scores on the practice tests will give you a rough idea of your range on the actual exam.

## Conversion Table

| Raw | Scaled | Raw | Scaled | Raw | Scaled | Raw | Scaled |
|:---:|:---:|:---:|:---:|:---:|:---:|:---:|:---:|
| 63 | 800 | 43 | 700 | 23 | 510 | 3 | 330 |
| 62 | 800 | 42 | 690 | 22 | 500 | 2 | 320 |
| 61 | 800 | 41 | 680 | 21 | 500 | 1 | 310 |
| 60 | 800 | 40 | 670 | 20 | 490 | 0 | 300 |
| 59 | 800 | 39 | 660 | 19 | 480 | -1 | 290 |
| 58 | 800 | 38 | 650 | 18 | 470 | -2 | 280 |
| 57 | 800 | 37 | 640 | 17 | 460 | -3 | 280 |
| 56 | 790 | 36 | 630 | 16 | 450 | -4 | 270 |
| 55 | 790 | 35 | 620 | 15 | 440 | -5 | 260 |
| 54 | 780 | 34 | 610 | 14 | 430 | -6 | 250 |
| 53 | 780 | 33 | 610 | 13 | 420 | -7 | 250 |
| 52 | 780 | 32 | 600 | 12 | 410 | -8 | 240 |
| 51 | 770 | 31 | 590 | 11 | 410 | -9 | 230 |
| 50 | 760 | 30 | 580 | 10 | 400 | -10 | 220 |
| 49 | 750 | 29 | 570 | 9 | 390 | -11 | 210 |
| 48 | 740 | 28 | 560 | 8 | 380 | -12 | 200 |
| 47 | 730 | 27 | 550 | 7 | 370 | -13 | 200 |
| 46 | 720 | 26 | 540 | 6 | 360 | -14 | 200 |
| 45 | 710 | 25 | 530 | 5 | 350 | | |
| 44 | 710 | 24 | 520 | 4 | 340 | | |

# Practice Test 2
## Answer Grid

1. Ⓐ Ⓑ Ⓒ Ⓓ Ⓔ
2. Ⓐ Ⓑ Ⓒ Ⓓ Ⓔ
3. Ⓐ Ⓑ Ⓒ Ⓓ Ⓔ
4. Ⓐ Ⓑ Ⓒ Ⓓ Ⓔ
5. Ⓐ Ⓑ Ⓒ Ⓓ Ⓔ
6. Ⓐ Ⓑ Ⓒ Ⓓ Ⓔ
7. Ⓐ Ⓑ Ⓒ Ⓓ Ⓔ
8. Ⓐ Ⓑ Ⓒ Ⓓ Ⓔ
9. Ⓐ Ⓑ Ⓒ Ⓓ Ⓔ
10. Ⓐ Ⓑ Ⓒ Ⓓ Ⓔ
11. Ⓐ Ⓑ Ⓒ Ⓓ Ⓔ
12. Ⓐ Ⓑ Ⓒ Ⓓ Ⓔ
13. Ⓐ Ⓑ Ⓒ Ⓓ Ⓔ
14. Ⓐ Ⓑ Ⓒ Ⓓ Ⓔ
15. Ⓐ Ⓑ Ⓒ Ⓓ Ⓔ
16. Ⓐ Ⓑ Ⓒ Ⓓ Ⓔ
17. Ⓐ Ⓑ Ⓒ Ⓓ Ⓔ
18. Ⓐ Ⓑ Ⓒ Ⓓ Ⓔ
19. Ⓐ Ⓑ Ⓒ Ⓓ Ⓔ
20. Ⓐ Ⓑ Ⓒ Ⓓ Ⓔ
21. Ⓐ Ⓑ Ⓒ Ⓓ Ⓔ

22. Ⓐ Ⓑ Ⓒ Ⓓ Ⓔ
23. Ⓐ Ⓑ Ⓒ Ⓓ Ⓔ
24. Ⓐ Ⓑ Ⓒ Ⓓ Ⓔ
25. Ⓐ Ⓑ Ⓒ Ⓓ Ⓔ
26. Ⓐ Ⓑ Ⓒ Ⓓ Ⓔ
27. Ⓐ Ⓑ Ⓒ Ⓓ Ⓔ
28. Ⓐ Ⓑ Ⓒ Ⓓ Ⓔ
29. Ⓐ Ⓑ Ⓒ Ⓓ Ⓔ
30. Ⓐ Ⓑ Ⓒ Ⓓ Ⓔ
31. Ⓐ Ⓑ Ⓒ Ⓓ Ⓔ
32. Ⓐ Ⓑ Ⓒ Ⓓ Ⓔ
33. Ⓐ Ⓑ Ⓒ Ⓓ Ⓔ
34. Ⓐ Ⓑ Ⓒ Ⓓ Ⓔ
35. Ⓐ Ⓑ Ⓒ Ⓓ Ⓔ
36. Ⓐ Ⓑ Ⓒ Ⓓ Ⓔ
37. Ⓐ Ⓑ Ⓒ Ⓓ Ⓔ
38. Ⓐ Ⓑ Ⓒ Ⓓ Ⓔ
39. Ⓐ Ⓑ Ⓒ Ⓓ Ⓔ
40. Ⓐ Ⓑ Ⓒ Ⓓ Ⓔ
41. Ⓐ Ⓑ Ⓒ Ⓓ Ⓔ
42. Ⓐ Ⓑ Ⓒ Ⓓ Ⓔ

43. Ⓐ Ⓑ Ⓒ Ⓓ Ⓔ
44. Ⓐ Ⓑ Ⓒ Ⓓ Ⓔ
45. Ⓐ Ⓑ Ⓒ Ⓓ Ⓔ
46. Ⓐ Ⓑ Ⓒ Ⓓ Ⓔ
47. Ⓐ Ⓑ Ⓒ Ⓓ Ⓔ
48. Ⓐ Ⓑ Ⓒ Ⓓ Ⓔ
49. Ⓐ Ⓑ Ⓒ Ⓓ Ⓔ
50. Ⓐ Ⓑ Ⓒ Ⓓ Ⓔ
51. Ⓐ Ⓑ Ⓒ Ⓓ Ⓔ
52. Ⓐ Ⓑ Ⓒ Ⓓ Ⓔ
53. Ⓐ Ⓑ Ⓒ Ⓓ Ⓔ
54. Ⓐ Ⓑ Ⓒ Ⓓ Ⓔ
55. Ⓐ Ⓑ Ⓒ Ⓓ Ⓔ
56. Ⓐ Ⓑ Ⓒ Ⓓ Ⓔ
57. Ⓐ Ⓑ Ⓒ Ⓓ Ⓔ
58. Ⓐ Ⓑ Ⓒ Ⓓ Ⓔ
59. Ⓐ Ⓑ Ⓒ Ⓓ Ⓔ
60. Ⓐ Ⓑ Ⓒ Ⓓ Ⓔ
61. Ⓐ Ⓑ Ⓒ Ⓓ Ⓔ

# Practice Test 2

*Questions 1–8 refer to the following poem. After reading the poem, choose the best answer to each question.*

When my mother died I was very young,
And my father sold me while yet my tongue
Could scarcely cry "'weep, 'weep, 'weep, 'weep,"*
So your chimneys I sweep & in soot I sleep.

*Line*
(5)   There's little Tom Dacre who cried when his head,
That curl'd like a lamb's back, was shav'd: so I said,
"Hush, Tom, never mind it, for when your head's bare
You know that the soot cannot spoil your white hair."

And so he was quiet, & that very night,
(10) As Tom was a sleeping, he had such a sight,
That thousands of sweepers, Dick, Joe, Ned & Jack,
Were all of them lock'd up in coffins of black.

And by came an Angel who had a bright key,
And he open'd the coffins & set them all free;
(15) Then down a green plain, leaping laughing, they run,
And wash in a river, and shine in the Sun.

Then naked & white, all their bags left behind,
They rise upon clouds, and sport in the wind;
And the Angel told Tom, if he'd be a good boy,
(20) He'd have God for his father & never want joy.

And so Tom awoke; and we rose in the dark,
And got with our bags & brushes to work.
Tho' the morning was cold, Tom was happy & warm;
So if all do their duty they need not fear harm.

(1789)

* "*'weep…'weep*" a contraction of the sweeper's call: "Sweep! Sweep!"

$\longrightarrow$

**GO ON TO THE NEXT PAGE**

1. The narrator of the poem

   (A) enjoys the responsibilities of his occupation.

   (B) is ready to leave his job for a new opportunity.

   (C) does not realize the lowliness of his work.

   (D) understands that he is close to dying.

   (E) wonders what might have been in another life.

2. The "'weep, 'weep, 'weep, 'weep" of line 3 could signify all of the following EXCEPT

   (A) the narrator's underdeveloped pronunciation.

   (B) an association between chimney sweeping and crying.

   (C) the repetitive drudgery of the narrator's occupation.

   (D) the pity that society feels for the narrator's situation.

   (E) the sadness of the narrator's losing a parent and being abandoned.

3. In the second stanza, Tom Dacre is portrayed as

   (A) innocent, but oppressed.

   (B) sad, but determined.

   (C) hopeless, but kind.

   (D) cruel, but rehabilitating.

   (E) sickly, but improving.

4. The coffins of line 12 most logically symbolize

   (A) the idea that Death is approaching quickly.

   (B) the narrator's horror concerning Tom's dream.

   (C) society's disapproval of the sweepers.

   (D) the abomination of the sweepers in God's eyes.

   (E) the sweepers' entrapment in their circumstances.

5. In lines 19–20, the Angel's admonition for Tom to "be a good boy" reveals that

   (A) God recognizes Tom as a wicked person.

   (B) Tom has suffered from the speaker's disapproval.

   (C) the code of conduct among chimney sweepers is firm.

   (D) Tom is beginning to enter into adulthood.

   (E) Tom dreams of a happiness he can earn.

6. The idea that "we rose in the dark" (line 21) could display all of the following EXCEPT

   (A) the sweepers' ignorance of their hopeless existence.

   (B) the contrast of the sweepers' lives to Tom's dream.

   (C) the eagerness that the sweepers hold for their work.

   (D) the earliness with which the sweepers must begin their jobs.

   (E) the awareness society lacks of the sweepers' bleak routine.

**GO ON TO THE NEXT PAGE**

7. The aphorism in line 24 is meant to be the narrator's

   (A) hopeful but ironically misled resolution of his existence.

   (B) acceptance of the treachery that life seems to offer.

   (C) dread of what is to come in the afterlife.

   (D) horror at the mistreatment of his fellow sweepers.

   (E) astute and sensible assessment of his situation.

8. The poem's meter and rhyme scheme reflect

   (A) the poet's lack of sophistication.

   (B) the narrator's innocence and simplicity.

   (C) a sweeper's ignorance and stupidity.

   (D) the poetic style of the late 1700s.

   (E) the comfort that God sends to the sweepers.

GO ON TO THE NEXT PAGE

*Questions 9–16 refer to the following passage. After reading the passage, choose the best answer to each question.*

My own sex, I hope, will excuse me, if I treat them like rational creatures, instead of flattering their fascinating graces, and viewing them as
Line if they were in a state of perpetual childhood,
(5) unable to stand alone. I earnestly wish to point out in what true dignity and human happiness consists—I wish to endeavor to acquire strength, both of mind and body, and to convince them that the soft phrases, susceptibility of heart,
(10) delicacy of sentiment, and refinement of taste, are almost synonymous with epithets of weakness, and that those beings who are only the objects of pity and that kind of love, which has been termed its sister, will soon become objects of contempt.
(15) Dismissing then those pretty feminine phrases, which the men condescendingly use to soften our slavish dependence, and despising that weak elegancy of mind, exquisite sensibility, and sweet docility of manners, supposed to be the
(20) sexual characteristics of the weaker vessel, I wish to shew that elegance is inferior to virtue, that the first object of laudable ambition is to obtain a character as a human being, regardless of the distinction of sex; and that secondary views
(25) should be brought to this simple touchstone.
This is a rough sketch of my plan; and should I express my conviction with the energetic emotions that I feel whenever I think of the subject, the dictates of experience and reflection
(30) will be felt by some of my readers. Animated by this important object, I shall disdain to cull my phrases or polish my style;—I aim at being useful, and sincerity will render me unaffected; for, wishing rather to persuade by the force of my
(35) arguments, than dazzle by the elegance of my language, I shall not waste my time in rounding periods,* or in fabricating the turgid bombast of

artificial feelings, which, coming from the head, never reach the heart.—I shall be employed about
(40) things, not words!—and, anxious to render my sex more respectable members of society, I shall try to avoid that flowery diction which has slided from essays into novels, and from novels into familiar letters and conversation.

(1792)

*rounding periods* using formal, elaborate sentences

9. The narrator in this passage regards women as

(A) surprisingly contemptible and base.
(B) overbearingly sentimental and cloying.
(C) irreparably coy and stupid.
(D) unquestionably devious and malignant.
(E) needlessly weak and subservient.

10. In relation to the first sentence, lines 5–8 imply that

(A) women need to expand their own femininity and childlike innocence.
(B) women who fulfill their expected social roles are respected by men.
(C) women are naturally inclined to behave immaturely in the presence of men.
(D) women who are mannerly and childish are neither happy nor dignified.
(E) women must supplant men in what have been traditionally patriarchal roles.

**GO ON TO THE NEXT PAGE**

11. In lines 7–14, the narrator emphasizes all of the following points EXCEPT that

    (A) she wants to uplift women while seeking her own self-improvement.

    (B) the strength sometimes exhibited by women can be misunderstood as contempt.

    (C) any love expressed toward women out of their pitifulness is temporary.

    (D) vulnerability, delicacy, and refinement are not actually desirable in a woman.

    (E) women who are pitied by men eventually will be despised by them.

12. The second paragraph begins to formulate a writing strategy that will

    (A) gradually reveal a social problem and the writer's ultimate purpose.

    (B) attempt to discuss what no previous writer has been brave enough to broach.

    (C) dispense with the feminine elegance that the narrator equates with weakness.

    (D) instruct the reader in ways to overthrow a corrupt social system.

    (E) not only mimic a masculine approach to writing but also generally mock men.

13. The narrator in lines 26–30 indicates that her writing style will

    (A) be an apt approach for her female readers.

    (B) prevent her ideas from being clearly understood.

    (C) reflect the strength of her human character.

    (D) offend some of her male readers.

    (E) help some of her readers empathize with her ideas.

14. The word "unaffected" in line 33 is closest in meaning to

    (A) "distant."

    (B) "stoic."

    (C) "forthright."

    (D) "absolute."

    (E) "causative."

15. The narrator's observation in lines 41–44 about "flowery diction" stresses that decorative language

    (A) is beneficial under certain conditions.

    (B) lacks both respectability and rarity.

    (C) interferes with the comprehension of text.

    (D) attempts to mask a writer's gender.

    (E) engages the wrong kind of reading public.

16. Throughout the passage, the narrator creates a link between

    (A) the roles shared by men and women and offers ways to maintain them.

    (B) the elegance of language and women and marks its problems in both.

    (C) the different trends in writing and speaking and tries to merge them.

    (D) the behavior and language of women and lauds the distinctness of each.

    (E) the literature and customs that ennoble women and attempts to perpetuate them.

**GO ON TO THE NEXT PAGE**

*Questions 17–26 refer to the following poem. After reading the poem, choose the best answer to each question.*

"The Author to Her Book"

Thou ill-formed offspring of my feeble brain,
Who after birth didst by my side remain,
Till snatched from thence by friends, less wise than true,
*Line*    Who thee abroad, exposed to public view,
(5)    Made thee in rags, halting to th' press to trudge,
Where errors were not lessened (all may judge).
At thy return my blushing was not small,
My rambling brat (in print) should mother call,
I cast thee by as one unfit for light,
(10)    Thy visage was so irksome in my sight;
Yet being mine own, at length affection would
Thy blemishes amend, if so I could:
I washed thy face, but more defects I saw,
And rubbing off a spot still made a flaw.
(15)    I stretched thy joints to make thee even feet,
Yet still thou run'st more hobbling than is meet;
In better dress to trim thee was my mind,
But nought save homespun cloth i' th' house I find.
In this array 'mongst vulgars may'st thou roam.      *vulgars* common people
(20)    In critic's hands beware thou dost not come,
And take thy way where yet thou art known
If for thy father asked, say thou hadst none;
And for thy mother, she alas is poor,
Which caused her thus to send thee out of door.

(1678)

**GO ON TO THE NEXT PAGE**

17. In this passage, the narrator is addressing her book as if it were a child who is

    (A) morally delinquent.

    (B) physically imperfect.

    (C) wholly unwanted.

    (D) desperately feeble.

    (E) precociously arrogant.

18. The narrator calls her friends "less wise than true" (line 3) because

    (A) they have proven to be more honest than they are intelligent.

    (B) their poor but well-intentioned decisions have nearly ruined her.

    (C) her truthfulness in dealing with them outshines their sagacity.

    (D) friendships tend to be founded more often on openness than intelligence.

    (E) she appreciates their loyalty to her more than their judgment of her work.

19. The parenthetical remark in line 6 reveals the narrator's

    (A) certainty about her work's flaws.

    (B) hope for critical acclaim.

    (C) interest in publishing.

    (D) low regard for the public.

    (E) previous disappointments in writing.

20. In lines 9–12, the narrator's attitude changes from rejection to

    (A) unconditional affection.

    (B) inescapable embarrassment.

    (C) childlike wonder.

    (D) maternal claim.

    (E) curbed delirium.

21. The narrator's actions in lines 13–14 are actually a description of her

    (A) attempting to cleanse herself of her work.

    (B) primping before meeting her publisher.

    (C) editing her work unsuccessfully.

    (D) translating a foreign language text.

    (E) erasing an editor's criticisms about her work.

22. The complaint in lines 15–16 reflects the narrator's inability to

    (A) understand the depth of her own poetry.

    (B) perfect the metrical quality of her poetry.

    (C) share the musical aspect of her poetry with the public.

    (D) relate the message of her poetry to the critics.

    (E) prepare her family for her newfound fame as a writer.

**GO ON TO THE NEXT PAGE**

23. Lines 17–19 express the narrator's realization that

    (A) her work is so amateurish that it might as well be written as a string of vulgarities.

    (B) unless she finds a generous publisher, she and her family may wind up destitute.

    (C) although her work is inelegant, it may find an audience among common people.

    (D) her poetry is so incomprehensible that it might as well wander in the gutter.

    (E) after her unnerving experiences with publishing, she would rather be domestic.

24. The warnings in lines 20–21 express the narrator's fear of

    (A) fame and desire for anonymity.

    (B) oblivion and desire for her work's glory.

    (C) death and desire for immortality through her work.

    (D) ridicule and desire for her family's unity.

    (E) criticism and desire for her work's acceptance.

25. During the course of the poem, the narrator's attitude moves from

    (A) self-criticism to conditional acceptance back to self-criticism.

    (B) self-doubt to fierce optimism back to self-doubt.

    (C) self-loathing to wild ecstasy back to self-loathing.

    (D) self-appreciation to writhing anguish back to self-appreciation.

    (E) self-torture to loving forgiveness back to self-torture.

26. All of the following appear in the poem EXCEPT

    (A) heroic couplets.

    (B) apostrophe.

    (C) metaphorical conceit.

    (D) classical allusion.

    (E) a humble tone.

**GO ON TO THE NEXT PAGE**

*Questions 27–37 refer to the following passage. After reading the passage, choose the best answer to each question.*

He sounded the clacker* till his arm ached, and at length his heart grew sympathetic with the birds' thwarted desires. They seemed, like
Line himself, to be living in a world which did not
(5) want them. Why should he frighten them away? They took upon them more and more the aspect of gentle friends and pensioners—the only friends he could claim as being in the least degree interested in him, for his aunt had often told him
(10) that she was not. He ceased his rattling, and they alighted anew.

"Poor little dears!" said Jude, aloud. "You *shall* have some dinner—you shall. There is enough for us all. Farmer Troutham can afford to let you
(15) have some. Eat, then, my dear little birdies, and make a good meal!"

They stayed and ate, inky spots on the nut-brown soil, and Jude enjoyed their appetite. A magic thread of fellow-feeling united his own life
(20) with theirs. Puny and sorry as those lives were, they much resembled his own.

His clacker he had by this time thrown away from him, as being a mean and sordid instrument, offensive both to the birds and to
(25) himself as their friend. All at once he became conscious of a smart blow upon his buttock, followed by a loud clack, which announced to his surprised senses that the clacker had been the instrument of offence used. The birds and Jude
(30) started up simultaneously, and the dazed eyes of the latter beheld the farmer in person, the great Troutham himself, his red face glaring down upon Jude's cowering frame, the clacker swinging in his hand.

(35) "So it's 'Eat my dear birdies,' is it, young man? 'Eat dear birdies,' indeed! I'll tickle your breeches, and see if you say 'Eat, dear birdies,' again in a hurry! And you've been idling at the schoolmaster's too, instead of coming here, ha'n't

(40) ye, hey? That's how you earn your sixpence a day for keeping the rooks off my corn!"

Whilst saluting Jude's ears with his impassioned rhetoric, Troutham had seized his left hand with his own left, and swinging his slim
(45) frame round him at arm's length, again struck Jude on the hind parts with the flat side of Jude's own rattle, till the field echoed with the blows, which were delivered once or twice at each revolution.

(50) "Don't 'ee sir—please don't 'ee" cried the whirling child, as helpless under the centrifugal tendency of his person as a hooked fish swinging to land, and beholding the hill, the rick, the plantation, the path, and the rooks going round
(55) and round him in an amazing circular race. "I— I—sir—only meant that—there was a good crop in the ground—I saw them sow it—and the rooks could have a little bit for dinner—and you wouldn't miss it, sir—and Mr. Phillotson† said I
(60) was to be kind to 'em—O, O, O!"

This truthful explanation seemed to exasperate the farmer even more than if Jude had stoutly denied saying anything at all; and he still smacked the whirling urchin, the clacks of the
(65) instrument continuing to resound all across the field and as far as the ears of distant workers—who gathered thereupon that Jude was pursuing his business with great assiduity—and echoing from the brand-new church tower just behind the
(70) mist, towards the building of which structure the farmer had largely subscribed, to testify his love for God and man.

(1896)

*a noisemaker for scaring crows
†the schoolmaster mentioned by Troutham

---

→

**GO ON TO THE NEXT PAGE**

27. The immediate conflict in this passage exists between

    (A) the protagonist and Nature.

    (B) a father and son.

    (C) Nature and society.

    (D) an employer and employee.

    (E) the protagonist and himself.

28. Jude probably "grew sympathetic with the birds' thwarted desires" (lines 2–3) for all of the following reasons EXCEPT that

    (A) their need makes him reflective.

    (B) their situation seems similar to his.

    (C) he has been recently punished.

    (D) he views them as comrades.

    (E) he feels ignored.

29. "The birds and Jude started up simultaneously" (lines 29–30) echoes the birds' and Jude's

    (A) readiness for danger.

    (B) awareness of opportunity.

    (C) independence from authority.

    (D) hope for the future.

    (E) similarity of circumstance.

30. The description of Farmer Troutham in lines 31–34 makes him sound

    (A) insightful.

    (B) formidable.

    (C) disappointed.

    (D) cranky.

    (E) inquisitive.

31. One can surmise all of the following about Troutham from lines 35–41 EXCEPT that

    (A) he has encountered Jude's laxity before.

    (B) he is capable of understatement.

    (C) he wants value for his money.

    (D) he does not esteem education highly.

    (E) he resorts to mockery when indignant.

32. For the phrase "Whilst saluting Jude's ears with his impassioned rhetoric" (lines 42–43), which statement seems best?

    (A) Troutham feels guilty; the narrator's tone is sympathetic.

    (B) Troutham feels like backing down; the narrator's tone is encouraging.

    (C) Troutham feels heroic; the narrator's tone is apathetic.

    (D) Troutham feels self-important; the narrator's tone is ironic.

    (E) Troutham feels triumphant; the narrator's tone is fearful.

33. All of the following demonstrate Jude's helplessness *except*

    (A) "centrifugal tendency" (lines 51–52).

    (B) "hooked fish" (line 52).

    (C) "round and round him" (lines 54–55).

    (D) "a good crop in the ground" (lines 56–57).

    (E) "O, O, O!" (line 60).

**GO ON TO THE NEXT PAGE**

34. The imagery in lines 50–60 is dominated by

    (A) light and dark.

    (B) animal husbandry.

    (C) entrapment.

    (D) circularity.

    (E) ambiguity.

35. From the series below, which items relate directly to the irony of Jude and Troutham's situation in the final paragraph?

    I. The clacker

    II. The mist

    III. The distant workers

    IV. Troutham's subscription to the brand-new church tower

    (A) I and II only

    (B) III and IV only

    (C) I, III, and IV only

    (D) I, II, and III only

    (E) I, II, III, and IV

36. The narrator's omniscience is best seen in

    (A) Jude's link with the birds.

    (B) Troutham's speeches to Jude.

    (C) Phillotson's comments about birds.

    (D) the distant workers' assumptions.

    (E) the mention of God.

37. Which statement below best embodies a theme of the passage?

    (A) Agricultural labor is monotonous and grueling.

    (B) Authority figures will dominate when attacked by scholars.

    (C) Education is less reliable than hard work.

    (D) The meek shall inherit the earth but must wait to do so.

    (E) Kindness will be misinterpreted, unrewarded, and/or punished.

GO ON TO THE NEXT PAGE

*Questions 38–45 refer to the following poem. After reading the poem, choose the best answer to each question.*

Come sleep, O sleep, the certain knot of peace,
The baiting place of wit, the balm of woe
The poor man's wealth, the prisoner's release,
Line    The indifferent judge between the high and low;
(5)    With shield of proof shield me from out the prease
Of those fierce darts Despair at me doth throw:
O make in me those civil wars to cease;
I will good tribute pay, if thou do so.
Take thou of me smooth pillows, sweetest bed,
(10)    A chamber deaf to noise, and blind to light,
A rose garland, and a weary head:
And if these things, as being thine by right,
Move not thy heavy grace, thou shalt in me,
Livelier than elsewhere Stella's image see.

*baiting place*  place of refreshment

*prease*  crowd

*tribute*  respectful payment

(1591)

38. In this poem, what the speaker wants most is to

(A) question sleep to discover why it has been so unhelpful.

(B) quiet his mind so that he may fall asleep.

(C) review his day so that he may dream more selectively.

(D) petition sleep so that he can achieve true love.

(E) remain awake so that he can think of his love.

39. In lines 1–4, the speaker discusses sleep using all of the following EXCEPT

(A) apostrophe.

(B) metaphor.

(C) paradox.

(D) respectful tone.

(E) dramatic irony.

40. In line 4, the word "indifferent" is closest in meaning to

(A) uncaring.

(B) unassuming.

(C) unbiased.

(D) unresponsive.

(E) unremarkable.

41. In lines 5–6, the speaker wishes sleep to shield him from

(A) the noisy crowd of people surrounding him.

(B) reminders of the conflicts plaguing the speaker's country.

(C) the despair of possible poverty and imprisonment.

(D) thoughts of hopelessness keeping him awake.

(E) the arrows with which Cupid assails him.

**GO ON TO THE NEXT PAGE**

42. The "civil wars" mentioned in line 7 must be a reference to

    (A) the speaker's memories of a recent military battle.

    (B) the conflict between the speaker's need to sleep and his recollection of Stella.

    (C) the memories of recent hardship, including imprisonment.

    (D) the inner turmoil of writing a poem to Stella.

    (E) the need to communicate with Stella versus the fear of being rejected by her.

43. The "good tribute" (line 8) itemized in lines 9–11 is later made ironic because it

    (A) will be withheld by the speaker if Stella appears.

    (B) has been stolen from Despair and thus does not belong to the speaker.

    (C) is only reluctantly offered by the speaker.

    (D) already belongs to, or is associated with, sleep.

    (E) is unwanted by sleep because of its material nature.

44. According to lines 12–14, if sleep does not help, then the speaker will

    (A) lie awake thinking of Stella.

    (B) long for Stella's presence in the room.

    (C) use this poem to communicate with Stella.

    (D) attempt to invade Stella's dreams.

    (E) dream of Stella all night.

45. Throughout the poem, sleep is treated as

    (A) a helpful friend.

    (B) a wise parent.

    (C) an insensitive lover.

    (D) a dangerous enemy.

    (E) a respected authority.

**GO ON TO THE NEXT PAGE**

Questions 46–54 refer to the following passage. After reading the passage, choose the best answer to each question.

Our house stood within a few rods of the Chesapeake Bay, whose broad bosom was ever white with sails from every quarter of the habitable globe. Those beautiful vessels, robed in
(5) purest white, so delightful to the eye of freemen, were to me so many shrouded ghosts, to terrify and torment me with thoughts of my wretched condition. I have often, in the deep stillness of a summer's Sabbath, stood all alone upon the lofty
(10) banks of that noble bay, and traced, with saddened heart and a tearful eye, the countless number of sails moving off to the mighty ocean. The sight of these always affected me powerfully. My thoughts would compel utterance; and there,
(15) with no audience but the Almighty, I would pour out my soul's complaint, in my rude way, with an apostrophe to the moving multitude of ships:—

"You are loosed from your moorings, and are free; I am fast in my chains, and am a slave! You
(20) move merrily before the gentle gale, and I sadly before the bloody whip! You are freedom's swift-winged angels, that fly round the world; I am confined in bands of iron! O that I were free! O, that I were on one of your gallant decks, and
(25) under your protecting wing! Alas! betwixt me and you, the turbid waters roll. Go on, go on. O that I could also go! Could I but swim! If I could fly! O, why was I born a man, of whom to make a brute! The glad ship is gone; she hides in the dim
(30) distance. I am left in the hottest hell of unending slavery. O God, save me! God, deliver me! Let me be free! Is there any God? Why am I a slave? I will run away. I will not stand it. Get caught, or get clear, I'll try it. I had as well die with ague* as
(35) with fever. I have only one life to lose. I had as well be killed running as die standing. Only think of it; one hundred miles straight north, and I am free! Try it? Yes! God helping me, I will. It cannot be that I shall live and die a slave. I will take to

(40) the water. This very bay shall yet bear me to freedom. The steamboats steered in a north-east course from North Point. I will do the same; and when I get to the head of the bay, I will turn my canoe adrift, and walk straight through Delaware
(45) into Pennsylvania. When I get there, I shall not be required to have a pass; I can travel without being disturbed. Let but the first opportunity offer, and come what will, I am off. Meanwhile, I will try to bear up under the yoke. I am not the
(50) only slave in the world. Why should I fret? I can bear as much as any of them. Besides, I am but a boy, and all boys are bound to some one. It may be my misery in slavery will only increase my happiness when I get free. There is a better day
(55) coming."

Thus I used to think, and thus I used to speak to myself; goaded almost to madness at one moment, and at last reconciling myself to my wretched lot.

(1845)

*ague* in this case, chills

46. The narrator in this passage is a slave who

(A) is about to escape to freedom in the North.

(B) longs for freedom but is too fearful to pursue it.

(C) wants to be free and is determined to achieve this goal.

(D) is an admirer of the sea and seagoing vessels.

(E) has just escaped from bondage but is beginning to regret this action.

**GO ON TO THE NEXT PAGE**

47. The narrator's contrasting opinions of the ships in lines 4–8 can be attributed to

(A) the various purposes which the ships fulfill for their owners.

(B) the difference between the beauty of the ships and the slave trading they support.

(C) the lack of knowledge he has concerning the ships' destinations and purposes.

(D) the contradictory orders his master has given him.

(E) the freedom that the ships exhibit but that he cannot have.

48. In lines 8–12, the narrator's diction demonstrates that, for him, freedom is

(A) a heated and maniacal desire.

(B) a dignified and sacred concept.

(C) a furtive and vengeful pursuit.

(D) a complex and confusing proposal.

(E) a hopeless and unachievable dream.

49. In line 18, the narrator begins his apostrophe to the ships because

(A) slavery has pushed him to the brink of madness.

(B) he has retained his old customs and believes the ships are alive.

(C) he hopes that someone on the decks will actually hear him.

(D) he wants God to deliver him from this unendurable fate.

(E) his musings about slavery have driven him to speak.

50. The ideas in lines 18–23 develop mainly through the use of

(A) antithesis.

(B) epic simile.

(C) local color.

(D) hyperbole.

(E) water imagery.

51. The narrator views the "turbid waters" in line 26 as

(A) a symbol of freedom.

(B) part of the bay's beauty.

(C) evidence of God's presence.

(D) an agitation reflecting the anger inside him.

(E) an obstacle keeping him from his goal.

52. Which of the following do lines 27–33 feature?

I. Rhetorical questions

II. A desperate tone

III. A philosophical and theological scope

IV. A new resolution

(A) I and II only

(B) I, II, and III only

(C) I, II, and IV only

(D) II, III, and IV only

(E) I, II, III, and IV

**GO ON TO THE NEXT PAGE**

53. In lines 47–55, the narrator's decision to escape enslavement has encouraged a new tone of

    (A) celebration and eagerness.

    (B) fear and dread.

    (C) perseverance and rationalization.

    (D) arrogance and command.

    (E) apathy and caution.

54. In the passage, the imagery describing the ships draws a parallel between escape and

    (A) an ideal childhood.

    (B) a joyous reunion.

    (C) a physical healing.

    (D) a heavenly afterlife.

    (E) a journey home.

**GO ON TO THE NEXT PAGE**

*Questions 55–61 refer to the following poem. After reading the poem, choose the best answer to each question.*

I have studied many times
The marble which was chiseled for me—
A boat with a furled sail at rest in a harbor.

*Line*
(5)
In truth it pictures not my destination
But my life.
For love was offered me and I shrank from its disillusionment;
Sorrow knocked at my door, but I was afraid;
Ambition called to me, but I dreaded the chances.
Yet all the while I hungered for meaning in my life.

(10)
And now I know that we must lift the sail
And catch the winds of destiny
Wherever they drive the boat.
To put meaning in one's life may end in madness,
But life without meaning is the torture

(15)
Of restlessness and vague desire —
It is a boat longing for the sea and yet afraid.

*marble* the narrator's tombstone;
he is speaking after his death

(1915)

55. In the poem, the speaker's tone is

(A) regretful.

(B) ominous.

(C) uplifting.

(D) indignant.

(E) resigned.

56. According to lines 3–5, the image
being discussed has all of the following
characteristics EXCEPT that

(A) it is part of the speaker's tombstone.

(B) the speaker rejects its intended meaning.

(C) it is designed to be symbolic or
metaphorical.

(D) the speaker invests the image with a new
meaning.

(E) the furled sail is an incorrect image of
the speaker's life.

57. In lines 6–9, the speaker's discussion of love,
sorrow, and ambition shows that

(A) he was given no opportunity to
experience these emotions.

(B) he was motivated by fear to avoid each
of these feelings.

(C) he has the same regard for these
emotions now as when he was alive.

(D) he is proving the original meaning of the
boat image to be true.

(E) he now sees emotions as destroyers of
life's meaning.

**GO ON TO THE NEXT PAGE**

58. Lines 10–12 have all of the following functions EXCEPT

  (A) to describe the consequences of the life the speaker has lived.

  (B) to change the speaker's focus from past experience to present insight.

  (C) to extend the speaker's observations from personal to universal.

  (D) to recapture a previous image's application to the speaker's life.

  (E) to provide an alternative to the way the speaker has spent his life.

59. At the end of the poem, the speaker implies that

  (A) the "torture/Of restlessness" is better than "madness."

  (B) "meaning in one's life" is better than "madness."

  (C) "life without meaning" is better than having emotions.

  (D) "madness" is better than "restlessness and vague desire."

  (E) "a boat longing for the sea" is better than "vague desire."

60. The poem features all of the following EXCEPT

  (A) metaphorical conceit.

  (B) personification.

  (C) discursive style.

  (D) biblical allusion.

  (E) free verse.

61. By the end of the poem, the speaker is calling for

  (A) a greater individual control of one's life.

  (B) a small degree of passion, energy, and enthusiasm.

  (C) an increased openness to uncontrollable forces.

  (D) a larger sense of stability and security.

  (E) a life dominated by artistic expression and aesthetic beauty.

## STOP!

**If you finish before time is up, you may check your work.**

**Turn the page
for answers and explanations
to Practice Test 2.**

# Answer Key
## Practice Test 2

| | | |
|---|---|---|
| 1. C | 22. B | 43. D |
| 2. D | 23. C | 44. A |
| 3. A | 24. E | 45. E |
| 4. E | 25. A | 46. C |
| 5. E | 26. D | 47. E |
| 6. C | 27. D | 48. B |
| 7. A | 28. C | 49. E |
| 8. B | 29. E | 50. A |
| 9. E | 30. B | 51. E |
| 10. D | 31. A | 52. E |
| 11. B | 32. D | 53. C |
| 12. C | 33. D | 54. D |
| 13. E | 34. D | 55. A |
| 14. C | 35. C | 56. E |
| 15. B | 36. D | 57. B |
| 16. B | 37. E | 58. A |
| 17. B | 38. B | 59. D |
| 18. E | 39. E | 60. D |
| 19. A | 40. C | 61. C |
| 20. D | 41. D | |
| 21. C | 42. B | |

# ANSWERS AND EXPLANATIONS

**1. (C)** Any references that the narrator makes to his occupation are matter of fact: "your chimneys I sweep" (line 4); "in soot I sleep" (line 4); "we rose in the dark/And got with our bags & brushes to work" (lines 21–22). The reader can surmise the lowliness of this work and can see how Tom's dream emphasizes a sweeper's drudgery, but the narrator's plainspoken tone demonstrates an innocence about his work's demeaning nature.

**2. (D)** Since the narrator is quoting himself here, any correlation to society in the quotation seems unlikely.

As the footnote indicates, the word 'weep is a contraction of Sweep! As this contraction is not normally found in English, one could surmise that it appears because of the narrator's childish speech pattern. So (A) doesn't work.

(B) is also faulty, because the footnote helps us see the link between 'weep and Sweep!

The quadruple repetition of 'weep [Sweep] helps us understand why one can't choose (C).

The narrator mentions losing his mother and being sold by his father in lines 1–2. His repetitive 'weep follows too soon to be coincidence. Thus, (E) is unlikely.

**3. (A)** The second stanza indicates that Tom's hair is similar to a lamb's, and a lamb typically is associated with innocence. Furthermore, Tom cries when his hair is being cut, so the experience of being "shorn" is oppressive to him; his hair is being cut against his will.

**4. (E)** The coffins are "lock'd up" (line 12) and contain all the sweepers. Likewise, these boys cannot escape their circumstances. The narrator, for instance, is abandoned to this occupation. Another example is that Tom has no control over what others do to him.

**5. (E)** Tom is told that if he is a good boy, God will take care of him and he will never lack joy.

**6. (C)** Again, the narrator has described their work very plainly and a little sadly. Tom's reaction to this life is to cry about his haircut and dream about locked coffins. We see no eagerness in any sweeper's actions.

Darkness is an archetype for ignorance or lack of knowledge. In addition, since we see no improvement occurring for the sweepers, even though the narrator remains optimistic at the end, and since we know society—exemplified by the narrator's father—is ignoring the plight of these boys, both (A) and (E) will not work.

The dream shows the sweepers being able to escape their circumstances. We see no such escape available in their waking lives. Thus, (B) is wrong.

(D) is not a logical choice, because if the sweepers are rising in the dark, then it must be early morning outside.

**7. (A)** Undoubtedly, the narrator's resolution at the end is hopeful, but it is also misled because he is using a workmate's unsubstantiated dream to guide his thinking. The circumstances of the narrator's life prove that nothing good will occur for the sweepers; real life is oppressing them. Yet the narrator would rather build his philosophy on a fantasy.

**8. (B)** The meter is uneven, but often takes on a sing-songy quality, as lines 9–10 exemplify. This technique, combined with a simple couplet rhyme, makes the narrator sound as if he is reciting a nursery poem.

**9. (E)** The narrator refers to the way women are regarded by using such phrases as "state of perpetual childhood" (line 4) and "epithets of weakness" (line 11). However, the whole point of this passage seems to be to bring women out of this maligning light. She wants to address them like "rational creatures" (line 2) and render them "more respectable members of society" (line 41).

10. (D) The important thing to note here is the opening of the stem: "In relation to the first sentence." Thus, one has to take into consideration lines 1–8 for the correct response. The narrator says that she wants to "point out in what true dignity and human happiness consists" after she has said that she will not flatter women's "fascinating graces" nor view them in a "state of perpetual childhood." The implication is that true human dignity does not lie in gracious or childish behavior.

11. (B) Since the narrator never refers to women as being strong, this response is the most likely.

12. (C) The narrator announces in lines 15–16 that she will be "Dismissing then those pretty feminine phrases" associated with the weakness of women. Her writing, like the new feminine behavior she wishes to encourage, will be forthright, virtuous, and devoid of affectedness.

13. (E) In these lines, the narrator says that the "energetic emotions" expressed in her writing will kindle "experience and reflection" in "some of [her] readers." So some will be able to relate to what she says.

14. (C) The narrator says, "sincerity will render me unaffected." She also says that she will write in an unpolished style and that she wishes to be "useful." All these are clues that she wants her writing to be forthright.

15. (B) The narrator wants to "render [her] sex more respectable" and has just previously said that she does not want to "waste [her] time" in the "turgid bombast of artificial feelings," so there must be a link between respectability and sincere expression. Additionally, she notes that "flowery diction" has found its way into several genres of writing, so it also must lack rarity.

16. (B) The first paragraph discusses the childishness and graciousness of women: in essence, their elegant submissiveness. The narrator then goes on to denounce this behavior. Later in the passage, the narrator notes that women are associated with flowery diction, and she condemns its insincerity. Both women and flowery diction have an artificiality that is not desirable.

17. (B) The narrator calls her poetry an "ill-formed offspring" (line 1) who is "unfit for light" (line 9) and whose "visage was so irksome" (line 10). It has "blemishes" (line 12), and its running is more akin to "hobbling" (line 16). All of these phrases point to perceived technical imperfections of her work.

18. (E) What the friends have done in line 4 is to expose the narrator's "child," her poetry, "to public view." In other words, they have sought to publish the narrator's work. This action shows that these friends are loyal to the narrator; however, if we remember how the narrator feels about her "child," we know also why she thinks this action to be unwise.

19. (A) She invites "all" to judge her poetry after she has criticized her work. She is certain that anyone can see how imperfect her book is.

20. (D) The narrator claims her poetry as "mine own" and says that "affection" motivates her to "amend" the "blemishes" of her text. We know that this claim is a maternal one because the narrator has already described the poetry in line 1 as her "offspring."

21. (C) The narrator "washes" her poetry's "face" but still sees more "defects." In "rubbing" away another error, she actually creates more ("still made a flaw").

22. (B) The narrator refers to her poetry as her child. Her child "runs" in its lines. Its "feet"—in this case, a pun—are its patterned cadence or its metrical feet (an iamb, for instance, is a type of foot; iambic pentameter features five iambic

feet per line, as seen in this poem). Even though she stretches the "joints" of her poem to make it "run" better, the lines are still more "hobbling" than is "meet," or appropriate. Thus, the meter is imperfect.

**23. (C)** The gloss note tells us that "vulgars" are "common people." The narrator says that she must dress her poetry in "homespun cloth" rather than in "better dress." In other words, the poetry lacks elegance, and for this reason it is appropriate for the common people.

**24. (E)** She warns her work to stay out of the hands of critics; if critics do not get hold of the work, then they cannot criticize it. She then tells her book to walk where it is known. Those familiar with the author's work would be more likely to accept it.

**25. (A)** By criticizing the technical features of her poetry, the narrator is really criticizing her own talent. She moves then to conditional acceptance when she claims the poetry for her own, but she still wants to edit what she has written. Finally, she returns to self-criticism when she implies that her work is plain ("homespun") and that she herself is "poor."

**26. (D)** The narrator makes no references to ancient Greco-Roman deities, customs, or history.

(A) is wrong because we see an AABBCC rhyme scheme in iambic pentameter—the definition of heroic couplets.

(B) is wrong because the narrator addresses her poetry as if it were human—an example of apostrophe.

Metaphorical conceit appears throughout the poem. The narrator begins with the idea that her poetry is her offspring; then she continues with other images that develop this initial idea. So (C) is wrong.

A humble tone predominates in this poem because the narrator is so self-effacing. Thus, (E) cannot work.

**27. (D)** Most of the passage is dedicated to the friction between Jude, hired to scare crows away from the corn, and his employer Farmer Troutham, who sees that Jude is too sympathetic with the birds to perform his job adequately.

**28. (C)** This answer assumes too much. The passage never reveals any previous punishment administered to Jude. For all we know, Farmer Troutham's thrashing is a first-and-only occurrence.

**29. (E)** The operative word in this question is "echoes." We are looking for this sudden action of starting up simultaneously to tie into some previous idea. Since the birds and Jude both start up, and since Jude has expressed a common link to the birds, (E) is the most likely answer.

**30. (B)** The farmer is described as "the great Troutham" who has a "red face glaring"; this character is imposing, indeed.

Since we aren't told what Troutham is thinking in these lines, and since we get no dialogue from him here, we cannot say that he is either insightful, disappointed, cranky, or inquisitive. So neither (A), (C), (D), or (E) will work.

**31. (A)** This response is wrong for the same reason that (C) is wrong in question 28: (A) assumes too much about Jude's recent past. We haven't been given any information about his relationship with Troutham prior to this incident.

In these lines, Troutham threatens to "tickle [Jude's] breeches." Then he proceeds to whack Jude with the clacker. Here, we have an example of understatement, and (B) becomes incorrect.

Troutham in these lines makes a reference to Jude's wages and implies that the boy has not been earning them. So (C) cannot work.

Troutham accuses Jude of "idling" at the schoolmaster's, so he must not highly esteem contact with educators; thus, (D) seems to be incorrect.

(E) doesn't work because, in lines 35–38, Troutham imitates Jude's speaking to the birds.

**32. (D)** Troutham's dialogue is described as "saluting" Jude's ears with "impassioned rhetoric;" certainly the farmer's comments are not as lofty as they are made to sound. Yet they are delivered by the farmer as if his ideas are crucial. In elevating what Troutham says, the narrator not only makes Troutham seem self-important but also betrays a mocking tone directed at Jude's irate employer.

**33. (D)** Since the crop in the ground has little to do with Jude's immediate situation, (D) is the most likely answer.

Jude has a "centrifugal tendency" because he is being swung around by Troutham; thus, (A) does not work.

(B) is incorrect because, in describing Jude as a "hooked fish," the narrator shows us that Jude has little control over his immediate situation.

The world is spinning "round and round him," thus demonstrating that Jude is helplessly whirled by Troutham; (C) is incorrect.

"O, O, O!" are the exclamations pouring out of Jude while he is being spun. He is so helpless that he cannot speak coherently. Therefore, (E) does not work.

**34. (D)** Lines 50–60 are full of images such as "whirling child," centrifugal tendency," and "amazing circular race." These lines even end with circular exclamations: "O, O, O!"

**35. (C)** The clacker relates directly to the situation's irony because it creates the noise being mistaken by the distant workers. The distant workers are a part of the irony because they are the ones mistaking the clacker's noise for Jude's tenacious crow scaring. The church tower is part of the irony because, even though Troutham has helped pay for it as a testament to his "love for God and man," he displays none of this love while beating Jude.

The mist is the only element that plays no direct part in this irony; if we leave the mist out of the description, we still see the irony of Troutham's behavior and of the workers' assumptions.

**36. (D)** In the last paragraph, the narrator is instantly able to shift his focus from Troutham and Jude to the workers, who are far away. The narrator is also able to peer into the thoughts of these workers without their saying anything. Such scope and insight are characteristic of the omniscient narrator.

**37. (E)** As depressing and unenlightening as this thought is, the text seems to support it. Jude is kind to the birds; Troutham misinterprets the action as laziness or willful dereliction of duty. Troutham does not reward Jude's kindness but rather punishes him for not doing his job.

**38. (B)** In the first two words, "Come sleep!" we understand that the speaker wants restfulness. In line 6, we know that it is Despair who is causing the disquiet in his mind, and by line 8, we even see that the speaker is willing to pay for sleep's services.

**39. (E)** In dramatic irony, the audience knows something in the narrative that a character does not. From the beginning to the end of this poem, however, we know as much as the speaker does; the text gives us no hidden information on sleep, Despair, or even Stella.

(A) is incorrect because the speaker is talking to sleep as if it were human; the apostrophe is there.

Direct comparisons are made between sleep and the following: a knot, a baiting place, a balm, wealth, and a release. These lines are full of metaphor, so (B) is wrong.

How can a poor man have wealth? How can a prisoner still be a prisoner and be released? These paradoxes are explained by the nature of sleep. Sleep is a luxury for a poor man, perhaps helping him to forget his impoverishment for a while; sleep also helps a prisoner to escape from confinement. These lines feature two paradoxes, so (C) is wrong.

Each of the metaphors describing sleep is a complimentary epithet: "sleep, the certain knot of peace," etc. Such a string of epithets is given to people of high rank. Thus, the respectful tone is present, and (D) is incorrect.

**40. (C)** Examining the context in which the word is used, we see that "indifferent" describes a judge. We would expect a judge to be impartial, so (C) makes sense. Furthermore, this judge deals with the "high and the low." If the judge is unbiased, then we have a logical relation to these groups of people. Finally, the rest of the epithets in the previous lines are complimentary, as is "unbiased." Thus, (C) is the logical choice from a contextual viewpoint.

**41. (D)** Despair is throwing those darts at the speaker, and since the speaker is asking to be shielded from Despair's darts, he wants protection from hopelessness.

**42. (B)** We have only the text to rely on, and (B) is the only response that stays within the text. We know that the speaker wants sleep, and we know that if he stays awake, he will think of Stella in a lively way. (B) deals with both of these conditions.

**43. (D)** The tribute consists of items such as "smooth pillows," the "sweetest bed," a dark, silent "chamber," and the like. These are obviously associated with sleep—in a sense, already belonging to it—so it seems strange that the speaker would be offering them as tribute. The speaker even admits that "these things" belong to sleep "by right" (line 12).

**44. (A)** If sleep does not accept the speaker's tribute—if the pillows, bed, and quiet chamber "Move not [sleep's] heavy grace" (line 13)—then it will observe "Stella's image" (line 14) in the speaker, who is left to lie awake ("livelier," line 14) and think of his love.

**45. (E)** The speaker opens the poem with respectful epithets. He then asks sleep for a kind of military protection against Despair and his own "civil wars." He ends by offering sleep a "tribute." All of these ideas show that the speaker is treating sleep as a respected authority.

**46. (C)** In lines 31–32, the narrator's exclamation of "Let me be free!" cannot make his desires more obvious. His determination to achieve his desires can be found in excerpts such as lines 47–48: "Let but the first opportunity offer, and come what will, I am off."

**47. (E)** The quality that the narrator admires about the ships is their ability to go anywhere, whereas he can go nowhere without his master's consent. Likewise, lines 4–8 describe the ships' sails from the freemen's point of view ("delightful") and from his own ("so many shrouded ghosts").

**48. (B)** The experience is made dignified by word choices such as "lofty," "noble," and "mighty." It seems sacred because he views the ships "in the deep stillness of a summer's Sabbath," as if he is part of a worship service.

**49. (E)** The most obvious evidence for this answer occurs in line 14: "My thoughts would compel utterance."

**50. (A)** We see the device in such paired opposites as "loosed" and "fast," "free" and "slave, merrily" and "sadly," and "fly" and "confined."

**51. (E)** The narrator notices these waters with an "Alas!" (line 25). They are a boundary keeping him from the ships that could take him to freedom.

**52. (E)** The narrator asks questions that are not answered, but that draw attention to his situation; therefore, they are rhetorical. His desperation can be seen in the exclamation points, in his description of slavery as the "hottest hell," and in his jumping from topic to topic. The question

"Is there any God?" offers a theological scope, and the succeeding question, "Why am I a slave?" has a metaphysical base. Finally, the speaker's new resolution occurs in this line: "I will run away."

**53. (C)** We see the narrator's perseverance in these lines: "Meanwhile, I will try to bear up under the yoke. I am not the only slave in the world. Why should I fret? I can bear as much as any of them." He uses the word *bear* twice. He is willing to endure much in order to be free eventually. His rationalizations come here: "Besides, I am but a boy, and all boys are bound to some one. It may be my misery in slavery will only increase my happiness when I get free." His slavery, he reasons, is like a young man's apprenticeship; it's tolerable for now if viewed as temporary. Furthermore, this misery that he must go through will actually increase his happiness in freedom later: a rationalization of his condition.

**54. (D)** The "beautiful vessels" are "robed in purest white" and are "delightful" when "freemen" see them (lines 4–5). Also, the narrator addresses them as "freedom's swift-winged angels" in lines 21–22.

**55. (A)** The speaker says that he has "studied many times" the engraving on his tombstone. This continual study leads him to a conclusion that he has misspent his life. Although he realizes now what life is supposed to be about, he makes this realization too late, after his death. He ends the poem not on an optimistic note but with an image that recalls the boat on his tombstone: the symbol of his fear.

**56. (E)** One has to be careful in examining the wording of this response. The speaker says that the furled sail was intended to describe the experience of death: docking the ship after a long voyage or something like that. However, according to the speaker, the furled sail *more accurately* describes his life: his playing it safe, his avoiding opportunity and emotional pain.

Line 2 helps us understand that the image is part of the speaker's tombstone, so (A) cannot be chosen.

Line 4 implies that the intended meaning of the image was to describe the speaker's destination: death. However, he says, "In truth, it pictures *not* my destination." So (B) does not work.

(C) cannot be right because the verb "pictures" in line 4 proves that the boat is supposed to be a metaphor.

Line 5 provides the speaker's new meaning for the boat image, a contrast to the intended meaning in line 4; thus, (D) is wrong.

**57. (B)** Clearly, the speaker "shrank" from the "disillusionment" of love, "was afraid" when "Sorrow knocked at [his] door," and "dreaded" the chances of ambition. Fear held him back in every instance.

**58. (A)** The speaker is explaining what life should be like: a series of accepted risks. Since he has already passed his time on earth and missed his chance, he is not talking about the consequences of his life but about an alternative to the safety in which he lived.

The speaker is discussing what he has learned now about the life from his past; (B) is therefore incorrect.

The speaker is using the personal details of his life to draw a lesson from which all people can learn: "*we* [emphasis added] must lift the sail/And catch the winds of destiny" (lines 10–11). Thus, (C) cannot work.

The image of lifting the sail in line 10 refers to the furled sail of the boat in line 3; (D) does not work.

The explanation for (A) discusses why (E) is wrong.

**59. (D)** These lines discuss a life with meaning versus a life without meaning. The speaker says that meaning may produce madness, "But life without meaning" leads to "restlessness and vague desire." He calls this last state of being a "torture." Thus, the implication is that madness is a better state than restlessness, etc.

**60.** **(D)** There are ships in the Bible but none described or used as this narrator does.

The metaphorical conceit appears as the extended comparison between the narrator and the boat. (A) therefore cannot be a choice.

(B) does not work because sorrow knocks at the speaker's door and ambition calls to him.

The poem is written in a discursive style because its point is to discuss a topic: here, the meaning of life. Thus, (C) is wrong.

There is no set meter or rhyme scheme in this poem, so it is written in free verse. (E) is now negated.

**61.** **(C)** The speaker says that we must "catch the winds of destiny/Wherever they drive the boat" (lines 11–12). Thus, we must be open to forces that we cannot control. The alternative is to rest in the harbor "longing for the sea and yet afraid" (line 16).

# HOW TO CALCULATE YOUR SCORE

**Step 1: Figure out your raw score.** Use the answer key to count the number of questions you answered correctly and the number of questions you answered incorrectly. (Do not count any questions you left blank.) Multiply the number wrong by 0.25 and subtract the result from the number correct. Round the result to the nearest whole number. This is your raw score.

## SAT Subject Test: Literature Practice Test 3

| Number right | Number wrong | Raw score |
|---|---|---|

$$\boxed{\phantom{00}} - \left(0.25 \times \boxed{\phantom{00}}\right) = \boxed{\phantom{00}}$$

**Step 2: Find your scaled score.** In the Score Conversion Table below, find your raw score (rounded to the nearest whole number) in one of the columns to the left. The score directly to the right of that number will be your scaled score.

A note on your practice test scores: Don't take these scores too literally. Practice test conditions cannot precisely mirror real test conditions. Your actual SAT Subject Test: Literature score will almost certainly vary from your practice test scores. However, your scores on the practice tests will give you a rough idea of your range on the actual exam.

## Conversion Table

| Raw | Scaled | Raw | Scaled | Raw | Scaled | Raw | Scaled |
|---|---|---|---|---|---|---|---|
| 63 | 800 | 43 | 700 | 23 | 510 | 3 | 330 |
| 62 | 800 | 42 | 690 | 22 | 500 | 2 | 320 |
| 61 | 800 | 41 | 680 | 21 | 500 | 1 | 310 |
| 60 | 800 | 40 | 670 | 20 | 490 | 0 | 300 |
| 59 | 800 | 39 | 660 | 19 | 480 | -1 | 290 |
| 58 | 800 | 38 | 650 | 18 | 470 | -2 | 280 |
| 57 | 800 | 37 | 640 | 17 | 460 | -3 | 280 |
| 56 | 790 | 36 | 630 | 16 | 450 | -4 | 270 |
| 55 | 790 | 35 | 620 | 15 | 440 | -5 | 260 |
| 54 | 780 | 34 | 610 | 14 | 430 | -6 | 250 |
| 53 | 780 | 33 | 610 | 13 | 420 | -7 | 250 |
| 52 | 780 | 32 | 600 | 12 | 410 | -8 | 240 |
| 51 | 770 | 31 | 590 | 11 | 410 | -9 | 230 |
| 50 | 760 | 30 | 580 | 10 | 400 | -10 | 220 |
| 49 | 750 | 29 | 570 | 9 | 390 | -11 | 210 |
| 48 | 740 | 28 | 560 | 8 | 380 | -12 | 200 |
| 47 | 730 | 27 | 550 | 7 | 370 | -13 | 200 |
| 46 | 720 | 26 | 540 | 6 | 360 | -14 | 200 |
| 45 | 710 | 25 | 530 | 5 | 350 | | |
| 44 | 710 | 24 | 520 | 4 | 340 | | |

# Practice Test 3
# Answer Grid

1. Ⓐ Ⓑ Ⓒ Ⓓ Ⓔ
2. Ⓐ Ⓑ Ⓒ Ⓓ Ⓔ
3. Ⓐ Ⓑ Ⓒ Ⓓ Ⓔ
4. Ⓐ Ⓑ Ⓒ Ⓓ Ⓔ
5. Ⓐ Ⓑ Ⓒ Ⓓ Ⓔ
6. Ⓐ Ⓑ Ⓒ Ⓓ Ⓔ
7. Ⓐ Ⓑ Ⓒ Ⓓ Ⓔ
8. Ⓐ Ⓑ Ⓒ Ⓓ Ⓔ
9. Ⓐ Ⓑ Ⓒ Ⓓ Ⓔ
10. Ⓐ Ⓑ Ⓒ Ⓓ Ⓔ
11. Ⓐ Ⓑ Ⓒ Ⓓ Ⓔ
12. Ⓐ Ⓑ Ⓒ Ⓓ Ⓔ
13. Ⓐ Ⓑ Ⓒ Ⓓ Ⓔ
14. Ⓐ Ⓑ Ⓒ Ⓓ Ⓔ
15. Ⓐ Ⓑ Ⓒ Ⓓ Ⓔ
16. Ⓐ Ⓑ Ⓒ Ⓓ Ⓔ
17. Ⓐ Ⓑ Ⓒ Ⓓ Ⓔ
18. Ⓐ Ⓑ Ⓒ Ⓓ Ⓔ
19. Ⓐ Ⓑ Ⓒ Ⓓ Ⓔ
20. Ⓐ Ⓑ Ⓒ Ⓓ Ⓔ
21. Ⓐ Ⓑ Ⓒ Ⓓ Ⓔ

22. Ⓐ Ⓑ Ⓒ Ⓓ Ⓔ
23. Ⓐ Ⓑ Ⓒ Ⓓ Ⓔ
24. Ⓐ Ⓑ Ⓒ Ⓓ Ⓔ
25. Ⓐ Ⓑ Ⓒ Ⓓ Ⓔ
26. Ⓐ Ⓑ Ⓒ Ⓓ Ⓔ
27. Ⓐ Ⓑ Ⓒ Ⓓ Ⓔ
28. Ⓐ Ⓑ Ⓒ Ⓓ Ⓔ
29. Ⓐ Ⓑ Ⓒ Ⓓ Ⓔ
30. Ⓐ Ⓑ Ⓒ Ⓓ Ⓔ
31. Ⓐ Ⓑ Ⓒ Ⓓ Ⓔ
32. Ⓐ Ⓑ Ⓒ Ⓓ Ⓔ
33. Ⓐ Ⓑ Ⓒ Ⓓ Ⓔ
34. Ⓐ Ⓑ Ⓒ Ⓓ Ⓔ
35. Ⓐ Ⓑ Ⓒ Ⓓ Ⓔ
36. Ⓐ Ⓑ Ⓒ Ⓓ Ⓔ
37. Ⓐ Ⓑ Ⓒ Ⓓ Ⓔ
38. Ⓐ Ⓑ Ⓒ Ⓓ Ⓔ
39. Ⓐ Ⓑ Ⓒ Ⓓ Ⓔ
40. Ⓐ Ⓑ Ⓒ Ⓓ Ⓔ
41. Ⓐ Ⓑ Ⓒ Ⓓ Ⓔ
42. Ⓐ Ⓑ Ⓒ Ⓓ Ⓔ

43. Ⓐ Ⓑ Ⓒ Ⓓ Ⓔ
44. Ⓐ Ⓑ Ⓒ Ⓓ Ⓔ
45. Ⓐ Ⓑ Ⓒ Ⓓ Ⓔ
46. Ⓐ Ⓑ Ⓒ Ⓓ Ⓔ
47. Ⓐ Ⓑ Ⓒ Ⓓ Ⓔ
48. Ⓐ Ⓑ Ⓒ Ⓓ Ⓔ
49. Ⓐ Ⓑ Ⓒ Ⓓ Ⓔ
50. Ⓐ Ⓑ Ⓒ Ⓓ Ⓔ
51. Ⓐ Ⓑ Ⓒ Ⓓ Ⓔ
52. Ⓐ Ⓑ Ⓒ Ⓓ Ⓔ
53. Ⓐ Ⓑ Ⓒ Ⓓ Ⓔ
54. Ⓐ Ⓑ Ⓒ Ⓓ Ⓔ
55. Ⓐ Ⓑ Ⓒ Ⓓ Ⓔ
56. Ⓐ Ⓑ Ⓒ Ⓓ Ⓔ
57. Ⓐ Ⓑ Ⓒ Ⓓ Ⓔ
58. Ⓐ Ⓑ Ⓒ Ⓓ Ⓔ
59. Ⓐ Ⓑ Ⓒ Ⓓ Ⓔ
60. Ⓐ Ⓑ Ⓒ Ⓓ Ⓔ
61. Ⓐ Ⓑ Ⓒ Ⓓ Ⓔ
62. Ⓐ Ⓑ Ⓒ Ⓓ Ⓔ
63. Ⓐ Ⓑ Ⓒ Ⓓ Ⓔ

# Practice Test 3

*Questions 1–9 refer to the following poem. After reading the poem, choose the best answer to each question.*

> Look in thy glass and tell the face thou viewest
> Now is the time that face should form another
> Whose fresh repair if now thou not renewest,
> Thou dost beguile the world, unbless some mother.

*Line*
*(5)* For where is she so fair whose uneared womb          *uneared* unplowed
> Disdains the tillage of thy husbandry?          *tillage* plowing
> Or who is he so fond will be the tomb
> Of his self-love to stop posterity?
> Thou art thy mother's glass, and she in thee

*(10)* Calls back the lovely April of her prime;
> So thou, in windows of thine age shalt see
> Despite of wrinkles, this, thy golden time.
> But if thou live, remembered not to be,
> Die single, and thine image dies with thee.

(1591)

1. The person being addressed in the poem is almost certainly

   (A) a baby.

   (B) a toddler.

   (C) a boy.

   (D) a young man.

   (E) an old man.

2. Within the context of the first four lines, the word *glass* must mean

   (A) the glassy surface of a still body of water.

   (B) a mirror belonging to the addressee.

   (C) the windowpane set in a house wall.

   (D) a goblet, mug, or tumbler.

   (E) eyeglasses.

**GO ON TO THE NEXT PAGE**

3. The principal imagery in lines 5–6 relates to

   (A) bureaucratic paperwork.

   (B) farming.

   (C) travel.

   (D) a county fair.

   (E) geology.

4. "Self-love" is called a "tomb" (lines 7–8) in this poem because

   (A) vanity always leads to the grave.

   (B) women often wish to kill narcissists.

   (C) egotism can cause one to ignore life-threatening circumstances.

   (D) unearthing a new discovery is a way of showing oneself love.

   (E) unlike love for someone else, self-love precludes procreation.

5. In lines 9–12, the narrator says that the addressee could do all of the following EXCEPT

   (A) act as a "glass" for his mother.

   (B) help his mother to recall her youth.

   (C) return to his mother when she calls for him.

   (D) find his [the addressee's] youth in his own offspring.

   (E) take time to reflect when he is older.

6. The most obvious example of structural parallelism occurs in what lines?

   (A) 1 and 2

   (B) 1 and 4

   (C) 4 and 8

   (D) 5 and 7

   (E) 9 and 10

7. The most obvious example of antithesis occurs in what line(s)?

   (A) 1 and 2

   (B) 5 only

   (C) 7 and 8

   (D) 10 only

   (E) 13 and 14

8. In lines 13–14, and throughout this sonnet, the narrator *mainly* wants the addressee to

   (A) stop maltreating women.

   (B) marvel at the way the mother in line 9 raised the addressee.

   (C) enjoy himself at the fair.

   (D) become a glass merchant.

   (E) perpetuate his [the addressee's] youth through reproduction.

9. The poem is an example of

   (A) a sonnet.

   (B) heroic couplets.

   (C) a pastoral.

   (D) an ode.

   (E) terza rima.

**GO ON TO THE NEXT PAGE**

*Questions 10–17 refer to the following passage. After reading the passage, choose the best answer to each question.*

[In the following passage, the narrator is proposing an idea "For Preventing the Children of Poor People in Ireland from Being a Burden to Their Parents or Country, and for Making Them Beneficial to the Public"]

I shall now therefore humbly propose my own thoughts, which I hope will not be liable to the least objection.

Line
(5)  I have been assured by a very knowing American of my acquaintance in London that a young healthy child well nursed is at a year old a most delicious, nourishing, and wholesome food, whether stewed, roasted, baked, or boiled; and I make no doubt that it will equally serve in a
(10) fricassee or a ragout.*

I do therefore humbly offer it to public consideration that of the hundred and twenty thousand children already computed†, twenty thousand may be reserved for breed, whereof only
(15) one-fourth part be males; which is more than we allow to sheep, black cattle, or swine; and my reason is that these children are seldom the fruits of marriage, a circumstance not much regarded by our savages; therefore one male will be
(20) sufficient to serve four females. That the remaining hundred thousand may, at a year old, be offered in sale to the persons of quality and fortune through the kingdom; always advising the mother to let them suck plentifully in the last
(25) month, so as to render them plump and fat for a good table. A child will make two dishes at an entertainment for friends; and when the family dines alone, the fore or hind quarter will make a reasonable dish, and seasoned with a little pepper
(30) or salt will be very good boiled on the fourth day, especially in winter.

I have reckoned upon a medium that a child just born will weigh twelve pounds, and in a solar year, if tolerably nursed, will increase to twenty-
(35) eight pounds.

I grant this food will be somewhat dear, and therefore very proper for landlords, who, as they have already devoured most of the parents, seem to have the best title to the children.

(1729)

*a spicy meat stew
†that is, the number of children annually born to Irish parents who cannot support them

10. In the passage, the narrator's tone is

(A) earnest.
(B) condescending.
(C) understated.
(D) doubtful.
(E) sentimental.

11. In the passage, the writer's purpose seems to be

(A) liberating.
(B) diplomatic.
(C) destructive.
(D) satirical.
(E) elevating.

12. By offering a variety of cooking methods in lines 8–10, the writer is trying to be

(A) shocking.
(B) helpful.
(C) thorough.
(D) contemplative.
(E) erudite.

**GO ON TO THE NEXT PAGE**

13. The number of male children that the narrator proposes for breeding in lines 11–15 is

    (A) 120,000.

    (B) 30,000.

    (C) 20,000.

    (D) 5,000.

    (E) 4.

14. In lines 15–20, how does the narrator suggest that this breeding number (question 13) is acceptable?

    I. Many of the poor do not marry anyway.

    II. It is a more humane consideration than that given livestock.

    III. The poor may be compared with uncivilized people.

    (A) I only

    (B) III only

    (C) I and II only

    (D) II and III only

    (E) I, II, and III

15. In lines 20–23, the narrator promotes what kind of people as the probable consumer for this new "product"?

    (A) The poor themselves

    (B) The rich

    (C) Savages

    (D) Europeans

    (E) Americans

16. The narrator's estimation in the fourth paragraph makes his general proposal appear

    (A) profitable and practical.

    (B) uncertain and unmanageable.

    (C) kind and considerate.

    (D) enlightening and entertaining.

    (E) serendipitous and serene.

17. The true purpose of the passage can best be seen in which aspect of the last paragraph?

    (A) The narrator's admission that the "food" will be expensive

    (B) The idea of landlords as herders

    (C) The narrator's switch from a humble proposal to an adamant demand

    (D) The mention of a "best title"

    (E) The double meaning of the word "devoured"

**GO ON TO THE NEXT PAGE**

Questions 18–27 refer to the following poem. After reading the poem, choose the best answer to each question.

See with what simplicity
This nymph begins her golden days!
In the green grass she loves to lie,
Line    And there with her fair aspect tames
(5)    The wilder flowers and gives them names,
But only with the roses plays,
            And them does tell
What color best becomes them, and what smell.

Who can foretell for what high cause
(10)    This darling of the gods was born!
Yet this is she whose chaster laws
The wanton love shall one day fear,
And under her command severe
See his bow broke and ensigns torn.            *ensigns*    flags
(15)            Happy who can
Appease this virtuous enemy of man!

O then let me in time compound
And parley with those conquering eyes            *parley*    speak
Ere they have tried their force to wound,
(20)    Ere, with their glancing wheels, they drive
In triumph over hearts that strive,
And them that yield but more despise:
            Let me be laid,
Where I may see thy glories from some shade.

(25)    Meantime, whilst every verdant thing
Itself does at thy beauty charm,
Reform the errors of the spring;
Make that the tulips may have share
Of sweetness, seeing they are fair:
(30)    And roses of their thorns disarm:
            But most procure
That violets may a longer age endure.

But O, young beauty of the woods,
Whom nature courts with fruit and flowers,
(35)    Gather the flowers, but spare the buds,
Lest Flora angry at thy crime            *Flora*    Roman goddess of flowers
To kill her infants in their prime,
Do quickly make th'example yours:
            And ere we see,
(40)    Nip in the blossom all our hopes and thee.

(1681)

18. The narrator's tone in the poem seems to be

    (A) appreciative, then commanding.
    (B) authoritative, then rebuking.
    (C) apologetic, then inquisitive.
    (D) admiring, then admonishing.
    (E) aggressive, then passive.

19. Within the context of lines 1–8, the relationship between nature and the "nymph" shows that

    (A) she is as innocent as nature, yet also has control over nature.
    (B) she is as lovely as nature, yet is as wild as nature.
    (C) she is as young as spring, yet as mature as winter.
    (D) she is as simple as nature, yet can create chaos in nature.
    (E) she is as delicate as a flower, but as robust as the narrator.

20. In the context of lines 11–14, the word *laws* must mean

    (A) society's rules of conduct.
    (B) government restrictions.
    (C) natural behavior.
    (D) religious guidelines.
    (E) self-determined morals.

21. In the context of lines 11–14, the personified "love" has all of the following characteristics EXCEPT that

    (A) he is portrayed as Cupid.
    (B) he represents sensuality or physical passion.
    (C) he desires more than the gods will allow.
    (D) he, like nature, is under the nymph's influence.
    (E) he has been defeated by "chaster laws."

22. The "virtuous enemy of man" in line 16 is

    (A) the narrator.
    (B) the nymph.
    (C) love.
    (D) poetry.
    (E) chastity.

23. What are the "hearts" of line 21 trying to accomplish?

    (A) They are trying to understand the mysteries of the nymph.
    (B) They want to convince the nymph of their honor.
    (C) They are desirous of sensual contact with the nymph.
    (D) They wish for the nymph to take control of them.
    (E) They wish to take control of nature.

**GO ON TO THE NEXT PAGE**

24. The tulips, roses, and violets of lines 28–32 serve what purpose in the poem?

    I. They are examples of natural flaws.

    II. They are opportunities to display the nymph's powers.

    III. They are symbols of the nymph's fleeting beauty.

    (A) I only

    (B) III only

    (C) I and II only

    (D) II and III only

    (E) I, II, and III

25. According to lines 33–40, if the nymph will "spare the buds" (line 35), she will also accomplish all of the following EXCEPT

    (A) to assure the future growth of well-loved flowers.

    (B) to avoid Flora's wrath.

    (C) to preserve the narrator's hopes for the nymph.

    (D) to prevent her own ruin.

    (E) to avert an offense against nature.

26. The "hopes" mentioned in line 40 are most closely aligned with the desires of

    (A) the "gods" in line 10.

    (B) "The wanton love" in line 12.

    (C) the "conquering eyes" in line 18.

    (D) "hearts" in line 21.

    (E) the "spring" of line 27.

27. The narrator's treatment of the addressee is both

    (A) exalting and demanding.

    (B) suggestive and rigorous.

    (C) chiding and condescending.

    (D) pejorative and threatening.

    (E) complimentary and seductive.

*Questions 28–37 refer to the following passage. After reading the passage, choose the best answer to each question.*

Mrs. Moreen, however, continued to be convincing; sitting there with her fifty francs she talked and repeated, as women repeat, and bored and irritated him, while he leaned against the
(5) wall with his hands in the pocket of his wrapper, drawing it together round his legs and looking over the head of his visitor at the grey negations of his window. She wound up with saying: "You see I bring you a definite proposal."

(10) "A definite proposal?"

"To make our relations regular, as it were—to put them on a comfortable footing."

"I see—it's a system," said Pemberton. "A kind of blackmail."

(15) Mrs. Moreen bounded up, which was what the young man wanted.

"What do you mean by that?"

"You practice on one's fears—one's fears about the child if one should go away."

(20) "And pray, with whom *should* a child be but those whom he loves most?"

"If you think that, why don't you dismiss me?"

"Do you pretend that he loves you more than he loves *us*?" cried Mrs. Moreen.

(25) "I think he ought to. I make sacrifices for him. Though I've heard of those *you* make, I don't see them.

Mrs. Moreen stared a moment; then, with emotion, she grasped Pemberton's hand. "*Will* you
(30) make it—the sacrifice?"

Pemberton burst out laughing. "I'll see—I'll do what I can—I'll stay a little longer. Your calculation is just—I *do* hate intensely to give him up; I'm fond of him and he interests me deeply, in
(35) spite of the inconvenience I suffer. You know my situation perfectly; I haven't a penny in the world, and, occupied as I am with Morgan, I'm unable to earn money."

Mrs. Moreen tapped her undressed arm with
(40) her folded banknote. "Can't you write articles? Can't you translate as *I* do?"

"I don't know about translating; it's wretchedly paid."

"I am glad to earn what I can," said Mrs.
(45) Moreen virtuously, with her head held high.

"You ought to tell me who you do it for." Pemberton paused a moment, and she said nothing; so he added: "I've tried to turn off some sketches, but the magazines won't have them—
(50) they've declined with thanks."

"You see then you're not such a phoenix—to have such pretensions," smiled his interlocutress.

"I haven't time to do things properly," Pemberton went on. Then as it came over him
(55) that he was almost abjectly good-natured to give these explanations he added: "If I stay on longer it must be on one condition—that Morgan shall know distinctly on what footing I am."

Mrs. Moreen hesitated. "Surely you don't want
(60) to show off* to a child?"

"To show *you* off, do you mean?"

Again Mrs. Moreen hesitated, but this time it was to produce a still finer flower. "And you talk of blackmail!"

(65) "You can easily prevent it," said Pemberton.

"And *you* talk of practicing on fears," Mrs. Moreen continued.

"Yes, there's no doubt I'm a great scoundrel."

(1892)

*show off* expose the situation

GO ON TO THE NEXT PAGE

28. The relationship between Mrs. Moreen and Morgan's tutor, Pemberton, is best described as

(A) informal and uncomplicated.

(B) romantic but stalled.

(C) amiable yet teasing.

(D) tense and unstable.

(E) competitive but friendly.

29. In lines 1–9, which of the following is physical evidence that Pemberton is "bored and irritated" (lines 3–4)?

I. His standing position

II. The condition of his "wrapper"

III. His gaze

IV. His facial expression

(A) I only

(B) III only

(C) I and II only

(D) I, II, and III only

(E) I, II, III, and IV

30. The topics of discussion in lines 10–27 include all of the following EXCEPT

(A) the possible termination of Pemberton's employment.

(B) a raise for Pemberton after a long period of devoted service.

(C) a concern for Morgan's emotional welfare.

(D) the stabilization of the employer/ employee relationship.

(E) the ethics of Mrs. Moreen's conduct.

31. The "sacrifice" to which Mrs. Moreen refers in line 30 must be

(A) a different method for Pemberton to approach Morgan's instruction.

(B) Pemberton's sustained endurance of Mrs. Moreen's advisements.

(C) the temporary postponement of Pemberton's departure.

(D) Pemberton's continued employment with additional duties added.

(E) the attempt to ignore Morgan's idiosyncratic behavior.

32. The internal conflict that Pemberton endures is a battle between

(A) his professional responsibilities and his attraction to his employer.

(B) his current employment and his desire to try a new vocation.

(C) his present attitude about Mrs. Moreen and his urge to change that attitude.

(D) his desire for his employer's respect and his own self-loathing.

(E) his need for increased finances and his devotion to Morgan.

33. One can infer in lines 39–52 that Mrs. Moreen feels

(A) superior to Pemberton.

(B) pity for Pemberton.

(C) attracted to Pemberton.

(D) hated by Pemberton.

(E) embarrassed by Pemberton.

**GO ON TO THE NEXT PAGE**

34. Pemberton's explanation in line 53 that he hasn't "time to do things properly" is

    (A) an implication that Mrs. Moreen interferes with his job.

    (B) a statement about the chaos in his private life.

    (C) a reminder of his dedication to Morgan's well-being.

    (D) a plea to spend less time with Morgan.

    (E) a complaint about the frustrations of being a tutor.

35. The exchange in lines 59–68 demonstrates all of the following EXCEPT that

    (A) the characters use the phrase "show off" differently from each other.

    (B) Pemberton is gaining an advantage over Mrs. Moreen.

    (C) Mrs. Moreen, in a way, is acknowledging her wrongdoing.

    (D) Mrs. Moreen is more concerned about Morgan than Pemberton.

    (E) both characters wish to be highly regarded by Morgan.

36. The quote "And you talk of blackmail" (lines 63–64) is called a "finer flower" because

    (A) it is a more original metaphor than Pemberton has used.

    (B) it is more difficult to understand than Mrs. Moreen's other comments.

    (C) it displays Mrs. Moreen's capacity for beautiful language.

    (D) it produces a devastating effect on Pemberton's composure.

    (E) it is a harsher retort than the one Pemberton has just given.

37. Throughout the passage, Pemberton represents himself as all of the following EXCEPT

    (A) talented.

    (B) burdened.

    (C) unhappy.

    (D) selfless.

    (E) concerned.

**GO ON TO THE NEXT PAGE**

*Questions 38–46 refer to the following poem. After reading the poem, choose the best answer to each question.*

        As if it were
forever that they move, that we
     keep moving—

*Line*      Under a wan sky where
(5)      as the lights went on a star
             pierced the haze and now
      follows steadily
               a constant
      above our six lanes
(10)     the dreamlike continuum...

And the people—ourselves!
   the humans from inside the
   cars apparent
   only at gasoline stops
(15)              unsure,
    eyeing each other

         drink coffee hastily at the
     slot machines & hurry
   back to the cars
(20)      vanish
     into them forever, to
     keep moving—

Houses now & then beyond the
sealed road, the trees / trees, bushes
(25)      passing by, passing
    the cars that
      keep moving ahead of
   us, past us, pressing behind us
             and
(30)        over left, those that come
     toward us shining too brightly
moving relentlessly

    in six lanes, gliding
north & south, speeding with
(35)  a slurred sound—

               (c. 1960)

38. The narrator regards humans in this poem as

(A) forever questioning.

(B) occasionally brilliant.

(C) constantly in motion.

(D) anxiously impatient.

(E) always at risk.

39. The "star" in line 5 serves what purpose for the second stanza?

(A) To give the lights of the highway an ethereal quality

(B) To provide a contrast of immobility to the continual action of the highway

(C) To draw the drivers' attention away from the monotony of routine action

(D) To lend a spiritual quality to the journey on the highway

(E) To symbolize the poet's yearning for rest

40. Considering the "wan sky" and the "haze" mentioned in the second stanza, what quality would the reader logically attach to the phrase "dreamlike continuum"?

(A) A sleepy state of being

(B) A progression of colorful images

(C) A grotesque masquerade

(D) A deceptively nightmarish existence

(E) An undisturbed fantasy

**GO ON TO THE NEXT PAGE**

41. The shift in focus within line 11 is most like the shift in

    (A) line 2.

    (B) line 4.

    (C) line 5.

    (D) line 6.

    (E) line 9.

42. All of the following could be said about the "humans" in lines 11–22 EXCEPT that

    (A) the appearances they make outside of their cars are brief.

    (B) their actions seem to be influenced by their cars.

    (C) their existence inside their cars seems more important than that outside.

    (D) the speed of their actions is different when they are outside of their cars.

    (E) they are uncommunicative and perhaps even suspicious of one another.

43. Within the context of the fifth stanza, the use of the word "sealed" (line 24) instead of tarred or paved creates an effect of

    (A) fatefulness.

    (B) sanitation.

    (C) isolation.

    (D) availability.

    (E) cessation.

44. Phrases such as "pressing behind us" (line 28) and "shining too brightly" (line 31) add not only speed to the experience of highway driving but also

    (A) friendship.

    (B) intensity.

    (C) expectation.

    (D) discord.

    (E) maliciousness.

45. The alliterated *s* in the last stanza serves to

    (A) portray the highway as an evil, hissing serpent.

    (B) exemplify the air let out of a tire to show the emptiness of this experience.

    (C) embody the wind as it whistles around a speeding car.

    (D) mimic the continuity of highway driving.

    (E) make the lines more memorable, as they are the most important of the poem.

46. The action and speed of the poem's subject matter are mimicked by which of the following?

    I.   The brevity of the lines

    II.  The use of the abbreviating ampersand (&) instead of the word *and*

    III. The six stanzas mirroring "our six lanes" (line 9)

    IV.  The jaggedness of the line spacing

    (A) I and II only

    (B) II and III only

    (C) I, II, and IV only

    (D) I, III, and IV only

    (E) I, II, III, and IV

**GO ON TO THE NEXT PAGE**

*Questions 47–57 refer to the following passage. After reading the passage, choose the best answer to each question.*

Line
(5)

(10)

(15)

(20)

(25)

(30)

(35)

Well, children, where there is so much racket there must be something out of kilter. I think that 'twixt the Negroes of the South and the women at the North, all talking about rights, the white men will be in a fix pretty soon. But what's all this here talking about?

That man over there says that women need to be helped into carriages, and lifted over ditches, and to have the best place everywhere. Nobody ever helps me into carriages, or over mud-puddles, or gives me any best place! And ain't I a woman? Look at me! Look at my arm! I have ploughed and planted, and gathered into barns, and no man could head me! And ain't I a woman? I could work as much and eat as much as a man—when I could get it—and bear the lash as well! And ain't I a woman? I have borne thirteen children, and seen them all sold off to slavery, and when I cried out with my mother's grief, none but Jesus heard me! And ain't I a woman?

Then they talk about this thing in the head; what's this they call it? ["Intellect," someone whispers.] That's it honey. What's that got to do with women's rights or Negro's rights? If my cup won't hold but a pint, and yours holds a quart, wouldn't you be mean not to let me have my little half-measure full?

Then that little man in black there, he says women can't have as much rights as men, 'cause Christ* wasn't a woman! Where did your Christ come from? Where did your Christ come from? From God and a woman! Man had nothing to do with Him.

If the first woman God ever made† was strong enough to turn the world upside down all alone, these women together ought to be able to turn it back, and get it right side up again! And now they is asking to do it, the men better let them.

(40)

Obliged to you for hearing me, and now old Sojourner ain't got nothing more to say.

(1851)

* Jesus, who most Christians believe was conceived of the virgin Mary and God
† Eve, who, according to Judeo-Christian tradition, ate a forbidden fruit that ended Paradise on Earth

47. The person making this speech seems to be

(A) growing increasingly angry.
(B) preaching to a church congregation in the North.
(C) emphasizing the ignorance and weakness of white men.
(D) encouraging newly empowered women to help end slavery.
(E) responding to previous speakers.

48. Lines 1–6 contain all of the following EXCEPT

(A) an adage about disagreement.
(B) colloquial language.
(C) a plea for racial and sexual equality.
(D) a prediction about a social dilemma.
(E) an interrogatory transition.

GO ON TO THE NEXT PAGE

49. Regarding the ideas of "That man over there," the speaker uses herself as an example in lines 10–15 so that she can

(A) point out the injustice of her situation.

(B) create awareness for the plight of the female slave.

(C) arouse suspicion about Southern slaveholders.

(D) prove how unnecessary it is to coddle women.

(E) find out why she has been treated differently from other women.

50. Within the context of line 14, the word "head" is closest in meaning to

(A) surpass.

(B) punish.

(C) overcome.

(D) correct.

(E) delay.

51. Compared to lines 9–14, how do lines 17–20 alter the speaker's argument?

(A) She moves from examples of physical achievement to emotional capacity.

(B) She becomes more intensely aware of her audience.

(C) She moves from emotional appeal to rationalization.

(D) She begins using rhetorical questions.

(E) She switches her focus from herself to the people around her.

52. Concerning the speaker's discussion of "intellect" in lines 21–27, all of the following are true EXCEPT that

(A) she knows what "intellect" means but cannot produce the word on her own.

(B) she hints that the white men in the audience are not as intellectual as they think.

(C) she does not see how a lack of intellect denies people of their rights.

(D) she creates a logical analogy to make her point, thus ironically revealing the intellect about which she is speaking.

(E) even though she is criticizing previous ideas, she still maintains a friendliness in her delivery.

53. In the analogy of lines 24–27, what do the cup and the cup's contents represent?

(A) The cup is a person's rights; the law fills the cup.

(B) The cup is a person's rights; intellect fills the cup.

(C) The cup is intellect; education fills the cup.

(D) The cup is social privilege; intellect fills the cup.

(E) The cup is intellect; a person's rights fill the cup.

GO ON TO THE NEXT PAGE

54. All of the following are true about lines 28–33 EXCEPT that

(A) the "little man in black" has used Christian belief to further his arguments.

(B) the speaker is arguing on the same terms as the "little man in black."

(C) the speaker simultaneously exalts women and denies men exaltation in her argument.

(D) the speaker's exclamation in line 30 and her use of "little man in black" demonstrate outrage.

(E) the speaker's repetition of "Where did your Christ come from?" magnifies the importance of her next idea.

55. The speaker's reference to Eve in lines 34–38 serves what purpose?

(A) To make an older biblical reference in case an audience member is unfamiliar with Christianity

(B) To reinforce the power of women and the need to exercise this power

(C) To beg that women be given the opportunity to right the wrongs they brought into the world

(D) To show that women are as blessed by divine authority as men

(E) To propose that it is easier to destroy than to rebuild

56. The last two lines of the speech demonstrate what quality about the speaker?

(A) Embarrassment

(B) Humility

(C) Fatigue

(D) Indignation

(E) Forgetfulness

57. Which of the following devices are most important in the speech's development?

(A) Rhetorical questions and repetition

(B) Antithesis and parallelism

(C) Ayllogism and Socratic method

(D) Sarcasm and irony

(E) Homily and anecdote

GO ON TO THE NEXT PAGE

*Questions 58–63 refer to the following poem. After reading the poem, choose the best answer to each question.*

Wife and servant are the same
But only differ in the name:
For when that fatal knot is tied,
*Line* Which nothing, nothing can divide:
(5) When she the word *obey* has said,
And man by law supreme has made,
Then all that's kind is laid aside,
And nothing left but state and pride:          *state* pomp
Fierce as an Eastern prince he grows,
(10) And all his innate rigor shows:
Then but to look, to laugh or speak,
Will the nuptial contract break.
Like mutes she signs alone must make,
And never any freedom take:
(15) But still be governed by a nod,
And fear her husband as her God:
Him still must serve, him still obey,
And nothing act, and nothing say,
But what her haughty lord thinks fit,
(20) Who with the power, has all the wit.          *wit* intelligence
Then shun, oh! shun that wretched state,
And all the fawning flatt'rers hate:
Value your selves, and men despise,
You must be proud if you'll be wise.

(1703)

58. The speaker in the poem denounces all of the following EXCEPT

(A) marriage.

(B) society's dependence on marriage.

(C) the tyranny of husbands.

(D) women's lack of self-esteem.

(E) the subservience of wives.

59. In lines 5–6, which of the following works against a wife?

(A) The husband's deception and society's apathy

(B) The wife's loyalty to her husband and his abuse of her

(C) Society's rules and the phrasing of the wedding vows

(D) The law's vagueness and our inability to change that law

(E) The world's need for procreation and our acceptance of this need

**GO ON TO THE NEXT PAGE**

60. Lines 11–18 explain that

    (A) a wife lives an immoderately restrictive existence.

    (B) it is good for a wife to treat her husband with respect.

    (C) a wife should be tractable, but a husband should be kind.

    (D) both a husband and a wife need to focus on God.

    (E) a silent wife is the happiest kind of housemate.

61. The "fawning flatt'rers" of line 22 are

    (A) new prospects for marriage after divorce.

    (B) women who try to make cruelty sound reasonable.

    (C) men before they go through the process of marriage.

    (D) husbands who realize that their marriages are in jeopardy.

    (E) wives who attempt to bolster each other's sagging egos.

62. The word "proud" in line 24 is closest in meaning to

    (A) haughty and arrogant.

    (B) noble and stately.

    (C) satisfied and whole.

    (D) disdainful and imperious.

    (E) independent and self-loving.

63. The poem is an example of

    (A) blank verse.

    (B) couplets.

    (C) an ode.

    (D) epic simile.

    (E) ballad form.

## STOP!

**If you finish before time is up, you may check your work.**

# Answer Key
# Practice Test 3

| | | |
|---|---|---|
| 1. D | 22. B | 43. C |
| 2. B | 23. C | 44. B |
| 3. B | 24. C | 45. D |
| 4. E | 25. A | 46. E |
| 5. C | 26. D | 47. E |
| 6. D | 27. E | 48. C |
| 7. E | 28. D | 49. D |
| 8. E | 29. D | 50. A |
| 9. A | 30. B | 51. A |
| 10. A | 31. C | 52. B |
| 11. D | 32. E | 53. E |
| 12. A | 33. A | 54. D |
| 13. D | 34. C | 55. B |
| 14. E | 35. A | 56. B |
| 15. B | 36. E | 57. A |
| 16. A | 37. A | 58. B |
| 17. E | 38. C | 59. C |
| 18. D | 39. B | 60. A |
| 19. A | 40. A | 61. C |
| 20. E | 41. A | 62. E |
| 21. C | 42. D | 63. B |

# ANSWERS AND EXPLANATIONS

**1. (D)** The addressee is being encouraged to reproduce: "that face should form another" (line 2); otherwise, he will "beguile the world, unbless some mother" (line 4), and his "image dies with [him]" (line 14). Having children will also help remind him of his youth, "this, [his] golden time" (line 12), when he is old and has "wrinkles" (line 12).

**2. (B)** If you are talking to "the face thou viewest" (line 1) when you "Look in thy glass," then that glass must have a reflective surface. The *thy* indicates a glass that the addressee would possess. A mirror is a more likely item to be owned than the surface of a body of water.

**3. (B)** The words "uneared" (line 5), "tillage," and "husbandry" (line 6) are all agricultural references. Even if you were not familiar with husbandry, or knew it as something relating to personal finances, the other two words make the farming aspect more obvious.

**4. (E)** In lines 7–8, self-love is a "tomb" because it will "stop posterity." If the addressee only loves himself, he will not join with another to procreate. He will then die without having created any more of himself. His identity ends when he ends.

**5. (C)** In line 10, the mother "Calls back the lovely April of her prime." In other words, she remembers a season of her life; she does not call *for* her son himself.

**6. (D)** Even though the lines are incomplete as ideas, they still mimic each other grammatically; therefore, they have a parallel structure. They are especially similar at these points: "where is she so fair" (line 5); "who is he so fond" (line 7).

**7. (E)** Antithesis is the pairing of opposites. Of the possible answers given, only lines 13 and 14 contain antithetical components: "live" in line 13 and "die" in line 14. The rest of the lines contain no such opposition.

**8. (E)** By now, it should be apparent what the narrator wants from the addressee. The narrator tells him, "Now is the time that [the addressee's] face should form another" (line 2). If he does not reproduce, he will "beguile the world, unbless some mother" (line 4); reproduction would be better for the world, as well as for a woman who would be a mother.

**9. (A)** A sonnet contains 14 lines, is written in iambic pentameter, has a set rhyme scheme, and is usually discursive.

**10. (A)** Phrases such as "I have been assured" (line 4), "I make no doubt" (lines 8–9), and "I have reckoned upon" (line 32) indicate how certain and careful the narrator is; he is very serious about this proposal.

**11. (D)** If you look at the bracketed introduction to this piece and read the outrageous propositions in the essay excerpt itself, you can see that the writer's purpose must be satire. Through dark humor, he is making more obvious the plight of the Irish poor: their economic entrapment and their being disregarded by those in power.

**12. (A)** Again, we have a distinction between writer and narrator. One might think that the narrator is either being helpful (B), thorough (C), contemplative (D), or erudite (E) by offering a variety of cooking methods. However, his earnestness would discourage him from being shocking; he might lose his audience.

It is the writer, with the purpose of satirizing society's disdain of the poor, who is being shocking.

**13. (D)** Not often will you find an arithmetical story problem in an SAT Subject Test: Literature, but we include it here because it requires some close reading.

If you chose (A), then you did not consider the computations following this number.

Answer (B) takes one quarter of the 120,000 previously mentioned; however, the narrator recommends that the one quarter be taken from the "twenty thousand ... reserved for breed" (lines 13–14).

This fact also eliminates (C) and locks in (D): $20{,}000 \times 0.25 = 5{,}000$.

Considering these previous figures, we're not sure how (E) could be considered an answer.

**14. (E)** Items I and III are correct because the narrator says that "these children are seldom the fruits of marriage" (lines 17–18) and that this fact is a "circumstance not much regarded by our savages" (lines 18–19). In other words, the children in question come from the lower classes, whose members rarely marry. In this sense, they may be compared to "savages," since marriage itself can easily be viewed as a rite of civilization. II is also correct because 5,000 human male breeders are "more than we allow to sheep, black cattle, or swine" (lines 15–16).

**15. (B)** The phrase "persons of quality and fortune" (lines 22–23) makes (B) correct.

**16. (A)** The narrator has already spoken of these babies as a commodity. By estimating the 133 percent increase in an infant's weight, he is indicating how economical raising these children will be in their first year.

**17. (E)** Since the narrator is proposing the eating of poor children, *devoured* has its literal meaning; the figurative meaning comes in the object "most of the parents" (line 38). One could take this as having a financial meaning: Landlords have "eaten" the money, or possibly the spirit, of their poor tenants. In this sentence, we also see the writer's purpose come through; the double meaning of *devoured* is a clue that the narrator's proposal is a satirical one.

**18. (D)** The narrator is complimentary on several occasions. He says the nymph has a "fair aspect" (line 4), "conquering eyes" (line 18), and "glories" (line 24); she is a "darling of the gods" (line 10) and a "beauty of the woods" (line 33). However, he begins his admonishment in line 35: "Gather the flowers, but spare the buds." This is not merely

a request, because it carries a warning: Flora will "nip" the nymph "in the blossom" (line 40) if the latter does not spare the buds.

**19. (A)** The nymph has a "simplicity" (line 1), which could be associated with any of the first adjectives in (A)–(E). However, when we see that she "tames/The wilder flowers and gives them names" (lines 4–5) and that she "does tell/What color best becomes [the roses]" (lines 7–8), we know that she has control over nature.

**20. (E)** The word "whose" preceding "laws" (line 11) shows us that the nymph's conduct is self-determined. The word "chaster," referring to the nymph's sexual purity, indicates that we are dealing with an issue of morality.

**21. (C)** The nymph's "chaster laws" are her own. She is a "darling of the gods," but they have imposed no rules on her or her associates. Therefore, "love" (Cupid) is not under the gods' authority when he is in the presence of the nymph.

**22. (B)** Her chaster laws make her "virtuous"; the narrator simply views this stance as antagonistic to males.

**23. (C)** The question asks the reader to consider the poem up to line 22. The issue having been discussed up to that point is the power and chastity of the nymph. (C) is therefore the best answer.

**24. (C)** I is right because the tulips, although "fair" (line 29), lack "sweetness" (of scent, one supposes); the roses have "thorns" (line 30); and the violets do not last long (lines 31–32).

II is right because the narrator supposes that the nymph has the power to correct these flaws (line 27).

However, since she does have this power, she would not be well represented by the flowers. Because they are flawed, the flowers do not symbolize her well. She can correct their imperfections, even give the violets longer life, so it is unlikely that there is something fleeting about the nymph. III, therefore, does not work.

**25. (A)** Although (A) is a logical answer for inclusion, it is not brought up by the narrator.

Instead, he refers directly to Flora's wrath (lines 36–38), so (B) is not an exception. Furthermore, since Flora embodies nature, (E) also could not be an exception.

Line 40 shows that both (C) and (D) cannot be excluded either, since both the narrator's hopes and the nymph might be "nipped" if the nymph does not heed the narrator's warning.

**26. (D)** The hearts are striving for the nymph's more sensual side, and the narrator has earlier hinted at his own physical interest in the maid: "Happy who can/Appease this virtuous enemy of man!/O then let me in time compound/And parley with those conquering eyes" (lines 15–18). He is not only opposed to her virginity, but the "then" of line 17 indicates a desire to eliminate it. This desire must be included in the "hopes" he refers to in line 40.

**27. (E)** Skillfully, the poet creates a narrator who intertwines an admiration for steadfastness with the desire to conquer it; the compliments of the first four stanzas lead to the suggestiveness of the last.

**28. (D)** Pemberton is "bored and irritated"(lines 3–4) by Mrs. Moreen. She is delivering a proposal to "make [their] relations regular" (line 11). These conditions imply that their relationship is tense and unstable. Other indicators of this negativity occur in these lines: "... it's a system ... a kind of blackmail" (lines 13–14); "You practice on one's fears" (line 18); "Yes, there's no doubt I'm a great scoundrel" (line 68).

**29. (D)** Pemberton is leaning against a wall in these lines; in doing so, he suggests a kind of detachment, perhaps either boredom or irritation. His wrapper is drawn "together round his legs," further closing him off from Mrs. Moreen. His gaze is directed not at her but out the window, so he is even more removed. However, we get no description of his facial features, other than his gaze. Thus, items I, II, and III are supported but not IV.

**30. (B)** Although the narrator has told us earlier that Mrs. Moreen holds 50 francs, we cannot say for certain if that money is for her or for Pemberton. Although the money, or some portion of it, is probably intended for Pemberton in Mrs. Moreen's "proposal," it may only be a one-time amount—not part of a regular raise for Pemberton.

**31. (C)** In the characters' conversation, Pemberton suggests, "why don't you dismiss me?" (line 22). So there is a hint that he may go. Yet when Mrs. Moreen asks if he will "make it—the sacrifice" (line 30), he replies "I'll stay a little longer." Now we know that he will delay his departure.

**32. (E)** The support for this answer is obviously located at lines 36–38: "I haven't a penny in the world, and, occupied as I am with Morgan, I'm unable to earn money."

**33. (A)** Mrs. Moreen's question at line 41, "Can't you translate as *I* do?" takes on a superior air. Additionally, she holds her head high and "virtuously" proclaims, "I am glad to earn what I can" (lines 44–45). She implies that he is *not* glad to do so and that her attitude, therefore, is morally superior to his.

**34. (C)** Pemberton's declaration echoes what he has previously said about Morgan in line 37: that the tutor is "occupied" with him. For this question, (E) may be an attractive distracter, but by Pemberton's own analysis, he is delivering his comment in a "good-natured" (line 55) way. Therefore, "I haven't time to do things properly" doesn't sound like a complaint about being a tutor.

**35. (A)** Both characters use "show off" in the sense of exposing something or someone, although Pemberton's usage might be more obvious. When Mrs. Moreen uses it, she is not asking Pemberton if he wishes to brag to Morgan but rather if Pemberton is threatening to expose his own financial situation—certainly an embarrassing and not a boastful thing to do.

**36. (E)** Mrs. Moreen's "finer flower" is a harsher retort for two reasons. First, she uses Pemberton's own words against him. Second, she sullies Pemberton's image as Morgan's tutor by implying that he is an extortionist.

**37. (A)** Pemberton never glorifies his talents either as a tutor or a writer. He is a devoted tutor and writer who needs to make extra money, but talent never enters into his evaluation of himself.

**38. (C)** Phrases such as "forever that they move" (line 2), "keep moving" (line 3), "dreamlike continuum" (line 10), "vanish/into them forever, to/keep moving—"(lines 20–22), and so on help determine the correct answer here.

**39. (B)** The star "pierced the haze" (line 6), it is steady (line 7), and the narrator calls it "a constant" (line 8). It is the only thing in the poem that stays still.

**40. (A)** Taken out of context, the phrase "dreamlike continuum" might be pleasant. However, when the sky in the second stanza is described as "wan" or pale, and a "haze" is also mentioned here, the dream becomes more of a sleepy distortion than a pleasant occurrence.

**41. (A)** Both line 11 and line 2 move from the third-person plural to the first-person plural; the narrator twice has excluded, then included, herself when discussing the highway journey.

**42. (D)** Both their actions inside and outside the cars is constant; at the gasoline stops, things are done "hastily." People "hurry/back to the cars."

**43. (C)** The actions in this stanza involve "passing" (line 25), "moving" (lines 27 and 32), "pressing behind us/and/over left" (lines 28–30), and coming "toward us" (line 31), but no contact is ever made. The "sealed" road, therefore, re-emphasizes the isolation of driving.

**44. (B)** Both "pressing" and "too" intensify the experience of this journey for us.

**45. (D)** From beginning to end, the poem has stressed how relentless this highway journey is. The sibilant *s*, because it has a continuous sound, can imitate this continuity, this slurring, mentioned in the final stanza.

**46. (E)** I can be right because one logically associates brevity with speed.

II can be right because an abbreviation creates brevity, which implies speed.

III and IV join to create a kind of emblematic poem, as if the six stanzas are highway lanes and the jagged lines are rows of speeding cars. Thus, all the choices in this set work.

**47. (E)** The most unamazing answer in the group, (E) is still the best. The speaker's replies to what "That man over there" (line 7), "they" (line 21), and "that little man in black" (line 28) have said. (C) might be attractive, since the speaker's arguments sometimes imply men's ignorance about what women can do and have done, but she never shows the men to be weak. By saying that she is their physical equal in lines 12–17, she is raising a woman to a man's level, not lowering the man. In claiming that men had nothing to do with Jesus's birth (lines 31–33) or in turning "the world upside down" (line 35), she accentuates what they have *not* done; she does *not* emphasize what they are *incapable* of doing. In these examples, she has again lifted women to a new level of power, not pulled men down.

**48. (C)** The speaker says that "Negroes of the South and the women at the North" are "all talking about rights" (lines 3–4), but she never makes a plea for their equality in these lines.

**49. (D)** "That man over there" has explained that women need special treatment (lines 7–9). To show that women obviously don't need to be handled delicately, the speaker points out her physical power and the fact that she has received no special treatment.

**50. (A)** The speaker is trying to demonstrate her physical equality with men, so (A) is the most pertinent choice.

**51. (A)** In lines 9–14, the speaker claims to have a strong arm, to be capable of great labors. In lines 17–20, she relates that she has borne great grief all alone, without a man's help.

**52. (B)** There may be other places where she calls male intellect into question, but in these lines, by saying that a man has a "quart" capacity while she has only a "pint," she allows that men have more intellect than she. (A) cannot be excepted because she needs to be coached on the word "intellect" (lines 22–23). The question in lines 23–24 proves that (C) can't be excluded. (D) is no exception because her analogy is logically constructed; intellect is required to be logical. Her use of the familiar "honey" in line 23 proves that she maintains her friendliness, so (E) cannot be excepted, either.

**53. (E)** The speaker does not believe that rights should be denied anyone, as she makes clear with her question in lines 23–24. For her analogy to coincide with this idea, the cup must represent intellect. She has not stated that her intellect is as great as other people's, only that her cup deserves to be filled. Thus her "pint" of lesser intellect deserves its "half measure" of rights just as a person of greater intellect can fill his "quart" with rights. Just because her cup holds less does not mean that it shouldn't be filled.

**54. (D)** Not hearing her tone of voice, and not seeing any declaration of anger, we cannot assume that she is outraged in these lines.

**55. (B)** The speaker refers to Eve's power to disrupt the world; she subsequently reasons that if one woman can upset it, then many women combined ought to be able to right the world and that "men better let them" (line 38).

**56. (B)** In the last two lines, the speaker acknowledges her debt to the audience ("Obliged to you") and refers to herself as "old Sojourner." Taken together, these phrases seem to make her subordinate to the audience; her humility shines through.

**57. (A)** The speech is peppered with rhetorical questions from line 5 to line 31. The question "Ain't I a woman?" is repeated four times, and it is not the speaker's only use of repetition.

**58. (B)** Although the speaker makes a reference to society's power in line 6 ("man by law supreme has made"), she never states that society relies on marriage to maintain that power. The poem is primarily addressed to wives and potential wives; it does not seem to be concerned with society as a whole.

**59. (C)** The word "obey" line 5 exposes the one-sidedness of marital power at this time, and the word "law" (line 6) refers to society's contemporary role in giving men superiority over women.

**60. (A)** According to these lines, the wife must never speak; in fact, she must "never any freedom take." Furthermore, she must "fear her husband" as she would God.

**61. (C)** The sentiment of line 22 is preceded by a warning to "shun that wretched state" of marriage; in line 23, the speaker says for women to "despise" men. Within this context, then, it seems logical that the "fawning flatt'rers" are men who might wish to marry a woman.

**62. (E)** The speaker has just told her audience that they must value themselves, despise men, and shun marriage. In this context, to be "proud" means to be independent and self-loving.

**63. (B)** The correct answer is couplets, since the rhyme scheme is AABBCCDD, etc.

# HOW TO CALCULATE YOUR SCORE

**Step 1: Figure out your raw score.** Use the answer key to count the number of questions you answered correctly and the number of questions you answered incorrectly. (Do not count any questions you left blank.) Multiply the number wrong by 0.25 and subtract the result from the number correct. Round the result to the nearest whole number. This is your raw score.

## SAT Subject Test: Literature Practice Test 4

| Number right | Number wrong | Raw score |
| --- | --- | --- |
| ☐ − (0.25 × ☐) | = | ☐ |

**Step 2: Find your scaled score.** In the Score Conversion Table below, find your raw score (rounded to the nearest whole number) in one of the columns to the left. The score directly to the right of that number will be your scaled score.

A note on your practice test scores: Don't take these scores too literally. Practice test conditions cannot precisely mirror real test conditions. Your actual SAT Subject Test: Literature score will almost certainly vary from your practice test scores. However, your scores on the practice tests will give you a rough idea of your range on the actual exam.

## Conversion Table

| Raw | Scaled | Raw | Scaled | Raw | Scaled | Raw | Scaled |
| --- | --- | --- | --- | --- | --- | --- | --- |
| 63 | 800 | 43 | 700 | 23 | 510 | 3 | 330 |
| 62 | 800 | 42 | 690 | 22 | 500 | 2 | 320 |
| 61 | 800 | 41 | 680 | 21 | 500 | 1 | 310 |
| 60 | 800 | 40 | 670 | 20 | 490 | 0 | 300 |
| 59 | 800 | 39 | 660 | 19 | 480 | -1 | 290 |
| 58 | 800 | 38 | 650 | 18 | 470 | -2 | 280 |
| 57 | 800 | 37 | 640 | 17 | 460 | -3 | 280 |
| 56 | 790 | 36 | 630 | 16 | 450 | -4 | 270 |
| 55 | 790 | 35 | 620 | 15 | 440 | -5 | 260 |
| 54 | 780 | 34 | 610 | 14 | 430 | -6 | 250 |
| 53 | 780 | 33 | 610 | 13 | 420 | -7 | 250 |
| 52 | 780 | 32 | 600 | 12 | 410 | -8 | 240 |
| 51 | 770 | 31 | 590 | 11 | 410 | -9 | 230 |
| 50 | 760 | 30 | 580 | 10 | 400 | -10 | 220 |
| 49 | 750 | 29 | 570 | 9 | 390 | -11 | 210 |
| 48 | 740 | 28 | 560 | 8 | 380 | -12 | 200 |
| 47 | 730 | 27 | 550 | 7 | 370 | -13 | 200 |
| 46 | 720 | 26 | 540 | 6 | 360 | -14 | 200 |
| 45 | 710 | 25 | 530 | 5 | 350 | | |
| 44 | 710 | 24 | 520 | 4 | 340 | | |

# Practice Test 4
# Answer Grid

1. Ⓐ Ⓑ Ⓒ Ⓓ Ⓔ
2. Ⓐ Ⓑ Ⓒ Ⓓ Ⓔ
3. Ⓐ Ⓑ Ⓒ Ⓓ Ⓔ
4. Ⓐ Ⓑ Ⓒ Ⓓ Ⓔ
5. Ⓐ Ⓑ Ⓒ Ⓓ Ⓔ
6. Ⓐ Ⓑ Ⓒ Ⓓ Ⓔ
7. Ⓐ Ⓑ Ⓒ Ⓓ Ⓔ
8. Ⓐ Ⓑ Ⓒ Ⓓ Ⓔ
9. Ⓐ Ⓑ Ⓒ Ⓓ Ⓔ
10. Ⓐ Ⓑ Ⓒ Ⓓ Ⓔ
11. Ⓐ Ⓑ Ⓒ Ⓓ Ⓔ
12. Ⓐ Ⓑ Ⓒ Ⓓ Ⓔ
13. Ⓐ Ⓑ Ⓒ Ⓓ Ⓔ
14. Ⓐ Ⓑ Ⓒ Ⓓ Ⓔ
15. Ⓐ Ⓑ Ⓒ Ⓓ Ⓔ
16. Ⓐ Ⓑ Ⓒ Ⓓ Ⓔ
17. Ⓐ Ⓑ Ⓒ Ⓓ Ⓔ
18. Ⓐ Ⓑ Ⓒ Ⓓ Ⓔ
19. Ⓐ Ⓑ Ⓒ Ⓓ Ⓔ
20. Ⓐ Ⓑ Ⓒ Ⓓ Ⓔ
21. Ⓐ Ⓑ Ⓒ Ⓓ Ⓔ

22. Ⓐ Ⓑ Ⓒ Ⓓ Ⓔ
23. Ⓐ Ⓑ Ⓒ Ⓓ Ⓔ
24. Ⓐ Ⓑ Ⓒ Ⓓ Ⓔ
25. Ⓐ Ⓑ Ⓒ Ⓓ Ⓔ
26. Ⓐ Ⓑ Ⓒ Ⓓ Ⓔ
27. Ⓐ Ⓑ Ⓒ Ⓓ Ⓔ
28. Ⓐ Ⓑ Ⓒ Ⓓ Ⓔ
29. Ⓐ Ⓑ Ⓒ Ⓓ Ⓔ
30. Ⓐ Ⓑ Ⓒ Ⓓ Ⓔ
31. Ⓐ Ⓑ Ⓒ Ⓓ Ⓔ
32. Ⓐ Ⓑ Ⓒ Ⓓ Ⓔ
33. Ⓐ Ⓑ Ⓒ Ⓓ Ⓔ
34. Ⓐ Ⓑ Ⓒ Ⓓ Ⓔ
35. Ⓐ Ⓑ Ⓒ Ⓓ Ⓔ
36. Ⓐ Ⓑ Ⓒ Ⓓ Ⓔ
37. Ⓐ Ⓑ Ⓒ Ⓓ Ⓔ
38. Ⓐ Ⓑ Ⓒ Ⓓ Ⓔ
39. Ⓐ Ⓑ Ⓒ Ⓓ Ⓔ
40. Ⓐ Ⓑ Ⓒ Ⓓ Ⓔ
41. Ⓐ Ⓑ Ⓒ Ⓓ Ⓔ
42. Ⓐ Ⓑ Ⓒ Ⓓ Ⓔ

43. Ⓐ Ⓑ Ⓒ Ⓓ Ⓔ
44. Ⓐ Ⓑ Ⓒ Ⓓ Ⓔ
45. Ⓐ Ⓑ Ⓒ Ⓓ Ⓔ
46. Ⓐ Ⓑ Ⓒ Ⓓ Ⓔ
47. Ⓐ Ⓑ Ⓒ Ⓓ Ⓔ
48. Ⓐ Ⓑ Ⓒ Ⓓ Ⓔ
49. Ⓐ Ⓑ Ⓒ Ⓓ Ⓔ
50. Ⓐ Ⓑ Ⓒ Ⓓ Ⓔ
51. Ⓐ Ⓑ Ⓒ Ⓓ Ⓔ
52. Ⓐ Ⓑ Ⓒ Ⓓ Ⓔ
53. Ⓐ Ⓑ Ⓒ Ⓓ Ⓔ
54. Ⓐ Ⓑ Ⓒ Ⓓ Ⓔ
55. Ⓐ Ⓑ Ⓒ Ⓓ Ⓔ
56. Ⓐ Ⓑ Ⓒ Ⓓ Ⓔ
57. Ⓐ Ⓑ Ⓒ Ⓓ Ⓔ
58. Ⓐ Ⓑ Ⓒ Ⓓ Ⓔ
59. Ⓐ Ⓑ Ⓒ Ⓓ Ⓔ
60. Ⓐ Ⓑ Ⓒ Ⓓ Ⓔ
61. Ⓐ Ⓑ Ⓒ Ⓓ Ⓔ
62. Ⓐ Ⓑ Ⓒ Ⓓ Ⓔ
63. Ⓐ Ⓑ Ⓒ Ⓓ Ⓔ

# Practice Test 4

*Questions 1–8 refer to the following passage. After reading the passage, choose the best answer to each question.*

RULES, by *the Observation of which, a Man of Wit And Learning, may nonetheless make himself a* disagreeable *Companion*

Line
(5)
Your Business is to shine; therefore you must by all means prevent the shining of others, for their Brightness may make yours less distinguished. To this End:

1. If possible engross the whole Discourse; and when other Matter fails, talk much of
(10) Yourself, your Education, your Knowledge, your Circumstances, your Successes in Business, Your Victories in Disputes, your own wise Sayings and Observations on particular Occasions, &c. &c. &c.

2. If when you are out of Breath, one of the
(15) Company should seize the Opportunity of saying something; watch his Words, and, if possible, find somewhat either in his Sentiment or Expression, immediately to contradict and raise a Dispute upon. Rather than fail, criticise even his
(20) Grammar.

3. If another should be saying an indisputably good Thing; either give no Attention to it; or interrupt him; or draw away the Attention of others; or, if you can guess what he would be at,
(25) be quick and say it before him; or, if he gets it said, and you perceive the Company pleased with it, own it to be a good Thing, and withal remark that it had been said by *Bacon*, *Locke*, *Bayle*, or some other eminent Writer; thus you deprive him
(30) of the Reputation he might have gained by it, and gain some yourself, as you hereby show your great Reading and Memory.

4. When modest Men have been thus treated by you a few times, they will choose ever after to
(35) be silent in your Company; then you may shine on without Fear of a Rival; rallying them at the same time for their Dullness, which will be to you a new Fund of Wit.

Thus will you be sure to please *yourself*. The
(40) polite Man aims at pleasing *others*, but you shall go beyond him even in that. A Man can be present only in one Company, but may at the same time be absent in twenty. He can please only where he is, you wherever you are *not*.

(1750)

**GO ON TO THE NEXT PAGE**

1.  The tone of the passage can best be described as

    (A) frank.

    (B) facetious.

    (C) inspirational.

    (D) presumptuous.

    (E) dilatory.

2.  The idea of "shining" in line 5 is a metaphor for being

    (A) ethereally handsome.

    (B) conspicuously intelligent.

    (C) theatrically entertaining.

    (D) physically splendid.

    (E) quietly intuitive.

3.  The advice in item 1 (lines 8–13) recommends that a person be

    (A) self-absorbed.

    (B) humorous.

    (C) helpful.

    (D) attentive.

    (E) generous.

4.  The advice in 2 (lines 14–20) assumes that the advisee will have been

    (A) just arriving for a gathering and in need of ways to join in the conversation.

    (B) almost forgetting what he had to say and in need of remembering the conversation.

    (C) momentarily distracted and in need of appearing attentive to the conversation.

    (D) constantly talking and in need of more methods for dominating the conversation.

    (E) frequently winded and in need of some manner of curbing the conversation.

5.  The strategy in item 3 (lines 21–32) is best described as

    (A) averring that another's ideas are one's own.

    (B) claiming for oneself the esteem given to someone else.

    (C) distracting others from the topic to save them from boredom.

    (D) displaying one's vast knowledge of classical authors.

    (E) emulating wise men such as Bacon, Locke, and Bayle.

**GO ON TO THE NEXT PAGE**

6. Although the advisee may interpret the silence of the "modest Men" (line 33) as "Dullness" (line 37), the reader may almost certainly regard this silence as a sign of

   (A) awe and dumbfoundedness.

   (B) cowardice and conspiracy.

   (C) stoicism and enlightenment.

   (D) resignation and displeasure.

   (E) cooperation and enthusiasm.

7. Lines 39–44 develop primarily with the use of

   (A) paradoxes.

   (B) rhetorical questions.

   (C) repetitions.

   (D) metaphors.

   (E) antithesis.

8. In the final paragraph, the advisee can consider himself superior to the "polite Man" (line 40) because

   (A) the advisee is ironically capable of pleasing a greater number of people.

   (B) the polite Man is ignorant of the advisee, but the reverse is not true.

   (C) the polite Man can engage only one, while the advisee can enthrall twenty.

   (D) the advisee is happier since he prefers to please himself over others.

   (E) the polite Man will strain himself by being too available for social functions.

*Questions 9–15 refer to the following poem. After reading the poem, choose the best answer to each question.*

In May, when sea-winds pierced our solitudes,
I found the fresh Rhodora in the woods,
Spreading its leafless blooms in a damp nook,
To please the desert and the sluggish brook.
(5)   The purple petals, fallen in the pool,
Made the black water with their beauty gay;
Here might the red-bird come his plumes to cool,
And court the flower that cheapens his array.
Rhodora! if the sages ask thee why
(10)  This charm is wasted on the earth and sky,
Tell them, dear, that if eyes were made for seeing,
Then Beauty is its own excuse for being:
Why thou wert there, O rival of the rose!
I never thought to ask, I never knew:
(15)  But, in my simple ignorance, suppose
The self-same Power that brought me there
brought you.

(1839)

9. The poem can be categorized as

  (A) a conversation.

  (B) an ode.

  (C) an elegy.

  (D) a polemic.

  (E) a sonnet.

10. Lines 1–4 give the rhodora all of the following characteristics EXCEPT that

  (A) it is in a natural setting.

  (B) it has a pleasing aspect.

  (C) like the speaker, it is solitary.

  (D) like the month of May, it has new life.

  (E) like the sea-winds, it rankles its environment.

11. The alliterated *p* in line 5 most logically mimics

  (A) the blooming of the rhodora.

  (B) the speaker's surprised sputtering.

  (C) the dripping of the pool's water.

  (D) the contact of pen to paper.

  (E) the rhodora's petals alighting on the water.

12. The red-bird in lines 7–8 is seen as

  (A) an inferior suitor.

  (B) a lively woodland creature.

  (C) a fellow poet seeking inspiration.

  (D) a natural judge of beauty.

  (E) a wise traveler.

13. In lines 9–12, the idea that "Beauty is its own excuse for being" justifies the flower's

  (A) falling petals.

  (B) effect on the water.

  (C) isolation in the woods.

  (D) purple blooms.

  (E) lack of popularity as a flower.

**GO ON TO THE NEXT PAGE**

14. Lines 13–17 feature all of the following
EXCEPT

(A) a humble tone.

(B) a belief in an external, controlling force.

(C) a comparison to a more traditional
symbol of beauty.

(D) a certainty counteracting the doubt of
the first four lines.

(E) a contrast between the speaker and the
"sages" of line 9.

15. The poem's development is marked by

(A) heroic couplets in villanelle form.

(B) couplets and quatrains.

(C) Petrarchan sestets.

(D) trochaic hexameter.

(E) ballad form.

GO ON TO THE NEXT PAGE

*Questions 16–25 refer to the following passage. After reading the passage, choose the best answer to each question.*

What shall we say to this new economic equality in a great laboring class? Some people within and without the race deplore it. "Back to the homes with the women," they cry, "and higher
(5) wage for the men." But how impossible this is has been shown by war conditions. Gessation of foreign migration has raised Negro men's wages, it has opened to them a score of new avenues of earning a living. Indeed, here, in microcosm and
(10) with differences emphasizing sex equality, is the industrial history of labor in the 19th and 20th centuries. We cannot imprison women again in a home or require them all on pain of death to be nurses and housekeepers.

(15) What is today the message of these black women to America and to the world? The uplift of women is, next to the problem of the color line and the peace movement, our greatest modern cause. When, now, two of these movements—
(20) woman and color—combine in one, the combination has deep meaning.

In other years women's way was clear: to be beautiful, to be petted, to bear children. Such has been their theoretic destiny and if
(25) perchance they have been ugly, hurt, and barren, that has been forgotten with studied silence. In partial compensation for this narrowed destiny the white world has lavished its politeness on womankind,—its chivalry and bows, its
(30) uncoverings and courtesies—all the accumulated homage disused for courts and kings and craving exercise. The revolt of white women against this preordained destiny has in these latter days reached splendid proportions, but it is the revolt
(35) of an aristocracy of brains and ability,—the middle class and rank and file still plod on in the appointed path, paid by the homage, the almost mocking homage, of men.

From black women of America, however, (and
(40) from some others, too, but chiefly from black women and their daughters' daughters) this gauze has been withheld and without semblance of such apology they have been frankly trodden under the feet of men. They are and have been objected
(45) to, apparently for reasons peculiarly exasperating to reasoning human beings. When in this world a man comes forward with a thought, a deed, a vision, we ask not, how does he look,—but what is his message? It is of but passing interest whether
(50) or not the messenger is beautiful or ugly,—the *message* is the thing. This, which is axiomatic among men, has been in past ages but partially true if the messenger was a woman. The world still wants to ask that a woman primarily be
(55) pretty and if she is not, the mob pouts and asks querulously, "What else are women for?" Beauty "is its own excuse for being,"* but there are other excuses, as most men know, and when the white world objects to black women because it
(60) does not consider them beautiful, the black world of right asks two questions: "What is beauty?" and, ""Suppose you think them ugly, what then? If ugliness and unconventionality and eccentricity of face and deed do not hinder men from doing
(65) the world's work and reaping the world's reward, why should it hinder women?"

(1920)

* *Beauty ... being*" from Emerson's "The Rhodora" (1839)

**GO ON TO THE NEXT PAGE**

16. The speaker's tone in the passage is best described as

    (A) enigmatic.

    (B) derisive.

    (C) satirical.

    (D) optimistic.

    (E) persuasive.

17. The "economic equality" being discussed by the speaker in lines 1–2 refers to the

    (A) increase in taxes for job stimulation.

    (B) advancement of women in the workplace.

    (C) rise of the American middle class.

    (D) new opportunities for all men of color.

    (E) stabilization of American spending.

18. One can infer from lines 1–6 that "war conditions"

    (A) disturbed the tranquility of American homes, to which women now do not wish to return.

    (B) created employment opportunities for women, who have now been told to relinquish their new jobs.

    (C) depleted the earning potential of American men, who now feel belittled and incapable of making enough money.

    (D) caused America to plummet into economic depression, the effects of which are only starting to be felt.

    (E) ended the need for several different types of jobs but started the need for several new types of jobs.

19. The "microcosm" to which the speaker refers in line 9 is which of the following?

    I. A reason women cannot be kept from the workplace

    II. The speaker's proposed economic utopia

    III. A representation of over 100 years of economic history

    IV. A result of the Emancipation Proclamation

    (A) I only

    (B) I and II only

    (C) I and III only

    (D) I, II, and III only

    (E) I, II, III, and IV

20. In the third paragraph, the speaker views "politeness on womankind" (lines 28–29) and "accumulated homage" (lines 30–31) as all of the following EXCEPT

    (A) unadulterated appreciation.

    (B) insincere veneration.

    (C) outdated behavior.

    (D) socialized excess.

    (E) insufficient recompense.

21. The speaker implies in lines 30–38 that this "accumulated homage" should be

    (A) acknowledged by upper-class women and ignored by lower-class women.

    (B) rebuffed by upper-class women and accepted by lower-class women.

    (C) accepted by all women, regardless of their social class.

    (D) ignored by all women, regardless of their social class.

    (E) rejected by all women, regardless of their social class.

22. The "gauze" to which the speaker refers in line 41 is a metaphor for

    (A) male politeness toward white women.

    (B) the need for healing among all women.

    (C) bureaucratic practices that prevent the advancement of women.

    (D) the economic situation of African American women.

    (E) the connection between generations of African American women.

23. The quote from "The Rhodora" in line 57 supports

    (A) the speaker's theme in this passage.

    (B) the views of white male society.

    (C) the opinions of upper class white women.

    (D) the plight of African American women.

    (E) the argument made by all American women.

24. The questions at the end of the passage call for all of the following EXCEPT

    (A) re-evaluating standards of beauty.

    (B) eliminating racial discrimination.

    (C) promoting equality between the sexes.

    (D) erasing judgments based on looks.

    (E) ending uprisings among the classes.

25. The speaker develops his argument mainly through the use of

    (A) generalization.

    (B) anecdote.

    (C) syllogism.

    (D) literary allusion.

    (E) rhetorical questions.

**GO ON TO THE NEXT PAGE**

*Questions 26–34 refer to the following poem. After reading the poem, choose the best answer to each question.*

Farewell, thou child of my right hand, and joy;
My sin was too much hope of thee, loved boy,
Seven years thou wert lent to me, and I thee pay,

Line    Exacted by thy fate, on the just day.
(5)     O, could I lose all father, now. For why
Will man lament the state he should envy?
To have so soon scaped world's and flesh's rage,
And, if no other misery, yet age?
Rest in soft peace, and asked, say here doth lie
(10)    Ben Jonson his best piece of poetry.
For whose sake, henceforth, all his vows be such,
As what he loves may never like too much.

child ... hand  literally, "Benjamin"

just  exact
lose ... father  give up thoughts of fatherhood

(1604)

26. This poem would most logically be found

    (A) in a leaflet.

    (B) in a theological text.

    (C) in a primer.

    (D) on a death certificate.

    (E) on a gravestone.

27. In lines 3–4, the financial imagery used to describe his son's life and death displays which of the following about the speaker?

    I.   His sense of the universe's balance

    II.  His resignation in giving up his son

    III. His self-loathing in his son's absence

    IV.  His inability to act on his own

    (A) I and II only

    (B) III and IV only

    (C) I, II, and III only

    (D) I, II, and IV only

    (E) II, III, and IV only

28. The question in lines 5–6 is posed as

    (A) a closure to the address in line 1.

    (B) an echo of the sentiment in line 2.

    (C) an explanation of the statement in line 5.

    (D) a contrast to the question in lines 7–8.

    (E) a reformulation of the question in line 9.

29. The "state" in line 6 is

    (A) fatherhood.

    (B) childhood.

    (C) death.

    (D) hope.

    (E) love.

GO ON TO THE NEXT PAGE

30. The observation in lines 7–8 describes the current condition of

   (A) the speaker.

   (B) the son.

   (C) all those living in the world.

   (D) the world itself.

   (E) all those who die of natural causes.

31. The "poetry" in line 10 is

   (A) the speaker.

   (B) the son.

   (C) this poem.

   (D) the poetic justice of the son's death.

   (E) the hope of future healing.

32. The "whose" of line 11 refers to

   (A) "rage" (line 7).

   (B) "misery" (line 8).

   (C) "age" (line 8).

   (D) "peace" (line 9).

   (E) "poetry" (line 10).

33. Lines 11–12 vow that the speaker will never again

   (A) be able to express love in his poetry.

   (B) experience another loved one's death.

   (C) hope for another son to be born to him.

   (D) grow too attached to that which he loves.

   (E) love those of whom he has grown fond.

34. The poem develops using all of the following EXCEPT

   (A) apostrophe.

   (B) rhetorical questions.

   (C) couplet rhyme.

   (D) personification.

   (E) imagery.

**GO ON TO THE NEXT PAGE**

*Questions 35–44 refer to the following passage. After reading the passage, choose the best answer to each question.*

Line
(5)

(10)

(15)

(20)

(25)

(30)

(35)

I quite enjoy the room, now it is bare again.
How those children did tear about here!
This bedstead is fairly gnawed!

But I must get to work.

I have locked the door and thrown the key
into the front path.

I don't want to go out, and I don't want to have
anybody come in, till John comes.

I want to astonish him.

I've got a rope up here that even Jennie did
not find. If that woman does get out, and tries to
get away, I can tie her!

But I forgot I could not reach far without
anything to stand on!

This bed will *not* move!

I tried to lift and push it until I was lame, and
then I got so angry I bit off a little piece at one
corner—but it hurt my teeth.

Then I peeled off all the paper I could reach
standing on the floor. It sticks horribly and the
pattern just enjoys it! All those strangled heads
and bulbous eyes and waddling fungus growths
just shriek with derision!

I am getting angry enough to do something
desperate. To jump out of the window would be
admirable exercise, but the bars are too strong
even to try.

Besides I wouldn't do it. Of course not. I know
well enough that a step like that is improper and
might be misconstrued.

I don't like to *look* out of the windows even—
there are so many of those creeping women, and
they creep so fast.

I wonder if they all come out of the wall-paper
as I did?

But I am securely fastened by my well-hidden
rope—you don't get *me* out in the road there!

I suppose I shall have to get back to the
pattern when it comes night, and that is hard!

(40)

(45)

(50)

(55)

(60)

(65)

It is so pleasant to be out in this great room
and creep around as I please!

I don't want to go outside. I won't, even if
Jennie asks me to.

For outside you have to creep on the ground,
and everything is green instead of yellow.

But here I can creep smoothly on the floor,
and my shoulder just fits in that long smooch
around the wall, so I cannot lose my way.

Why, there's John at the door!

It's no use, young man, you can't open it!

How he does call and pound!

Now he's crying for an axe.

It would be a shame to knock down that
beautiful door!

"John dear!" said I in the gentlest voice, "the
key is down by the front steps, under a plantain
leaf!"

That silenced him for a few moments.

Then he said—very quietly indeed, "Open the
door my darling!"

"I can't," said I. "The key is down by the front
door under a plantain leaf!"

And then I said it again, several times, very
gently and slowly, and said it so often that he had
to go and see, and he got it of course, and came
in. He stopped short by the door.

"What is the matter?" he cried. "For God's
sake, what are you doing!"

I kept on creeping just the same...

(1892)

GO ON TO THE NEXT PAGE

35. The narrator of this passage has

    (A) a domineering husband.

    (B) a disturbed mind.

    (C) a sharp memory.

    (D) a lack of financial security.

    (E) a haughty demeanor.

36. In lines 2–3, the condition of the bedstead *seems* to have been

    (A) created long before the narrator is speaking.

    (B) stopped short by outside interference.

    (C) caused by the children.

    (D) aggravated over time.

    (E) inspired by anger.

37. Lines 16–18 imply that the bedstead's condition was caused by the narrator after

    (A) more than one attempt to move the bed.

    (B) Jennie's discovery of the rope.

    (C) the abduction of "the woman" in line 11.

    (D) John's initial return to the room.

    (E) throwing the key into the front path.

38. In lines 19–23, the wallpaper is personified as

    (A) antagonistic.

    (B) playful.

    (C) teasing.

    (D) commanding.

    (E) oblivious.

39. If one considers the narrator's previous comments, then the reason why it is so "hard" to "get back to the pattern when it turns night" (lines 38–39) is that

    (A) her state of being alters in the absence of light.

    (B) she wishes her husband to go with her.

    (C) Jennie is a constant obstacle to the narrator's plans.

    (D) she desperately wants to peel off the wallpaper.

    (E) it is more difficult to find the pattern in the dark.

40. The observation in line 45 that outside "everything is green instead of yellow" demonstrates which of the following?

    I. The narrator's difficulty in coping with the outside world

    II. Another reason for the narrator to stay in her room

    III. The narrator's fear that madness will soon overtake her

    IV. The narrator's need for continuity

    (A) I and II only

    (B) I and III only

    (C) I, II and IV only

    (D) I, III, and IV only

    (E) I, II, III, and IV

**GO ON TO THE NEXT PAGE**

41. Lines 49–62 create a tension that is caused by

    (A) the narrator's seemingly composed delight contrasted with John's anxiety.

    (B) the narrator's limitations in the room contrasted with her outside opportunities.

    (C) the narrator's evil inclinations contrasted with John's essential good.

    (D) the narrator's regard for the door contrasted with John's desire to destroy it.

    (E) the narrator's respect for John contrasted with John's disrespect for her.

42. The many paragraph indentations appearing in this passage demonstrate

    (A) the random flow of the narrator's thoughts.

    (B) a journalistic approximation in the passage.

    (C) a conventional approach to first-person narration.

    (D) John's awkward communication with his wife.

    (E) Jennie's control over the narrator's thought processes.

43. What the narrator seems to desire most in this passage is

    (A) sanity and order.

    (B) love and compassion.

    (C) fear and awe.

    (D) freedom and isolation.

    (E) healing and attention.

44. The wallpaper symbolizes the narrator's sense of

    (A) obligation.

    (B) nurturing.

    (C) entrapment.

    (D) marital bliss.

    (E) revelation.

**GO ON TO THE NEXT PAGE**

Questions 45–53 refer to the following poem. After reading the poem, choose the best answer to each question.

So Gareth all for glory underwent
The sooty yoke of kitchen-vassalage,*
Ate with young lads his portion by the door
And couch'd at night with grimy kitchen-knaves.

Line
(5)   And Lancelot ever spake him pleasantly,
But Kay, the seneschal†, who loved him not,
Would hustle and harry him, and labor him
Beyond his comrades of the hearth, and set

To turn the broach, draw water or hew wood
(10)  Or grosser tasks; and Gareth bowed himself
With all obedience to the King, and wrought
All kind of service with a noble ease
That graced the lowliest act in doing it.
And when the thralls had talk among themselves
(15)  And one would praise the love that linkt the King
And Lancelot—how the king had saved his life
In battle twice, and Lancelot once the King's—
For Lancelot was first in the tournament,
But Arthur mightiest on the battlefield—
(20)  Gareth was glad. Or if some other told
How once the wandering forester at dawn
Far over the blue tarns and hazy seas,
On Caer-Eryri's highest found the King
A naked babe, of whom the prophet spake,
(25)  "He passes to the isle of Avilion,‡
He passes and is healed and cannot die"—
Gareth was glad. But if their talk were foul,
Then would he whistle rapid as any lark,
Or carol some old roundelay, and so loud
(30)  That first they mocked, but after, reverenced him.
Or Gareth, telling some prodigious tale
Of knights who sliced a red-life bubbling way
Thro' twenty folds of twisted dragon, held
All in a gap-mouth'd circle his good mates
(35)  Lying or sitting round him, idle hands,
Charm'd; till Sir Kay, the seneschal, would come
Blustering upon them, like a sudden wind

Among dead leaves and drive them all apart.
Or when the thralls had sport among themselves,
(40)  So there were any trial of mastery,
He, by two yards in casting bar or stone
Was counted best; and if there chanced a joust,
So that Sir Kay nodded him leave to go
Would hurry thither, and when he saw the knights
(45)  Clash like the coming and retiring wave,
And the spear spring, and good horse reel, the
boy was half beyond himself for ecstasy.

1869

* *vassalage* servitude, especially in Medieval times
† Sir Kay is King Arthur's foster brother and *seneschal*, or estate manager.
‡ Avilion, or Avalon, is the island where Arthur will go to heal himself until his predicted return to the throne.

45. The passage depicts Gareth primarily as

(A) a commoner who admires the Round Table Knights.

(B) a demoted knight who regrets his past behavior.

(C) a disguised sorceror who is awaiting his chance to ruin Arthur.

(D) a lazy vassal who is planning to escape from his kitchen duties.

(E) a brother of Sir Kay who is helping out until other vassals are found.

**GO ON TO THE NEXT PAGE**

46. Lines 1–2 indicate Gareth's attitude toward his job as

    (A) pessimistic.

    (B) anarchistic.

    (C) apathetic.

    (D) dogmatic.

    (E) optimistic.

47. The alliteration in lines 6–8 could most logically be mimicking the sound of

    (A) Gareth's speed or fatigue.

    (B) Sir Lancelot's boxing of Gareth's ears.

    (C) the clanking of kitchen pots.

    (D) the howling wind outside.

    (E) the sobbing of Gareth's fellow workers.

48. In lines 10–13, what seems to be true of Gareth?

    (A) He thinks that if he works hard, he will be rewarded.

    (B) He works hard to avoid disfavor with Kay, Lancelot, and Arthur.

    (C) He won't perform lowly tasks, only noble or graceful ones.

    (D) He works with dignity so that even his most menial job honors the king.

    (E) He is sad while performing his tasks but does them anyway.

49. All of the following indicate Arthur's superiority EXCEPT

    (A) "the King had saved his life/In battle twice, and Lancelot once the King's" (lines 16–17).

    (B) "mightiest on the battlefield" (line 19).

    (C) "On Caer-Eryi's highest found the King" (line 23).

    (D) "A naked babe" (line 24).

    (E) "'He passes and is heal'd and cannot die'" (line 26).

50. Gareth's method for dealing with "foul" (line 27) talk of Lancelot or Arthur could be described best as

    (A) violent.

    (B) uncaring.

    (C) distracting.

    (D) unaware.

    (E) reiterative.

51. All of the following could be reasons why his fellow workers admire Gareth EXCEPT that

    (A) he speaks no evil.

    (B) he is energetic.

    (C) he is favored by Kay.

    (D) he tells engaging stories.

    (E) he is a good athlete.

**GO ON TO THE NEXT PAGE**

52. The incongruency in Sir Kay's behavior occurs where?

    (A) lines 6–9

    (B) lines 16–17

    (C) lines 25–26

    (D) lines 36–38

    (E) line 43

53. The passage may be best described as

    (A) an historical account of the Camelot legend.

    (B) a polemic arguing against child labor laws.

    (C) a foreshadowing of trouble between Arthur and Lancelot.

    (D) a study of a hardworking, likeable character.

    (E) a contrast between a playful youth and his demanding master.

**GO ON TO THE NEXT PAGE**

*Questions 54–63 refer to the following passage. After reading the passage, choose the best answer to each question.*

I will therefore speak to you as supposing Lady
Mary not only capable, but desirous of learning:
in that case by all means let her be indulged in it.
*Line* You will tell me I did not make it a part of your
(5) education: your prospect was very different from
hers. As you had no defect either in mind
or person to hinder, and much in your
circumstances to attract the highest offers, it
seemed your business to learn how to live in the
(10) world, as it is hers to know how to be easy* but of
it. It is the common error of builders and parents
to follow some plan they think beautiful (and
perhaps is so), without considering that nothing is
beautiful that is misplaced. Hence we see so many
(15) edifices raised that the raisers can never inhabit,
being too large for their fortunes. Vistas are laid
open over barren heaths, and apartments
contrived for a coolness very agreeable in Italy,
but killing in the north of Britain: thus every
(20) woman endeavors to breed her daughter a fine
lady, qualifying her for a station in which she will
never appear, and at the same incapacitating her
for that retirement† to which she is destined.
Learning, if she has a real taste for it, will not only
(25) make her contented, but happy in it. No
entertainment is so cheap as reading, nor any
pleasure so lasting. She will not want new
fashions, nor regret the loss of expensive
diversions, or variety of company, if she can be
(30) amused with an author in her closet.‡ To render
this amusement extensive, she should be
permitted to learn the languages. I have heard it
lamented that boys lose so many years in mere
learning of words: this is no objection to a girl,
(35) whose time is not so precious: she cannot advance

herself in any profession, and has therefore more
hours to spare: and as you say her memory is
good, she will be very agreeably employed this
way.

(1763)

* *how to be easy* how to be comfortable in the world of society
† *retirement* life of solitude
‡ *closet* a private study chamber

54. The identity of the narrator seems to be
   (A) a landlord.
   (B) a teacher.
   (C) Lady Mary's mother.
   (D) Lady Mary's grandmother.
   (E) a marriage prospect for Lady Mary.

55. In lines 4–11, the narrator views Lady Mary as different from the addressee in all of the following ways EXCEPT that
   (A) the addressee was not encouraged to learn when younger.
   (B) the addressee was less capable of learning than Lady Mary.
   (C) the addressee is somehow more attractive than Lady Mary.
   (D) Lady Mary appears less capable of the "highest offers" than the addressee.
   (E) the narrator considers the addressee more worldly without learning.

**GO ON TO THE NEXT PAGE**

56. The building analogy in lines 11–23 is used to emphasize that

    (A) social refinement is appropriate in the upbringing of only some young women.

    (B) architecture is a much maligned discipline and deserves a higher regard.

    (C) engineering often favors practical considerations over aesthetic values.

    (D) the addressee is among those who cannot fulfill the needs of the younger generation.

    (E) Lady Mary has no chance of surviving in isolation for the rest of her life.

57. The narrator employs the adage that "nothing is beautiful that is misplaced" (lines 13–14) so that she may

    (A) point out both Lady Mary and the addressee's eccentric behavior and looks.

    (B) justify the addressee's lack of academics and explain Lady Mary's need for them.

    (C) deny that either Lady Mary or the addressee has proven worthy of her social role.

    (D) encourage the addressee to build an appropriate dwelling for Lady Mary.

    (E) hold herself up as both a social and scholastic ideal to the addressee and Lady Mary.

58. In lines 19–23, the narrator implies that the breeding of a "fine lady"

    (A) does not require a scholarly education.

    (B) is a process that is easily mastered.

    (C) requires only small amounts of time and patience.

    (D) is best left to parents than to professionals.

    (E) lasts only for the duration of a woman's youth.

59. The antecedent for "it" in line 25 is

    (A) "coolness" (line 18).

    (B) "Italy" (line 18).

    (C) "station" (line 21).

    (D) "retirement" (line 23).

    (E) "Learning" (line 24).

60. Lines 27–30 explain that Lady Mary would not want the worldly trappings of society if

    (A) an author were to marry her.

    (B) she were to become a book collector.

    (C) the addressee were to find her a husband.

    (D) she were pleased to occupy herself with reading.

    (E) she were to maintain an intriguing secret.

**GO ON TO THE NEXT PAGE**

61. In lines 30–39, the narrator views learning in all of the following ways EXCEPT that

(A) foreign language education is not as important to a man as other areas of knowledge.

(B) foreign language education can be described merely as the learning of words.

(C) foreign language acquisition is more useful to a woman's education than a man's.

(D) some education can be a waste of time, especially for men.

(E) education is the best means by which a woman can advance herself in a profession.

62. Throughout the passage, the narrator's opinion of Lady Mary is that she is

(A) bright but not marriageable.

(B) dull but capable of a limited education.

(C) ill-suited for high society but marriageable if educated.

(D) ugly but worldly enough to make her attractive.

(E) desperate but too shy to attract a suitable husband.

63. Throughout the passage, the narrator's opinion of education is that it is

(A) an undertaking better suited to men of high social status than to women.

(B) reserved for only the most discerning and well-bred people.

(C) secondary to fine breeding but highly desirable under certain circumstances.

(D) a necessary pursuit to enlighten, advance, and expand any individual.

(E) a trend that is desirable for Lady Mary's generation but not the addressee's.

## STOP!

**If you finish before time is up,
you may check your work.**

# Answer Key
## Practice Test 4

| | | |
|---|---|---|
| 1. B | 22. A | 43. D |
| 2. B | 23. B | 44. C |
| 3. A | 24. E | 45. A |
| 4. D | 25. A | 46. E |
| 5. B | 26. E | 47. A |
| 6. D | 27. D | 48. D |
| 7. E | 28. C | 49. D |
| 8. A | 29. C | 50. C |
| 9. B | 30. B | 51. C |
| 10. E | 31. B | 52. E |
| 11. E | 32. E | 53. D |
| 12. A | 33. D | 54. D |
| 13. C | 34. D | 55. B |
| 14. D | 35. B | 56. A |
| 15. B | 36. C | 57. B |
| 16. E | 37. A | 58. A |
| 17. B | 38. A | 59. D |
| 18. B | 39. D | 60. D |
| 19. C | 40. C | 61. E |
| 20. A | 41. A | 62. A |
| 21. E | 42. A | 63. C |

# ANSWERS AND EXPLANATIONS

**1. (B)** With enthusiasm and brightness, the narrator is recommending ways in which his advisee may be a "disagreeable Companion" (line 3). Such an approach can best be called facetious. Why would someone give this advice seriously?

**2. (B)** The text continually makes recommendations about the advisee's conversation: that it should display his "Knowledge" and his "Victories in Disputes" (lines 10–12), that he should "criticise... Grammar" (lines 19–20), and that he should display his "great Reading and Memory" (lines 31–32). So the advisee's intellect seems to be of utmost importance to the narrator.

**3. (A)** The idea is best summed up in the advice to "talk much of Yourself." On a more basic level, the narrator uses the possessive pronoun *your* six times in three lines. Such excess demonstrates the self-absorption that the narrator recommends.

**4. (D)** In number 1, the narrator has recommended that the advisee "talk much" on various topics. Number 2 follows with the hypothetical supposition that the advisee would be out of breath. It is logical to assume, then, that this breathlessness was caused by "talking much."

**5. (B)** According to the narrator, the advisee can claim that a speaker's clever remark is actually a quote from someone else; the advisee can therefore deprive the speaker "of the Reputation he might have gained" by the remark. The narrator further states that in taking this action, the advisee is gaining some recognition for himself. (C) contains some truth here, except that the strategy of distracting others is not meant to save them from boredom but to draw attention away from the "indisputably good Thing" that someone else has said.

**6. (D)** Leading up to this silence, the advisee would have dominated the conversation, spoken only about himself, and put down others' attempts to speak. Not only would the advisee's companions

be understandably displeased by this conduct, but they also would be resigned to the idea that they could not get a word in edgewise.

**7. (E)** Opposites paired throughout these lines include "*yourself*" and "*others*" (lines 39–40), "present" and "absent" (lines 42–43), and "where he is" and "wherever you are *not*" (line 44).

**8. (A)** Because a man can be absent among 20 men, and because people would prefer not to be in the company of an overbearing conversationalist, the advisee can make 20 men happy by being absent. However, the polite Man can please only the one person to whom he is speaking. Thus, the advisee can be superior to the polite Man.

**9. (B)** An ode is a poem of praise, and this poem praises the beauty of the rhodora flower. The language is too elevated for it to be a conversation (A), and because this poem has 17 lines, it is not a sonnet (E), which has 14 lines. An elegy (C) is a poem of mourning, or a lament for the dead. A polemic (D) is a controversial argument, especially one attacking a specific opinion.

**10. (E)** Line four describes the rhodora as actually pleasing its environment, not rankling it.

**11. (E)** Line five describes the rhodora's petals falling on top of the water. So in a contextual sense, the alliteration of the line is most logically mimicking this occurrence.

**12. (A)** Since the red-bird would come to "court the flower," he is a suitor of sorts. Additionally, the beauty of the rhodora "cheapens his array," or makes his plumage look bad, so he is not as beautiful as the flower.

**13. (C)** The rhodora's "charm" is its beauty, and a sage might say that that charm is "wasted on the earth and sky" (line 10) because there is no one to see the flower's beauty. However, the speaker suggests that beauty does not have to be seen to be justified.

**14. (D)** The first four lines relate the speaker's encounter with the rhodora. His descriptions of the plant, however, are complimentary and assured; there is no doubt here.

**15. (B)** Lines 1–4 have an AABB rhyme scheme, while lines 9–12 have an EEFF rhyme; these are couplets. On the other hand, lines 5–8 have a CDCD rhyme scheme, and lines 13–16 follow a pattern of GHGH; these sets are quatrains, not only because they follow a certain four-line rhyme scheme but also because they each contain a complete thought.

**16. (E)** The narrator's aim is to promote social equality and financial independence for women, especially women of color. He is at his most persuasive in statements such as "We cannot imprison women again," (line 12) and rhetorical questions such as "If ugliness and unconventionality and eccentricity of face and deed do not hinder men from doing the world's work and reaping the world's reward, why should it hinder women?" (lines 63–66).

**17. (B)** The narrator refers to the situation as "*this* [emphasis added] new economic equality," so it is an economic equality of a certain kind. He notes that "Some people…deplore" (lines 2–3) this equality. Then he imagines that they would exclaim, "Back to the homes with the women" (lines 3–4). Thus, women are involved in the concept. Finally, when he further imagines people crying "higher wage for the men" (lines 4–5), we can infer that women have been paid workers outside the home but that there is now a strong sentiment to revert to the more traditional economic situation of women working only in the home.

**18. (B)** The quotes cited in the explanation of question 17 above help to support this answer, also. The women have been working outside the home, but the war made it necessary for them to do so. Probably so many men joined the military that job positions were left vacant and had to be filled by women.

**19. (C)** The "microcosm" to which the narrator refers is the new economic opportunities opening up for women in the 20th century. It is a microcosm "with differences" (line 10) from the improved wages gained by African American males when "foreign migration" (lines 6–7) ceased, but these are only differences "emphasizing sex equality" (line 10). Essentially, in both cases, a formerly downtrodden group achieves new economic advancement, and once that has been attained, the narrator says that it cannot be taken away. Thus, item I has support.

The narrator further states that the microcosm is a model for "the industrial history of labor in the 19th and 20th centuries" (lines 10–12), so item III is also supported.

However, the microcosm is not a utopia, an ideal society. Rather, it is discussed as another step in the economic evolution of a country: The utopia has not yet been achieved. Additionally, the economic equality of women has come about because of recent war, not because of the document that freed slaves in the middle 1800s. Thus, neither II nor IV is supported.

**20. (A)** When the narrator calls this politeness an "almost mocking homage" (lines 37–38), we see that, if it can be called appreciation, then it is tainted by scorn.

**21. (E)** The narrator observes that white women "of an aristocracy of brains and ability" (line 35) have been able to "revolt ... against this preordained destiny" (lines 32–33) of condescending male politeness. If they are rejecting it, and they have brains and ability, then we can infer that these women are doing the intelligent thing, according to the narrator. However, in lines 35–37, the narrator complains that the women of "the middle class and rank and file still plod on in the appointed path." They are not rejecting the politeness paid to them by men, but the narrator has established that this kind of revolt is the intelligent way to go. Thus, he is encouraging all women to refuse the politeness of men.

**22. (A)** The narrator uses the image of "this gauze," and he has just been speaking about the "almost mocking homage" of men. Thus, there is a correlation. The metaphor is appropriate here because gauze is a thin cloth that is translucent but not transparent. The politeness of men is portrayed as a hazy veneer behind which hide oppression and mockery.

**23. (B)** Men are described as those who objectify women. For them, beauty—especially feminine beauty—would need no other excuse to exist than its own being. The narrator, however, is able to see women as intelligent and capable beings; he cares more about their "message" than their looks.

**24. (E)** The narrator has previously spoken admiringly of privileged white women's revolt against male politeness. He has suggested that other women should do the same. Thus, he does not seek an end to social uprising.

**25. (A)** Ideas are delivered in this essay with references to large groups of people: "a great laboring class" (line 2), women, "Negro men" (line 7), black women, "America and…the world" (line 16), "womankind" (line 29), and "the mob" (line 55). Generalizations thus dominate the text.

**26. (E)** The speaker is addressing his recently dead son and tells him in lines 9–10 to say—if asked— "here doth lie/Ben Jonson." The poem would then most logically appear on a tombstone.

**27. (D)** We see the universe's balance of item I in the idea that payment is "Exacted by thy fate, on the just day." He considers his son, while alive, a loan that must be paid back in full as his fate demands. The image also shows that even though there is no joy in making this payment, there is also no hesitation; the speaker is bitterly submitting to the boy's fate. Thus, II and IV are also supported.

**28. (C)** The speaker says in line 5 that he could abandon all thoughts of being a father. The "For" of the following question means "because," so the speaker is offering an explanation for his statement. In essence, there is no point in bringing another life into the world when death is a preferred state of being—or such is how he attempts to comfort himself.

**29. (C)** As explained in #28, the narrator says that death is the enviable state. What makes it so enviable is that, in death, one has escaped the "rage" of the world (perhaps the hardships of life, or natural disasters or war) and of flesh (perhaps disease). If we encounter none of these during life, then death will at least save us from "age." The claim is logical but darkly facetious.

**30. (B)** Since line 6 describes the "state [one] should envy" and the son is the one who is in that state, (B) is the logical choice. (E) may be an attractive distracter, but part of this enviable state is that the son has "so soon" escaped the rage of the world, etc. That is, he has died as a child—not from old age.

**31. (B)** The son is told to say, "here doth lie/ Ben Jonson his best piece of poetry." The gloss note explains that, in line 1, the speaker is saying farewell to the "child of [his] right hand," meaning "Benjamin." It is highly likely, then, that "Ben Jonson" is the Benjamin of the first line; the *his* is grammatically confusing in modern usage but contextually sound—the possessive pronoun refers to the speaker, the father. So figuratively speaking, the son is the poetry of the speaker.

**32. (E)** The speaker is about to make a vow or series of vows. He is doing so for the sake of, or because of, his "poetry." The "whose" seems a strange possessive pronoun to use here until one realizes that the poetry is a metaphor for the son.

**33. (D)** The phrase "what he loves" shows that the speaker is capable or will be capable of loving. However, he will "never like too much"—never show a fondness for or attachment to—anything he loves from now on. The speaker has learned a dark lesson from this episode in his life.

**34. (D)** The very opposite of personification may be occurring here. The speaker discusses the death of his son as if it were part of a business transaction; then he compares his son to poetry. In his deep grief, the father is dehumanizing or "depersonifying" the son, almost detaching himself from his son's loss.

**35. (B)** Some signs of the narrator's mental disturbance are her biting the bed (lines 17–18), tearing the wallpaper (line 19–23), and imagining herself originating *from* the wallpaper (lines 34–35).

**36. (C)** In the pertinent lines, the narrator claims that children have torn through the room, then observes that the bedstead has been gnawed. One would logically assume that the chewed bed furniture is part of the children's rampage.

**37. (A)** After trying to "lift and push" the bed unsuccessfully, the narrator says that she "bit off a little piece" of the bed. She has now become a more likely candidate for the bed chewing than the children she mentioned previously. Furthermore, since the bedstead is "fairly gnawed," there has been more than one bite taken out of it; thus, more than one attempt to move the bed.

**38. (A)** Not only does the wallpaper stick "horribly" when the narrator tries to peel it, but the pattern "enjoys" sticking and "shriek[s] with derision" when the narrator is tearing.

**39. (D)** The desire to get back to the wallpaper and the action of peeling it off the wall seem contradictory. None of the other choices is as contextually sound as this one.

**40. (C)** In line 42, the narrator says that she does not want to go outside. Line 44 begins with a "For," so she is about to provide reasons she does not want to go; one of those reasons is that everything outside is green and not yellow. Tracing this process, we understand that a mere color change distresses her, so she has problems coping with the outside world; item I is proven.

She has already stated that she likes to "creep around" as she pleases (line 41), and she has implied that she prefers not to "creep on the ground" (line 44) outside, so the color preference is one more reason to stay inside; II is thus proven. She prefers to remain in a yellow interior rather than risk a green exterior, so IV is supported, also.

However, the narrator has not expressed a fear of going mad. Lines 28–30 come closest to her admitting that she is disturbed, but even in that excerpt, she thinks that someone *else* will "misconstrue" her actions. Therefore, III lacks support.

**41. (A)** The exclamation "Why there's John at the door!" in line 49 sounds as if the narrator is pleased that he has come. Furthermore, by her own admission, she is speaking to him in "the gentlest voice" (line 55). On the other hand, and on the other side of the door, John is in a frenzy; the narrator reports that "he does call and pound" and that he is "crying for an axe" (lines 51–52). The differing emotional and mental states of these characters create an obvious tension.

**42. (A)** A basic understanding of mechanics tells us that one begins a new paragraph with every new idea. Many of the speaker's "paragraphs" last for a single, short sentence; therefore, several new ideas are coming to her in quick succession.

**43. (D)** The narrator is happy that she can creep around as she pleases (line 41); she takes delight in a certain kind of freedom. However, she does not want to leave the room, and she wants no one to come in; therefore, she desires isolation also.

**44. (C)** Although the narrator feels secure in the room, she appears trapped by other people's desires and expectations, primarily Jennie's and John's. The orderly and controlled thing for her to do would be to leave the wallpaper up. She chooses, however to peel it off, to be chaotic, to fly in the face of Jennie's and John's expectations. John's exclamation of

"For God's sake, what are you doing!" (lines 67–68) when he sees the condition of the room shows that she has successfully shocked him and, thus, expressed her desire for independence.

Also, if we infer that the wallpaper is the source of the room's yellow color, and we remember that the narrator prefers the yellow to the green outside, then we see how trapped she is by her need for sameness.

**45. (A)** Gareth is a kitchen servant, as we see in lines 1–2; thus, he has the appearance of a commoner. In line 20, he is "glad" when the other servants speak well of Arthur and Lancelot, and he is "half beyond himself for ecstasy" (line 47) when he watches the Round Table knights compete.

**46. (E)** Anyone who will undertake kitchen drudgery "all for glory" has to be optimistic.

**47. (A)** It is the *h* sound that is alliterated, and since Gareth is being ordered around and is working assiduously, the *h* most logically mimics the vassal's possible panting.

**48. (D)** In these lines, Gareth obeys the king, but we are not given any motivation for his doing so; we may only infer that Gareth's high regard for Arthur makes him obey. Furthermore, Gareth performs "All kind of service with a noble ease." There is not any task we see him refusing, and he performs even the "lowliest" service with grace.

**49. (D)** One need not even review the passage for this answer. Arthur is superior to Lancelot in (A) and superior to all fighters in (B). (C) shows him as superlative in being found on the highest mountain. (E) demonstrates that he is supreme among humans in that he cannot die. (D) is the only option that shows him as ordinary, in fact, as vulnerable.

**50. (C)** Gareth whistles or sings when others talk badly of the knights; thus, he distracts himself and his comrades from an ignoble pastime. We can infer that his actions are intentional, because

the other vassals eventually "reverence" him for what he has done. They appreciate his drawing them away from gossip and slander or admire his wish not to indulge in it.

**51. (C)** Early on, line 6 tells us that Kay does not love Gareth. We also see that Kay drives him as hard as or harder than the other vassals.

**52. (E)** By nodding Gareth "leave to go," Kay is giving Gareth an unaccustomed break.

**53. (D)** The passage is full of examples of Gareth's hard work. What makes him likable is his admiration for the knights, his goodness, and his unflappable attitude. The fact that he eventually wins over his fellow vassals shows how likable he is.

**54. (D)** The narrator says in lines 19–21 that "every woman endeavors to breed her daughter a fine lady," and the entire passage offers advice on the rearing of Lady Mary. We can infer from these facts that the person being addressed is Lady Mary's mother. Furthermore, when the narrator anticipates that "You will tell me I did not make [learning] a part of your education" (lines 4–5), she is at once announcing herself as the addressee's parent and quelling the notion that she is a teacher.

**55. (B)** The narrator flatly says that the addressee had "no defect either in mind or person." Thus she was *capable* of attaining an academic education—but the narrator believed that this lack of imperfection made the addressee better suited for marriage and society.

**56. (A)** The building analogy shows that some structures are not appropriate for their environments. Likewise, some young women are bred to be ladies of high society when they "will never appear" in that "station" (lines 21–22). Apparently, Lady Mary is one of these unfit women, and that is why the narrator thinks that an academic rather than a social education is better for her.

**57. (B)** The narrator has already noted that, since the addressee had no mental or personal barriers to well-placed marriage, she did not need an education. She therefore was less dependent on an education. The implication is that Lady Mary lacks some qualities that her mother has, so the daughter, who would be ill placed in society, is better off acquiring some "learning."

**58. (A)** The narrator expresses the opinion that the addressee did not need a scholarly education since she "had no defect either in mind or person to hinder" (lines 6–7) her prospects for a society marriage and the life of a "fine lady." The explanations for Questions 56 and 57 apply here also.

**59. (D)** We have some shaky pronoun references going on here. The *it* of line 24 obviously refers to "Learning," but the second *it* of that statement does not. The *it* of line 25 would be unnecessary if it *were* referring to "Learning." However, the narrator's purpose here is to convince the addressee that a life of solitude—"retirement"—will be pleasing to Lady Mary if she is educated.

**60. (D)** The narrator has been expounding on the appropriateness of Lady Mary becoming learned. Option (D) is the only response that contextually fits with this line of thought.

**61. (E)** The narrator's idea is that Lady Mary should pursue education because, unlike a male, "she cannot advance herself in any profession, and has therefore more hours to spare" (lines 35–37). The wording here tells us that foreign language education is something to be attained in lieu of the more practical training required for a profession.

**62. (A)** Earlier in the passage, the narrator said that the addressee was capable of attracting the "highest offers" (line 8); yet the narrator recommends a life of solitude, or "retirement" (line 23), for Lady Mary. We can infer, then, that Lady Mary is not marriageable to someone of high status, even though her mother's prospects were outstanding. Still, the narrator believes the addressee when the latter describes Lady Mary as "capable" and "desirous" of learning (lines 1–2). So the narrator thinks that the girl is bright, even though it is doubtful that she could be married to someone from privileged society.

**63. (C)** Fine breeding is for someone like the addressee, who has no deficiencies. The implication is that those who may not marry to financial advantage, like Lady Mary, can benefit from education.

# HOW TO CALCULATE YOUR SCORE

**Step 1: Figure out your raw score.** Use the answer key to count the number of questions you answered correctly and the number of questions you answered incorrectly. (Do not count any questions you left blank.) Multiply the number wrong by 0.25 and subtract the result from the number correct. Round the result to the nearest whole number. This is your raw score.

## SAT Subject Test: Literature Practice Test 5

| Number right | Number wrong | Raw score |
|---|---|---|
| ☐ | – (0.25 × ☐) = | ☐ |

**Step 2: Find your scaled score.** In the Score Conversion Table below, find your raw score (rounded to the nearest whole number) in one of the columns to the left. The score directly to the right of that number will be your scaled score.

A note on your practice test scores: Don't take these scores too literally. Practice test conditions cannot precisely mirror real test conditions. Your actual SAT Subject Test: Literature score will almost certainly vary from your practice test scores. However, your scores on the practice tests will give you a rough idea of your range on the actual exam.

## Conversion Table

| Raw | Scaled | Raw | Scaled | Raw | Scaled | Raw | Scaled |
|---|---|---|---|---|---|---|---|
| 63 | 800 | 43 | 700 | 23 | 510 | 3 | 330 |
| 62 | 800 | 42 | 690 | 22 | 500 | 2 | 320 |
| 61 | 800 | 41 | 680 | 21 | 500 | 1 | 310 |
| 60 | 800 | 40 | 670 | 20 | 490 | 0 | 300 |
| 59 | 800 | 39 | 660 | 19 | 480 | -1 | 290 |
| 58 | 800 | 38 | 650 | 18 | 470 | -2 | 280 |
| 57 | 800 | 37 | 640 | 17 | 460 | -3 | 280 |
| 56 | 790 | 36 | 630 | 16 | 450 | -4 | 270 |
| 55 | 790 | 35 | 620 | 15 | 440 | -5 | 260 |
| 54 | 780 | 34 | 610 | 14 | 430 | -6 | 250 |
| 53 | 780 | 33 | 610 | 13 | 420 | -7 | 250 |
| 52 | 780 | 32 | 600 | 12 | 410 | -8 | 240 |
| 51 | 770 | 31 | 590 | 11 | 410 | -9 | 230 |
| 50 | 760 | 30 | 580 | 10 | 400 | -10 | 220 |
| 49 | 750 | 29 | 570 | 9 | 390 | -11 | 210 |
| 48 | 740 | 28 | 560 | 8 | 380 | -12 | 200 |
| 47 | 730 | 27 | 550 | 7 | 370 | -13 | 200 |
| 46 | 720 | 26 | 540 | 6 | 360 | -14 | 200 |
| 45 | 710 | 25 | 530 | 5 | 350 | | |
| 44 | 710 | 24 | 520 | 4 | 340 | | |

# Practice Test 5
# Answer Grid

1. (A) (B) (C) (D) (E)
2. (A) (B) (C) (D) (E)
3. (A) (B) (C) (D) (E)
4. (A) (B) (C) (D) (E)
5. (A) (B) (C) (D) (E)
6. (A) (B) (C) (D) (E)
7. (A) (B) (C) (D) (E)
8. (A) (B) (C) (D) (E)
9. (A) (B) (C) (D) (E)
10. (A) (B) (C) (D) (E)
11. (A) (B) (C) (D) (E)
12. (A) (B) (C) (D) (E)
13. (A) (B) (C) (D) (E)
14. (A) (B) (C) (D) (E)
15. (A) (B) (C) (D) (E)
16. (A) (B) (C) (D) (E)
17. (A) (B) (C) (D) (E)
18. (A) (B) (C) (D) (E)
19. (A) (B) (C) (D) (E)
20. (A) (B) (C) (D) (E)
21. (A) (B) (C) (D) (E)

22. (A) (B) (C) (D) (E)
23. (A) (B) (C) (D) (E)
24. (A) (B) (C) (D) (E)
25. (A) (B) (C) (D) (E)
26. (A) (B) (C) (D) (E)
27. (A) (B) (C) (D) (E)
28. (A) (B) (C) (D) (E)
29. (A) (B) (C) (D) (E)
30. (A) (B) (C) (D) (E)
31. (A) (B) (C) (D) (E)
32. (A) (B) (C) (D) (E)
33. (A) (B) (C) (D) (E)
34. (A) (B) (C) (D) (E)
35. (A) (B) (C) (D) (E)
36. (A) (B) (C) (D) (E)
37. (A) (B) (C) (D) (E)
38. (A) (B) (C) (D) (E)
39. (A) (B) (C) (D) (E)
40. (A) (B) (C) (D) (E)
41. (A) (B) (C) (D) (E)
42. (A) (B) (C) (D) (E)

43. (A) (B) (C) (D) (E)
44. (A) (B) (C) (D) (E)
45. (A) (B) (C) (D) (E)
46. (A) (B) (C) (D) (E)
47. (A) (B) (C) (D) (E)
48. (A) (B) (C) (D) (E)
49. (A) (B) (C) (D) (E)
50. (A) (B) (C) (D) (E)
51. (A) (B) (C) (D) (E)
52. (A) (B) (C) (D) (E)
53. (A) (B) (C) (D) (E)
54. (A) (B) (C) (D) (E)
55. (A) (B) (C) (D) (E)
56. (A) (B) (C) (D) (E)
57. (A) (B) (C) (D) (E)
58. (A) (B) (C) (D) (E)
59. (A) (B) (C) (D) (E)
60. (A) (B) (C) (D) (E)
61. (A) (B) (C) (D) (E)
62. (A) (B) (C) (D) (E)
63. (A) (B) (C) (D) (E)

# Practice Test 5

*Questions 1–7 refer to the following poem. After reading the poem, choose the best answer to each question.*

Love like a juggler comes to play his prize          *prize* game
And all minds draw his wonders to admire,
To see how cunningly he, wanting eyes,
*Line*     Can yet deceive the best sight of desire;
(5)     The wanton child, how he can feign his fire
So prettily as none sees his disguise,               *prettily* skillfully
How finely do his tricks, while we fools hire
The badge and office of his tyrannies,               *badge and office* signs and service
For in the end, such juggling he doth make
(10)     As he our hearts, instead of eyes, doth take;
For men can only by their sleights abuse
The sight with nimble and delightful skill,
But if he play, his gain is our lost will;
Yet, childlike, we cannot his sports refuse.          *sports* games

(1621)

**GO ON TO THE NEXT PAGE**

1. Love is viewed in this poem as all of the following EXCEPT

   (A) skillful.

   (B) tender.

   (C) despotic.

   (D) playful.

   (E) deceptive.

2. Within the context of the first four lines, the idea that Love is "wanting eyes" (line 3) means which of the following?

   I. Being blind

   II. Desiring an audience

   III. Lacking insight

   IV. ignoring our attention

   (A) I only

   (B) I and II only

   (C) I, II, and III only

   (D) I, II, and IV only

   (E) I, II, III, and IV

3. In lines 5–8, "we fools" (line 7) act in a manner best described as

   (A) uneducated.

   (B) inexperienced.

   (C) enterprising.

   (D) deceitful.

   (E) naïve.

4. The antecedent for the word "their" in line 11 is

   (A) "men" (line 11).

   (B) "eyes" (line 10).

   (C) "hearts" (line 10).

   (D) "tyrannies" (line 8).

   (E) "tricks" (line 7).

5. In lines 11–12, what is the consequence of Love's taking our hearts during his juggling act?

   (A) Our stolen hearts cause our eyes to be fooled by love.

   (B) Love keeps our stolen hearts forever by his side.

   (C) We eventually win our stolen hearts back from love.

   (D) Much to love's delight, we grow thin and wan.

   (E) Until our hearts are returned, we abuse love.

6. The last two lines feature all of the following EXCEPT

   (A) antithesis concerning what Love obtains from us.

   (B) a parallel between great labor and casual play.

   (C) an ironic observation that we, like Love, seem childlike.

   (D) the idea that, inevitably, we fall prey to Love.

   (E) the claim that we are unable to overcome Love's power.

**GO ON TO THE NEXT PAGE**

7. The irony of the poem is found in the idea that

   (A) while we constantly seek Love's approval, in reality, we already have that Approval.

   (B) love wants to be serious with us, yet all we can do is play childish games with him.

   (C) the speaker is never aware of Love's power, although Love has had a domineering hold on her.

   (D) despite the speaker's knowledge of Love's duplicity, she still finds Love irresistible.

   (E) even though several lines describe Love as a child, his behavior is not in the least childish.

GO ON TO THE NEXT PAGE

*Questions 8–17 refer to following passage. After reading the passage, choose the best answer to each question.*

Well, I think I'll finish that story for the editor
of the "Dutchman." Let me see; where did I leave
off? The setting sun was just gilding with his last
ray—"Ma, I want some bread and molasses"—
*Line*
(5) (yes, dear,) gilding with his last ray the church
spire—"Wife, where's my Sunday pants?" (*Under
the bed, dear,*) the church spire of Inverness,
when a—"There's nothing under the bed, dear,
but your lace cap"—(Perhaps they are in the coal
(10) hod* in the closet,) when a horseman was seen
approaching—"Ma'am, the pertators is out; not
one for dinner"—(Take some turnips,)
approaching, covered with dust, and—"Wife! the
baby has swallowed a button"—(*Reverse him,*
(15) dear—take him by the heels,) and waving in his
hand a banner, on which was written—"Ma! I've
torn my pantaloons"—liberty or death! The
inhabitants rushed *en masse*—"Wife! *will* you
leave off scribbling?" (Don't be disagreeable,
(20) Smith, I'm just getting inspired,) to the public
square, where De Begnis, who had been
secretly—"Butcher wants to see you, ma'am"—
secretly informed of the traitors'—"Forgot *which*
you said, ma'am, sausages or mutton chop"—
(25) movements, gave orders to fire; not less than
twenty—"My gracious! Smith, you haven't been
*reversing* that child all this time; he's as black as
your coat; and that boy of *yours* has torn up the
first sheet of my manuscript. There! it's no use for
(30) a married woman to cultivate her intellect—
Smith, hand me those twins."

(1853)

\* *hod* pail for storing coal

8. The narrator of this passage splits her
attention between

(A) reading the newspaper and quieting her
rambunctious family.

(B) reveling in a daydream and filtering out
several interruptions.

(C) writing a narrative and tending to
various household matters.

(D) editing a romance novel and rejecting
her family's demands.

(E) critiquing an editorial and quelling
memories of the day's events.

9. All of the following are true of the sun image
in lines 3–4 EXCEPT that

(A) it is an example of personification.

(B) it is interrupted by a demand.

(C) it humorously juxtaposes the house's
tranquil exterior and chaotic interior.

(D) its *s* consonance helps create a peaceful
scene within the image.

(E) its loftiness is ironically contrasted by the
triviality of the subsequent quotation.

**GO ON TO THE NEXT PAGE**

10. The discussion of the "Sunday pants" in lines 6–10 exemplifies all of the following EXCEPT

    (A) the disorder of the household.

    (B) the narrator's attention to her present task.

    (C) the lack of love between the narrator and her husband.

    (D) the husband's disregard for the narrator's present task.

    (E) the husband's dependency on the narrator.

11. The quotation in lines 11–12 is most likely spoken by

    (A) a visiting grocer taking an order.

    (B) a household servant planning a meal.

    (C) an irritated husband becoming increasingly sarcastic.

    (D) an obstinate child complaining of his hunger.

    (E) a minor character speaking from the narrator's text.

12. The sentence, "Ma! I've torn my pantaloons" in lines 16–17 is humorous in relation to

    (A) "a horseman was seen approaching" (lines 10–11).

    (B) "Take some turnips" (line 12).

    (C) "'Wife! the baby has swallowed a button'" (lines 13–14).

    (D) "take him by the heels" (line 15).

    (E) "a banner, on which was written" (line 16).

13. "The inhabitants rushed *en masse*" (lines 17–18) is a parallel between

    (A) the freedom fighters' cause and the narrator's secret desires.

    (B) the narrator's thoughts about her future and the words on the page.

    (C) the use of a French expression and the house's French bourgeois ambience.

    (D) the crowd in the narrator's text and the people surrounding the narrator.

    (E) the speed of the "inhabitants" and the alacrity with which the narrator works.

14. The narrator's address of her husband as "Smith" in line 20 could indicate all of the following EXCEPT

    (A) her growing irritation.

    (B) a sudden lapse in recognition.

    (C) the diminishment of her affection.

    (D) a sudden formality in speaking.

    (E) a distancing from her surroundings.

15. At line 26, the last interruption is permanent because of which of the following?

    I.   A child's safety being endangered

    II.  The narrator's text being sabotaged

    III. The butcher's appearance making the situation finally unbearable

    IV.  The narrator's feeling guilty about working on something unrelated to her family

    (A) I and II only

    (B) II and III only

    (C) I, II, and III only

    (D) II, III, and IV only

    (E) I, II, III, and IV

**GO ON TO THE NEXT PAGE**

16. The narrator's observation in lines 29–30 that "it's no use for a married woman to cultivate her intellect" is

    (A) a relieved capitulation to the unenlightened beliefs of the time.

    (B) a curious parallel to the themes of the text in which she is engaged.

    (C) a welcome acknowledgment that family duties eclipse a career.

    (D) a needed break from the grind of her previous literary tasks.

    (E) a resigned acceptance of overwhelming domestic responsibilities.

17. The passage develops mainly through the use of

    (A) antithesis and metaphor.

    (B) contrasts and parallels.

    (C) epigrams and aphorisms.

    (D) simile and personification.

    (E) banter and understatement.

**GO ON TO THE NEXT PAGE**

*Questions 18–29 refer to the following passage. After reading the poem, choose the best answer to each question.*

To be or not to be—that is the question.
Whether 'tis nobler in the mind to suffer
The slings and arrows of outrageous fortune
Or to take arms against a sea of troubles

*Line*
(5)    And by opposing, end them. To die, to sleep—
No more, and by a sleep to say we end
The heartache and the thousand natural shocks
Which flesh is heir to. 'Tis a consummation
Devoutly to be wished. To die, to sleep,

(10)    To sleep—perchance to dream. Aye, there's the rub,     *rub* obstacle
For in that sleep of death what dreams may come
When we have shuffled off this mortal coil     *shuffled...coil* cast off life's problems
Must give us pause. There's the respect     *respect* reason
That makes calamity of so long life.     *calamity...life* long life a hardship

(15)    For who would bear the whips and scorns of time,
The oppressor's wrong, the proud man's contumely     *contumely* insulting behavior
The pangs of despised love, the law's delay,
The insolence of office and the spurns
That patient merit of the unworthy takes,

(20)    When he himself might his quietus make     *quietus* final settlement (e.g., death)
With a bare bodkin? Who would fardels bear,     *bodkin* dagger    *fardels* burdens
To grunt and sweat under a weary life,
But that the dread of something after death,
The undiscovered country from whose bourn     *bourn* boundary

(25)    No traveler returns, puzzles the will,
And makes us rather bear those ills we have
Than fly to others that we know not of?
Thus conscience does make cowards of us all,     *conscience* consciousness
And thus the native hue of resolution

(30)    Is sicklied o'er with the pale cast of thought,
And enterprises of great pitch and moment
With this regard, their currents turn awry
And lose the name of action.

(1602)

GO ON TO THE NEXT PAGE

18. Which statement seems most accurate about the speaker?

    (A) He feels rejected by both his friends and family.

    (B) He is uncertain about either living or dying.

    (C) He is pining for both an unrequited love and unfulfilled plans.

    (D) He is mourning the deaths of both a hated enemy and a beloved relative.

    (E) He is fatigued by the stress and routine of life.

19. The choices he refers to in lines 2–5 can best be summed up by which of the following pairs?

    (A) Passivity versus assertiveness

    (B) War on land versus war at sea

    (C) Armed combat versus unarmed combat

    (D) Sensitivity versus coldness

    (E) Moderation versus intemperance

20. Starting with the phrase "To die, to sleep," lines 5–13 demonstrate

    (A) choices the speaker faces.

    (B) fearful fits of sleep experienced by the speaker.

    (C) a way of looking at sleep.

    (D) a way of looking at death.

    (E) the speaker's open-mindedness.

21. The "rub" (line 10) mentioned by the speaker refers to an idea suggested by the phrase

    (A) "the thousand natural shocks" (line 7).

    (B) "a consummation" (line 8).

    (C) "To die" (line 9).

    (D) "to sleep" (line 9).

    (E) "to dream" (line 10).

22. In lines 10–14, the conflicting ideas are

    (A) that sleep is soothing but death can be horrifying.

    (B) that mortality is frightening but immortality offers hope.

    (C) that death is comforting but what may come after is troubling.

    (D) that life is coiled with trouble but we have moments of pleasure.

    (E) that we must pause to reflect but take action after reflecting.

23. In lines 15–21, "he himself" (line 20) refers to

    (A) "the unworthy" (line 19).

    (B) "despised love" (line 17).

    (C) "the proud man" (line 16).

    (D) "The oppressor" (line 16).

    (E) "who" (line 15).

**GO ON TO THE NEXT PAGE**

24. What does the question in lines 15–21 propose?

    (A) That death seems relatively easy in the face of life's various hardships

    (B) That some avocation may distract one from life's dulling routine

    (C) That revenge is the best response to the many wrongdoers in one's life

    (D) That the only way to survive life's hardship is to become as heartless as others

    (E) That the many roles that one plays in life will ultimately end with death

25. The subject for the predicates "puzzles the will" (line 25) and "makes us rather bear the ills we have/Than fly to others that we know not of" (lines 26–27) is

    (A) "traveler" (line 25).

    (B) "The undiscovered country" (line 24).

    (C) "death" (line 23).

    (D) "dread" (line 23).

    (E) "Who" (line 21).

26. The phrase "The undiscovered country from whose bourn/No traveler returns" (lines 24–25) is

    (A) a symbol of the narrator's hope.

    (B) a metaphor for "death" (line 23).

    (C) a foreshadowing of revelation.

    (D) a reason for the "action" named in line 33.

    (E) an analogy to "conscience" (line 28).

27. Following the question in lines 15–21, the next question in lines 21–27 does all of the following EXCEPT

    (A) continue to discuss life's difficulties.

    (B) answer the question in lines 15–21.

    (C) offer a way to mediate the problems of life.

    (D) rationalize why we prefer life to death.

    (E) suggest that the afterlife may be as difficult as life itself.

**GO ON TO THE NEXT PAGE**

28. What is the speaker's meaning in the phrase "With this regard, their currents turn awry" (line 32)?

    (A) Fear of what may come after death impedes remarkable achievements.

    (B) Sleep prevents any great enterprises from ever occurring.

    (C) Narrow-mindedness gets in the way of spiritual development.

    (D) Action cannot take place without wise advice.

    (E) Nothing can be resolved without change.

29. The entire soliloquy can best be summed up as

    (A) a perverse death wish.

    (B) an unresolved contemplation.

    (C) a plea for change.

    (D) a diatribe against society.

    (E) an incoherent polemic.

**GO ON TO THE NEXT PAGE**

*Questions 30–38 refer to the following passage. After reading the passage, choose the best answer to each question.*

I had rarely had reason to enter my father's room
prior to this occasion and I was newly struck by the
smallness and starkness of it. Indeed, I recall my
*Line* impression at the time was of having stepped into
(5) a prison cell, but then, this might have had as
much to do with the pale early light as with the size
of the room or the bareness of its walls. For my
father had opened his curtains and was sitting,
shaved and in full uniform, on the edge of his bed
(10) from where evidently he had been watching the
sky turn to dawn. At least one assumed he had
been watching the sky, there being little else to
view from his small window other than roof-tiles
and guttering. The oil lamp beside his bed had
(15) been extinguished, and when I saw my father
glance disapprovingly at the lamp I had brought to
guide me up the rickety staircase, I quickly
lowered the wick. Having done this, I noticed all
the more the effect of the pale light coming into
(20) the room and the way it lit up the edges of my
father's craggy, lined, still awesome features.

"Ah," I said, and gave a short laugh, "I might
have known Father would be up and ready for the
day."

(25) "I've been up for the past three hours," he said,
looking me up and down rather coldly.

"I hope Father is not being kept awake by his
arthritic troubles."

"I get all the sleep I need."

(30) My father reached forward to the only chair in
the room, a small wooden one, and placing both
hands on its back, brought himself to his feet.
When I saw him stood upright before me, I could
not be sure to what extent he was hunched over
(35) due to his infirmity and what extent due to the
habit of accommodating the steeply sloped
ceilings of the room.

"I have come here to relate something to you,
Father."

(40) "Then relate it briefly and concisely. I haven't
all morning to listen to your chatter."

"In that case, Father, I will come straight to
the point."

"Come to the point then and be done with it.
(45) Some of us have work to be getting on with."

"Very well. Since you wish me to be brief, I will
do my best to comply. The fact is, Father has
become increasingly infirm. So much so that even
the duties of the under-butler are now beyond his
(50) capabilities. His lordship is of the view, as indeed I
am myself, that while Father is allowed to
continue with his present round of duties, he
represents an ever-present threat to the smooth
running of this household, and in particular to
(55) next week's important international gathering."

My father's face, in the half-light, betrayed no
emotion whatsoever.

"Principally," I continued, "it has been felt that
Father should no longer be asked to wait at table,
(60) whether or not guests are present."

"I have waited at table every day for the last
fifty-four years," my father remarked, his voice
perfectly unhurried.

"Furthermore, it has been decided that Father
(65) should not carry laden trays of any sort for even
the shortest distance. In view of these limitations,
and knowing Father's esteem for conciseness, I
have listed here the revised round of duties he
will from now on be expected to perform."

(70) I felt disinclined actually to hand him the piece of
paper I was holding, and so put it down on the end of
his bed. My father glanced at it then returned his gaze
to me. There was still no trace of emotion discernible
in his expression, and his hands on the back of the
(75) chair appeared perfectly relaxed. Hunched over or
not, it was impossible not to be reminded of the
sheer impact of his physical presence—

(1988)

GO ON TO THE NEXT PAGE

30. The narrator's feelings about his father can best be described as

    (A) nervously awed.

    (B) bitterly condescending.

    (C) wistfully disappointed.

    (D) coldly callous.

    (E) quietly affable.

31. The narrator's behavior toward his father can best be described as

    (A) austere and short-tempered.

    (B) encouraging and advising.

    (C) demonstrative and giddy.

    (D) polite and officious.

    (E) playful and teasing.

32. In the first paragraph, the condition of the room and the staircase leading to it could symbolize all of the following about the father EXCEPT his

    (A) age.

    (B) stolidity.

    (C) work experience.

    (D) professional demeanor.

    (E) infirmity.

33. The oil lamps in lines 14–18 could represent what about the father and the narrator?

    (A) The extinguished lamp could symbolize the father's impending demotion; the lit lamp could represent the narrator's household power.

    (B) The extinguished lamp could represent the narrator's hope of reunion with his father; the lit lamp could symbolize the narrator's new professional relationship with his father.

    (C) The extinguished lamp could symbolize the end of the father's life; the lit lamp could represent the rejuvenating effect the narrator has on his father.

    (D) The extinguished lamp could symbolize the father's lack of opportunities in life; the lit lamp could represent the narrator's abundance of opportunities.

    (E) The extinguished lamp could symbolize the father's bitterness; the lit lamp could represent the narrator's seeking of new knowledge about his father.

34. The use of "Father" in lines 23, 27, 47, 51, 59, and 64 indicates which of the following about the narrator?

    I. Respect for his father

    II. Emotional attachment to his father

    III. Discomfort in addressing his father

    (A) I only

    (B) III only

    (C) I and III only

    (D) II and III only

    (E) I, II, and III

**GO ON TO THE NEXT PAGE**

35. In lines 46–55, which of the following apparently holds the *least* importance for the narrator?

    (A) The opinions of "his lordship"

    (B) The manner in which the household is run

    (C) The upcoming "international gathering"

    (D) Maintaining a professional attitude

    (E) His personal relationship with his father

36. The response to the father in lines 64–69 demonstrates that the narrator

    (A) does not hear what his father has just said.

    (B) refuses to realize the emotional weight of what the father has just said.

    (C) is staying focused on the professional angle of the discussion.

    (D) wants to indicate to his father that the demotion is not so shameful.

    (E) fears that his father might berate him unless the narrator continues uninterrupted.

37. The last paragraph makes apparent that the narrator

    (A) desperately wants his father to quit so that they may have a normal relationship.

    (B) remains aloof from his father because of their mutually destructive past.

    (C) has been reaching out to his father all this time but to no effect.

    (D) honors his father and emulates his purposefulness, ironically driving them apart.

    (E) has confidence that his father will overcome this hurtful but temporary setback.

38. This passage is best described as

    (A) a social commentary on working-class issues.

    (B) an example of people failing to communicate fully.

    (C) a description of a typical father-son relationship.

    (D) a model for employee/employer communication.

    (E) a polemic arguing against single-parent families.

**GO ON TO THE NEXT PAGE**

*Questions 39–48 refer to the following poem. After reading the poem, choose the best answer to each question.*

"Ode to Ethiopia"

O Mother Race! to thee I bring
This pledge of faith unwavering,
   This tribute to thy glory.
*Line* I know the pangs which thou didst feel,
(5) When Slavery crushed thee with its heel,
   With thy dear blood all gory.

Sad days were those—ah, sad indeed!
But through the land the fruitful seed
   Of better times was growing.
(10) The plant of freedom upward sprung,
And spread its leaves so fresh and young
   Its blossoms now are blowing.

On every hand in this fair land,
Proud Ethiope's swarthy children stand
(15)    Beside their fairer neighbor;
The forests flee before their stroke,
Their hammers ring, their forges smoke,
   They stir in honest labour.

They tread the fields where honour calls;
(20) Their voices sound through senate halls
   In majesty and power.
To right they cling; thy hymns they sing
Up to the skies in beauty ring,
   And bolder grow each hour.

(25) Be proud, my Race, in mind and soul;
Thy name is writ on Glory's scroll
   In characters of fire.
High 'mid the clouds of Fame's bright sky
Thy banner's blazoned folds now fly,
(30)    And truth shall lift them higher.

Thou hast the right to noble pride,
Whose spotless robes were purified
   By blood's severe baptism.
Upon thy brow the cross was laid,
(35) And labour's painful sweat-beads made
   A consecrating chrism.

No other race, or white or black,
When bound as thou wert, to the rack,
   So seldom stooped to grieving;
(40) No other race, when free again,
Forgot the past and proved them men
   So noble in forgiving.

Go on and up! Our souls and eyes
Shall follow thy continuous rise;
(45)    Our ears shall list thy story
From bards who from thy root shall spring,
And proudly tune their lyres to sing
   Of Ethiopia's glory.

               (1896)

39. In the poem, the speaker is making an apostrophe to

   (A) the African Americans of his time.

   (B) all African Americans—past, present, and future.

   (C) all people of color.

   (D) the Africans who came before him.

   (E) the human race.

**GO ON TO THE NEXT PAGE**

40. The plant imagery of the second stanza describes all of the following EXCEPT the

    (A) end of hard labor.

    (B) growth of freedom.

    (C) changing times.

    (D) thriving of a people.

    (E) new course for a society.

41. The "fairer neighbor" of line 15 is

    (A) anyone willing to erase the memory of slavery.

    (B) America.

    (C) any white American.

    (D) Canada.

    (E) anyone treating African Americans with respect.

42. The speaker portrays Ethiopia's African American decendants in lines 16–24 as

    (A) hardworking in their present situation but mindful of their origins.

    (B) generous with each other but understandably cautious with others.

    (C) content for the present but getting ready for social revolution.

    (D) moving westward to find opportunity but still building in the East.

    (E) capable of great achievement but harboring deep resentment.

43. The speaker's expectation in lines 25–30 is that

    (A) the fame he will derive from writing this poem will serve to advance all African Americans.

    (B) a newly commissioned flag will honor the sacrifices and achievements of the African race in America.

    (C) the history and accomplishments of his people will become better known than they are now.

    (D) the recognition that his people deserve has already reached its acme, but they can take comfort in this knowledge.

    (E) after a great battle, African Americans will emerge victorious over their white enslavers.

44. In lines 31–36, the speaker uses all of the following EXCEPT

    (A) Christian imagery.

    (B) a righteous tone.

    (C) paradox.

    (D) personification.

    (E) foreshadowing.

45. In lines 37–42, the speaker attributes what two things to the addressee?

    (A) Stoicism and a capacity for absolution

    (B) A need to forgive and a justifiable sadness

    (C) Pride and an ability to see beyond racial differences

    (D) Noble accomplishments and a penchant for gratitude

    (E) Bravado and a manliness facing the threat of emasculation

**GO ON TO THE NEXT PAGE**

46. The speaker's comment about "bards" (line 46) makes an ironic reference to

    (A) slave spirituals.

    (B) Shakespeare.

    (C) African mythology.

    (D) the fall of white America.

    (E) poets like himself.

47. Throughout the poem, the narrator views the addressee as

    (A) formerly abused but noble.

    (B) dangerously weak but recovering.

    (C) spiritually distant but emotionally available.

    (D) physically strong but in need of guidance.

    (E) presently downtrodden but optimistic.

48. According to the poem, the future seems hopeful for African Americans because

    (A) the spirit of ancient Ethiopia will be reincarnated in them.

    (B) natural social change will right the wrongs of the past.

    (C) their own honor and hard work will promote them.

    (D) God will punish those who have taken advantage of them.

    (E) the abuse of slavery makes them deserving of advancement.

**GO ON TO THE NEXT PAGE**

*Questions 49–57 refer to the following passage. After reading the passage, choose the best answer to each question.*

By a passage in one of your late Papers, I
understand that the Government at home will
not suffer our mistaken Assemblies to make any
Law for the preventing or discouraging the
*(5)* importation of convicts from Great Britain, for
this kind Reason, '*That such Laws are against the
Publick Utility, as they tend to prevent the
Improvement and Well Peopling of the Colonies.*'

Such a tender parental Concern in our *Mother
(10) Country* for the *Welfare* of her Children, calls
aloud for the highest Returns of Gratitude and
Duty. This every one must be sensible of: But 'tis
said, that in our present Circumstances it is
absolutely impossible for us to make *such* as are
*(15)* adequate to the Favour. I own it; but nevertheless
let us do our Endeavour. 'Tis something to show
a grateful Disposition.

In some of the uninhabited Parts of the
Provinces, there are Numbers of these venomous
*(20)* Reptiles we call rattlesnakes; Felons-convict from
the Beginning of the World: These, whenever we
meet with them, we put to Death, by Virtue of an
old Law, *Thou Shall bruise his Head.** But as this
is a sanguinary Law, and may be too cruel; and as
*(25)* however mischievous those Creatures are with
us, they may possibly change their Natures, if
they were to change the Climate; I would humbly
propose, that this general Sentence of *Death* be
changed for *Transportation*.
*(30)* In the Spring of the Year, when they first creep
out of their Holes, they are feeble, heavy, slow, and
easily taken; and if a small Bounty were allowed *per*
Head, some Thousands might be collected
annually, and *transported* to Britain. There I would
*(35)* propose to have them carefully distributed in *St.
James Park*, in the *Spring-Gardens*, and other Places
of Pleasure about *London*; in the Gardens of all the
Nobility and Gentry throughout the Nation; but

particularly in the Gardens of the *Prime Ministers*,
*(40)* the *Lords of Trade* and *Members of Parliament*; for
to them we are *most particularly* obliged.

There is no human Scheme so perfect, but
some Inconveniences may be objected to it: Yet
when the Conveniencies far exceed, the Scheme
*(45)* is judged Operational, and fit to be executed.
Thus Inconveniencies have been objected to
that good *wise* Act of Parliament, by virtue of
which all *Newgates†* and *Dungeons* in *Britain* are
emptied into the colonies. It has been said, that
*(50)* these Thieves and Villains introduced among us,
spoil the Morals of Youth in the Neighborhoods
that entertain them, and perpetrate many horrid
Crimes: But let not *private Interests* obstruct
publick Utility. Our Mother knows what is best
*(55)* for us.

(1751)

---

* *bruise his Head* a reference to God's curse on the serpent in
the Garden of Eden (*Genesis* 3:15)

† *Newgate* an infamous London prison

49. The tone in the passage above is

   (A) solemn.

   (B) obsequious.

   (C) carefree.

   (D) sarcastic.

   (E) endearing.

**GO ON TO THE NEXT PAGE**

50. As related in lines 1–8, the problem addressed by the narrator includes all of the following EXCEPT

    (A) power taken away from American lawmakers.

    (B) British disregard for American government and society.

    (C) British criminals being exported, without hindrance, to America.

    (D) British opinion that criminal exports to America will have positive results.

    (E) American criminals being forced to remain on American soil.

51. The narrator's proposal in lines 18–29 parallels the previously discussed problem in all of the following ways EXCEPT that

    (A) the snakes are referred to as "Felons-convict" (line 20).

    (B) the proposal seemingly mimics the humanity and utility of the criminal importation to America.

    (C) the snakes may change their ways in Great Britain as the exported criminals are supposed to have done in America.

    (D) the proposal offers an exchange of one evil for another.

    (E) the snakes are as easily transported to Britain as they were destroyed in America.

52. In lines 30–34, how does the narrator make the gathering of snakes sound agreeable?

    (A) It could be both easy and profitable.

    (B) The event could become an annual holiday.

    (C) It would be a chance to regain contact with Britain.

    (D) It would be pleasurable and sporting.

    (E) The result would gain America favor with Britain.

53. In lines 34–41, the distribution of snakes in various British garden spots could represent all of the following EXCEPT

    (A) the need to awaken British government officials to their own callous judgment.

    (B) the importation of British criminals to America.

    (C) the narrator's negative reaction to British criminal importation.

    (D) the spoiling of an ideal place with a foreign evil.

    (E) the American desire to take over British government.

**GO ON TO THE NEXT PAGE**

54. The narrator says that Americans are "*most particularly* obliged" to "*Prime Ministers*, the *Lords of Trade*, and *Members of Parliament*" (lines 39–41) because these groups

    (A) are most interested in American welfare.

    (B) have helped establish America as a land of freedom.

    (C) are most responsible for the idea of British criminal exportation.

    (D) have championed America's causes in the British government.

    (E) understand the positive implications of criminal emigration.

55. The word "Inconveniencies" in line 46 is an example of

    (A) hyperbole.

    (B) metonymy.

    (C) understatement.

    (D) left-handed compliment.

    (E) antithesis.

56. The phrase "let not *private Interests* obstruct publick Utility" (lines 53–54) is an example of all of the following EXCEPT

    (A) antithesis.

    (B) personification.

    (C) an allusion to a phrase "in one of your late Papers" (line 1).

    (D) a satirical attempt to emphasize the flaw of British criminal importation.

    (E) a reference to one of the "Inconveniencies" (line 46) that the narrator has described.

57. The sentence, "Our mother knows what is best for us" (lines 54–55) is an example of all of the following EXCEPT

    (A) irony.

    (B) personification.

    (C) an admission of British superiority.

    (D) a continuation of the maternal imagery in lines 9–17.

    (E) the tone of the entire passage.

**GO ON TO THE NEXT PAGE**

*Questions 58–63 refer to the following poem. After reading the poem, choose the best answer to each question.*

### 1

The gray sea and the long black land;
And the yellow half-moon large and low;
And the startled little waves that leap
*Line* In fiery ringlets from their sleep,
(5) As I gain the cove with pushing prow,
And quench its speed i' the slushy sand.

### 2

Then a mile of warm sea-scented beach;
Three fields to cross till a farm appears;
A tap at the pane, the quick sharp scratch
(10) And blue spurt of a lighted match,
And a voice less loud, through its joys and fears,
Than the two hearts beating each to each!

(1845)

58. This poem is a description of

  (A) a nighttime tryst.

  (B) a fisherman's return.

  (C) a Viking invasion.

  (D) a nightly voyage.

  (E) a clandestine elopement.

59. All of the following are part of the first stanza's nocturnal imagery EXCEPT

  (A) "gray sea" (line 1).

  (B) "black land" (line 1).

  (C) "yellow half-moon" (line 2).

  (D) "little waves…/…from their sleep" (lines 3–4).

  (E) "pushing prow" (line 5).

60. The word "quench" in line 6 does all of the following EXCEPT

  (A) symbolize the narrator's thirst for the sea's power.

  (B) indicate the end of the narrator's voyage.

  (C) act as part of a compound verb phrase.

  (D) create a feeling of satisfaction in having reached shore.

  (E) join the alliterated *s* in mimicking the sounds of the beach.

61. The description of the sounds of the "voice" and the "two hearts" in lines 11–12 is called

  (A) apostrophe.

  (B) anachronism.

  (C) euphemism.

  (D) simile.

  (E) hyperbole.

62. Both stanzas are constructed using

  (A) elegiac verse.

  (B) sonnet sestets.

  (C) sentence fragments.

  (D) heroic couplets.

  (E) third-person point of view.

**GO ON TO THE NEXT PAGE**

63. The type of construction mentioned in question 62 creates the feeling that

    (A) the people in the poem are doomed to tragedy.

    (B) the people in the poem are being discussed analytically.

    (C) we are seeing only a segment of a larger, longer story.

    (D) the poem has several characteristics of an epic.

    (E) we are seeing these characters from a great distance.

## STOP!

**If you finish before time is up,
you may check your work.**

# Answer Key
## Practice Test 5

| | | |
|---|---|---|
| 1. B | 22. C | 43. C |
| 2. B | 23. E | 44. E |
| 3. E | 24. A | 45. A |
| 4. C | 25. D | 46. E |
| 5. A | 26. B | 47. A |
| 6. B | 27. C | 48. C |
| 7. D | 28. A | 49. D |
| 8. C | 29. B | 50. E |
| 9. C | 30. A | 51. E |
| 10. C | 31. D | 52. A |
| 11. B | 32. C | 53. E |
| 12. E | 33. A | 54. C |
| 13. D | 34. C | 55. C |
| 14. B | 35. E | 56. B |
| 15. A | 36. C | 57. C |
| 16. E | 37. D | 58. A |
| 17. B | 38. B | 59. E |
| 18. B | 39. D | 60. A |
| 19. A | 40. A | 61. E |
| 20. D | 41. C | 62. C |
| 21. E | 42. A | 63. C |

# ANSWERS AND EXPLANATIONS

**1. (B)** In this poem, Love is a "juggler," (line 1) who operates "cunningly" (line 3) and "Can…deceive" (line 4). He is a "wanton child" (line 5) who does "tricks" (line 7) and is associated with "tyrannies" (line 8). There appears to be no tenderness in this description of love.

**2. (B)** *Wanting* can mean both "desiring" and "lacking." Here, Love is a juggler, a performer who desires to have eyes watching him; thus, Item II makes sense. Furthermore, love is traditionally portrayed as blind, and his lacking sight here sets up an irony in line 4: the blind deceiving the sighted. So item I is also sensible. However, because he is cunning, Love hardly lacks insight. Additionally, if he wanted to ignore us, then he would not have so much interaction with us. Therefore, III and IV do not work.

**3. (E)** The word "fools" would make only (A), (B), or (E) right. The present tense of lines 5–8, however, implies that love's machinations are an ongoing process. In other words, we have *experience* with love and that experience should *educate* us, but we remain naïve in thinking love will actually turn out for the good.

**4. (C)** Line 10 tells us that love takes our "hearts." The speaker continues this idea in lines 11–12, where she says that it is only because our hearts have been abducted by love that we can "abuse," or fool, our sight. In other words, in spite of what our eyes register, we pay no attention to our eyes, because love has our hearts. It isn't that love is blind—our stolen hearts fool our eyesight.

**5. (A)** Love's juggling act does "abuse/The sight with nimble and delightful skill." Skillfully, Love manipulates our sight.

**6. (B)** There is no great labor here. When he is at play, Love saps our wills easily; we cannot resist. There is antithesis in Love's gain being our loss

(line 13); Love is a "wanton child" (line 5) and we are "childlike" (line 14); we "cannot his sports refuse" (line 14), so we fall prey to him and our "will" is "lost" (line 13).

**7. (D)** As seen in question 1's explanation, Love deals with us in cunning and deceitful ways. The speaker describes this behavior, yet she notes that we do not "refuse" his sporting with us (line 14).

**8. (C)** The narrator says in lines 1–2 that she wants to "finish that story for the editor of the 'Dutchman.'" Since she is engaged in a concrete activity, (B) is out. The identification of the editor for something called the "Dutchman" and the content of the story she is finishing rule out (D). Because she is doing something *for* the editor and not reading something *by* him, we can eliminate (A). Later in line 29, when she claims the item on which she is working as "my manuscript," we have a strong indicator that she is the one doing the writing, not an editor. When presented with various household matters, she attempts to address them all, not simply ignore them.

**9. (C)** The sun image is part of the narrator's story for the "Dutchman." Although this story takes place outside, we never see the outside of the narrator's home. True, the interior of the house is chaotic, but the house's exterior is unknown to us.

**10. (C)** We really don't have enough in the dialogue to determine how much love is shared by the narrator and her husband. If anything, their mutual use of "dear" in addressing each other shows at least some affection.

**11. (B)** The line comes from someone who is noting not only the lack of potatoes in the house but also that there will be none for dinner. Furthermore, the person quoted has a dialect different from the narrator and her husband, and the narrator uses no "dear" or "Smith" when talking to this character. Of the options offered in this question, the most likely speaker is the servant.

**12. (E)** The child's interruption comes right after the banner is described, humorously suggesting that the banner has written on it, "Ma! I've torn my pantaloons!"

**13. (D)** In the narrator's text, a crowd in a church is rushing a horseman who is waving a banner. Likewise, the narrator is being rushed at from all sides by her family and servant(s).

**14. (B)** The narrator is engaged with her text but not to the point of failing to recognize her husband. She uses "Smith" again when she makes a final break with her manuscript (line 26), and at that point, she would be the most aware of her surroundings. So "Smith" is hardly an amnesiac title for her husband.

**15. (A)** In her address to her husband in lines 26–30, the narrator is alarmed that the husband has held the button-swallowing child upside down for so long. In that same sentence, she also exclaims that a child has torn the first page of her narrative. Once she has noticed these two events, she stops writing. Items I and II thus have evidence to support them.

Since the butcher's appearance happens a few lines before her exclamations and she makes no reference to it in lines 26–30, item III seems unlikely. Then, by the end of the passage, the narrator declares that "it's no use for a married woman to cultivate her intellect." She has not ceased her writing out of guilt but out of exasperation; item IV thus lacks credibility.

**16. (E)** The narrator has been so engaged by her text that she seems loath to abandon it. However, because several household matters—especially her button-swallowing son—need her immediate attention, she sees that it is "no use" to "cultivate her intellect" by writing.

**17. (B)** The passage is a constant back-and-forth between the narrator's manuscript and household interruptions. Some of these interruptions contrast with her story—the noble slogan on the banner compared with the triviality of her child's torn pantaloons, for instance—and other interruptions parallel her story—such as the crowds that rush both the horseman of her story and the narrator herself.

**18. (B)** The very opening, "To be or not to be," shows that the speaker is facing a choice between existence and nonexistence. He discusses the difficulty of the choice in later lines.

**19. (A)** To answer either with (B) or (C) would be to take the figurative language of these lines as the speaker's *actual* problem. He uses the military metaphors to distinguish between his inaction ("suffer/The slings and arrows of outrageous fortune") and the possible action he might take ("take arms against a sea of troubles").

**20. (D)** Choice (A) might be true for the entire passage, but lines 5–13 deal with a single option; no other choice is discussed here. Both (B) and (C) miss the figurative use of "sleep." Every time sleep is mentioned, it occurs as an appositive for death ("To die, to sleep"); "sleep" renames "die"—sleep is a metaphor. "Open-mindedness" in (E) connotes that the speaker is keeping several options open. However, in lines 5–13, he is only discussing death and only seems to have a negative view of it. (D) refers to the death/sleep connection and the speaker's uncertainty about death.

**21. (E)** The speaker doesn't mention the "rub" until he has brought up the concept of dreaming. The reason that dreams are an obstacle is that they "give us pause." There is an uncertainty to the dreams that may occur in the sleep of death. So death does not offer an assured comfort.

**22. (C)** Choice (A) does not consider sleep as a metaphor for death. There is nothing hopeful about the speaker's outlook on a possible afterlife, so choice (B) is out. (D) ignores the discussion of death taking place in the lines. (E) may be true in other parts of the soliloquy but not here; there is action in "[shuffling] off this mortal coil," but that action occurs before "pausing," not after. (C) makes death sound comforting ("sleep of death") but shows that what may come after can make us hesitate.

23. **(E)** Answers (A) through (D) all refer to examples of what the "who" might endure in life. The "who" in line 15 puts up with these difficulties but could end the conflict with a single "bare bodkin," stabbing himself. Thus, he could easily escape life's abuses.

24. **(A)** After listing the many hardships associated with living, the speaker suggests that they all could be relieved through death.

25. **(D)** A new clause start with "But that" at line 23. Then we have the noun "dread," which is modified by the prepositional phrase "of something." The object "something" is in turn modified by "after death," and the object "death" has a modifying appositive that runs from "The undiscovered country" to "traveler returns." The key here is to eliminate the prepositional and appositive phrases. Then we are left with "dread ... puzzles the will/ And makes us rather bear the ills we have." In simpler language, our dread of what may happen after death—and death is like an undiscovered country from which no one returns—saps our will and makes us put up with life's hardships; the alternative is dealing with death's unknowns.

26. **(B)** See the discussion of the word *death* in the explanation for question 25. The appositive phrase is acting as a metaphor comparing death to a country.

27. **(C)** Choice (A) seems a possibility because of the phrase "grunt and sweat under a weary life." The answer to the question in lines 15–21 occurs after the word "But" in line 23, so (B) could work. Answers (D) and (E) are just other ways of stating

answer (B). (C), then, is the only option that does not work; there is a sense in these lines that the speaker is caught in the middle of something, but he is not mediating—actively balancing to achieve middle ground. Rather, he seems indecisive, unable to escape from the middle.

28. **(A)** The "enterprises of great pitch and moment" (line 31), or remarkable achievements, lose their "current" or course of action "with this regard": that death, being an unknown, is something to be dreaded. The statement at line 32 is in response to the question of lines 21–27, whose idea is summed up in "Thus conscience does make cowards of us all" (line 28).

29. **(B)** The passage weighs the pros and cons of staying alive or seeking death, of remaining passive or becoming active. It ends with commentary but no resolution.

30. **(A)** The narrator describes his father as having "still awesome features" (line 21) and is "reminded of the sheer impact of his physical presence" (lines 76–77). If we combine these descriptions with the narrator's act of turning down the lamp, at which the father looks disapprovingly (lines 14–18), then we see a nervously awed narrator.

31. **(D)** In his narration, we see the son awed by his father. When he speaks to his father, though, he is very businesslike. In lines 22–24, he compliments his father's work ethic. He politely expresses concern—but not too much—for his father's arthritis in lines 27–28. In lines 46–55, he is compliant with his father's wishes but still emotionally remote when delivering the news of the demotion.

32. **(C)** We have information on (A), (B), (D), and (E) but none on (C), making it the likely exception. Since the room is stark, this feature could represent both the father's stolid treatment of his son (B) and the brisk professionalism with which he approaches his job (D). The staircase is described as "rickety" (line 17), thus symbolizing either the father's age

(A) or the infirmity he demonstrates when rising from his bed in lines 30–32 (E).

**33. (A)** An extinguished lamp represents an end. Since this lamp is used by the father, it easily represents the end of his career as he has known it. The lit lamp belongs to the son, who not only still has power in the household but exercises that power over his father. Even his hiding of the lamp shows the narrator's slight discomfort in displaying his power.

**34. (C)** Item I is correct because the respect the narrator has for his father borders on fear; the respect is obviously apparent.

Item III is correct because we see his discomfort when he hides the lamp; also, we know that the son has uncomfortable news to relay: the demotion of his own father.

Item II might be attractive because an overuse of the word *Father* could be a sign of endearment; however, every instance of the word *Father* cited in the question is a third-person reference. When the narrator should be talking *to* his father, he seems to be talking about his father—while the old man is in the room. Such pronominal distancing is a sign of detachment, not attachment.

**35. (E)** The emotional distance and shallow professionalism with which he treats his father both show that their personal relationship has little immediate priority for the narrator.

**36. (C)** Choice (C) is correct for a very simple reason: It does not make an assumption about the narrator. In this part of the dialogue, he makes no comment about what the father has just said—no comment to the father, no comment to us. We know from the content of lines 64–69 that the son talks only about the job, so (C) has to be right.

**37. (D)** He has expressed an awe of his father, already discussed in the answer for question 30. His father is very single-minded about his job; the son's speeches to the father show this same kind of focus.

Logically, one would expect respect and emulation to bring a son closer to his father. However, here we see the opposite occurring: The father is becoming an emotionally distant subordinate to the son.

**38. (B)** Other answers here may be worded more impressively, but one should not be fooled; as ordinary as (B) sounds, it is the correct answer. Rather than express surprise or anger or any emotional reaction to the news of his demotion, the father simply states that he has "waited at table every day for the last fifty-four years" (lines 61–62). The son tells *us* about the awe he feels for his father but chooses to maintain a distant professionalism with him. Neither one of them expresses his true feelings to the other.

**39. (D)** The poem is entitled "Ode to Ethiopia." The speaker is addressing his "Mother Race." It follows that he is speaking to his African ancestors. If he were speaking to contemporary African Americans—the ones who live in his time—he would use a term such as "Brother Race" or "Fellow Race." In fact, he often refers to his contemporaries in this poem, but he talks *about* them, not *to* them.

**40. (A)** We might be able to infer that there is *continued* labor here, since there is so much growth and thriving mentioned, but there is certainly no *end* to labor—if labor is really discussed at all in this stanza.

**41. (C)** The "fairer neighbor" of line 15 is a contrast to the Mother Race's "swarthy children" of line 14. The term *fairer* is simply a reference to skin color.

**42. (A)** Phrases such as "they stir in honest labor" (line 18) prove that African Americans are working hard in their present situation in America. But they are also mindful of their origins, as seen when they sing the "hymns" of Ethiopia (line 22).

**43. (C)** The "banner" of the Mother Race now flies "'mid the clouds of Fame's bright sky" (line 28).

That is, the speaker's African predecessors have gained fame. But the folds of the flag shall be lifted "higher" by "truth" (line 30). Logically continuing the metaphor, we see that truth will cause the African race to gain even greater fame.

**44. (E)** The imagery discusses only what the Africans have endured in the past, not what will happen in the future.

**45. (A)** According to the speaker, even in the face of great physical pain (line 38), African Americans have displayed stoicism because they have "So seldom stooped to grieving" (line 39). But in spite of the injustices of slavery, they have also been "So noble in forgiving" (line 42). In fact, the speaker feels that they have shown the kind of forgiveness that can be called "absolution," because it even "Forgot the past" (line 41).

**46. (E)** A bard is traditionally a traveling singer, but he can also be simply a poet. The speaker has predicted that black poets will write poems about the Mother Race: "bards ... from thy root shall spring/And proudly tune their lyres to sing/Of Ethiopia's glory." Yet, ironically, we already have a poem here that is written presumably by an African American poet and that glorifies Africans. The speaker has already fulfilled his own prophecy.

**47. (A)** Lines 31–39 are clearest about the agonies that Africans had to endure under slavery. Yet the speaker sees the nobility of his race, past and present, in lines 14, 19, 31 and 40–42.

**48. (C)** The speaker makes several references to the honor and honest labor of Africans in America. Furthermore, because of their hard work, "Proud Ethiope's swarthy children stand" (line 14) next to white Americans. Black Americans also "bolder grow each hour" (line 24) in their work and in their voices. Thus, the speaker sees only advancement for his people.

**49. (D)** The narrator declares that Britain's government (the "Government at home" in line 2) has a "tender parental Concern" (line 9) for the colonies. This concern is expressed by mandating that British criminals be exported to America for the colonies' "*Improvement and Well Peopling*" (line 8). To foist lawbreakers on a region innocent of these criminals' wrongs hardly seems tender or parental. Thus, at this point, and continuing in the passage, we see the narrator's sarcasm.

**50. (E)** Only "convicts from Great Britain" are discussed in lines 1–8.

**51. (E)** The narrator speaks of the snakes' destruction in America as commonplace but not necessarily as easy; lines 30–34 will later discuss the ease of snake killing. Furthermore, he says that the snakes may be transported to Great Britain but does not indicate how easy the transportation will be.

**52. (A)** The snakes are described as "feeble, heavy, slow, and easily taken" in lines 31–32. The narrator later proposes that a small bounty may be may be paid out for each collected snake. Thus, snake gathering can be both easy and profitable.

**53. (E)** The implication is that the snakes would be troublesome to the British—as British criminals would be to American colonists—but there is no description of the snakes defeating or subduing the British. Thus, the analogy in (E) does not work here.

**54. (C)** These groups include lawmakers and those who would benefit financially from criminal exportation. Thus, they are most responsible for the export of British convicts.

**55. (C)** Criminal importation into the colonies is obviously far more than an inconvenience; great social problems could arise because of this mandate. Thus, merely to call it an inconvenience is to downplay its effects.

**56. (B)** The act of obstruction is not necessarily a human one. All things, animate or inanimate, may obstruct.

**57. (C)** If the tone of the passage is satirical, then the narrator does not truly believe in British superiority.

**58. (A)** The "yellow half-moon" of line 2 is the strongest indicator that the setting occurs at night. The "tap at the pane" (line 9) demonstrates a desire to gain someone's attention at the farmhouse, and the "voice less loud" (line 11) appears to be a response from within. The "two hearts beating each to each" (line 12) implies a romantic motivation for the meeting.

**59. (E)** One need not return to the text for this answer. A prow may be pushing at any time of day, so it is not necessarily nocturnal. It is also noted that the sea is "gray" (A) and the land is "black" (B), both indicative of night. The moon is out, and the waves have been sleeping (D), both associated with night.

**60. (A)** The sea is merely a conveyor for the narrator; it helps him reach the shore and, ultimately, the farmhouse. Furthermore, the sea is described as "gray" in line 1, and it has "little waves" (line 3). Therefore, the sea is not really portrayed as powerful here.

**61. (E)** The idea here is that the voice within the farmhouse is not as loud as the beating of the two characters' hearts. To claim that two heartbeats can drown out even a whisper must be exaggeration.

**62. (C)** Neither stanza has a complete sentence.

**63. (C)** The stanzas are brief—they tell a very short story. But the fragmented narration adds to the feeling that we are only viewing a partial picture. We know almost nothing about these characters' histories, personalities, or futures.

# HOW TO CALCULATE YOUR SCORE

**Step 1: Figure out your raw score.** Use the answer key to count the number of questions you answered correctly and the number of questions you answered incorrectly. (Do not count any questions you left blank.) Multiply the number wrong by 0.25 and subtract the result from the number correct. Round the result to the nearest whole number. This is your raw score.

## SAT Subject Test: Literature Practice Test 6

| Number right | Number wrong | Raw score |
|:---:|:---:|:---:|

$$\Box \;-\; \left(0.25 \times \Box\right) \;=\; \Box$$

**Step 2: Find your scaled score.** In the Score Conversion Table below, find your raw score (rounded to the nearest whole number) in one of the columns to the left. The score directly to the right of that number will be your scaled score.

A note on your practice test scores: Don't take these scores too literally. Practice test conditions cannot precisely mirror real test conditions. Your actual SAT Subject Test: Literature score will almost certainly vary from your practice test scores. However, your scores on the practice tests will give you a rough idea of your range on the actual exam.

## Conversion Table

| Raw | Scaled | Raw | Scaled | Raw | Scaled | Raw | Scaled |
|:---:|:---:|:---:|:---:|:---:|:---:|:---:|:---:|
| 63 | 800 | 43 | 700 | 23 | 510 | 3 | 330 |
| 62 | 800 | 42 | 690 | 22 | 500 | 2 | 320 |
| 61 | 800 | 41 | 680 | 21 | 500 | 1 | 310 |
| 60 | 800 | 40 | 670 | 20 | 490 | 0 | 300 |
| 59 | 800 | 39 | 660 | 19 | 480 | -1 | 290 |
| 58 | 800 | 38 | 650 | 18 | 470 | -2 | 280 |
| 57 | 800 | 37 | 640 | 17 | 460 | -3 | 280 |
| 56 | 790 | 36 | 630 | 16 | 450 | -4 | 270 |
| 55 | 790 | 35 | 620 | 15 | 440 | -5 | 260 |
| 54 | 780 | 34 | 610 | 14 | 430 | -6 | 250 |
| 53 | 780 | 33 | 610 | 13 | 420 | -7 | 250 |
| 52 | 780 | 32 | 600 | 12 | 410 | -8 | 240 |
| 51 | 770 | 31 | 590 | 11 | 410 | -9 | 230 |
| 50 | 760 | 30 | 580 | 10 | 400 | -10 | 220 |
| 49 | 750 | 29 | 570 | 9 | 390 | -11 | 210 |
| 48 | 740 | 28 | 560 | 8 | 380 | -12 | 200 |
| 47 | 730 | 27 | 550 | 7 | 370 | -13 | 200 |
| 46 | 720 | 26 | 540 | 6 | 360 | -14 | 200 |
| 45 | 710 | 25 | 530 | 5 | 350 | | |
| 44 | 710 | 24 | 520 | 4 | 340 | | |

# Practice Test 6
## Answer Grid

1. Ⓐ Ⓑ Ⓒ Ⓓ Ⓔ
2. Ⓐ Ⓑ Ⓒ Ⓓ Ⓔ
3. Ⓐ Ⓑ Ⓒ Ⓓ Ⓔ
4. Ⓐ Ⓑ Ⓒ Ⓓ Ⓔ
5. Ⓐ Ⓑ Ⓒ Ⓓ Ⓔ
6. Ⓐ Ⓑ Ⓒ Ⓓ Ⓔ
7. Ⓐ Ⓑ Ⓒ Ⓓ Ⓔ
8. Ⓐ Ⓑ Ⓒ Ⓓ Ⓔ
9. Ⓐ Ⓑ Ⓒ Ⓓ Ⓔ
10. Ⓐ Ⓑ Ⓒ Ⓓ Ⓔ
11. Ⓐ Ⓑ Ⓒ Ⓓ Ⓔ
12. Ⓐ Ⓑ Ⓒ Ⓓ Ⓔ
13. Ⓐ Ⓑ Ⓒ Ⓓ Ⓔ
14. Ⓐ Ⓑ Ⓒ Ⓓ Ⓔ
15. Ⓐ Ⓑ Ⓒ Ⓓ Ⓔ
16. Ⓐ Ⓑ Ⓒ Ⓓ Ⓔ
17. Ⓐ Ⓑ Ⓒ Ⓓ Ⓔ
18. Ⓐ Ⓑ Ⓒ Ⓓ Ⓔ
19. Ⓐ Ⓑ Ⓒ Ⓓ Ⓔ
20. Ⓐ Ⓑ Ⓒ Ⓓ Ⓔ
21. Ⓐ Ⓑ Ⓒ Ⓓ Ⓔ

22. Ⓐ Ⓑ Ⓒ Ⓓ Ⓔ
23. Ⓐ Ⓑ Ⓒ Ⓓ Ⓔ
24. Ⓐ Ⓑ Ⓒ Ⓓ Ⓔ
25. Ⓐ Ⓑ Ⓒ Ⓓ Ⓔ
26. Ⓐ Ⓑ Ⓒ Ⓓ Ⓔ
27. Ⓐ Ⓑ Ⓒ Ⓓ Ⓔ
28. Ⓐ Ⓑ Ⓒ Ⓓ Ⓔ
29. Ⓐ Ⓑ Ⓒ Ⓓ Ⓔ
30. Ⓐ Ⓑ Ⓒ Ⓓ Ⓔ
31. Ⓐ Ⓑ Ⓒ Ⓓ Ⓔ
32. Ⓐ Ⓑ Ⓒ Ⓓ Ⓔ
33. Ⓐ Ⓑ Ⓒ Ⓓ Ⓔ
34. Ⓐ Ⓑ Ⓒ Ⓓ Ⓔ
35. Ⓐ Ⓑ Ⓒ Ⓓ Ⓔ
36. Ⓐ Ⓑ Ⓒ Ⓓ Ⓔ
37. Ⓐ Ⓑ Ⓒ Ⓓ Ⓔ
38. Ⓐ Ⓑ Ⓒ Ⓓ Ⓔ
39. Ⓐ Ⓑ Ⓒ Ⓓ Ⓔ
40. Ⓐ Ⓑ Ⓒ Ⓓ Ⓔ
41. Ⓐ Ⓑ Ⓒ Ⓓ Ⓔ
42. Ⓐ Ⓑ Ⓒ Ⓓ Ⓔ

43. Ⓐ Ⓑ Ⓒ Ⓓ Ⓔ
44. Ⓐ Ⓑ Ⓒ Ⓓ Ⓔ
45. Ⓐ Ⓑ Ⓒ Ⓓ Ⓔ
46. Ⓐ Ⓑ Ⓒ Ⓓ Ⓔ
47. Ⓐ Ⓑ Ⓒ Ⓓ Ⓔ
48. Ⓐ Ⓑ Ⓒ Ⓓ Ⓔ
49. Ⓐ Ⓑ Ⓒ Ⓓ Ⓔ
50. Ⓐ Ⓑ Ⓒ Ⓓ Ⓔ
51. Ⓐ Ⓑ Ⓒ Ⓓ Ⓔ
52. Ⓐ Ⓑ Ⓒ Ⓓ Ⓔ
53. Ⓐ Ⓑ Ⓒ Ⓓ Ⓔ
54. Ⓐ Ⓑ Ⓒ Ⓓ Ⓔ
55. Ⓐ Ⓑ Ⓒ Ⓓ Ⓔ
56. Ⓐ Ⓑ Ⓒ Ⓓ Ⓔ
57. Ⓐ Ⓑ Ⓒ Ⓓ Ⓔ
58. Ⓐ Ⓑ Ⓒ Ⓓ Ⓔ
59. Ⓐ Ⓑ Ⓒ Ⓓ Ⓔ
60. Ⓐ Ⓑ Ⓒ Ⓓ Ⓔ
61. Ⓐ Ⓑ Ⓒ Ⓓ Ⓔ
62. Ⓐ Ⓑ Ⓒ Ⓓ Ⓔ

# Practice Test 6

Questions 1–7 refer to the following poem. After reading the poem, chose the best answer to each question.

I saw thee once—once only—years ago;
I must not say *how* many—but *not* many.
It was a July midnight; and from out
*Line* A full-orbed moon, that, like thine own soul, soaring,
(5) Sought a precipitate pathway up through heaven,
There fell a silvery-silken veil of light,
With quietude, and sultriness, and slumber,
Upon the upturned faces of a thousand
Roses that grew in an enchanted garden,
(10) Where no wind dared to stir, unless on tiptoe—
Fell on the upturned faces of these roses
That gave out, in return for the love-light,
Their odorous souls in an ecstatic death—
Fell on the upturned faces of these roses
(15) That smiled and died in this parterre, enchanted
By thee, and by the poetry of thy presence.

(1845)

1. This stanza is an example of

   (A) a hurried supplication.

   (B) an ode to flowers.

   (C) a sonnet discussing beauty.

   (D) a holy catechism.

   (E) an idealized recollection.

2. Lines 1–6 contain all of the following EXCEPT

   (A) a self-imposed restriction.

   (B) a nocturnal setting.

   (C) a simile describing the addressee.

   (D) a farewell to the addressee's soul.

   (E) a line of *l* consonance.

3. The primary subject and verb in the clause beginning after the semicolon in line 3 are

   (A) "moon" and "soaring" (line 4).

   (B) "soul" and "soaring" (line 4).

   (C) "moon" (line 4) and "Sought" (line 5).

   (D) "pathway" (line 5) and "fell" (line 6).

   (E) "veil" and "fell" (line 6).

**GO ON TO THE NEXT PAGE**

4. Which of the following are personified in the stanza?

   I. The July midnight

  II. The wind

 III. The roses

 IV. The parterre

(A) I and II only

(B) II and III only

(C) I, II, and III only

(D) II, III, and IV only

(E) I, II, III, and IV

5. The moon's radiance in the stanza seems to have an effect on

(A) the addressee's soul.

(B) the roses' abundance.

(C) the roses' fragrance.

(D) the addressee's departure.

(E) the narrator's nervousness.

6. The death of the roses in line 15 pertains to all of the following EXCEPT

(A) a lack of strong winds.

(B) the addressee's presence.

(C) the roses' fragrance.

(D) a repayment for something given them.

(E) the narrator's use of metaphor.

7. The stanza develops using all of the following EXCEPT

(A) imagery.

(B) understatement.

(C) repetition.

(D) complex sentence structure.

(E) an admiring tone.

GO ON TO THE NEXT PAGE

*Questions 8–17 refer to the following passage. After reading the passage, choose the best answer to each question.*

It was about the beginning of spring 1757, when I arrived in England and I was near twelve years of age at that time. I was very much struck
Line with the buildings and the pavement of the streets
(5) in Falmouth; and, indeed, every object I saw, filled me with new surprise. One morning, when I got upon deck, I saw it covered all over with the snow that fell over-night. As I had never seen anything of the kind before, I thought it was salt; so I
(10) immediately ran down to the mate and desired him, as well as I could, to come and see how somebody in the night had thrown salt all over the deck. He, knowing what it was, desired me to bring some of it down to him. Accordingly, I took
(15) up a handful of it, which I found very cold indeed; and when I brought it to him he desired me to taste it. I did so, and I was surprised beyond measure. I then asked him what it was; he told me it was snow, but I could not in anywise
(20) understand him. He asked me if we had no such thing in my country; I told him, No. I then asked him the use of it, and who made it; he told me a great man in the heavens, called God. But here again I was to all intents and purposes at a loss to
(25) understand him; and the more so, when a little after I saw the air filled with it in a heavy shower, which fell down on the same day. After this, I went to church; and having never been at such a place before, I was again amazed at seeing and
(30) hearing the service. I asked all I could about it; and they gave me to understand it was worshipping God, who made us and all things. I was still at a great loss, and soon got to an endless field of inquiries, as well as I was able to speak
(35) and ask about things. However, my little friend Dick used to be my best interpreter; for I could make free with him, and he always instructed me with pleasure. And from what I could understand by him of this God, and in seeing these white

(40) people did not sell one another as we did, I was much pleased: and in this I thought they were much happier than we Africans. I was astonished at the wisdom of the white people in all things I saw; but was amazed at their not sacrificing, or
(45) making any offerings, and eating with unwashed hands, and touching the dead. I likewise could not help remarking that particular slenderness of their women, which I did not at first like; and I thought they were not so modest and shame faced
(50) as the African women.

I had often seen my master and Dick employed in reading; and I had a great curiosity to talk to the books, as I thought they did; and so to learn how all things had a beginning: for that purpose I
(55) have often taken up a book, and have talked to it, and then put my ears to it, when alone, in hopes that it would answer me; and I have been very much concerned when I found it remained silent.

(1789)

8. In this passage, the narrator is primarily portrayed as

(A) callous but needy.

(B) introverted but imaginative.

(C) aloof but importunate.

(D) religious but mischievous.

(E) inexperienced but curious.

**GO ON TO THE NEXT PAGE**

9. In lines 3–6, the narrator seems unaccustomed to

   (A) being a slave.

   (B) the warmth of spring.

   (C) urban development.

   (D) his own emotions.

   (E) attaining the age of twelve.

10. The incident with the snow in lines 6–27 demonstrates that the mate and the narrator are

    (A) forming a friendly, if unequal, relationship.

    (B) continuing a master/slave relationship.

    (C) competing against each other.

    (D) trying each other's patience.

    (E) attempting to rid the other of past prejudices.

11. The snow could symbolize all of the following EXCEPT

    (A) the narrator's displacement, as the snow occurs in spring.

    (B) the narrator's ignorance, as he knows nothing about snow.

    (C) the mate's culture, as the snow is both unfamiliar to the narrator and white.

    (D) the narrator's situation, as the snow is both foreign and unexpected to him.

    (E) the benevolence of God, as the mate uses the snow to discuss God's being.

12. In line 27, the narrator moves from a discussion of snow to a description of his first church service. This move seems to be prompted by

    (A) the narrator's discoveries about God.

    (B) the taunting that the mate directs at him .

    (C) the need to become a good citizen of Falmouth.

    (D) the mate's encouragement to seek divine truth.

    (E) the narrator's fear of living away from his home.

13. In lines 35–39, Dick offers information about God the same way that

    (A) the narrator offers the mate information about snow.

    (B) the people of Falmouth offer information about religion.

    (C) the mate offers information about snow.

    (D) the narrator offers information to the reader about slavery.

    (E) Dick also offers information about the church.

14. In lines 41–50, the narrator regards white people with all of the following EXCEPT

    (A) exasperation.

    (B) awe.

    (C) confusion.

    (D) abasement.

    (E) admiration.

**GO ON TO THE NEXT PAGE**

15. In lines 54–58, the narrator speaks to books for all of the following reasons EXCEPT that

    (A) he wants to understand the meaning of life.

    (B) he does not understand the purpose of reading.

    (C) he confuses reading aloud with direct address.

    (D) he thinks he is imitating his master and Dick.

    (E) he wants to learn to read.

16. In this passage, snow, God, and books all have which of the following in common?

    (A) They portray the narrator as incapable of grasping basic concepts.

    (B) They all originate from European beliefs and customs.

    (C) They show how patronizing, and even cruel, white society can be.

    (D) They demonstrate the difficulties of acclimating to another culture.

    (E) They create an antagonism between the narrator and white society.

17. This passage is narrated by someone who

    (A) has since become more educated and acculturated.

    (B) will never again see his homeland or his people.

    (C) wants to enter into privileged white society.

    (D) cannot forget the wrongs committed by Dick and the mate.

    (E) attempts to overcome racial prejudice and social inequality.

GO ON TO THE NEXT PAGE

*Questions 18–27 refer to the following poem. After reading the poem, choose the best answer to each question.*

I hate inconstancy—I loathe, detest,
    Abhor, condemn, abjure the mortal made
Of such quicksilver clay that in his breast
Line    No permanent foundation can be laid;
(5)  Love, constant love, has been my constant guest—
    And yet, last night, being at a masquerade,
I saw the prettiest creature, fresh from Milan,
Which gave me some sensations like a villain.

But soon Philosophy came to my aid,
(10)    And whispered, "Think of every sacred tie!"
"I will, my dear Philosophy!" I said,
    "But then her teeth, and then, oh, Heaven, her eye!
I'll just inquire if she be wife or maid,
    Or neither—out of curiosity."
(15)  "Stop!" cried Philosophy, with air so Grecian
    (Though she was masked then as a fair Venetian);

"Stop!" so I stopped.—But to return: that which
    Men call inconstancy is nothing more
Than admiration due where nature's rich
(20)    Profusion with young beauty covers o'er
Some favored object; and as in the niche
    A lovely statue we almost adore,
This sort of adoration of the real
    Is but a heightening of the "beau ideal."        *beau ideal*  ideal beauty

(25)  'Tis the perception of the beautiful,
    A fine extension of the faculties,
Platonic, universal, wonderful,
    Drawn from the stars, and filtered through the skies,
Without which life would be extremely dull;
(30)    In short, it is the use of our own eyes,
With one or two small senses added, just
To hint that flesh is formed of fiery dust.

Yet 'tis a painful feeling, and unwilling,
    For surely if we always could perceive
(35)  In the same object graces quite as killing
    As when she rose upon us like an Eve,
'Twould save us many a heartache, many a shilling
    (For we must get them anyhow, or grieve),
Whereas, if one sole lady pleased forever,
(40)  How pleasant for the heart, as well as liver.

(1819)

⟶

**GO ON TO THE NEXT PAGE**

18. In the passage above, the speaker's tone is best described as

    (A) off-the-cuff.

    (B) cautionary and worrisome.

    (C) melancholy and languorous.

    (D) tongue-in-cheek.

    (E) earnest and severe.

19. The topic of discussion in the passage is the speaker's

    (A) struggle with romantic fidelity.

    (B) enjoyment of costume balls.

    (C) preferences for a lifelong companion.

    (D) appreciation for Greek philosophy.

    (E) need to be completely adored.

20. In lines 1–4, what aspect of the "mortal" (line 2) is criticized?

    (A) His fear of taking risks

    (B) His irresolute disposition

    (C) His inured emotions

    (D) His many prejudices

    (E) His fast-paced society

21. The speaker treats the "prettiest creature" (line 7) as

    (A) an annoyance that he would rather ignore.

    (B) a braggart that displays her ostentation.

    (C) a competitor who could steal focus from him.

    (D) a complication that disturbs his adamant beliefs.

    (E) a challenge that he will not accept any cost.

22. The phrase "out of curiosity" in line 14 emphasizes the speaker's

    (A) flat denial of his own philosophical hypocrisy.

    (B) insatiable quest for ultimate knowledge.

    (C) intense interest in the creature's familial origins.

    (D) sudden awakening to his Philosophy's shortcomings.

    (E) clear obsession with the degradations of marriage.

23. The third and fourth stanzas are best summarized as

    (A) a reinforcement of the ideas in lines 1–5.

    (B) a rationalization of the speaker's feelings toward the creature.

    (C) an epiphany that the speaker has struggled to achieve.

    (D) a discussion of the manner in which the senses operate.

    (E) an aside that reveals the speaker's desire for unconditional acceptance.

**GO ON TO THE NEXT PAGE**

24. What is the "painful … and unwilling" feeling referred to in line 33?

    (A) Past heartbreaks the speaker has suffered

    (B) The obligation of fidelity to one person

    (C) An attraction to multiple women

    (D) The speaker's fear of rejection by the creature

    (E) The complications in a new relationship

25. The final stanza includes all of the following EXCEPT

    (A) a hypothetical situation treating constancy as an actual possibility.

    (B) an admission that romances are costly both emotionally and financially.

    (C) a change in the narrator's tone, brought about by new considerations.

    (D) a simultaneous glorification and denigration of women.

    (E) a reconsideration of the narrator's previous philosophy.

26. Which of the items listed above are personified in the passage?

    I. "Love, constant love" (line 5)

    II. "Philosophy" (line 9, et al.)

    III. "faculties" (line 26)

    IV. "graces" (line 35)

    (A) II only

    (B) I and II only

    (C) I, II, and IV only

    (D) II, III, and IV only

    (E) I, II, III, and IV

27. The masquerade setting can be seen as appropriate for this passage, because

    (A) the speaker could not meet the creature so easily elsewhere.

    (B) the masks reflect the speaker's own falseness to his convictions.

    (C) the creature's costume helps the speaker to notice her more readily.

    (D) the masquerade's festive atmosphere brings the speaker out of his depression.

    (E) the party symbolizes the creature's shallowness and capriciousness.

**GO ON TO THE NEXT PAGE**

*Questions 28–39 refer to the following passage. After reading the passage, choose the best answer to each question.*

Every object, on which his eyes rested, seemed to announce the presence of Ellena; and the very flowers that so gaily embellished the apartment,
*Line*
(5) breathed forth a perfume, which fascinated his senses and affected his imagination. Before Signora Bianchi appeared, his anxiety and apprehension had encreased so much, that, believing he should be unable to support himself in her presence, he was more than once upon the
(10) point of leaving the house. At length, he heard her approaching step from the hall, and his breath almost forsook him. The figure of Signora Bianchi was not of an order to inspire admiration, and a spectator might have smiled to
(15) see the perturbation of Vivaldi, his faultering step and anxious eye, as he advanced to meet the venerable Bianchi, as he bowed upon her faded hand, and listened to her querulous voice. She received him with an air of reserve, and some
(20) moments passed before he could recollect himself sufficiently to explain the purpose of his visit; yet this, when he discovered it, did not apparently surprise her. She listened with composure, though with somewhat of a severe countenance,
(25) to his protestations of regard for her niece, and when he implored her to intercede for him in obtaining the hand of Ellena, she said, 'I cannot be ignorant that a family of your rank must be averse to an union with one of mine; nor am I
(30) unacquainted that a full sense of the value of birth is a marking feature in the characters of the Marchese and Marchesa di Vivaldi. This proposal must be disagreeable or, at least, unknown to them; and I am to inform you, Signor, that,
(35) though Signora di Rosalba* is their inferior in rank, she is their equal in pride.'

Vivaldi disdained to prevaricate, yet was shocked to own the truth thus abruptly. The

ingenuous manner, however, with which he at
(40) length did this, and the energy of a passion too eloquent to be misunderstood, somewhat soothed the anxiety of Signora Bianchi, with whom other considerations began to arise. She considered that from her own age and infirmities
(45) she must very soon, in the course of nature, leave Ellena a young and friendless orphan; still somewhat dependent upon her own industry, and entirely so on her discretion. With much beauty and little knowledge of the world, the
(50) dangers of her future situation appeared in vivid colours to the affectionate mind of Signora Bianchi; and she sometimes thought that it might be right to sacrifice considerations, which in other circumstances would be laudable, to the
(55) obtaining for her niece the protection of a husband and a man of honour. If in this instance she descended from the lofty integrity, which ought to have opposed her consent that Ellena should clandestinely enter any family, her
(60) parental anxiety may soften the censure she deserved.

But, before she determined upon this subject, it was necessary to ascertain that Vivaldi was worthy of the confidence she might repose in
(65) him. To try, also, the constancy of his affection, she gave little present encouragement to his hopes. His request to see Ellena she absolutely refused, till she should have considered further of his proposals; and his enquiry whether he had a
(70) rival, and, if he had, whether Ellena was disposed to favour him, she evaded, since she knew that a reply would give more encouragement to his hopes, than it might hereafter be proper to confirm.

GO ON TO THE NEXT PAGE

(75)    Vivaldi, at length, took his leave, released, indeed, from absolute despair, but scarcely encouraged to hope; ignorant that he had a rival, yet doubtful whether Ellena honoured himself with any share of esteem.

(1797)

*Signora di Rosalba*  Signora Bianchi

28. Vivaldi's mood in lines 1–10 can best be described as

 (A) romanticized but nervous anticipation.

 (B) concentrated but mocking self-reflection.

 (C) curious but intense agony.

 (D) sincere but reserved affability.

 (E) undeserved but acute alienation.

29. In lines 12–18, "a spectator might have smiled to see the perturbation of Vivaldi" because

 (A) Vivaldi is a lovestruck youth, impatiently awaiting news of Ellena.

 (B) Signora Bianchi is an unimposing figure, hardly inspiring anxiety.

 (C) Ellena is barely likeable enough even for Vivaldi to bother with her.

 (D) love has made Vivaldi into a mirror image of Signora Bianchi.

 (E) impatience has caused Vivaldi to forget common courtesies.

30. In lines 18–25, Signora Bianchi's behavior can best be described as

 (A) contemptuous.

 (B) serene.

 (C) timid.

 (D) haughty.

 (E) conservative.

31. In lines 27–34, Signora Bianchi observes that Vivaldi's parents

 (A) would disapprove of Vivaldi and Ellena marrying, since she is lower in social rank.

 (B) would disapprove of Vivaldi and Ellena marrying, since she is higher in social rank.

 (C) would approve of Vivaldi and Ellena marrying, since she is higher in social rank.

 (D) would only consider Vivaldi's marriage to Ellena if rank were not important to her.

 (E) would consider Vivaldi's marriage to Ellena if the union would elevate her rank.

**GO ON TO THE NEXT PAGE**

32. Signora Bianchi's observation about herself in lines 34–36 is a signal to Vivaldi that

(A) she will seek her niece's marriage even if Vivaldi's parents disapprove of Ellena.

(B) she would prefer that Vivaldi court other young women instead of Ellena.

(C) she wishes that Ellena would pursue other prospects before settling on Vivaldi.

(D) she at one time was more powerful even than Vivaldi's parents.

(E) she will not seek her niece's marriage if Vivaldi's parents disapprove of Ellena.

33. Vivaldi is able to calm Signora Bianchi's apprehensions in lines 37–46 because he

(A) vehemently denies any obstacle preventing his marriage to Ellena.

(B) openly admits his parents' possible misgivings about his marrying Ellena.

(C) shyly confesses an undying commitment to both Ellena and the signora.

(D) solemnly promises to do whatever it takes to win the signora's approval.

(E) sadly relates that he has lost his family birthright in seeking Ellena's hand.

34. All of the following pertain to Signora Bianchi's "other considerations" (line 43) about Ellena marrying Vivaldi EXCEPT

(A) Ellena's lack of worldly experience.

(B) Vivaldi's sincerity and earnest passion.

(C) Signora Bianchi's own impending death.

(D) Ellena's fragile health and feelings.

(E) Ellena's sole dependence on her aunt.

35. The device used in lines 56–61 is known as

(A) antithesis.

(B) hyperbole.

(C) synecdoche.

(D) narrative intrusion.

(E) character inversion.

36. In lines 56–61, Signora Bianchi may deserve a softened kind of "censure" because

(A) she might give up Ellena to Vivaldi's family, but only for her niece's education.

(B) she might succumb to Vivaldi's pleas, but only because she knows her niece's heart.

(C) she might abandon her ethics, but only because she must secure her niece's future.

(D) she might not trust Vivaldi's arguments, but only because she is wary for her niece.

(E) she might be treating Vivaldi with disrespect, but only because she is his elder.

37. In lines 62–74, Signora Bianchi refuses Vivaldi's requests of visitation and further information for all of the following reasons EXCEPT that

(A) she wishes to test his faithfulness and fortitude.

(B) she needs more time to consider his proposal.

(C) she suspects that he is projecting a false front.

(D) she requires proof that he is the right man for her niece.

(E) she wants to delay encouraging him until a more appropriate time.

**GO ON TO THE NEXT PAGE**

38. In the final paragraph of the passage, Vivaldi's mood has

    (A) reversed completely since he first entered the signora's residence.

    (B) improved only slightly since he first entered the signora's residence.

    (C) remained unchanged since he first entered the signora's residence.

    (D) lessened in intensity concerning his feelings toward Ellena.

    (E) caused him to abandon his hopes of marrying Ellena.

39. Throughout the passage, the narrator observes these two characters with

    (A) jaded apathy.

    (B) outright disdain.

    (C) slight aloofness.

    (D) quiet awe.

    (E) amused sympathy.

GO ON TO THE NEXT PAGE

*Questions 40–46 refer to the following poem. After reading the poem, choose the best answer to each question.*

And yet I cannot reprehend the flight
Or blame th'attempt presuming so to soar;
The mounting venture for a high delight
*Line*    Did make the honour of the fall the more.
*(5)*    For who gets wealth, that puts not from the shore?
Danger hath honour, great designs their fame;
Glory doth follow, courage comes before;
And though th'event oft answers not the same—
Suffice that high attempts have never shame.
*(10)*    The mean observer, whom base safety keeps,
Lives without honour, dies without a name,
And in eternal darkness ever sleeps.—
     And therefore, *Delia*, 'tis to me no blot
     To have attempted, tho' attained thee not.

                (1592)

40. The above poem is an example of

     (A) an ode.

     (B) heroic couplets.

     (C) a sonnet.

     (D) an idyll.

     (E) a mock epic.

41. In lines 1–4, all of the following ideas about the "flight" (line 1) are true EXCEPT that

     (A) the narrator cannot find anything wrong with it.

     (B) the goals for the flight, from the outset, have been impossible.

     (C) the flight's purpose has been to gain a lofty kind of pleasure.

     (D) the attempt at flight has ultimately failed.

     (E) the flight's success was not a condition of its greatness.

42. In the metaphor of line 5, what is necessary to attain wealth?

     (A) Digging in sand

     (B) Avoiding the beach

     (C) Preventing pollution

     (D) Leaving land behind

     (E) Desiring treasure

43. In the context of lines 6–9, the best translation for the phrase "th'event oft answers not the same" is that

     (A) different people have different experiences.

     (B) the unexpected rarely occurs if one is prepared.

     (C) the lessons of history are too often ignored.

     (D) people do not often answer the call of glory.

     (E) a venture does not always end in success.

**GO ON TO THE NEXT PAGE**

44. Which of the following are true about the "observer" in line 10?

    I.   He is inconsequential compared to someone who takes risks.

    II.  His lack of daring causes him dishonor, obscurity, and ignorance.

    III. Risk prevents him from being more than an observer.

    (A) I only

    (B) II only

    (C) I and III only

    (D) II and III only

    (E) I, II, and III

45. How do lines 13–14 relate to the rest of the poem?

    (A) They provide an example of its ideas.

    (B) They provide a contrast to its ideas.

    (C) They provide a riddle for Delia to solve.

    (D) They provide an answer to Delia's question.

    (E) They provide a decision for Delia to make.

46. The narrator's purpose seems to be to

    (A) chastise Delia as an unworthy observer and promote himself as a "doer."

    (B) prove to Delia his worthiness of her love and ask for a second chance with her.

    (C) encourage the reader to take more risks, no matter what the cost.

    (D) praise Delia as a lofty endeavor and claim pride even in failing to win her.

    (E) explore both the happiness and the responsibilities that love provides.

**GO ON TO THE NEXT PAGE**

Questions 47–54 refer to the following poem. After reading the poem, choose the best answer to each question.

The flower that smiles to-day
    To-morrow dies:
All that we wish to stay
    Tempts and then flies.
*Line*
(5)   What is this world's delight?
Lightning that mocks the night,
    Brief even if bright.

Virtue how frail it is!
    Friendship how rare!
(10)  Love how it sells poor bliss
    For proud despair!
But we, though soon they fall,
Survive their joy, and all
    Which ours we call.

(15)  Whilst skies are blue and bright,
    Whilst flowers are gay,
Whilst eyes that change ere night
    Make glad the day,
Whilst yet the calm hours creep,
(20)  Dream thou—and from thy sleep
    Then wake to weep.

(1821)

47. The speaker's tone in the poem is best described as

(A) reticent.
(B) foreboding.
(C) disenchanted.
(D) devil-may-care.
(E) elated.

48. The flower of line 1 is all of the following EXCEPT

(A) a personified entity.
(B) an example of fleetingness.
(C) a symbol of nature's great power.
(D) an illustration of the idea in lines 3–4.
(E) a parallel to "Lightning" in line 6.

49. The "Lightning" of line 6 is all of the following EXCEPT

(A) a personified entity.
(B) an answer to the question in line 5.
(C) a metaphor for "delight" in line 5.
(D) an illustration of the idea in lines 3–4.
(E) an image of the speaker's pain.

50. In the second stanza, the speaker uses "we" (line 12) to exhibit

(A) human mortality.
(B) comparative longevity.
(C) earthly brevity.
(D) racial disparity.
(E) global equality.

51. The word "Survive" in line 13 is closest in meaning to

(A) "outlast."
(B) "endure."
(C) "exist."
(D) "thrive."
(E) "experience."

GO ON TO THE NEXT PAGE

52. The main verb phrase for the sentence in
    lines 15–21 is

    (A) "are" (lines 15 and 16).

    (B) "change" (line 17).

    (C) "make" (line 18).

    (D) "creep" (line 19).

    (E) "Dream" (line 20).

53. Lines 20–21 feature all of the following
    EXCEPT

    (A) imperative mood.

    (B) antithesis.

    (C) anticlimax.

    (D) assonance.

    (E) thematic unity.

54. The first two stanzas develop mainly through
    the use of

    (A) aphorism, then the third uses repetition.

    (B) a unifying image, then the third uses a
        contrasting image.

    (C) simile, then the third uses deductive
        reasoning.

    (D) alliteration, then the third uses
        personification.

    (E) informal diction, then the third uses
        formalized language.

**GO ON TO THE NEXT PAGE**

Questions 55–62 refer to the following passage. After reading the passage, choose the best answer to each question.

(*In the following passage, the 18th century composer Wolfgang Mozart has just submitted an idea for an opera based on the French play* The Marriage of Figaro. *Various officials in the court of Joseph, Emperor of Austria—including Mozart's musical rival Salieri—have expressed doubts about the adaptation; they believe the subject matter to be too commonplace.*)

If you are honest—each one of you—which of you isn't more at home with his hairdresser than Hercules? or Horatius? [*To* Salieri] Or your
Line stupid Danaius,* come to that! Or *mine—mine!*
(5) *Idomeneo, King of Crete!* All those anguished antiques! They're all bores! Bores, bores, bores! [Suddenly he springs up and jumps onto a chair, like an orator. Declaring it] All serious operas written this century are boring!
(10) [They turn and look at him in shocked amazement. A pause. He gives his little giggle, and then jumps down again.]
Look at us! Four gaping mouths. What a perfect quartet! I'd love to write it—just this second of
(15) time, this now, as you are! Herr Chamberlain thinking: "Impertinent Mozart. I must speak to the Emperor at once!" Herr Prefect thinking: "Ignorant Mozart. Debasing opera with his vulgarity!" Herr Court Composer thinking:
(20) "German Mozart! What can he finally know about music?" And Mozart himself, in the middle, thinking: "I'm just a good fellow. Why do they all disapprove of me?" [*Excitedly to* Van Swieten] That's why opera is important, Baron.
(25) Because it's realer than any play! A dramatic poet would have to put all those thoughts down one after another to represent this second of time. The composer can put them all down at once— and still make us hear each one of them.
(30) Astonishing device—a vocal quartet! [*More and*

*more excited*] I tell you I want to write a finale lasting half an hour! A quartet becoming a quintet becoming a sextet. On and on, wider and wider—all sounds multiplying and rising
(35) together—and the together making a sound entirely new! ... I bet you that's how God hears the world. Millions of sounds ascending at once and mixing in His ear to become an unending music, unimaginable to us! [*To* Salieri] That's our
(40) job! That's our *job*, we composers: to combine the inner minds of him and him and him, and her and her—the thoughts of chambermaids and Court Composers—and turn the audience into God.
(45) [Pause. Salieri stares at him, fascinated.]

(1981)

*Danaius* a character in one of Salieri's lofty operas

55. In this passage, Mozart's monologue can best be described as

(A) passionate and radical.

(B) disdainful and deceitful.

(C) sorrowful and anguished.

(D) respectful and solemn.

(E) restrained and abashed.

GO ON TO THE NEXT PAGE

56. Mozart's first question proposes the idea that

   (A) we would rather look good than be entertained.

   (B) we favor contemporary style to ancient custom.

   (C) we would choose close friends over brief acquaintances.

   (D) we prefer ordinary situations to ennobling ideas.

   (E) we fancy relaxation more than physical or mental strain.

57. The passage suggest that *Idomeneo, King of Crete* (line 6) is all of the following EXCEPT

   (A) a contrast to Salieri's Danaius.

   (B) a work of Mozart's.

   (C) an opera.

   (D) part of a self-criticism..

   (E) an illustration of Mozart's argument.

58. The quartet that Mozart imagines in lines 13–23 is

   (A) an obvious impossibility from a musical standpoint.

   (B) an example of an operatic style opposing loftiness.

   (C) the kind of ensemble one would see in *Idomeneo.*

   (D) an intriguing idea to the men he is addressing.

   (E) an attempt to humiliate the men he is addressing.

59. The parallel structure with which Mozart constructs the others' dialogue in the quartet emphasizes

   (A) the agreement between Mozart and the others.

   (B) the trouble that Mozart is acquiring for himself.

   (C) the harmony of a vocal ensemble.

   (D) the musicality of disapproval.

   (E) the unity of Emperor Joseph's Austria.

60. For Mozart, the vocal music of an opera is superior to dialog in a play, because

   (A) opera offers a loftier ideal than the ordinary dialog of a play.

   (B) the audience member's ear must be trained to appreciate opera.

   (C) God himself prefers music over ordinary human speech.

   (D) a composer of opera is more talented than a mere playwright.

   (E) dialog is linear, but vocal music can have simultaneous voices.

61. All of the following are true concerning Mozart's discussion of God in lines 36–44 EXCEPT that

   (A) Mozart suggests that opera mimics the way the world sounds to God.

   (B) Mozart's discussion of vocal ensemble has broached the topic of God.

   (C) Mozart places the composer of opera on a level with God.

   (D) Mozart's ideas about God have led him back to his initial ideas about opera.

   (E) Mozart's speech has stunned at least one of his listeners.

**GO ON TO THE NEXT PAGE**

62. Mozart's monologue reveals him to be all of the following EXCEPT

    (A) revolutionary in his ideas.

    (B) heedful of others' advice.

    (C) free-flowing in his delivery.

    (D) negligent about decorum.

    (E) mindful of a composer's audience.

# STOP!

**If you finish before time is up,
you may check your work.**

# Answer Key
# Practice Test 6

| | | |
|---|---|---|
| 1. E | 22. A | 43. E |
| 2. D | 23. B | 44. E |
| 3. E | 24. C | 45. A |
| 4. B | 25. C | 46. D |
| 5. C | 26. B | 47. C |
| 6. A | 27. B | 48. C |
| 7. B | 28. A | 49. E |
| 8. E | 29. B | 50. B |
| 9. C | 30. E | 51. A |
| 10. A | 31. A | 52. E |
| 11. E | 32. E | 53. D |
| 12. A | 33. B | 54. A |
| 13. C | 34. D | 55. A |
| 14. A | 35. D | 56. D |
| 15. A | 36. C | 57. A |
| 16. D | 37. C | 58. B |
| 17. A | 38. B | 59. C |
| 18. D | 39. E | 60. E |
| 19. A | 40. C | 61. C |
| 20. B | 41. B | 62. B |
| 21. D | 42. D | |

# ANSWERS AND EXPLANATIONS

**1. (E)** The speaker remembers a "July midnight" (line 3) in an "enchanted garden" (line 9) where "a thousand/Roses" (lines 8–9) were giving up their "odorous souls" (line 13) because they had been charmed by the "poetry" of the addressee's "presence" (line 16). The scene is too perfect; it makes the addressee's influence supernatural. Overall, this is an idealized recollection.

**2. (D)** The speaker compares the addressee's soul to the "full-orbed moon," as both seek "a precipitate pathway up through heaven." Yet a soaring soul is not one that has necessarily left the body for good; sometimes, a soaring soul is a metaphor for joy. Certainly, the roses receive a kind of joyousness from the addressee, because they are "enchanted …by the poetry" (lines 15–16) of her presence. If her soul had left and the narrator had bade it farewell, then these roses would be charmed by a corpse—hardly part of the ideal image that the speaker is trying to create.

**3. (E)** The prepositional phrase "from out/A full-orbed moon" begins the clause. The adjective clause "that, like thine own … through heaven" modifies "moon." These items may be eliminated as mere modifiers. Then, when we come to line 6, we see that "There fell a silvery-silken veil of light" or, without the inversion, "A silvery silken veil of light fell there." The prepositional phrase "of light" can be removed as a modifier, as can "silvery" and "silken." Thus, the subject is "veil," and the verb is "fell." The rest of the stanza is part of the predicate starting with "fell."

**4. (B)** The phrase "no wind dared to stir, unless on tiptoe" (line 10) shows not only the human quality of daring but also the physical action of tiptoeing; so there is evidence for item II. Likewise, the roses have both "faces" (line 8, et al.) and "souls" (line 13), and as they died, they smiled (line 15); item III then has support. The July midnight is described in the most direct way possible in line 3, and the "parterre"

is simply a location for the roses to have their death scene. Therefore, items I and IV go unsupported.

**5. (C)** The roses give up their "odorous souls" (line 13) "in return for the love-light" (line 12) of the moon. The moon shines on them, and they have a pleasing scent.

**6. (A)** The roses die, having been influenced by the addressee's presence and the moonlight. They are only figuratively dying, however. Their fragrance is compared to a soul leaving the body. The wind, or lack thereof, seems to be neither a cause nor an effect of the roses' condition.

**7. (B)** The idealization of both the setting and the addressee diminishes the chance of understatement in this stanza. Enchanted gardens and women who charm flowers belong more in the realm of hyperbole than understatement.

**8. (E)** The narrator has never before encountered snow, books, or the concept of God. Thus, he is inexperienced with these things. Still, he is not afraid to ask questions about these things or to experiment with them; therefore, his curiosity is obvious.

**9. (C)** The narrator says, "I was very much struck with the buildings and the pavement of the streets." Falmouth's urbanity has made an impression on him.

**10. (A)** The relationship is friendly enough on the narrator's side, because he has no qualms about approaching the mate with questions about snow. As for the mate, he seems friendly enough to share his knowledge openly with the narrator, even to steer the conversation into a theological discussion. Of course, the relationship is unequal because the mate is a part of white society, is knowledgeable about matters valued by that society, and is a free man.

**11. (E)** The mate certainly credits God with creating the snow, but he never places a value or benefit on it; neither does the narrator view snow as a kind of benevolence.

**12. (A)** In lines 27–28, the narrator says, "After this, I went to church." The "this" is his confusion following the conversation with the mate about God and snow. Yet going to church seems to be his own decision: The mate has told him *about* God but not overtly encouraged the narrator to *seek* God.

**13. (C)** Once in a while, you will see an analogy as an SAT Subject Test: Literature question. The "Dick: God" connection is that Dick teaches the narrator about God. In fact, the narrator relates that "he always instructed me with pleasure" (lines 37–38). We see a similar connection in the "the mate: snow" set. The mate has taught the narrator about snow.

**14. (A)** Even when the narrator disapproves of whites or European customs, he tempers his criticisms: he does not "at first" (line 48) like the "slenderness" of white women, an implication that he becomes accustomed to their size later. Furthermore, he does not call white women "immodest" or "brazen"; he merely remarks that they are "not so modest and shame faced as the African women" (lines 49–50). Such mildness of critique does not adequately demonstrate exasperation.

**15. (A)** This option is too broad. The last paragraph is focused solely on the narrator's relationship with books, not his desire for such broad, general knowledge.

**16. (D)** In encountering snow, God, and books, the narrator always begins by being understandably confused. All these things are part of a region or a culture that are foreign to him. Thus, he has to spend a period of time being educated about each.

**17. (A)** Ironically, a narrator who describes his ignorance concerning Falmouth's climate and culture is able to relate his story with clarity and sophistication. While at first he literally "talked" to books, now he seems quite literate.

**18. (D)** To express such strong feelings about inconstancy, and then to abandon those feelings at the first sight of a pretty "creature," shows a humorous lack of self-restraint. And the narrator continues this tone in the rest of the stanzas while he improbably rationalizes his inconstant behavior.

**19. (A)** The pertinent excerpts to prove this point appear in the first stanza: "I hate inconstancy ... And yet ... I saw the prettiest creature ... Which gave me some sensations like a villain." The struggle continues as "Philosophy" tells the speaker to "Think of every sacred tie!" (line 10), yet the speaker is still distracted by "her teeth" and "her eye" (line 12). He gives up the pursuit in line 17 but still cannot stop thinking about inconstancy in the abstract for the rest of the passage.

**20. (B)** In these lines, the speaker says that he hates inconstancy, or unfaithfulness, and then he criticizes the mortal who has no "permanent foundation" (line 4) laid in his "breast" because he is made of "quicksilver clay" (line 3). Quicksilver is liquid at room temperature, and clay is soft and malleable, so if one is made of these substances, he metaphorically is too weak to be faithful. A foundation of quicksilver clay would be a temporary one indeed, and if laid in the breast where the heart is located, that foundation will fail to support romantic faithfulness.

**21. (D)** By noticing that she is pretty and in desiring to speak with her, the speaker shows that he is interested in the creature. But Philosophy intercedes at lines 9–10, 15, and 17 to remind the speaker of his values and of his previous commitments. So the creature is causing the speaker to act against his belief system.

**22. (A)** The phrase comes after a dash's pause; the speaker is somehow aware that asking the creature whether or not she is married places him in moral danger. So the phrase "out of curiosity" provides an innocent reason for his inquiry. However, his previous struggles with Philosophy prove to us that curiosity is an unlikely motivator for the question.

**23. (B)** The speaker changes his tune in lines 17–19, saying that "that which/Men call inconstancy is nothing more/Than admiration." Eighteen lines ago, he said that he hated inconstancy. In the next stanza, he also calls inconstancy the "perception of the beautiful" and "A fine extension of the faculties." He is treating an inevitably hurtful and potentially destructive behavior as if it were something sublime. Thus, he is rationalizing, and doing it badly.

**24. (C)** In line 33, the speaker says that "[it] is a painful feeling." "It" has also been discussed in the previous stanza and appears to have "This sort of adoration" (line 23)—another name for inconstancy—as its antecedent. So the "painful feeling" is inconstancy. After line 33, the speaker explains that the reason inconstancy is so painful is that it causes "many a heartache" (line 37).

**25. (C)** The narrator's tone is still flippant. He is romantic enough to say that constancy can prevent heartache but callous enough to admit that constancy can also save money: not as many women to woo. (D) may seem an attractive option, but here is its reasoning: the narrator's hypothetical situation glorifies a woman by comparing her newness and appeal to Eve's in the Garden of Eden. Yet, at the same time, this consideration is merely a hypothesis; the implication is that constancy is not possible, so a woman truly can be called an "object," as the speaker does in line 35. According to the narrator, Eve may have had "graces," but they were eventually "killing" for Adam and the human race.

**26. (B)** "Love, constant love" has been the speaker's "guest," so it sounds human. Philosophy actually converses with the speaker, so it, too, is personified: items I and II are thus proven.

The word "faculties," however, is referred to as being extended, and nonhuman things can extend. Also, "graces" are referred to as "killing," but nonhuman things can kill. So items III and IV have little evidence for support.

**27. (B)** Just as partygoers at a masquerade hide their true identities behind masks, so too does the speaker expose another identity when he spies the creature. Either he has been false to his previous convictions, or those convictions were always a façade.

**28. (A)** Vivaldi has "anxiety and apprehension" (lines 6–7), but not so much that he fails to notice the sights and smells of his surroundings. The effect that the environment has on him is to "announce the presence of Ellena" (line 2). By associating virtually everything he sees with his beloved, he is romanticizing his visit.

**29. (B)** Choice (A) is an attractive distracter, but the context of lines 12–18 favor option (B): "The figure of Signora Bianchi was not of an order to inspire admiration." So why does Vivaldi's step falter? Why are his eyes "anxious"? Despite her unimposing form, he is still nervous.

**30. (E)** Signora Bianchi greets Vivaldi with "an air of reserve." She listens to him "with composure." She has a "severe countenance," but her frail form and humble station prevent her from being contemptuous or haughty. The severity of her look does, however, show a lack of timidity.

**31. (A)** Signora Bianchi says she is aware "that a full sense of the value of birth is a marking feature in the characters of the Marchese and Marchesa di Vivaldi." The "birth" she speaks of is noble birth or birth into a social station. She knows, then, that Vivaldi's proposal of marriage to Ellena "must be disagreeable or, at least, unknown" to Vivaldi's parents, because Ellena is of lower social rank.

**32. (E)** If Vivaldi's parents disapprove of Ellena, then for Signora Bianchi to pursue the matter would be undignified. She would be putting herself in the position of supplication or antagonism with Vivaldi's family, and either state would be beneath her pride.

**33. (B)** Vivaldi does not want to "prevaricate" or hedge with the signora; in fact, he admits the truth to her in an "ingenuous" fashion: Innocently, he tells her that she is right about his parents. This admission would come as a relief to the signora, possibly because she knows she is dealing with an honest man.

**34. (D)** Evidence for the other options can be found in lines 48–49 (A), lines 37–41 (B), lines 43–46 (C), and lines 45–48 (E). Although the signora is described as having infirmities, Ellena is not described as infirm or in bad health, so (D) is correct.

**35. (D)** The third-person narrator faithfully relates the scene between the two characters and stays out of the action until these lines. Here, she makes a personal judgment about a character and suggests that the signora may deserve a kind of softened "censure."

**36. (C)** She has implied to Vivaldi that if his parents disapprove of Ellena, the signora will not further seek for Ellena to marry him; Signora Bianchi has asserted her dignity. However, after she has considered Ellena's fate following her own death, she now thinks that dignity may have to be sacrificed so that Ellena will live in domestic security.

**37. (C)** Lines 37–42 have described Signora Bianchi's relief to find Vivaldi so earnest. Nothing has since happened for her relief to change. Yet in spite of his forthrightness, she has further considerations to make, as the rest of the options point out.

**38. (B)** Vivaldi was full of "anxiety and apprehension" when he first entered the household. At the end of the passage, he is "released, indeed, from absolute despair" but still has doubts about his chances with Ellena. His feelings for her have not lessened, nor has his resolve, but his certainty about their future together has increased only a little.

**39. (E)** In the case of the young man, the narrator notes in lines 14–15 that "a spectator might have smiled to see the perturbation of Vivaldi." His awkwardness in meeting this frail but dignified lady is amusing, but because we know that he is partly flustered by love, his faltering is charming. The narrator also says in lines 56–61 that Signora Bianchi is deserving of reprimand but of a softened kind, since she, too, is motivated by love for Ellena. Thus the narrator is sympathetic to both and just a little amused.

**40. (C)** The poem has 14 lines; it is written in iambic pentameter; it has a Shakespearean sonnet rhyme scheme. Yes, it's a sonnet.

**41. (B)** The speaker says that the flight is presumptuous (line 2) and he calls it a "mounting venture" (line 3), but these ideas imply difficulty or grandeur—not impossibility.

**42. (D)** Even if the reader is not familiar with the phrase *putting from shore* as a term meaning "going out to sea," the context of the phrase makes (D) the right choice. Compared to the other options, (D) is the most adventurous, and the speaker is talking about taking risks in this sonnet.

**43. (E)** The "event" of this phrase may not answer the courage, honor, or "great designs" previously mentioned. In other words, courage and the rest are not enough to ensure an outcome; the event may not equal the courage, honor, and planning that went into it. However, line 9 suggests that if an attempt is noble, there is no shame in it, no matter what the outcome.

**44. (E)** The observer "lives without honour, dies without a name" and sleeps in "eternal darkness." Compared to a risk taker, the observer is dishonorable and will become obscure and inconsequential. Furthermore, because "base safety keeps" him, it is risk that prevents him from moving out of his role as an observer. Thus, all three items have support.

**45. (A)** The narrator is relating his failed attempt at Delia's favor to the rest of the poem's theme: Even though he has failed, his was a noble try, so there is no shame in it.

**46. (D)** The narrator spends much of the poem discussing the importance and honor of attempting lofty endeavors, regardless of outcome. In lines 13–14, he relates his attempt to win Delia as an example of such a conquest, noting that it is "no blot" to have failed. The honor was in the risk he took rather than being an "observer" (line 10).

**47. (C)** The speaker does not just discuss the brevity of earthly things; he does so with a callous abruptness. After the first line, we might expect a continued description of the flower's beauty; instead, the narrator halts his line with "To-morrow dies." Usually positive aspects of life such as virtue, friendship, and love are scorned by the speaker in the second stanza. Then, at the end of the poem, he commands us to "wake to weep." His is a disenchanted voice.

**48. (C)** Since the flower dies "To-morrow," it is not an example of nature's great power. If nature's power is in the flower's life force, then that power is snuffed out fairly quickly. If nature's power has allowed the flower to die, then nature has not exerted much strength.

**49. (E)** If this poem is an expression of the speaker's pain, then that pain seems to be a lasting one. By the end of the poem, he has not changed his pessimistic views. The brevity of lightning, then, as he describes it, does not adequately parallel whatever longer-lasting pain he feels.

**50. (B)** Normally, in discussing earthly fleetingness, a poet laments human mortality. But here, the speaker says that we outlive or "survive" all other earthly things. Compared to virtue, friendship, and love, "we" live on, alone.

**51. (A)** In the context of the second stanza, "we" humans "survive," or outlive, the brevity of "frail" virtue, "rare" friendship, and lost love, as "soon they fall."

**52. (E)** The lines beginning with "Whilst" or "While" are subordinate clauses—modifying but not a part of the main clause. After we eliminate them, we are left with the command to "Dream," the sentence's main verb.

**53. (D)** No vowel sounds are conspicuously repeated in either line.

**54. (A)** The sentences in the first two stanzas are brief enough and imagistic enough and clever enough to be aphoristic observations about life—pessimistic though they are. Then, in the third stanza, we have an elongated sentence that contains three similarly constructed adverb clauses. Aphorism leads to repetition.

**55. (A)** Mozart's passion can be seen in his use of exclamation and in the stage direction "Suddenly he springs up and jumps onto a chair, like an orator" (lines 7–8). His declaration that operas are "Bores, bores, bores!" is, in a sense, a defense of his radical choice for an opera, *The Marriage of Figaro*. Salieri and the rest think that it is too commonplace, while Mozart thinks that mythological and historical subjects like Hercules and Horatius are too dreary.

**56. (D)** Again, he is defending the ordinariness, the "vulgarness," of *The Marriage of Figaro*. Mozart believes that we prefer to be in the company of ordinary people—such as a hairdresser—rather than with distant, lofty characters like Hercules.

**57. (A)** On the contrary, Mozart groups Idomeneo and Danaius together. He calls Danaius "stupid" in lines 3–4, then he follows immediately with "Or *mine—mine! Idomeneo, King of Crete!* All those anguished antiques!" So both characters are stuffy relics that Mozart would like to move beyond.

**58. (B)** Mozart takes what for him is an ordinary situation—a discussion of opera with his colleagues—and imagines it as a musical ensemble. There are no mythological or historical characters involved—only contemporary ones. Thus, he is modeling his argument.

**59. (C)** Mozart envisions each of the other characters beginning in the same way: "Impertinent Mozart" (line 16), "Ignorant Mozart" (line 18), and "German Mozart" (line 20). This pattern mimics the blending of voices in a vocal quartet. The other options are either contradictory to the text or do not have enough evidence for support.

**60. (E)** Mozart says it himself: "A dramatic poet would have to put all those thoughts down one after another to represent this second of time. The composer can put them all down at once" (lines 25–28). Mozart observes that the poet would have to put the thoughts down in a linear progression. It has nothing to do with the dramatist's talent but with the restrictions of his craft.

**61. (C)** In lines 40–44, Mozart exclaims that it is the composer's job to "turn the audience into God." It is not the composer whom Mozart deifies but the audience.

**62. (B)** The only advice of which we would be aware is that implied in the introductory note: Mozart should not write an opera based on *The Marriage of Figaro*. However, by the end of his monologue, he seems to have increased his determination to proceed.

# HOW TO CALCULATE YOUR SCORE

**Step 1: Figure out your raw score.** Use the answer key to count the number of questions you answered correctly and the number of questions you answered incorrectly. (Do not count any questions you left blank.) Multiply the number wrong by 0.25 and subtract the result from the number correct. Round the result to the nearest whole number. This is your raw score.

## SAT Subject Test: Literature Practice Test 7

| Number right | Number wrong | Raw score |
|:---:|:---:|:---:|

$$\boxed{\phantom{00}} - \left(0.25 \times \boxed{\phantom{00}}\right) = \boxed{\phantom{00}}$$

**Step 2: Find your scaled score.** In the Score Conversion Table below, find your raw score (rounded to the nearest whole number) in one of the columns to the left. The score directly to the right of that number will be your scaled score.

A note on your practice test scores: Don't take these scores too literally. Practice test conditions cannot precisely mirror real test conditions. Your actual SAT Subject Test: Literature score will almost certainly vary from your practice test scores. However, your scores on the practice tests will give you a rough idea of your range on the actual exam.

## Conversion Table

| Raw | Scaled | Raw | Scaled | Raw | Scaled | Raw | Scaled |
|:---:|:---:|:---:|:---:|:---:|:---:|:---:|:---:|
| 63 | 800 | 43 | 700 | 23 | 510 | 3 | 330 |
| 62 | 800 | 42 | 690 | 22 | 500 | 2 | 320 |
| 61 | 800 | 41 | 680 | 21 | 500 | 1 | 310 |
| 60 | 800 | 40 | 670 | 20 | 490 | 0 | 300 |
| 59 | 800 | 39 | 660 | 19 | 480 | -1 | 290 |
| 58 | 800 | 38 | 650 | 18 | 470 | -2 | 280 |
| 57 | 800 | 37 | 640 | 17 | 460 | -3 | 280 |
| 56 | 790 | 36 | 630 | 16 | 450 | -4 | 270 |
| 55 | 790 | 35 | 620 | 15 | 440 | -5 | 260 |
| 54 | 780 | 34 | 610 | 14 | 430 | -6 | 250 |
| 53 | 780 | 33 | 610 | 13 | 420 | -7 | 250 |
| 52 | 780 | 32 | 600 | 12 | 410 | -8 | 240 |
| 51 | 770 | 31 | 590 | 11 | 410 | -9 | 230 |
| 50 | 760 | 30 | 580 | 10 | 400 | -10 | 220 |
| 49 | 750 | 29 | 570 | 9 | 390 | -11 | 210 |
| 48 | 740 | 28 | 560 | 8 | 380 | -12 | 200 |
| 47 | 730 | 27 | 550 | 7 | 370 | -13 | 200 |
| 46 | 720 | 26 | 540 | 6 | 360 | -14 | 200 |
| 45 | 710 | 25 | 530 | 5 | 350 | | |
| 44 | 710 | 24 | 520 | 4 | 340 | | |

# Practice Test 7
# Answer Grid

1. (A) (B) (C) (D) (E)
2. (A) (B) (C) (D) (E)
3. (A) (B) (C) (D) (E)
4. (A) (B) (C) (D) (E)
5. (A) (B) (C) (D) (E)
6. (A) (B) (C) (D) (E)
7. (A) (B) (C) (D) (E)
8. (A) (B) (C) (D) (E)
9. (A) (B) (C) (D) (E)
10. (A) (B) (C) (D) (E)
11. (A) (B) (C) (D) (E)
12. (A) (B) (C) (D) (E)
13. (A) (B) (C) (D) (E)
14. (A) (B) (C) (D) (E)
15. (A) (B) (C) (D) (E)
16. (A) (B) (C) (D) (E)
17. (A) (B) (C) (D) (E)
18. (A) (B) (C) (D) (E)
19. (A) (B) (C) (D) (E)
20. (A) (B) (C) (D) (E)
21. (A) (B) (C) (D) (E)

22. (A) (B) (C) (D) (E)
23. (A) (B) (C) (D) (E)
24. (A) (B) (C) (D) (E)
25. (A) (B) (C) (D) (E)
26. (A) (B) (C) (D) (E)
27. (A) (B) (C) (D) (E)
28. (A) (B) (C) (D) (E)
29. (A) (B) (C) (D) (E)
30. (A) (B) (C) (D) (E)
31. (A) (B) (C) (D) (E)
32. (A) (B) (C) (D) (E)
33. (A) (B) (C) (D) (E)
34. (A) (B) (C) (D) (E)
35. (A) (B) (C) (D) (E)
36. (A) (B) (C) (D) (E)
37. (A) (B) (C) (D) (E)
38. (A) (B) (C) (D) (E)
39. (A) (B) (C) (D) (E)
40. (A) (B) (C) (D) (E)
41. (A) (B) (C) (D) (E)
42. (A) (B) (C) (D) (E)

43. (A) (B) (C) (D) (E)
44. (A) (B) (C) (D) (E)
45. (A) (B) (C) (D) (E)
46. (A) (B) (C) (D) (E)
47. (A) (B) (C) (D) (E)
48. (A) (B) (C) (D) (E)
49. (A) (B) (C) (D) (E)
50. (A) (B) (C) (D) (E)
51. (A) (B) (C) (D) (E)
52. (A) (B) (C) (D) (E)
53. (A) (B) (C) (D) (E)
54. (A) (B) (C) (D) (E)
55. (A) (B) (C) (D) (E)
56. (A) (B) (C) (D) (E)
57. (A) (B) (C) (D) (E)
58. (A) (B) (C) (D) (E)
59. (A) (B) (C) (D) (E)
60. (A) (B) (C) (D) (E)
61. (A) (B) (C) (D) (E)
62. (A) (B) (C) (D) (E)
63. (A) (B) (C) (D) (E)

# Practice Test 7

*Questions 1–8 refer to the following poem. After reading the poem, choose the best answer to each question.*

Thou wast that all to me, my love,
    For which my soul did pine—
    A green isle in the sea, love,
Line      A fountain and a shrine,
(5)   All wreathed with fairy fruits and flowers,
    And all the flowers were mine.

Ah, dream too bright to last!
    Ah, starry Hope! That didst arise
But to be overcast!
(10)    A voice from out the Future cries,
"On! on!"—but o'er the Past
    (Dim gulf!) my spirit hovering lies
Mute, motionless, aghast!

For, alas! alas! with me
(15)    The light of Life is o'er!
    "No more—no more—no more—"
(Such language holds the solemn sea
    To the sands upon the shore)
Shall bloom the thunder-blasted tree,
(20)    Or the stricken eagle soar!

And all my days are trances,
    And all my nightly dreams
Are where thy dark eye glances,
    And where thy footstep gleams—
(25)   In what ethereal dances,
    By what eternal streams.

(1845)

1. This poem discusses primarily the speaker's
   (A) reasons he lost his love.
   (B) outlook on life after losing his love.
   (C) preparations for returning to his love.
   (D) plans for revenge against his love.
   (E) hopes for his love's future happiness.

2. The "green isle," the "fountain," and the "shrine" of lines 3–4 are
   (A) metaphors for the speaker's love.
   (B) actual meeting places for the speaker and his love.
   (C) imagined meeting places for the speaker and his love.
   (D) places where the speaker's love isolates herself.
   (E) symbols of the speaker's soul.

GO ON TO THE NEXT PAGE

3. Lines 5–6 contain all of the following EXCEPT

(A) an indication that the speaker's love has died.

(B) alliteration creating a soft and pleasing mood.

(C) repetition emphasizing an aspect of "the flowers."

(D) a hint that the speaker and his love were once united.

(E) modifying phrases for a noun or nouns in lines 3–4.

4. The "dream" of line 7 has all of the following characteristics EXCEPT that

(A) it represents the situation in the first stanza.

(B) it is synonymous with the "starry Hope" of line 8.

(C) it suggests an eternal bond felt by the speaker and his love.

(D) it is a metaphor for the speaker's impermanent happiness.

(E) it has an intensity that prevents its longevity.

5. The main idea of the second stanza is that

(A) the speaker continues to move forward after heartbreak.

(B) the speaker's love tries to draw him away from the past.

(C) the speaker's existence is a battle between light and darkness.

(D) the speaker's spirit falsifies and debases the past.

(E) the speaker is fixated on thoughts of his past romance.

6. The parenthetical remark in lines 17–18 expresses which of the following?

I. A comment about the quote in line 16

II. An observation about life's fixed course

III. A hope that life will improve in the future

IV. A blessing on the beauty of nature

(A) I only

(B) I and II only

(C) I, II, and III only

(D) I, II, and IV only

(E) I, II, III, and IV

7. The "thunder-blasted tree" and the "stricken eagle" in lines 19–20 are both

(A) symbols of rebirth that capture the speaker's resurrected hopes.

(B) images of the speaker's altered relationship with his love.

(C) homage to the glory of a long lost ideal.

(D) parallels to the "green isle," imagery of lines 3–4.

(E) objects of the verb phrase "Shall bloom."

8. The last stanza's use of repetition helps to convey the idea that

(A) the speaker cannot break away from his past.

(B) the speaker is fated to repeat the mistakes of the past.

(C) the speaker's love is waiting for him in the future.

(D) time will heal the wounds that the speaker suffers.

(E) love has become dreadful monotony to the speaker.

**GO ON TO THE NEXT PAGE**

*Questions 9–16 refer to the following passage. After reading the passage, choose the best answer to each question.*

The women—or rather girls, for they were mostly young—wore drawn cotton bonnets with great flapping curtains to keep off the sun, and
*Line*
(5)  gloves to prevent their hands being wounded by the stubble. There was one wearing a pale pink jacket, another in a cream-coloured, tight-sleeved gown, another in a petticoat as red as the arms of a reaping-machine; and others, older in the brown-rough "wropper," or over-all—the old-
(10)  established and most appropriate dress of the field-woman, which the young ones were abandoning. This morning, the eye returns involuntarily to the girl in the pink cotton jacket, she being the most flexuous and finely drawn
(15)  figure of them all. But her bonnet is pulled so far over her brow that none of her face is disclosed while she binds, though her complexion may be guessed from a stray twine or two of dark brown hair which extends below the curtain of her
(20)  bonnet. Perhaps one reason why she seduces casual attention is that she never courts it, though the other women often gaze around them.

Her binding proceeds with clock-like monotony. From the sheaf last finished she draws
(25)  a handful of ears, patting their tips with her left palm to bring them even. Then, stooping low, she moves forward, gathering the corn with both hands against her knees and pushing her left gloved hand under the bundle to meet the right
(30)  on the other side, holding the corn in an embrace like that of a lover. She brings the ends of the bond together and kneels on the sheaf while she ties it, beating back her skirts now and then when lifted by the breeze. A bit of her naked arm is
(35)  visible between the buff leather of the gauntlet and the sleeve of her gown; and as the day wears on, its feminine smoothness becomes scarified by the stubble and bleeds.

At intervals she stands up to rest, and to retie
(40)  her disarranged apron, or to pull her bonnet straight. Then one can see the oval face of a handsome young woman with deep, dark eyes and long, heavy, clinging tresses, which seem to clasp in a beseeching way anything they fall
(45)  against. The cheeks are paler, the teeth more regular, the red lips thinner than is usual in a country-bred girl.

(1891)

9. The passage is best described as

   (A) a psychological study of a character's personality.

   (B) a sweeping portrait of nature in autumn.

   (C) a drab rendering of farmland routine.

   (D) an exposé of 19th-century agricultural labor abuses.

   (E) a gradual focusing on a single individual.

10. The discussion of the workers' garb in lines 1–12 does all of the following EXCEPT

   (A) add color to the description of the fields.

   (B) reflect the workers' longing for a new order.

   (C) link some of the workers to the machines that aid them.

   (D) show the difference between the young and the old.

   (E) demonstrate some practical responses to the work environment.

**GO ON TO THE NEXT PAGE**

11. In lines 12–22, the girl in the pink cotton jacket seems different from the other workers for what reason?

   I.   She is less exposed facially.
   II.  She is less diligent.
   III. She is not seeking attention.
   IV.  She is more traditional.

   (A) I and III only
   (B) III and IV only
   (C) I, II, and IV only
   (D) II, III, and IV only
   (E) I, II III, and IV

12. Lines 1–2, 12–13, and 20–22 indicate what about the narrator?

   (A) He is hoping for his heroine's release from this situation.
   (B) He is falling in love with the subject of the narration.
   (C) He is given to overstatement, deceit, and arrogance.
   (D) He is capable of mistakes, distractions, or uncertainty.
   (E) He is concerned that she will not keep up with the other workers.

13. The activity described in lines 23–38 seems indicative of

   (A) routine.
   (B) memory.
   (C) necessity.
   (D) optimism.
   (E) ambition.

14. Starting in the second paragraph, the narrator's shift from past tense to present indicates all of the following EXCEPT

   (A) a reflection of the newness of morning.
   (B) a change to a more immediate focus.
   (C) an embellishment of the subject's work ethic.
   (D) a move from the general to the specific.
   (E) an emphasis on this worker's difference from the others.

15. Lines 39–47 demonstrate what about the narrator and "the country-bred girl"?

   (A) They would make a nice couple, if only temporarily.
   (B) He seems to be preparing himself for an encounter with her; she would enjoy it.
   (C) He is suspicious of her motives and origins; she is avoiding social contact.
   (D) He is noticing an emerging physical beauty; she does not fit in with this society.
   (E) Her manner tells him that she is someone from his own shire.

16. The way the passage develops suggests that the narrator might best be described as

   (A) a restrained admirer.
   (B) a shocked passerby.
   (C) a methodical archaeologist.
   (D) a bored tourist.
   (E) a nosy employer.

**GO ON TO THE NEXT PAGE**

*Questions 17–24 refer to the following poem. After reading the poem, choose the best answer to each question.*

Fly envious time, till thou run out thy race,
Call on the lazy leaden-stepping hours,
Whose speed is but the heavy plummet's pace;          *plummet* pendulum
*Line*   And glut thyself with what thy womb devours,
(5)      Which is no more than what is false and vain,
And merely mortal dross;                              *dross* debris, garbage
So little is our loss,
So little is thy gain.
For whenas each thing bad thou hast entombed,
(10)     And last of all thy greedy self consumed,
Then long eternity shall greet our bliss
With an individual kiss;
And joy shall overtake us as a flood,
When everything that is sincerely good
(15)     And perfectly divine,
With truth, and peace and love shall ever shine
About the supreme throne
Of him, to whose happy-making sight alone,
When once our heavenly-guided soul shall climb,
(20)     Then all this earthly grossness quit,          *quit* be rid of
Attired with stars, we shall forever sit,
Triumphing over death, and chance, and thee O time.

(1690)

17. The entire poem uses

(A) iambic pentameter.

(B) couplets.

(C) a doubtful tone.

(D) apostrophe.

(E) quatrains.

18. The consonance of *l* in line 2 creates what effect?

(A) It creates a musical mood that mocks time's intentions.

(B) It emphasizes the power that time has over all of creation.

(C) It creates barriers of sound, thus demonstrating the weakness of time.

(D) It recalls the flapping sound of time as it runs.

(E) It elongates the sound of the line, thus demonstrating time's slow pace.

**GO ON TO THE NEXT PAGE**

19. The running imagery in lines 1–3 and the eating imagery in lines 4–6 do all of the following EXCEPT

    (A) point out the finite quality of time.

    (B) reveal how time destroys earthly things.

    (C) parallel the fast pace and greed of mortals.

    (D) speak of time with an insulting tone.

    (E) emphasize the triviality of earthly things.

20. All the following could be said of lines 7–8 EXCEPT that

    (A) their parallel structure reinforces the vanity of earthly things.

    (B) their brevity represents time's lack of power.

    (C) their antithesis stresses the unimportance of time's acquisitions.

    (D) their metrical shift imitates the chaos of eternity.

    (E) their matter-of-fact tone causes the speaker to sound assured.

21. In lines 13–22, what can one understand about "us" (line 13) after time has its "greedy self consumed" (line 10)?

    (A) The loss of our individuality is a comfort rather than a curse.

    (B) With heavenly assistance, we are essentially victorious and eternal.

    (C) Punishment awaits us if we hold earthly things important.

    (D) We are self-governing, and even our earthly life foreshadows immortality.

    (E) Eternity is one more struggle to face after the hardship of life on earth.

22. The word "grossness" in line 20 is closest in meaning to

    (A) disgust.

    (B) obesity.

    (C) paltriness.

    (D) multitude.

    (E) vulgarity.

23. With which of the following conflicts does the poem concern itself?

    I.   Earthly versus heavenly

    II.  Ephemeral versus eternal

    III. Limitation versus limitlessness

    IV.  Fate versus free will

    (A) I and II only

    (B) I and III only

    (C) I, II, and III only

    (D) I, III, and IV only

    (E) I, II, III, and IV

24. The speaker's outlook in the poem

    (A) remains positive, even gloating.

    (B) changes from positive to negative.

    (C) is initially angry, then becomes serene.

    (D) is resentful against time and earthly things.

    (E) alters from meekness to boldness.

**GO ON TO THE NEXT PAGE**

*Questions 25–32 refer to the following passage. After reading the passage, choose the best answer to each question.*

...men of low birth, and no breeding, have found themselves suddenly translated into a state of affluence, unknown to former ages; and no
Line
(5)   wonder that their brains should be intoxicated with pride, vanity, and presumption. Knowing no other criterion of greatness, but the ostentation of wealth, they discharge their affluence without taste or conduct, through every channel of the most absurd extravagance; and all of them hurry
(10)  to Bath,* because here, without any further qualification, they can mingle with the princes and nobles of the land. Even the wives and daughters of low tradesmen, who, like shovel-nosed sharks, prey upon the blubber of those
(15)  uncouth whales of fortune, are infected with the same rage of displaying their importance; and the slightest indisposition serves them for a pretext to insist upon being conveyed to Bath, where they may hobble country-dances and cotillons
(20)  among lordlings, squires, counsellors, and clergy. These delicate creatures, from Bedforbury, Butcher-row, Crutched-friers, and Botolph–lane,† cannot breathe in the gross air of the Lower Town,‡ or conform to the vulgar rules of the
(25)  common lodging-house; the husband, therefore, must provide an entire house, or elegant apartments in the new buildings. Such is the composition of what is called the fashionable company at Bath; where a very inconsiderable
(30)  proportion of genteel people are lost in a mob of impudent plebeians, who have neither understanding nor judgment, nor the least idea of propriety and decorum; and seem to enjoy nothing so much as an opportunity of insulting
(35)  their betters.
        Thus the number of people, and the number of houses continue to increase; and this will ever be the case, till the streams that swell this irresistible torrent of folly and extravagance,
(40)  shall either be exhausted, or turned into other channels, by incidents and events which I do not pretend to foresee. This, I own, is a subject on which I cannot write with any degree of patience; for the mob is a monster I never could abide,
(45)  either in its head, tail, midriff, or members; I detest the whole of it, as a mass of ignorance, presumption, malice, and brutality; and, in this term of reprobation, I include, without respect of rank, station, or quality, all those of both sexes,
(50)  who affect its manners, and court its society.

(1771)

*Bath  resort town in southern England, famous for its spas
†Bedfordbury...Botolph-lane  streets in the commercial section
‡Lower Town  the city of London

25.  The narrator of this passage is someone who

(A)  despises those without money.

(B)  keeps a residence in Lower Town.

(C)  admires anyone making his own fortune.

(D)  favors the gentility of the noble classes.

(E)  likes seeing Bath socially integrated.

26.  In lines 1–10, the narrator complains that

(A)  too many wealthy people are vacationing in Bath.

(B)  those who are newly wealthy do not exercise refinement.

(C)  affluence corrupts those who have been wealthy for generations.

(D)  the residents of Bath confuse affluence with ostentation.

(E)  no one is able to improve upon or even maintain past standards of living.

**GO ON TO THE NEXT PAGE**

27. In lines 9–12, the narrator implies that, for those not belonging to the noble classes, Bath is

    (A) too accessible.

    (B) dreadfully boring.

    (C) very dirty.

    (D) surprisingly vulgar.

    (E) unceasingly active.

28. The narrator would say all of the following about the "wives and daughters of low tradesmen" (lines 12–13) EXCEPT that

    (A) they are as hungry as sea predators.

    (B) their behavior is as bad as their husbands'.

    (C) they are unfit for upper-class social events.

    (D) their tastes belie their backgrounds and run to the extravagant.

    (E) their conduct has had many of them evicted from the Lower Town.

29. Which of the following contribute to "the number of people, and the number of houses [that] continue to increase" (lines 36–37) in Bath?

    I. The arrival of the newly wealthy

    II. The tastes of tradesmen's wives and daughters

    III. The popularity of Bath

    IV. The accessibility of Bath

    (A) I and II only

    (B) I and III only

    (C) I and IV only

    (D) I, III, and IV only

    (E) I, II, III, and IV

30. In lines 36–42, the recent changes occurring in Bath and their possible future outcomes are described mainly through the use of

    (A) a fascinated tone.

    (B) antithesis.

    (C) water imagery.

    (D) a tonal shift.

    (E) personification.

31. All of the following can be said about the "monster" (line 44) EXCEPT that

    (A) it is a metaphor for "the mob."

    (B) the narrator hates the monster.

    (C) its analogy is restricted to the lower classes.

    (D) its behavior is boorish and presumptuous.

    (E) the narrator's time in Bath has inspired this image.

32. The narrator's tone in this passage would LEAST LIKELY be described as

    (A) egalitarian.

    (B) exasperated.

    (C) critical.

    (D) stuffy.

    (E) consistent.

**GO ON TO THE NEXT PAGE**

Questions 33–44 refer to the following poem. After reading the poem, choose the best answer to each question.

### To a Fish

You strange, astonished-looking, angle-faced,
Dreary-mouthed, gaping wretches of the sea,
Gulping salt-water everlastingly,

*Line*    Cold-blooded, though with red your blood be graced,
(5)    And mute, though dwellers in the roaring waste;
And you, all shapes beside, that fishy be—
Some round, some flat, some long, all devilry,
Legless, unloving, infamously chaste—

O scaly, slippery wet, swift, staring wights,          *wights* creatures
(10)    What is't ye do? What life lead? Eh, dull goggles?
How do ye vary your vile days and nights?
How pass your Sundays? Are ye still but joggles
In ceaseless wash? Still nought but gapes, and bites,
And drinks, and stares, diversified with boggles?          *boggles* sudden movements

### A Fish Answers

(15)    Amazing monster! That, for aught I know,
With the first sight of thee didst make our race
Forever stare! Oh flat and shocking face,
Grimly divided from the breast below!
Thou that on dry land horribly dost go
(20)    With a split body and ridiculous pace,
Prong after prong, disgracer of all grace,
Long-useless-finned, haired upright, unwet, slow!

O breather of unbreathable, sword-sharp air,
How canst exist? How bear thyself, thou dry
(25)    And dreary sloth? What particle canst share
Of the only blessed life, the watery?
I sometimes see of ye an actual *pair*
Go by! Linked fin by fin! odiously.

*(The poem continues on the next page)*

**GO ON TO THE NEXT PAGE**

*The Fish Turns Into a Man, and Then Into*
*a Spirit, and Again Speaks*

*Line*   Indulge thy smiling scorn, if smiling still,
(30)    O man! And loathe, but with a sort of love;
     For difference must its use by difference prove,
     And in such sweet clang, the spheres with music fill.
     One of the spirits am I, that at his will
     Live in whate'er has life—fish, eagle, dove—
(35)    No hate, no pride, beneath nought, nor above,
     A visitor of the rounds of God's sweet skill.

     Man's life is warm, glad, sad, 'twixt loves and graves,
     Boundless in hope, honored with pangs austere,
     Heaven-gazing; and his angel-wings he craves:
(40)    The fish is swift, small-needing, vague yet clear,
     A cold, sweet, silver life, wrapped in round waves,
     Quickened with touches of transporting fear.

                    (1836)

33. Which of the following can be said of the fish?

    (A) The fish loathes the human for the entirety of the poem.

    (B) The fish disdains the human, then begins to understand the value of all creatures.

    (C) The fish is amazed by the human, then finally considers man to be ordinary.

    (D) The fish fears the human, then realizes that no creature should be feared.

    (E) The fish honors the human for the entirety of the poem.

34. In the first four lines of the passage, what dominates the description of the fish?

    (A) Infinitive phrases

    (B) Prepositional phrases

    (C) Gerund phrases

    (D) Noun phrases

    (E) Participial phrases

35. In the first stanza, the only seemingly positive aspect of the fish that the speaker states is in line

    (A) 1.

    (B) 2.

    (C) 4.

    (D) 5.

    (E) 7.

**GO ON TO THE NEXT PAGE**

36. In lines 1–14, the human narrator has all of the following problems with fish *except* that they

    (A) lack human physiology.

    (B) cannot justify their existence with any redeeming value.

    (C) must be jealous of human ease and contentment.

    (D) seem more associated with the satanic than the godly.

    (E) lead dull, repetitive lives.

37. In lines 13–14, what dominates the description of fish?

    (A) Alliteration

    (B) Simile

    (C) Syllogism

    (D) Synecdoche

    (E) Antithesis

38. In lines 15–17, the fish's response to the human explains

    (A) why humans are so ill-tempered.

    (B) why fish became water dwellers.

    (C) why fish have a gawking appearance.

    (D) why fish are immobilized forever.

    (E) why humans remained on the land.

39. The "prong" referred to in line 21 must be

    (A) Poseidon's trident.

    (B) a human being.

    (C) a fishing implement.

    (D) a seaweed strand.

    (E) a human leg.

40. The fish remarks on all of the following human characteristics in lines 15–28 EXCEPT

    (A) physiognomy and other physical features.

    (B) lack of grace and agility.

    (C) the ability to walk arm in arm with others.

    (D) air-breathing capabilities.

    (E) the link with water that the fish shares.

41. The fish's statement that the human should "loathe, but with a sort of love" (line 30) is a type of

    (A) paradox.

    (B) poor judgment.

    (C) sarcasm.

    (D) elision.

    (E) euphemism.

**GO ON TO THE NEXT PAGE**

42. The fish's aphorism that "difference must its use by difference prove" (line 31) means that

    (A) there is a value in differences, which is made apparent by their very distinctions.

    (B) if one is truly to be different, he must first make his differences conspicuous.

    (C) we should accept all creatures, because there really are no differences among us.

    (D) different creatures will never accept each other until disparity is eliminated.

    (E) we can accept others' differences, but ultimately, we will gravitate to like species.

43. In lines 33–36, becoming a spirit has taught the fish that

    (A) God is intolerant of conflict among his creatures.

    (B) we may become any creature we wish after death.

    (C) humans are the highest life forms on earth.

    (D) fish are made of the same cosmic energy as humans.

    (E) creation is beautiful, equal, and virtuous.

44. The final stanza demonstrates the idea that

    (A) earthly creatures' differences make them doomed to remain in conflict for eternity.

    (B) earthly creatures have always had the capacity to understand and tolerate each other.

    (C) despite their differences, earthly creatures are beings of complexity and virtue.

    (D) because of their shared Creator, earthly creatures have an obligation to love each other.

    (E) the future of earthly creatures is uncertain until they learn to love each other.

**GO ON TO THE NEXT PAGE**

*Questions 45–54 refer to the following passage. After reading the passage, choose the best answer to each question.*

The young man swung in from the corridor, breathless. He was shaking his head with laughter and triumph. Here! he said. And waggled the lion
Line at her. One-and-six!*
(5)   What? she said.

He laughed. I was arguing with him for fun, bargaining—when the train had pulled out already, he came tearing after....One-and-six baas!† So there's your lion.
(10)  She was holding it away from her, the head with the open jaws, the pointed teeth, the black tongue, the wonderful ruff of fur facing her. She was looking at it with an expression of not seeing, of seeing something different. Her face was
(15)  drawn up, wryly, like the face of a discomforted child. Her mouth lifted nervously at the corner. Very slowly, cautious, she lifted her finger and touched the mane, where it was joined to the wood.
(20)  But how could you, she said. He was shocked by the dismay in her face.

Good heavens, he said, what's the matter?

If you wanted the thing, she said, her voice rising and breaking with the shrill impotence of
(25)  anger, why didn't you buy it in the first place? If you wanted it, why didn't you pay for it? Why did you have to wait for him to run after the train with it and give him one-and-six? One-and-six!

She was pushing it at him, trying to force him
(30)  to take it. He stood astonished, his hand hanging at his sides.

But you wanted it! You liked it so much?
—It's a beautiful piece of work, she said fiercely, as if to protect it from him.
(35)  You liked it so much! You said yourself it was too expensive—

Oh *you*—she said, hopeless and furious. *You*... She threw the lion into the seat.

He stood looking at her.

(40)  She sat down again in the corner and, her face slumped in her hand, stared out of the window. Everything was turning around inside her. One-and-six. One-and-six. One-and-six for the wood and the carving and the sinews and the legs and
(45)  the switch of the tail. The mouth open like that and the teeth. The black tongue, rolling, like a wave. The mane around the neck. To give one-and-six for that. The heat of shame mounted through her legs and body and sounded in her
(50)  ears like the sound of sand pouring. Pouring, pouring. She sat there, sick. A weariness, a tastelessness, the discovery of a void made her hands slacken their grip, atrophy emptily, as if the hour was not worth their grasp. She was feeling
(55)  like this again. She had thought it was something to do with singleness, with being alone and belonging too much to oneself.

She sat there not wanting to move or speak, or to look at anything, even; so that the mood
(60)  should be associated with nothing, no object, word or sight that might recur and so recall the feeling again....Smuts blew in grittily, settled on her hands. Her back remained at exactly the same angle, turned against the young man sitting with
(65)  his hands drooping between his sprawled legs, and the lion, fallen on its side in the corner.

(1952)

*One-and-six   one shilling and sixpence
†baas   African dialect for "boss," a deferential address, usually to a white male

45. The man and the woman in the passage are having a disagreement concerning

 (A) the quality of a small wooden lion.

 (B) the priorities of their relationship.

 (C) his wastefulness with money.

 (D) her easily discontented nature.

 (E) the rightness of his conduct.

46. In lines 1–4, the attitude of the man can best be described as

 (A) proud.

 (B) aghast.

 (C) surprised.

 (D) cheated.

 (E) incredulous.

47. The woman's reaction in lines 10–19 to the lion is best summed up as

 (A) fearful.

 (B) troubled.

 (C) disdainful.

 (D) grateful.

 (E) shocked.

48. Since the man has paid "one-and-six" for the lion, the woman's question of "why didn't you pay for it?" (line 26) must be

 (A) a recognition of the payment's inadequacy.

 (B) a statement about her distaste for the lion.

 (C) a revelation of the woman's own forgetfulness.

 (D) an attempt to make the man return the lion.

 (E) an inquiry about the transaction's validity.

49. The young man is finding the woman's behavior about the lion to be

 (A) amusing and entertaining.

 (B) familiar and tiresome.

 (C) contradictory and confounding.

 (D) bubbly and energetic.

 (E) melodramatic and embarrassing.

50. All of the following can be said about the phrase "The black tongue, rolling, like a wave" (lines 46–47) EXCEPT that

 (A) it is the most figurative description of the lion between lines 43–51.

 (B) it expresses the young woman's admiration for the lion's beauty.

 (C) it reflects her desire to leave the train and the young man behind.

 (D) it is a simile remarking on the sculptor's skill.

 (E) it helps to explain why she is behaving as she is.

**GO ON TO THE NEXT PAGE**

51. Lines 54–57 suggest which of the following?

   I. The incident with the lion has stirred a familiar feeling within the woman.

   II. Part of the woman's sadness stems from not being married.

   III. The woman feels solely responsible for the lion's purchase.

   (A) I only

   (B) II only

   (C) I and III only

   (D) II and III only

   (E) I, II, and III

52. The "Smuts," or dirt particles, of line 62 could symbolize

   (A) that progress means nothing without genuine caring.

   (B) how greed corrupts upper-class white society.

   (C) how the young man has tried to please the woman.

   (D) that the woman feels tainted by the incident.

   (E) how the lion has affected the young woman.

53. The lion, "fallen on its side in the corner" (line 66), could symbolize for the couple that

   (A) their problems have moved beyond the lion incident.

   (B) neither one of them is thinking about the lion anymore.

   (C) just as the lion has been discarded, so has their relationship.

   (D) just as the lion appears to be sleeping, so are they both tired.

   (E) they both feel "cornered" by the other's behavior.

54. The passage develops with the use of a

   (A) first-person major character narrator.

   (B) first-person minor character narrator.

   (C) third-person observer.

   (D) third-person limited omniscient narrator.

   (E) third-person omniscient narrator.

**GO ON TO THE NEXT PAGE**

*Questions 55–63 refer to the following poem. After reading the poem, choose the best answer to each question.*

Ha! tott'ring Johnny strut and boast,
But think of what your feathers cost;
Your crowing days are short at most,
Line      You bloom but soon to fade.
(5)    Surely you could not stand so wide,
If strictly to the bottom tried;
The wind would blow your plume aside,
      If half your debts were paid.
            Then boast and bear the crack,
(10)          With the Sheriff at your back,
            Huzza for dandy Jack,
                  My jolly fop, my Jo—

The blue smoke from your segar flies          *segar* cigar
Offensive to my nose and eyes,
(15)    The most of people would be wise,
      Your presence to evade.
Your pockets jingle loud with cash,
And thus you cut a foppish dash,
But alas! dear boy, you would be trash,
(20)      If your accounts were paid.
            Then boast and bear the crack, etc.

My duck bill boots would look as bright,
Had you in justice served me right,
Like you, I then could step as light,
(25)      Before a flaunting maid.
And nicely could I clear my throat,
And to my tights, my eyes devote,
But I'd leave you bear, without coat,          *bear* bare
For which you have not paid.
(30)          Then boast and bear the crack, etc.

I'd toss myself with a scornful air,
            And to a poor man pay no care,
I could rock cross-legged in my chair,
      Within the cloister shade.
(35)    I'd gird my neck with a light cravat,
And creaming wear my bell-crown hat;
But away my down would fly at that,
      If once my debts were paid.
            Then boast and bear the crack,
(40)          With the Sheriff at your back,
            Huzza for dandy Jack,
                  My jolly fop, my Jo—

(1845)

**GO ON TO THE NEXT PAGE**

55. In this poem, Johnny is best identified as
    (A) a neighbor of the speaker.
    (B) the narrator of the poem.
    (C) a respected aristocrat.
    (D) a victimized outcast.
    (E) a well-dressed debtor.

56. The "feathers" of line 2 are Johnny's
    (A) female companions.
    (B) life experience.
    (C) expensive clothes.
    (D) muddled thinking.
    (E) hidden identity.

57. In the context of the poem, lines 3–4 are a warning that Johnny must eventually
    (A) face the reality of death.
    (B) reveal his extended past.
    (C) lose his continued stubbornness.
    (D) change his view of humanity.
    (E) come to a financial reckoning.

58. Within the context of the first stanza, "the bottom" (line 6) must be a reference to
    (A) the "bottom rung" of the social ladder.
    (B) a kind of corporal punishment that Johnny deserves.
    (C) the "bottom line"—a tally of debits and credits.
    (D) Johnny's vulgarity—his "bottom feeder" attitude.
    (E) a kind of dungeon to which Johnny should be sent.

59. Lines 11–12 carry a tone of
    (A) true acclaim.
    (B) paternal pride.
    (C) funereal mourning.
    (D) bitter anger.
    (E) exclamatory irony.

60. Considering its effect on the speaker, one could view the "blue smoke" of line 13 as a symbol of
    (A) Johnny's unfounded brashness.
    (B) Johnny's fantastic wealth.
    (C) the speaker's attitude about Johnny.
    (D) public opinion concerning Johnny.
    (E) Johnny's aristocratic origins.

61. The third stanza reveals all of the following EXCEPT
    (A) a hypothetical situation created by the speaker.
    (B) the speaker viewing himself as Johnny's equal.
    (C) Johnny involved in a flirtation with a woman.
    (D) a reference to the speaker's pending lawsuit against Johnny.
    (E) a new reason why the speaker is so critical of Johnny's conduct.

62. Lines 31–38 do all of the following EXCEPT
    (A) continue the idea started in the third stanza.
    (B) use first-person pronouns that really refer to Johnny.
    (C) allude to a set of images begun in the first stanza.
    (D) further the description of Johnny's audacity.
    (E) reiterate the advice of lines 11–12.

63. The poem can best be described as
    (A) a slanted character description.
    (B) a narrative with a surprise ending.
    (C) an exposé of the upper class.
    (D) an economic polemic.
    (E) a passionate elegy.

## STOP!

**If you finish before time is up,
you may check your work.**

# Answer Key
# Practice Test 7

1. B
2. A
3. A
4. C
5. E
6. B
7. B
8. A
9. E
10. B
11. A
12. D
13. A
14. A
15. D
16. A
17. D
18. E
19. C
20. D
21. B
22. C

23. C
24. A
25. D
26. B
27. A
28. E
29. E
30. C
31. C
32. A
33. B
34. E
35. C
36. C
37. D
38. C
39. E
40. E
41. A
42. A
43. E
44. C

45. E
46. A
47. B
48. A
49. C
50. C
51. A
52. D
53. A
54. D
55. E
56. C
57. E
58. C
59. E
60. A
61. D
62. E
63. A

# ANSWERS AND EXPLANATIONS

**1. (B)** From the first stanza, we know that, at one time, the "love" and the speaker were together: All the "flowers" that decked the images representing her were his. But that "dream" (line 7) could not last, and even though the "Future" calls to the speaker, his "spirit" hovers over the past. Since then, for him, "the light of Life is o'er" (line 15), and the speaker will never again be able to have what once was. In the final stanza, he tells us that he spends all his days and nights thinking about his love, and there is no indication that this routine will stop. In summary, he has lost his love, and life is now worse for him. The rest of the options are too active; (B) allows for him to remain linked to the past.

**2. (A)** The speaker says to his love, "Thou wast that all to me" (line 1). The phrase "that all" is exemplified by the "green isle" and the other images. His soul pined for her (line 2) as it would for these things.

**3. (A)** Decking a shrine or even a fountain or an isle does not indicate death, necessarily. Flowers are used as decorations for many kinds of events, many of them happier than death. Furthermore, the first stanza is a happy recollection. The flowers would be better suited for a festive mood.

**4. (C)** Because the "dream" did not last, thinking of it as an eternal bond would be a poor analogy. Also, this poem is narrated from the speaker's point of view; we never know what his love's feelings were.

**5. (E)** The speaker says that his spirit hovers over the "Past," which to him is a "Dim gulf!" Some voice from the "Future" encourages him to move forward, to get "On! on!" with his life. The "but" of line 11 shows us, however, that he is not heeding that voice.

**6. (B)** The parenthetical remark starts with, "Such language," a reference to the phrase "No more," etc. This phrase, "No more," has a finality to it, demonstrated by the sea's being held to the "sands upon the shore." Thus, there is a fixedness to the sea's course; items I and II are supported.

Since the parenthetical remark is commenting on such a terminal thought as "No more," one cannot see any hope in the image; thus, item III lacks support. It is the routine of nature and its finality that are being described in the parentheses, not its beauty, so item IV does not work.

**7. (B)** Paraphrasing the inverted sentence in which these images appear, we read, "The thunder-blasted tree shall bloom 'No more—no more—no more,' nor shall the eagle soar." The implication is that, at one time, the tree bloomed and the eagle soared. Had both the tree and the eagle remained healthy, they could have been linked to the "green isle" images of the first stanza, which talked of better days between the speaker and his love. However, nature has blasted the tree and the eagle is stricken—in much the way that the speaker's relationship with his love has changed for the worse.

**8. (A)** The repetitions show us how routine his behavior is. During all his days, he is in a trance: a reference to his "Mute, motionless" soul hovering over the Past. His love haunts his "nightly dreams," also. If he routinely obsesses about her, then he cannot break away from his past.

**9. (E)** The narrator begins—almost like a movie—in a "wide shot" of the field. We see many women at once performing agricultural labor. Then the narrator "pans" among the women, until "the eye returns involuntarily" (lines 12–13) to the worker in the pink jacket. The next two paragraphs deal solely with her actions and features in "close-up." However, we never see the inner workings of her mind, so (A) cannot work.

**10. (B)** To know their longing, we would first have to see what is going on in their hearts or heads. The narrator in this passage gives us only physical descriptions, or exteriors.

**11. (A)** The evidence for item I is in this excerpt from lines 15–16: "her bonnet is pulled so far over her brow that none of her face is disclosed." Item III is proven by this sentence: "Perhaps one reason why she seduces casual attention is that she never courts it" (lines 20–21). The narrator hazards a guess that she never seeks to be noticed, her closely drawn bonnet being evidence of that behavior.

We see that "she binds" in 12–22, words that do not indicate whether she is working more or less diligently than the others—although the second paragraph displays her as a hard worker. Furthermore, her pink jacket distinguishes her from the older workers, who wear the traditional "wropper." Therefore, items II and IV have no support.

**12. (D)** The narrator corrects himself in line 1: "or rather girls." He says in lines 12–13 that "the eye returns involuntarily" to the girl in the pink jacket, as if he cannot help this distraction from the general picture. His "Perhaps" in line 20 shows a degree of uncertainty, as well.

**13. (A)** According to the narrator, the girl works with "clock-like monotony" (lines 23–24). Furthermore, she continues to work like this "as the day wears on" (lines 36–37) and until her hands become "scarified" (line 37). Thus, the work is repetitive and ongoing to the point of physical damage.

**14. (A)** The time of day *is* morning, but the second paragraph focuses only on the worker. As lines 36–37 indicate, the paragraph follows her work over the course of the day.

**15. (D)** The beauty is emerging because the narrator is beginning to see what lies beneath that drawn bonnet: "Then one can see the oval face of a handsome young woman" (lines 41-42). She does not fit in with this society because her "cheeks are paler, the teeth more regular, the red lips thinner than is usual in a country-bred girl" (lines 45–47). She is in a rural setting, working among other country girls, but she seems different.

**16. (A)** The narrator notices the girl's beauty, but he does so cautiously, even reluctantly. His eye is drawn to her "involuntarily," and he guesses at, but is not certain of, reasons why she "seduces casual attention."

**17. (D)** This poem features a variety of meters and rhyme schemes. It is also expressed with certainty. However, from beginning to end, it addresses time as if that entity were a living, reasoning being.

**18. (E)** Time does, indeed, have a slow pace in these lines, because its hours are "lazy" and step with feet of lead. The *l* is a fluid sound, unlike a *b* or *t* for instance, and thus can lengthen the pace of a line.

**19. (C)** In lines 1–6, nothing is fast paced; time moves slowly. Time may also devour earthly things in a greedy way here. However, nothing about human beings is discussed in these lines. We are focusing on time's qualities. Moreover, they are not parallel to ours, because the speaker gives us a different fate than time's.

**20. (D)** Their meter is identical. If one interprets "metrical shift" as a change in meter from previous lines, lines 7–8 still do not mimic eternity's chaos. According to the narrator, God seems to have a definite plan for time's end and our salvation.

**21. (B)** We are eternal as "we…forever sit" (line 21) in God's presence. We are victorious because we are "Triumphing over death" (line 22). Furthermore, we are able to do these things because our souls are "heavenly-guided" (line 19); thus, we have divine assistance.

**22. (C)** Anything earthly in this poem has been discussed as "false," "vain," and "dross." When we lose earthly materials, "So little is our loss" (line 7). Therefore, all earthly things are unimportant, insignificant, or *paltry*.

23. **(C)** The end of earthly things is discussed in the first half of the poem, and a prediction about our heavenly lives is made in the second, so item I is covered. Ephemeral things are temporary, and earthly things in this poem will not last—they are limited. On the other hand, we will endure in heaven—there is no limit to our existence. Thus items II and III have support. Item IV lacks evidence, because humans do not seem to be exercising any will at all here. We are taken into heaven with no regard to our earthly conduct.

24. **(A)** The outlook is obviously positive, because the poem ends with a prediction that we will be eternally blissful. The speaker's words approach the level of gloating when he tells time that it can consume all it wants but its gain is "So little," as is our loss. There is almost an arrogance here, because the speaker implies that all he has to do is wait for God to "make his move" and time—no matter how much it consumes—will end at that moment.

25. **(D)** In the opening lines, the narrator says that "men of low birth," or those not of the noble classes, have gained sudden wealth and thereby are "intoxicated with pride, vanity, and presumption." He complains that they act with no "taste or conduct" (line 8) and display "absurd extravagance" (line 9). He later is dismayed that an "inconsiderable proportion of genteel people are lost in a mob of impudent plebeians" (lines 29–31). The implication is that genteel people are preferable to those of the lower classes. Finally, in the last lines of the passage, we know that the narrator does not favor the noble classes outright, only the proper conduct associated with nobility; he says that if anyone "without respect of rank, station, or quality" imitates the behavior or seeks the company of the ill-behaved class, then they also are included in his "term of reprobation."

26. **(B)** The narrator explains that newly wealthy people, "Knowing no other criterion of greatness" besides "ostentation of wealth," behave "without taste or conduct." They have money but no manners.

27. **(A)** The narrator remarks that, in Bath, the newly moneyed may mingle with the nobility "without any further qualification." The implication is that money alone should not qualify people of a lower class to interact with the noble classes.

28. **(E)** It is not that the Lower Town has sent these women away but that newly acquired wealth has made the women too haughty to "breathe in the gross air of the Lower Town, or conform to the vulgar rules of the common lodging-house." The women have, in essence, removed *themselves* from the lower-class environment of Lower Town, because they think they are too good for it.

29. **(E)** Item I is proven in the passage's first five lines. The tastes of tradesmen's wives and daughters are partially expressed in their refusal to stay in lodging houses, so that "an entire house, or elegant apartments in the new buildings" must be constructed; item II therefore has proof. As for items III and IV, the narrator has already discussed that "all" of the newly affluent "hurry to Bath" and that they need no "further qualification" (lines 9–11) to do so.

30. **(C)** The influx of people into Bath is described as "streams" and a "torrent." He sees no end to Bath's increasing population until the numbers of people entering into the city are either exhausted or "turned into other channels," the way a river would have its course changed.

31. **(C)** The "monster" analogy also applies to those of the upper classes who behave in the same way as the newly wealthy. The narrator explains in lines 47–49: "and, in this term of reprobation, I include, without respect of rank, station, or quality."

32. **(A)** The narrator sees a definite and proper distinction between the classes; moreover, he does not believe that the resources of Bath are deserved by all people.

**33. (B)** The fish is disdainful of the man, using such invectives as "Amazing monster" (line 15), "shocking face" (line 17), "ridiculous pace" (line 20), and "disgracer of all grace" (line 21). However, in the stanzas starting at line 29, the fish's spirit form has witnessed the skill of God's creation and is now able to see not only that a fish is "A cold, sweet, silver life" (line 41) but also that man is "Boundless in hope" and "Heaven-gazing" (lines 38–39).

**34. (E)** Participial phrases are verbals that have -*ing* and -*ed* suffixes and that are used as adjectives. The words "astonish*ed*-look*ing*," "angle-fac*ed*," "Dreary-mouth*ed*," "gap*ing*," "Gulp*ing*," and "Cold-blood*ed*" are all participles describing the fish.

**35. (C)** The human speaker notes that the fish at least has "red ... blood," so it does have something human—and therefore acceptable by the speaker's terms—about it.

**36. (C)** The human speaker directs all his comments to and about the fish. Only once does he hint at a comparison between humans and sea creatures: in line 4, when he talks about the fish's red blood. Otherwise, he never suggests that fish are unhappy in their existence or wishing to trade it for a human one. He is simply repulsed by the fish's form and manner.

**37. (D)** The various parts or actions of the fish—gapes, bites, drinks, and stares—are used to represent the whole of the fish.

**38. (C)** The lines indicate that the human form is so shocking, it may have caused fish forever to be staring.

**39. (E)** In line 20, the fish has described the man's "split body," a reference to the "fork" created where our legs join the hips. Immediately after, the fish remarks that we move at a "ridiculous pace" and then it uses the phrase "Prong after prong." In context, the fish must be describing the way we walk: "Prong after prong," our legs moving back and forth.

**40. (E)** The fish does not see the human linked to the sea. In fact, it asks the rhetorical question, "What particle canst share/Of the only blessed life, the watery?" The implication is humans are too land oriented to share the water's blessed life.

**41. (A)** A paradox is a seeming contradiction with a deeper meaning. On the surface, it would be contradictory to loathe and love something at the same time. As we see in the final stanzas, however, the fish is talking about noticing differences but appreciating them as well.

**42. (A)** Again, we have an inverted sentence that makes more sense when rearranged and slightly modified. The line could be read this way: "Difference must prove its use by being different." In other words, differences have worth simply because they are differences. The implication is that there is even a beauty in differences. This idea is similar to "Beauty is its own excuse for being," a line found in two other works in this volume's other practice tests.

**43. (E)** Creation is beautiful, because God has made it with "sweet skill." It is equal, because "whate'er has life" is "beneath nought, nor above." Finally, it is virtuous, because living things have "No hate, nor pride."

**44. (C)** Note that this question refers to the *last* stanza of the poem. The last stanza's descriptions of man and fish show that the two are still very different. However, they are both virtuous because man is "Heaven-gazing"—seeking the divine—and the fish is "small-needing"—lacking greed. They are also both complex: Man's life is both "glad" and "sad;" the fish is "vague yet clear."

**45. (E)** The woman's musings about the lion in the 4th and 14th paragraphs show her appreciation for the sculpture. Her concern is that the young man has not only paid little for the craft but has also haggled that price down from what must have already been a modest price.

**46. (A)** The young man swings in from the corridor, as if he is doing something heroic. He also shakes his head with "laughter and triumph." If he feels triumphant about his purchase, then he must be proud of himself.

**47. (B)** She must be admiring the lion, because she notices its "wonderful" ruff of fur. But her admiration turns into something else when we see her face drawing up "wryly, like the face of a discomforted child" (lines 15–16). Her mouth lifts "nervously" and she touches the lion's mane with caution (lines 16–18). The juxtaposition of her admiration for the work and her nervous behavior indicates that she is troubled.

**48. (A)** The amount that the young man paid for the lion has already been made clear. Her question implies that the small amount which he has shelled out can hardly be considered payment, especially if one considers the lion's craftsmanship—an aspect she has already noted.

**49. (C)** He has entered their compartment in triumph, yet she acts as if she is not grateful for his accomplishment. His confusion about her reaction is recorded in "Good heavens … what's the matter?" (line 22). In line 32, he says, "But you wanted it! You liked it so much?" He is reviewing the recent past because he cannot make sense of the present; her behavior now seems contradictory to her desires then.

**50. (C)** She definitely wants to close the young man out; her silence and the toss of the lion into the corner explain this idea clearly. Yet, in her musings, she has not displayed a desire to leave the young man, and she certainly has no intention or desire to leave the train.

**51. (A)** The proof for item I occurs in lines 54–55: "She was feeling like this again." The lion has awakened something inside her that she has felt before.

Item II could be proven in the passage, except for the use of past perfect verb tense: "She had thought it was something to do with singleness." The *had* implies that this thought occurred previously, when these feelings *first* came to her, before the time of this passage. Now that she is experiencing them again, the *had* indicates that singleness is not motivating the feelings, but something else is.

Item III is not valid because, even though shame is welling within the woman, she is not placing that shame specifically. Is she feeling shameful about her role in this incident? Is she ashamed of the young man's conduct? Or both? Since the options are open, III is not definite.

**52. (D)** The smuts are settling on her hands, thus getting them dirty. Likewise, the lion incident has caused her to feel troubled and has driven a wedge between the young man and herself.

**53. (A)** Lines 54–57 imply that this familiar feeling experienced by the woman has nothing to do with being alone. The young man's actions, then, are causing her to realize that there would be nothing wrong in being single. The lion incident may even be causing her to reconsider the relationship that she has with him. Also, the lion that she so much admired has been left carelessly to fall on its side, unattended. We see in his silence and his hands "drooping between his sprawled legs" (line 65) an attitude of defeat. If the lion were all that was bothering him, would the young man really be this abject? Both of the characters seem to be aware that there is something going on beyond the lion episode.

**54. (D)** The narrator is outside the story, so only (C), (D), or (E) could work. (D) is the best option, because the narrator tells us what the woman is feeling, but we do not know the young man's thoughts.

**55. (E)** Johnny's "feathers" are his expensive clothes. By hypothetically putting himself in Johnny's place, the speaker implies in lines 22–28 that Johnny is wearing fashionable boots, is devoting attention to his tights—presumably primping—and is wearing a coat. The problem, however, as the speaker notes in several places, is that Johnny has not settled his debts. For example, the coat previously mentioned is one "For which [Johnny has] not paid" (line 29).

**56. (C)** In this context, Johnny's "feathers" are his fancy clothes that he shows off (like a peacock and its plumage, for example).

**57. (E)** Johnny crows and blooms now—that is, he is stylish in his clothes—but he will soon fade, as line 10 tells us, because "the Sheriff" will be "at [his] back." Johnny's indebtedness will soon be discovered, and the law will pursue him.

**58. (C)** Johnny is in debt. If he were "tried" to the bottom line, or held responsible for the debts tallied up on an accounting document, then Johnny "could not stand so wide" in a posture of self-assurance.

**59. (E)** "Huzza" is an exclamation. What makes these lines ironic is that they follow a series of critical revelations and vindictive predictions. If lines 11–12 were sincere, they would contradict the attitude of the previous lines.

**60. (A)** The speaker finds the smoke "offensive." Just as offensive to him is the roosterlike arrogance that Johnny displays. Yet, as the speaker points out, Johnny's self-confidence is ill founded, since the young man has secret debts soon to be discovered. Also, to the speaker, Johnny's pretensions are as transparent as smoke.

**61. (D)** There is a mention of "justice" here but not in relation to a future lawsuit; rather, "justice" alludes to a past event. The new reason for the speaker to be critical is that Johnny has not done the speaker justice. These lines imply a reason for the speaker to be so vituperative: One of Johnny's creditors is the speaker himself.

**62. (E)** By continuing to describe Johnny's audacious behavior, the stanza does not reiterate a cheer for Johnny; its tone, in fact, would have the opposite effect.

**63. (A)** Certainly, the poem describes the character of Johnny. It is a biased description, however, because we only have the speaker's point of view. We have not heard from other creditors, witnesses to Johnny's financial transactions, or even Johnny himself. That is not to imply that Johnny is innocent of the speaker's charges—merely that we have a one-sided view here.

# HOW TO CALCULATE YOUR SCORE

**Step 1: Figure out your raw score.** Use the answer key to count the number of questions you answered correctly and the number of questions you answered incorrectly. (Do not count any questions you left blank.) Multiply the number wrong by 0.25 and subtract the result from the number correct. Round the result to the nearest whole number. This is your raw score.

## SAT Subject Test: Literature Practice Test 8

| Number right | Number wrong | Raw score |
|---|---|---|

$$\boxed{\phantom{00}} \; - \; \left(0.25 \times \boxed{\phantom{00}}\right) \; = \; \boxed{\phantom{00}}$$

**Step 2: Find your scaled score.** In the Score Conversion Table below, find your raw score (rounded to the nearest whole number) in one of the columns to the left. The score directly to the right of that number will be your scaled score.

A note on your practice test scores: Don't take these scores too literally. Practice test conditions cannot precisely mirror real test conditions. Your actual SAT Subject Test: Literature score will almost certainly vary from your practice test scores. However, your scores on the practice tests will give you a rough idea of your range on the actual exam.

## Conversion Table

| Raw | Scaled | Raw | Scaled | Raw | Scaled | Raw | Scaled |
|---|---|---|---|---|---|---|---|
| 63 | 800 | 43 | 700 | 23 | 510 | 3 | 330 |
| 62 | 800 | 42 | 690 | 22 | 500 | 2 | 320 |
| 61 | 800 | 41 | 680 | 21 | 500 | 1 | 310 |
| 60 | 800 | 40 | 670 | 20 | 490 | 0 | 300 |
| 59 | 800 | 39 | 660 | 19 | 480 | -1 | 290 |
| 58 | 800 | 38 | 650 | 18 | 470 | -2 | 280 |
| 57 | 800 | 37 | 640 | 17 | 460 | -3 | 280 |
| 56 | 790 | 36 | 630 | 16 | 450 | -4 | 270 |
| 55 | 790 | 35 | 620 | 15 | 440 | -5 | 260 |
| 54 | 780 | 34 | 610 | 14 | 430 | -6 | 250 |
| 53 | 780 | 33 | 610 | 13 | 420 | -7 | 250 |
| 52 | 780 | 32 | 600 | 12 | 410 | -8 | 240 |
| 51 | 770 | 31 | 590 | 11 | 410 | -9 | 230 |
| 50 | 760 | 30 | 580 | 10 | 400 | -10 | 220 |
| 49 | 750 | 29 | 570 | 9 | 390 | -11 | 210 |
| 48 | 740 | 28 | 560 | 8 | 380 | -12 | 200 |
| 47 | 730 | 27 | 550 | 7 | 370 | -13 | 200 |
| 46 | 720 | 26 | 540 | 6 | 360 | -14 | 200 |
| 45 | 710 | 25 | 530 | 5 | 350 | | |
| 44 | 710 | 24 | 520 | 4 | 340 | | |

# Practice Test 8
# Answer Grid

1. Ⓐ Ⓑ Ⓒ Ⓓ Ⓔ
2. Ⓐ Ⓑ Ⓒ Ⓓ Ⓔ
3. Ⓐ Ⓑ Ⓒ Ⓓ Ⓔ
4. Ⓐ Ⓑ Ⓒ Ⓓ Ⓔ
5. Ⓐ Ⓑ Ⓒ Ⓓ Ⓔ
6. Ⓐ Ⓑ Ⓒ Ⓓ Ⓔ
7. Ⓐ Ⓑ Ⓒ Ⓓ Ⓔ
8. Ⓐ Ⓑ Ⓒ Ⓓ Ⓔ
9. Ⓐ Ⓑ Ⓒ Ⓓ Ⓔ
10. Ⓐ Ⓑ Ⓒ Ⓓ Ⓔ
11. Ⓐ Ⓑ Ⓒ Ⓓ Ⓔ
12. Ⓐ Ⓑ Ⓒ Ⓓ Ⓔ
13. Ⓐ Ⓑ Ⓒ Ⓓ Ⓔ
14. Ⓐ Ⓑ Ⓒ Ⓓ Ⓔ
15. Ⓐ Ⓑ Ⓒ Ⓓ Ⓔ
16. Ⓐ Ⓑ Ⓒ Ⓓ Ⓔ
17. Ⓐ Ⓑ Ⓒ Ⓓ Ⓔ
18. Ⓐ Ⓑ Ⓒ Ⓓ Ⓔ
19. Ⓐ Ⓑ Ⓒ Ⓓ Ⓔ
20. Ⓐ Ⓑ Ⓒ Ⓓ Ⓔ
21. Ⓐ Ⓑ Ⓒ Ⓓ Ⓔ

22. Ⓐ Ⓑ Ⓒ Ⓓ Ⓔ
23. Ⓐ Ⓑ Ⓒ Ⓓ Ⓔ
24. Ⓐ Ⓑ Ⓒ Ⓓ Ⓔ
25. Ⓐ Ⓑ Ⓒ Ⓓ Ⓔ
26. Ⓐ Ⓑ Ⓒ Ⓓ Ⓔ
27. Ⓐ Ⓑ Ⓒ Ⓓ Ⓔ
28. Ⓐ Ⓑ Ⓒ Ⓓ Ⓔ
29. Ⓐ Ⓑ Ⓒ Ⓓ Ⓔ
30. Ⓐ Ⓑ Ⓒ Ⓓ Ⓔ
31. Ⓐ Ⓑ Ⓒ Ⓓ Ⓔ
32. Ⓐ Ⓑ Ⓒ Ⓓ Ⓔ
33. Ⓐ Ⓑ Ⓒ Ⓓ Ⓔ
34. Ⓐ Ⓑ Ⓒ Ⓓ Ⓔ
35. Ⓐ Ⓑ Ⓒ Ⓓ Ⓔ
36. Ⓐ Ⓑ Ⓒ Ⓓ Ⓔ
37. Ⓐ Ⓑ Ⓒ Ⓓ Ⓔ
38. Ⓐ Ⓑ Ⓒ Ⓓ Ⓔ
39. Ⓐ Ⓑ Ⓒ Ⓓ Ⓔ
40. Ⓐ Ⓑ Ⓒ Ⓓ Ⓔ
41. Ⓐ Ⓑ Ⓒ Ⓓ Ⓔ
42. Ⓐ Ⓑ Ⓒ Ⓓ Ⓔ

43. Ⓐ Ⓑ Ⓒ Ⓓ Ⓔ
44. Ⓐ Ⓑ Ⓒ Ⓓ Ⓔ
45. Ⓐ Ⓑ Ⓒ Ⓓ Ⓔ
46. Ⓐ Ⓑ Ⓒ Ⓓ Ⓔ
47. Ⓐ Ⓑ Ⓒ Ⓓ Ⓔ
48. Ⓐ Ⓑ Ⓒ Ⓓ Ⓔ
49. Ⓐ Ⓑ Ⓒ Ⓓ Ⓔ
50. Ⓐ Ⓑ Ⓒ Ⓓ Ⓔ
51. Ⓐ Ⓑ Ⓒ Ⓓ Ⓔ
52. Ⓐ Ⓑ Ⓒ Ⓓ Ⓔ
53. Ⓐ Ⓑ Ⓒ Ⓓ Ⓔ
54. Ⓐ Ⓑ Ⓒ Ⓓ Ⓔ
55. Ⓐ Ⓑ Ⓒ Ⓓ Ⓔ
56. Ⓐ Ⓑ Ⓒ Ⓓ Ⓔ
57. Ⓐ Ⓑ Ⓒ Ⓓ Ⓔ
58. Ⓐ Ⓑ Ⓒ Ⓓ Ⓔ
59. Ⓐ Ⓑ Ⓒ Ⓓ Ⓔ
60. Ⓐ Ⓑ Ⓒ Ⓓ Ⓔ
61. Ⓐ Ⓑ Ⓒ Ⓓ Ⓔ
62. Ⓐ Ⓑ Ⓒ Ⓓ Ⓔ
63. Ⓐ Ⓑ Ⓒ Ⓓ Ⓔ

# Practice Test 8

*Questions 1–10 refer to the following passage. After reading the passage, choose the best answer to each question.*

She had seen some beautiful patterns, veritable bargains in the shop windows. And still there would be left enough for new stockings—two
*Line*
(5) pairs apiece—and what darning that would save for a while! She would get caps for the boys and sailor hats for the girls. The vision of her little brood looking fresh and dainty and new for once in their lives excited her and made her restless and wakeful with anticipation.

(10) The neighbors sometimes talked of "better days" that little Mrs. Sommers had known before she had ever thought of being Mrs. Sommers. She herself indulged in no such morbid retrospection. She had no time—no second of time to devote
(15) to the past. The needs of the present absorbed her every faculty. A vision of the future like some dim, gaunt monster sometimes appalled her, but luckily to-morrow never comes.

Mrs. Sommers was one who knew the value of
(20) bargains; who could stand for hours making her way inch by inch toward the desired object that was selling below cost. She would elbow her way if need be; she had learned to clutch a piece of goods and hold it and stick to it with persistence
(25) and determination till her turn came to be served, no matter when it came.

But that day she was a little faint and a little tired. She had swallowed a light luncheon—no! when she came to think of it, between getting the
(30) children fed and the place righted, and preparing herself for the shopping bout, she had actually forgotten to eat any luncheon at all!

She sat herself upon a revolving stool before a counter that was comparatively deserted,
(35) trying to gather strength and courage to charge through an eager multitude that was besieging breastworks* of shirting and figured lawn. An all-gone limp feeling had come over her and she rested her hand aimlessly upon the
(40) counter. She wore no gloves. By degrees she grew aware that her hand had encountered something very soothing, very pleasant to touch. She looked down to see that her hand lay upon a pile of silk stockings. A placard near by announced that they
(45) had been reduced in price from two dollars and fifty cents to one dollar and ninety-eight cents; and a young girl who stood behind the counter asked her if she wished to examine their line of silk hosiery. She smiled, just as if she had been
(50) asked to inspect a tiara of diamonds with the ultimate view of purchasing it. But she went on feeling the soft, sheeny luxurious things—with both hands now, holding them up to see them

**GO ON TO THE NEXT PAGE**

glisten, and to feel them glide serpent-like
(55) through her fingers.

Two hectic blotches came suddenly into her pale cheeks. She looked up at the girl.

"Do you think there are any eights-and-a-half among these?"

(1894)

* *breastworks* an image of temporary, breast-high fortifications

1. The woman in this passage is all of the following EXCEPT

    (A) the mother of at least four children.

    (B) a skillful bargain hunter.

    (C) a weary shopper.

    (D) someone on the verge of a change.

    (E) a happy woman.

2. In the first paragraph, the woman is primarily concerned with

    (A) cheaply but tastefully clothing her children.

    (B) saving enough money for her own needs.

    (C) enjoying her day by browsing through shops.

    (D) daydreaming about her children's future.

    (E) trying to stay awake in the midst of fatigue.

3. Mrs. Sommers does not indulge in the "morbid retrospection" (line 13) of what might have been, because

    (A) such thinking would be detrimental to her happiness.

    (B) she is too consumed with her life as it is now.

    (C) she is already preoccupied with fears of the future.

    (D) she wants to avoid giving her neighbors any fuel for gossip.

    (E) her husband would be displeased if she were having second thoughts.

4. The phrase "luckily, to-morrow never comes" (line 19) expresses Mrs. Sommers's

    (A) refusal to grow old with grace and dignity.

    (B) fear that debt will finally catch up to her.

    (C) postponement of facing her dissatisfaction.

    (D) acknowledgment that she has seen "better days."

    (E) happiness to have found a life of security.

5. The narrator in lines 27–32 is

    (A) making fun of Mrs. Sommers's middle-class values.

    (B) portraying Mrs. Sommers as an organized mother.

    (C) helping Mrs. Sommers to recall very basic information.

    (D) aligning the narration with Mrs. Sommers's thoughts.

    (E) expressing concern for Mrs. Sommers's situation.

**GO ON TO THE NEXT PAGE**

6. The difference between the "multitude" (line 36) and Mrs. Sommers is one of

   (A) energy.

   (B) purpose.

   (C) funds.

   (D) experience.

   (E) obligation.

7. The word "lawn" in line 38 must refer to

   (A) the back yard of the store.

   (B) the carpet on which the "multitude" stands.

   (C) a type of cloth piled up in the store.

   (D) sculpted bushes accenting the store's décor.

   (E) the predominant color of the sale items.

8. The fact that the stockings "glide serpent-like through her fingers" (lines 54–55) suggests that the stockings have all of the following characteristics EXCEPT

   (A) a serpentine sheen.

   (B) a cold-blooded nature.

   (C) a snake's length.

   (D) a reptilian smoothness.

   (E) a tempting appeal.

9. The question at the end of the passage implies that Mrs. Sommers is

   (A) getting caught up in the buying frenzy of the "multitude."

   (B) considering a personal luxury over her children's more basic needs.

   (C) becoming delusional from having missed a meal.

   (D) succumbing to the salesperson's clever selling tactics.

   (E) needing a special accessory for an upcoming social event.

10. What most likely makes us sympathize with Mrs. Sommers's action at the end of the passage is

    (A) her children and her obligation to them.

    (B) her malnutrition and her ensuing forgetfulness.

    (C) her finances and her stubborn pride.

    (D) her location and the "multitude's" behavior.

    (E) her neighbors' comments and her prospects.

**GO ON TO THE NEXT PAGE**

*Questions 11–18 refer to the following poem. After reading the poem, choose the best answer to each question.*

> Oh, talk not to me of a name great in story;
> The days of our youth are the days of our glory;
> And the myrtle and ivy of sweet two-and-twenty
> Are worth all your laurels, though ever so plenty.
>
> *Line*
> (5)   What are garlands and crowns to the brow that is wrinkled?
> 'Tis but as a dead flower with May-dew besprinkled.
> Then away with all such from the head that is hoary!
> What care I for the wreaths that can *only* give glory?
>
> Oh FAME!—if I e'er took delight in thy praises,
> (10)  'Twas less for the sake of thy high sounding phrases,
> Than to see the bright eyes of the dear one discover
> She thought that I was not unworthy to love her.
>
> *There* chiefly I sought thee, *there* only I found thee;
> Her glance was the best of the rays that surround thee;
> (15)  When it sparkled o'er aught that was bright in my story,
> I knew it was love, and I felt it was glory.
>
> (1821)

11. This poem is best described as

    (A) couplets praising a certain kind of fame.

    (B) a sonnet discussing aging and its benefits.

    (C) an elegy for an old man.

    (D) a comic ballad.

    (E) an ode to fame.

12. The speaker's main idea in the first stanza is that

    (A) talking about renowned people lessens their glory.

    (B) myrtle and ivy symbolize glory better than laurels.

    (C) the only real glory is found during youth.

    (D) real-life heroes are better than fictional ones.

    (E) youth quickly fades into old age.

**GO ON TO THE NEXT PAGE**

13. The image in line 6 is all of the following EXCEPT

    (A) a metaphor composed of an unlikely pair.

    (B) an illustration of the idea in line 5.

    (C) a rationale for the exclamation at line 7.

    (D) an example of the futility in honoring the old.

    (E) a symbol of old age's inevitability.

14. The implication of line 8 is that

    (A) glory has no intrinsic value.

    (B) wreaths are inappropriate symbols of glory.

    (C) the speaker has grown apathetic about life.

    (D) glory is a mystery to the speaker.

    (E) wreaths should do more than symbolize glory.

15. In the third stanza, the speaker regards fame as

    (A) the ultimate goal of a young man's life.

    (B) an excuse for falling in love with a woman.

    (C) a way by which to hear "high sounding phrases."

    (D) the downfall of the reckless man.

    (E) a means by which to impress a woman.

16. The "*There*" of line 13 is actually

    (A) the "FAME" of the third stanza.

    (B) the heart of the speaker.

    (C) the lives of the young.

    (D) the heads of the old.

    (E) the "eyes of the dear one."

17. The last two stanzas feature

    (A) several similes.

    (B) an analogy between fame and the dear one.

    (C) images of darkness.

    (D) an apostrophe to fame.

    (E) a contrast between the young and the old.

18. Under what conditions would the speaker prefer to experience his fame?

    I. In the vigor of youth

    II. As a memory during his old age

    III. Among several admirers

    IV. From his dear one's perspective

    V. Throughout history

    (A) I and III only

    (B) I and IV only

    (C) I, III, and IV only

    (D) II, III, and V only

    (E) II, III, IV, and V only

**GO ON TO THE NEXT PAGE**

Questions 19–27 refer to the following passage. After reading the passage, choose the best answer to each question.

"The *nosferatu** do not die like the bee when he sting once. He is only stronger, and being stronger, have yet more power to work evil. This
Line vampire which is amongst us is of himself so
(5) strong in person as twenty men; he is of cunning more than mortal, for his cunning be the growth of ages; he have still the aid of necromancy, which is, as his etymology imply, the divination of the dead, and all the dead that he can come
(10) nigh to are for him to command; he is brute, and more than brute; he is devil in callous, and the heart of him is not; he can within limitations, appear at will when, and where, and in any of the forms that are to him; he can, within his range,
(15) direct the elements; the storm, the fog, the thunder; he can command all the meaner things; the rat the owl, and the bat—the moth, and the fox, and the wolf; he can grow and become small; and he can at times vanish and become
(20) unknown. How then are we to begin our strike to destroy him? How shall we find his where; and having found it, how can we destroy? My friends, this is much; it is a terrible task that we undertake, and there may be consequences to
(25) make the brave shudder. For if we fail in this our fight he must surely win; and then where end we? Life is nothings; I heed him not. But to fail here, is not mere life and death. It is that we become as him; that we henceforward become foul things of
(30) the night like him—without heart or conscience, preying on the bodies and the souls of those we love best. To us, for ever are the gates of heaven shut; for who shall open them to us again? We go on for all time abhorred by all; a blot on the face
(35) of God's sunshine; an arrow in the side of Him who died for man.† But we are face to face with duty; and in such case must we shrink? For me, I say, no; but then I am old, and life with his sunshine, his fair places, his song of birds, his

(40) music and his love, lie far behind. You others are young. Some have seen sorrow; but there are fair days yet in store. What say you?"

Whilst he was speaking, Jonathan had taken my hand. I feared, oh so much, that the appalling
(45) nature of our danger was overcoming him when I saw his hand stretch out; but it was life to me to feel its touch—so strong, so self-reliant, so resolute. A brave man's hand can speak for itself; it does not even need a love to hear its music.
(50) When the Professor had done speaking my husband looked in my eyes, and I in his; there was no need for speaking between us.

"I answer for Mina and myself," he said.

(1897)

*nosferatu* the undead; vampires

†*Him who died for man* According to Christian belief, Jesus's death by crucifixion was a sacrifice so that all people could be freed from sin and joined to God eternally.

19. Which of the following may be surmised about the first speaker in this passage?

(A) He is a native speaker of English.

(B) His purpose is to describe.

(C) He has been recently attacked by a vampire.

(D) He has had no effect on his listeners.

(E) He is knowledgeable about his subject matter.

**GO ON TO THE NEXT PAGE**

20. The word "his" in line 8 refers to

    (A) the first speaker himself.

    (B) Jonathan.

    (C) the word "necromancy."

    (D) the vampire.

    (E) the word "mortal."

21. The vampire is described as a "devil in callous" (line 11) to make the point that

    (A) he is a demon in disguise.

    (B) he is without human compassion.

    (C) he cannot be harmed by conventional weapons.

    (D) he periodically lashes out with satanic force.

    (E) he hardens those who live long enough to oppose him repeatedly.

22. For the speaker, "Life is nothings" (line 27) probably because

    I. he is old.

    II. his Christian beliefs offer him hope of the afterlife.

    III. duty is more important than his own life.

    (A) I only

    (B) I and II only

    (C) II and III only

    (D) I and III only

    (E) I, II, and III

23. In lines 27–36, failure to defeat the vampire includes what consequences for the listeners?

    (A) The loss of their humanity and spiritual salvation

    (B) The end of their civilization

    (C) The sacrifice of their lives

    (D) The guilt of not having tried their utmost in combating evil

    (E) The burden of restless wandering until the vampire is defeated

24. In lines 37–42, the speaker reminds his listeners of his age and their youth because

    (A) their strength can bolster his ego.

    (B) his experience can fill in the gaps of their naivete.

    (C) their stamina can complement his wisdom.

    (D) their youth gives them an excuse not to endanger themselves.

    (E) his age proves how incompetent they are.

25. The phrase "it was life to me to feel its touch" (lines 46–47) seems

    (A) appropriate, since Jonathan and she have been married for so long.

    (B) foreboding, since neither Jonathan nor the first speaker knows that she is a vampire.

    (C) unexpected, since we did not know Jonathan and she were holding hands.

    (D) ironic, since Jonathan and she are about to face death together.

    (E) humorous, since Jonathan is so obviously frightened by the speaker's words.

**GO ON TO THE NEXT PAGE**

26. What attitude does the narrator seem to have about her own power in this situation?

   (A) She is resentful that the men are taking control.

   (B) She is content to comply with the men's decisions.

   (C) She will allow them their plans for now but will assume control later.

   (D) She feels paralyzed when thinking of taking a leadership role in the situation.

   (E) She would like more control but defers to their authority for the sake of expediency.

27. The passage can best be described as following what pattern?

   (A) Description to persuasion to conviction

   (B) Explanation to cooperation to humiliation

   (C) Inspiration to degradation to duty

   (D) Antithesis to harmony to chaos

   (E) Metaphor to reality to fantasy

**GO ON TO THE NEXT PAGE**

*Questions 28–35 refer to the following poem. After reading the poem, choose the best answer to each question.*

When our two souls stand up erect and strong,
Face to face, silent, drawing nigh and nigher,
Until the lengthening wings break into fire
*Line* At either curvéd point,—what bitter wrong
*(5)* Can the earth do to us, that we should not long
Be here contented? Think. In mounting higher,
The angels would press on us and aspire
To drop some golden orb of perfect song
Into our deep, dear silence. Let us stay
*(10)* Rather on earth, Belovéd,—where the unfit
Contrarious moods of men recoil away
And isolate pure spirits, and permit
A place to stand and love in for a day,
With darkness and the death-hour rounding it.

(1850)

28. In the poem, the speaker requests

   (A) a blessed, joyful eternity with the angels.

   (B) a quick but glorious "death-hour."

   (C) an eternal, thoughtful repayment of her passion.

   (D) a fiery but complete absolution of her sins.

   (E) an isolated, earthly afterlife with her love.

29. The process being described in lines 1–4 demonstrates

   (A) shared loathing.

   (B) eternal suffering.

   (C) fulfilled hopes.

   (D) passionate harmony.

   (E) spiritual erosion.

30. The rhetorical question of lines 4–6 implies all of the following EXCEPT that

   (A) the earth is powerless to harm the couple referred to in lines 1–4.

   (B) the process in lines 1–4 makes the couple impervious to earthly harm.

   (C) the couple can be happy even if they remain on the earth.

   (D) the couple must remain on earth only for a short while.

   (E) the speaker actually wants to share an afterlife on earth with her love.

31. The speaker regards the "perfect song" of line 8 as

   (A) sudden but welcome.

   (B) surprising but fitting.

   (C) beautiful but unwanted.

   (D) complex but melodious.

   (E) soothing but ill-timed.

32. All of the following can be said about the "Contrarious moods" of line 11 EXCEPT that

   (A) they belong to those who are still physical beings.

   (B) they contrast with the couple's harmony.

   (C) they can dangerously infect the couple.

   (D) they help give the speaker what she wants.

   (E) they are repelled by beings like the couple.

33. The speaker talks of "darkness and the death-hour" (line 14) with

    (A) great fear.

    (B) high hopes.

    (C) idle curiosity.

    (D) final resignation.

    (E) wondrous awe.

34. A verb in the imperative mood can be found in line

    (A) 2.

    (B) 4.

    (C) 6.

    (D) 7.

    (E) 12.

35. The speaker treats her subject matter

    (A) traditionally.

    (B) unconventionally.

    (C) scientifically.

    (D) tearfully.

    (E) imploringly.

**GO ON TO THE NEXT PAGE**

*Questions 36–46 refer to the following passage. After reading the passage, choose the best answer to each question.*

And one day he came to me, as I was in the summer-house in the little garden, at work with my needle, and Mrs. Jervis was just gone from
Line me; and I would have gone out; but he said,
(5) "Don't go, Pamela: I have something to say to you; and you always fly me, when I come near you, as if you were afraid of me."

I was much out of countenance you may well think; and began to tremble, and the more when
(10) he took me by the hand; for no soul was near us.

"Lady Davers," said he, (and seemed, I thought, to be as much at a loss for words as I) "would have had you live with *her*; but she would not do for you what I am resolved to do, if you
(15) continue faithful and obliging. What say you, my girl?" said he, with some eagerness; "had you not rather stay with me than go to Lady Davers?" He looked so, as filled me with fear; I don't know how; wildly, I thought.

(20) I said, when I could speak, "Your Honour will forgive me; but as you have no lady for me to wait upon, and my good lady has been now dead this twelvemonth, I had rather, if it would not displease you, wait upon Lady Davers, *because—*"

(25) I was proceeding, and he said a little hastily, "—*Because* you are a little fool, and know not what's good for yourself. I tell you, I will make a gentlewoman of you, if you are obliging, and don't stand in your own light." And so saying, he
(30) put his arm about me, and kissed me.

Now, you will say, all his wickedness appeared plainly. I struggled, and trembled, and was so benumbed with terror, that I sunk down, not in a fit, and yet not myself; and I found myself in his
(35) arms, quite void of strength; and he kissed me two or three times, with frightful eagerness. At last I burst from him, and was getting out of the summer-house; but he held me back, and shut the door.

(40) I would have given my life for a farthing.*
And he said, "I'll do you no harm, Pamela; don't be afraid of me."

I said, "I won't stay."

"You *won't*, hussy!† Do you know who you
(45) speak to?"

I lost all fear, and all respect, and said, "Yes, I do, sir, too well! Well may I forget that I am your servant, when you forget what belongs to a master."

(50) I sobbed and cried most sadly. "What a foolish hussy you are!" said he: "Have I done you any harm?" "Yes, sir," said I, "the greatest harm in the world: You have taught me to forget myself, and what belongs to me; and have lessened the
(55) distance that fortune has made between us, by demeaning yourself, to be so free to a poor servant. Yet, sir, I will be bold to say, I am honest, though poor: And if you were a prince, I would not be otherwise than honest."

(60) He was angry, and said, "Who, little fool, would have you otherwise? Cease your blubbering. I own I have undervalued myself; but it was only to try you. If you can keep this matter secret, you'll give me the better opinion
(65) of your prudence: And here's something," added he, putting some gold in my hand, "to make you amends for the fright I put you in. Go, take a walk in the garden, and don't go in till your blubbering is over: And I charge you say nothing
(70) of what has passed, and all shall be well, and I'll forgive you."

(1740)

*farthing* former British coin equaling 1/4 of a penny
†*hussy* here, a disrespectful girl

**GO ON TO THE NEXT PAGE**

36. The passage shows Pamela's opinion of the gentleman as

    (A) fearful, then reproachful.

    (B) respectful, then fearful.

    (C) seductive, then standoffish.

    (D) bold, then meek.

    (E) playful, then serious.

37. Pamela's greatly punctuated comment at lines 17–19 demonstrates her

    (A) careful control.

    (B) lack of education.

    (C) satirical mimicry.

    (D) inclination toward excess.

    (E) recollected consternation.

38. In lines 20–24, Pamela's refusal of the gentleman's proposition is all of the following EXCEPT

    (A) logical.

    (B) interrupted.

    (C) hurried.

    (D) understandable.

    (E) polite.

39. Concerning the gentleman's response in lines 25–30, all of the following can be supported EXCEPT that the gentleman

    (A) is insulting to Pamela after she has refused him.

    (B) seems obligated to alter his previous proposition.

    (C) suggests that her cooperative behavior will gain status for Pamela.

    (D) hints that Pamela's improved status would not be grounds for her vanity.

    (E) concludes his new proposition by indicating his underlying intentions.

40. The gentleman is able to kiss Pamela "two or three times" (lines 35–36) because

    (A) she is secretly attracted to him.

    (B) she is slowly mustering the strength to repel him.

    (C) her respect for his position outweighs her morals.

    (D) she is going limp to squelch his desire.

    (E) her fear of him has paralyzed her.

**GO ON TO THE NEXT PAGE**

41. The phrase "I would have given my life for a farthing" (line 40) is best interpreted as

    (A) "My life was not worth much after his advances."

    (B) "It would have cost very little to coax my death and escape my situation."

    (C) "No one ever could have made me believe that he would have been so forward."

    (D) "I would have been happy to trade places with anyone at that very moment."

    (E) "I would have paid any amount to start my life over again."

42. In lines 46–49, Pamela suggests to the gentleman that he

    (A) would not act this way if she were actually in his employ.

    (B) needs to master his emotions or he will face a downfall.

    (C) is neither the master of her body nor her will.

    (D) will gain her respect once he proposes marriage.

    (E) could not think he was able to deceive her even for a moment.

43. Of the following, the word that best defines "free" in line 56 is

    (A) *lax.*

    (B) *licentious.*

    (C) *exempt.*

    (D) *independent.*

    (E) *firm.*

44. The word "honest" in line 57 is used to mean

    (A) truthful.

    (B) fair.

    (C) worthy.

    (D) unreserved.

    (E) chaste.

45. The gentleman's speech in the final paragraph contains all of the following EXCEPT

    (A) a thinly veiled bribe.

    (B) a questionable justification.

    (C) a command for silence.

    (D) a promise of future good conduct.

    (E) an audacious exoneration.

46. Through the interaction of these characters, the passage demonstrates

    (A) the presumption of power and rank.

    (B) the moral frailty of the female sex.

    (C) the peripheral offenses of slavery.

    (D) the insanity of deference and servitude.

    (E) the mysteries of love and attraction.

GO ON TO THE NEXT PAGE

*Questions 47–55 refer to the following passage. After reading the passage, choose the best answer to each question.*

"Don't touch me, please," she said softly. "I am part egg-shell" Or perhaps I had better put it in a safe place." She began unfastening the collar of her gown.

(5) "What is it?" said her lover.

"An egg-a cochin's* egg. I am hatching a very rare sort. I carry it about everywhere with me, and it will get hatched in about three weeks."

"Where do you carry it?"

(10) "Just here." She put her hand into her bosom and drew out the egg, which was wrapped in wool, outside it being a piece of pig's bladder, in case of accidents. Having exhibited it to him she put it back, "Now mind you don't come near me. I

(15) don't want to get it broke, and have to begin another."

"Why do you do such a strange thing?"

"It's an old custom, I suppose it is natural for a woman to want to bring live things into the

(20) world."

"It is very awkward for me just now," he said, laughing.

"It serves you right. There—that's all you can have of me."

(25) She had turned round her chair, and reaching over the back of it, presented her cheek to him gingerly.

"That's very shabby of you!"

"You should have catched me a minute ago

(30) when I had put the egg down! There!" she said defiantly, "I am without it now!" She had quickly withdrawn the egg a second time; but before he could quite reach her she had put it back as quickly, laughing with the excitement of her

(35) strategy. Then there was a little struggle, Jude made a plunge for it and capturing it triumphantly. Her face flushed; and becoming suddenly conscious he flushed also.

They looked at each other, panting; till he

(40) rose and said: "One kiss, now I can do it without damage to property; and I'll go!"

But she had jumped up too. "You must find me first!" she cried.

Her lover followed her as she withdrew. It was

(45) now dark inside the room, and the window being small he could not discover for a long time what had become of her, till a laugh revealed her to have rushed up the stairs, whither Jude rushed at her heels.

*cochin   a type of chicken

(1896)

47.  The people in the passage are primarily

(A) concerned about protecting the cochin's egg.

(B) working to establish boundaries of mutual respect.

(C) curious about each other's innermost thoughts.

(D) seeking each other's amorous attentions.

(E) beginning a future with one another.

GO ON TO THE NEXT PAGE

48. In lines 1–2, when the woman says "I am part egg-shell," she is both referring to the egg in her bosom and

    (A) coyly alluding to her feminine vulnerability.

    (B) facetiously understating her coarse robustness.

    (C) anxiously anticipating her romantic rebirth.

    (D) quietly attempting to point out her skin's creaminess.

    (E) matter-of-factly declaring her inaccessibility.

49. The description of the cochin's egg in lines 10–16 reflects both

    (A) the woman's working-class background and her naturally maternal instincts.

    (B) the love with which the woman surrounds Jude and the inception of their relationship.

    (C) the woman's need for physical warmth and Jude's emotional "shell."

    (D) the woman's fondness for poultry and the true self that she hides from Jude.

    (E) the care with which the woman protects the egg and the elaborateness of her deception.

50. The awkwardness that Jude expresses in line 21 could be caused by which of the following?

    I. His inability to grasp the woman's purpose in incubating the egg

    II. His need for the woman's unequivocal acceptance and approval

    III. The woman's maternal desires expressed during a romantic tension

    IV. The difficulty of getting close to the woman while she retains the egg

    (A) I only

    (B) II only

    (C) I and III only

    (D) I, III, and IV only

    (E) II, III, and IV only

51. Jude's exclamation, "That's very shabby of you!" (line 28) is a response to

    (A) the brazenness of the woman's behavior.

    (B) the woman's apparent romantic coolness.

    (C) the delay in his departure that the woman is causing.

    (D) the impoliteness of the woman in not walking him out.

    (E) the woman's incomplete explanation about the egg.

**GO ON TO THE NEXT PAGE**

52. The woman's "strategy" (line 35) is to

    (A) amuse Jude with her playfulness, thus expressing her desire for a friend.

    (B) demonstrate her indecisiveness, thus forcing Jude to be more forceful.

    (C) alternate her state of accessibility, thus enticing Jude.

    (D) display the egg repeatedly, thus hinting that Jude should take it.

    (E) emphasize the egg's delicacy, thus driving Jude away.

53. In lines 37–38, the faces of the couple flush because

    (A) they are embarrassed by their immature behavior.

    (B) they are overheated from their strenuous playfulness.

    (C) they realize that they came close to damaging the egg.

    (D) they understand that this will be their last night together.

    (E) they know they have crossed a boundary of propriety.

54. It is obvious that the two characters' objectives differ, because

    (A) Jude continually approaches her, but the woman has said she does not want to be touched.

    (B) Jude is full of questions about her, but the woman refuses to delve into Jude's background.

    (C) Jude has a serious proposal for her, but all the woman can do is play games and make jokes.

    (D) Jude declares an intent to leave, but the woman's actions at the end suggest that he stay.

    (E) Jude expresses a clear respect for her, but the woman frequently mocks Jude.

55. The darkness described in lines 44–49 is a symbolic indication that

    (A) the future looks grim for both Jude and the woman.

    (B) both Jude and the woman are engaged in a kind of evil.

    (C) Jude is beginning to feel sullied by their behavior.

    (D) the woman's past, if discovered by Jude, would damage her.

    (E) Jude is ignorant of the woman's machinations.

**GO ON TO THE NEXT PAGE**

*Questions 56–63 refer to the following poem. After reading the poem, choose the best answer to each question.*

```
        And I            and your eyes
        Draw round about a ring of gold
        And sing their circle of sparks
Line    And I            and your eyes
 (5)    Hold untold tales and conspire
        With moon and sun to shake my soul.

        And I            and your eyes
        If I could hold your hillside smile
        Your seashore laughter  your lips

(10)    Then I
        Could stand alone    the pain
        Of flesh     alone  the time and space
        And steel    alone  but I am shaken
        It has taken         your eyes
(15)    To move this stone.
```

                    (1980)

56. The poem primarily describes

    (A) the effect the addressee's image has on the speaker.

    (B) a wedding performed between a hill and the sea.

    (C) the physical features of the addressee.

    (D) the speaker's preference for solitude.

    (E) the addressee's feelings for the speaker.

57. In lines 1–3, images of continuity and connection develop with all of the following EXCEPT

    (A) the first "And," which implies a beginning before the poem.

    (B) the gap between "I" and "and your eyes," which creates a profound pause.

    (C) the "ring of gold," whose shape denotes no beginning and no end.

    (D) the pronoun "their," which joins "I," "your eyes," and the "ring of gold."

    (E) the "circle of sparks," another symbol of no beginning and no end.

58. The implication about the "I" in lines 4–6 is that

    (A) it is a different person from the "I" of line 1.

    (B) it has a greater intensity than the "I" of line 1.

    (C) it is incapable of verbal expression.

    (D) it has resulted from a union of the moon and sun.

    (E) it acts independently of the speaker's soul.

59. The "hillside smile" and "seashore laughter" of lines 8–9 are images that

    (A) do not affect the speaker the way the addressee's lips do.

    (B) connote the eternal presence of the addressee within the speaker.

    (C) hint at the addressee's recent mockery of the speaker.

    (D) demonstrate the addressee's profound but elusive effect on the speaker.

    (E) replace the addressee's eyes as her most important features.

60. The last stanza suggests that

    (A) the effect of the addressee on the speaker helps make life more bearable.

    (B) the speaker is begging for a life separate from the addressee.

    (C) the pain of life helps to make him aware of society's hurt.

    (D) "time and space/And steel ..." are all that is left of the addressee's image.

    (E) the speaker has a lack of motivation that "steels" him against the addressee.

61. The "but I am shaken" of line 13 implies that

    (A) the speaker is weary of the pain of life and wants to be ignored.

    (B) the loneliness of life has disturbed the speaker unutterably.

    (C) because of the addressee's presence in his life, the speaker has become maladjusted.

    (D) even though the addressee wants to be a part of his life, the speaker is unable to let her in.

    (E) even if he may not be able to cling to the addressee's image, he acknowledges her previous influence on him.

62. The "stone" of the final line is

    (A) the speaker.

    (B) the addressee.

    (C) "steel."

    (D) life's pain.

    (E) love.

63. The gaps of the poem suggest

    (A) pauses constructed by the speaker to give him time to think.

    (B) the addressee's attempts to remove herself from the speaker.

    (C) the speaker's isolation in spite of the addressee's effects on him.

    (D) the doubt that the speaker and addressee share about the future.

    (E) the couple's failed attempts at reaching out to each other.

# STOP!

**If you finish before time is up, you may check your work.**

**Turn the page
for answers and explanations
to Practice Test 8.**

# Answer Key
# Practice Test 8

| | | |
|---|---|---|
| 1. E | 22. E | 43. B |
| 2. A | 23. A | 44. E |
| 3. B | 24. D | 45. D |
| 4. C | 25. D | 46. A |
| 5. D | 26. B | 47. D |
| 6. A | 27. A | 48. A |
| 7. C | 28. E | 49. E |
| 8. B | 29. D | 50. D |
| 9. B | 30. D | 51. B |
| 10. E | 31. C | 52. C |
| 11. A | 32. C | 53. E |
| 12. C | 33. B | 54. D |
| 13. E | 34. C | 55. E |
| 14. A | 35. B | 56. A |
| 15. E | 36. A | 57. B |
| 16. E | 37. E | 58. E |
| 17. D | 38. C | 59. D |
| 18. B | 39. B | 60. A |
| 19. E | 40. E | 61. E |
| 20. C | 41. B | 62. A |
| 21. B | 42. C | 63. C |

# ANSWERS AND EXPLANATIONS

**1. (E)** Mrs. Sommers has every reason to feel pressured and unhappy. Her neighbors gossip about the "'better days' that little Mrs. Sommers had known before" (lines 10–11). If the narrator were going to contradict the neighbors' observations, it would have been here. However, all the narrator can tell us is that Mrs. Sommers refuses to think about the past: "She herself indulged in no such morbid retrospection. She had no time..." (lines 12–14). So then, we know she is not unhappy, because she has no time for regret. Yet she also has no time for happiness.

**2. (A)** Mrs. Sommers is shopping for clothing, but she is also mindful of "veritable bargains in the shop windows" (lines 1–2). The recipients of her shopping will be the boys, for whom she will get caps, and the girls, for whom she will get sailor hats (lines 5–6). The children will also receive new stockings. We know that these are not for Mrs. Sommers because the narrator notes that there will "be left enough for ...two pairs *apiece*" (lines 3–4)—each *child* will receive two pairs of stockings, and this acquisition will save a significant amount of stocking repair for a while (lines 4–5).

**3. (B)** This idea is supported in lines 15–16: "The needs of the present absorbed her every faculty." She has no time to think of the past.

**4. (C)** Tomorrow "luckily" never comes because, if it did, Mrs. Sommers would be face to face with "A vision of the future like some dim, gaunt monster" (lines 16–17). The present preoccupies her; she has no time to think about the dissatisfaction of her present life, of which the past could remind her—as her neighbors explain—or that the future will make known to her.

**5. (D)** Mrs. Sommers is not directly quoted here, but the narrator seems to be picking up on the mother's thought patterns, especially at the "—no! when she came to think of it..." (lines 28–29).

The narrator's self-correction also sounds like Mrs. Sommers's realizing why she is so "faint and a little tired" (lines 27–28).

**6. (A)** The multitude is "eager" and is "besieging breastworks of shirting and figured lawn" (lines 36–38), as if they are a medieval mob attacking a castle. On the other hand, Mrs. Sommers has "An all-gone limp feeling" (line 38).

**7. (C)** "Lawn" is one of the things composing the "breastworks," or fortifications, in the store. The only thing shoppers would besiege would be store items for sale, so "lawn" must be some kind of merchandise that has been placed in breast-high piles. Furthermore, the breastworks are also composed of shirting, so it is logical to assume that lawn is associated with shirting. In context then, the most likely choice for lawn is a type of cloth.

**8. (B)** If we say that the stockings had a cold-bloodedness, we would be personifying them as merciless. Silk stockings do not universally symbolize this quality; moreover, they seem to be rather passive in this instance. On the other hand, (E) follows the line of thought that snakes are a cultural symbol of temptation, reminiscent of the serpent in the Garden of Eden.

**9. (B)** The narrator has established in the first and third paragraphs that Mrs. Sommers is an able bargain hunter. The information from the neighbors implies that Mrs. Sommers's financial situation forces her to hunt bargains. These stockings, then, are a luxury, that will throw her clothing budget off-balance and leave less money for her children's more basic need for everyday stockings.

**10. (E)** The neighbors know that Mrs. Sommers has seen "better days." Her future is a "gaunt monster" that leers at her from a distance. With such a contrasted bright past and bleak future, and an attitude of self-neglect in favor of her children, she perhaps deserves to treat herself this one time.

**11. (A)** This poem is not an ode to fame in general; the speaker stipulates that, if he enjoyed the praises of fame, it was "less for the sake of [its] high sounding phrases/Than to see the bright eyes of the dear one discover/She thought that I was not unworthy to love her" (lines 10–12). In other words, the best fame for him is the kind that resides in his dear one's eyes; if she thinks him famous, and that fame sparks her love, then he is happy.

**12. (C)** Line 2 makes this idea obvious. The speaker will expand on the same idea in the second stanza.

**13. (E)** The focus of the image is the unlikeliness of finding the dew of May—a symbol of springtime youthfulness—on a dead flower. The two do not go together. It is true that old age is inevitable, but the image is not portraying that particular truth. We do not see the flower's progression into old age; it is simply dead.

**14. (A)** There are two points to make about line 8. The first is that the wreaths are probably laurel wreaths—symbols of victory and emblems of fame—and that the narrator notes their inability to do anything *except* give glory. The second point is that the narrator does not care about these wreaths. One may infer almost syllogistically, then, that the narrator does not care for a general kind of fame. He is about to make a transition into discussing the fame for which he *does* care: the kind that his dear one holds for him.

**15. (E)** The third stanza tells us the following: What is important about fame is that it causes the "dear one" to find the speaker worthy of her love. For this reason, fame has value, more so than for its "high sounding phrases."

**16. (E)** The third stanza's last two lines talk about the dear one's eyes discovering the speaker's worth. "*There*" in line 13, then, makes the dear one's eyes a location for fame. The narrator continues this idea in the subsequent lines; the dear one's "glance" displays fame best.

**17. (D)** The speaker talks to fame as if it were sentient. All the second-person pronouns are then addresses to fame, not to the dear one. She is only talked *about*, not talked *to*.

**18. (B)** The first two stanzas concentrate on the superiority of fame—or "glory"—in youth. Fame is wasted on the old. The last two stanzas discuss its superiority in the dear one's eyes. Her perception of the speaker makes his fame worthwhile.

**19. (E)** The quoted speaker is an encyclopedia on vampires. One can see how many facts he spouts in his sentence constructions: "He is only stronger…"; "This vampire … is … so strong in person …"; "he is of cunning…"; "…he have still the aid of necromancy"; "he is brute…"; "he can … appear at will" (lines 1–13), etc. However, his purpose is not merely to describe; he wants to convince his audience that they face danger in undertaking to defeat the vampire.

**20. (C)** Normally, the third-person masculine pronouns are reserved for the vampire; however, as the context of this sentence suggests, our speaker's lack of fluency in English has caused him to use *his* instead of *its* for *necromancy*; the etymology of *necromancy* clearly defines the word as the "divination of the dead."

**21. (B)** We can tell early on that our speaker is not a master of English. Here, as his context implies, the speaker uses the adjective "callous" for the noun "callousness." Thus, the human trait of compassion is missing in the vampire. The next part of this sentence, "the heart of him is not" helps to confirm this idea.

**22. (E)** After the speaker makes this statement, he refers to the following: Item I is found at lines 38–40; item II is in lines 32–33; item III is in lines 36–38. The speaker is discussing success in defeating the vampire vs. failure. For the speaker, death is not a thing to worry about: Most of life's pleasures are behind him, and his eternal reward is guaranteed if he dies performing his duty in the fight against evil. But if the vampire wins, he and his listeners risk becoming one of the undead, "abhorred by all; a blot on the face of God's sunshine" (lines 34–35).

23. (A) The loss of their humanity is confirmed by the idea "that we henceforward become foul things of the night like him—without heart or conscience" (lines 29–30). The loss of their spiritual salvation is described in this image: "To us, for ever are the gates of heaven shut; for who shall open them to us again?" (lines 32–33). Thus, it is in the listeners' best interests to succeed in defeating the vampire.

24. (D) After describing his age and the fact that he has already experienced life's pleasures, he turns to his listeners and says, "You others are young … there are fair days in store." The implication is that they risk losing these fair days whether they die fighting the vampire or succumb to his undead influence. The speaker's final question, "What say you?" gives the listeners a chance to back out.

25. (D) Mina strongly implies that Jonathan is ready to go fight the undead. His touch—which is enlivening to her—is "so strong, so self-reliant, so resolute" (lines 47–48) that his decision is unquestionable. Furthermore, they seem to have an implicit agreement that they will fight the vampire together (lines 50–52). We know also from the speaker's information that this fight will imperil the couple. Thus, Jonathan's enlivening touch has a bit of irony, if we consider what is in store for Mina and him.

26. (B) The first speaker offers them the choice. Mina looks at Jonathan and knows implicitly what they are about to do. She allows Jonathan, in his own words, to answer for her and himself. She makes no commentary on this action. Furthermore, her adoration of her husband and her comment that his touch gives her life both strongly imply that she defers to him willingly.

27. (A) The speaker first describes the vampire; then he persuades the couple of the rightness in defeating it and of the dangers of pursuing it. In the end, Jonathan expresses the couple's mutual conviction that they will take the risk.

28. (E) In lines 7–9, the speaker notes that angelic music would enter into the couple's "deep, dear silence" in the afterlife. Then, she recommends that she and her love "stay/Rather on earth." Thus, she prefers quiet isolation on earth in her afterlife.

29. (D) The passion appears in such descriptors as "strong" and "lengthening wings break into fire"; fire, in fact, is a traditional symbol of passion. The harmony appears in the two souls drawing "nigh and nigher" and in experiencing this spiritual process together. In the context of the rest of the poem, (D) is the best answer. (C) may be an attractive distracter, but the speaker's hopes are merely expressed in this poem, not yet fulfilled.

30. (D) The question implies that earth cannot do them harm, so their stay on it can be a long one.

31. (C) It is a "golden orb of perfect" song, giving the music an ideal quality. However, it would "drop" into the couple's "deep, dear silence," causing the speaker to suggest that the couple remain on earth—away from the angels and their pretty, but unwanted, music.

32. (C) The speaker's rhetorical question in lines 4–6 has already implied that the earth can do the couple no harm. These earthly beings then have no chance of infecting the speakers.

33. (B) These ideas are part of the speaker's vision for the afterlife with her love. Since she has spoken in a positive way about this vision throughout the poem, (B) seems consistent with the poem's development. Also, the "darkness and the death-hour" will "round" the couple's "place to stand and love in for a day." They are visualized as happy in this state.

**34. (C)** Here, the word "Think" stands alone. It is a command to her love, with *you* as the understood subject. Thus, it is an imperative.

**35. (B)** First, the speaker would prefer an afterlife on earth rather than in heaven. She does not deny heaven's existence but simply does not want to spend all of eternity there. Most people expressing a belief in heaven see it as a perfect existence; she does not. Second, if we deem something perfect, it follows that that thing is desirable or at least pleasant. However, the perfect song of the angels is not something that the speaker wishes to experience. Thus, she is unconventional on two counts.

**36. (A)** In lines 5–7, the gentleman himself notices that Pamela is "afraid of" him. Pamela confirms this observation when she says that the sight of him makes her "tremble" (line 9). Later, she is "benumbed with terror" (line 33) when he kisses her. However, after this insult, she loses "all fear, and all respect" (line 46) for him and begins to reproach him for his inappropriate behavior. In lines 56–57, for instance, she says that he has demeaned himself by being so free with her.

**37. (E)** The content of the sentence tells us how fearful she is in that moment. The punctuation causes her speech to fragment and helps to accentuate the discomfiture of her fear.

**38. (C)** The response's complex construction and natural pauses—indicated by properly employed commas and a semicolon—make it sound rather fluid.

**39. (B)** Many motivators could obligate him to change his proposition: social propriety, a personal sense of honor, a sensitivity to Pamela's feelings. Yet, in each instance, the gentleman would be *obligated* to make his proposition more respectful. Instead, he resorts to bribery and forcefulness in trying to get Pamela to change her mind. Thus, it is not obligation which changes his proposition but a kind of lustful persistence.

**40. (E)** Pamela says it herself in lines 32–33: "I struggled, and trembled, and was so benumbed with terror, that I sunk down." She is paralyzed by fear.

**41. (B)** She is in a situation that she does not want to experience. The idea of "giving" one's life could have a connotation of surrendering to death. Since a farthing is not worth much, then it would take very little to get her to "give up" her life: She would give her life for a farthing. (A) may seem an attractive distracter, but the pride and vehemence with which she later declares her "honest" nature (line 57) shows that she still values herself.

**42. (C)** Her reproach that "you forget what belongs to a master" refers to his recent misconduct. By forcing himself on her, he has supposed that her body and will belonged to him, as her master. She reminds him how wrong he was in that supposition.

**43. (B)** In context, Pamela considers his behavior to be immoral.

**44. (E)** Because she has refused his amorous and lustful advances, *honest* must mean "chaste." Her lower social and economic status does not mean that she is unchaste.

**45. (D)** The gentleman gives her gold to soothe her (A); he says that he meant only to test or "try" her (B); he tells her to "say nothing of what has passed" (C); and he has the gall to say "I'll forgive you" when he was the one who wronged her (E). This last statement is his only reference to the future; any other mention of his own conduct is relegated to the past. He makes no promises of forthcoming good behavior.

**46. (A)** As Pamela points out to him in lines 45–49, the gentleman has presumed that taking advantage of her is acceptable conduct. She strongly implies that their difference in social rank influenced his reasoning.

**47. (D)** Several times, Jude approaches the woman for a kiss. Although she playfully keeps him at bay for a while, we see in lines 34–35 that she laughs at the "excitement of her strategy." Thus, her incubation of the cochin's egg has been a ruse to entice him. They are both desirous of each other.

**48. (A)** Her action is coy because, as we see later, she has really intended to be "touched" all along. The softness of her speech and the content of her request both refer to her feminine vulnerability: she is alone with a man and, thus, could be taken advantage of by the standards of the time.

**49. (E)** In these lines, there are several steps to the woman's revelation and re-placement of the egg. So, too, her "strategy" to keep him at her house and entice him has an intricacy to it. (A) may be an attractive distracter, but we are told nothing of the woman's background up to this point, and she doesn't mention maternal instinct until lines 18–20.

**50. (D)** The character Jude is getting in deep. He has just asked the woman in line 17 why she is incubating the egg. After she gives a reason, he expresses his feelings of awkwardness. It is possible that this statement is in reference to her explanation: Perhaps he just does not get what she means. Item I therefore is allowable.

Furthermore, this moment clearly reveals itself as one of romantic tension when she offers him her cheek to kiss and says, "… that's all you can have of me" (lines 23–24). His commenting "That's very shabby of you!" two lines later shows that, even though her coyness prevents it for now, he has been wanting a more intimate kiss. The awkwardness he previously has expressed may have been in reference to this desire. After all, he brings it up when she admits to having maternal desires. Perhaps he feels awkward about interpreting a certain kind of romantic signal from her. So, item III has some support.

Then, there are also grounds for item IV. We know that Jude wants a kiss, but the egg is setting up a supposed barrier between the two of them. Expressing his awkwardness could be a reference to his frustration.

The item that does not work is II. It must be true that he wants enough acceptance from the woman to get a kiss, but this can be rather a superficial kind of approval. To say that Jude wants unequivocal acceptance from her is assuming too much.

**51. (B)** The woman is teasing Jude, who is expecting something more than a kiss on the cheek, given her flirtatious behavior (including unfastening her gown collar). When she turns her back on him and offers only a cheek for him to kiss, she is feigning coolness in response to his desires.

**52. (C)** The woman alternately removes and replaces the egg, thereby alternating her state of accessibility to Jude. Whenever he may think it's safe to advance, she replaces the fragile egg in her gown, forcing him to wait in anticipation for his next opportunity for intimacy.

**53. (E)** Jude has just stuck his hand in her cleavage, an intimate gesture. The fact that the woman isn't stopping him suggests that she has hoped for this action. They have just crossed a line and now know that more overt behavior is mutually acceptable: hence, the flushed faces.

**54. (D)** Jude and the woman are obviously experiencing mutual sexual attraction, but Jude declares his intent to leave in lines 40–41. When the woman hears this, she races upstairs with an implied invitation for him to follow.

**55. (E)** The narrator lets us know in lines 34–35 that the woman is scheming. Jude, however, is unaware of her designs. For all he knows, what is happening between them is a spontaneous occurrence. While Jude is unfamiliar with his surroundings in the dark room, the woman seems to know exactly where she is going.

**56. (A)** The addressee's "eyes" are the image that threads through this poem. The eyes "Draw round" with him and "sing … a circle of sparks" (lines 2–3). They also "Hold untold tales" with him (line 5). They have already had these effects, but he wants always to be able to "hold" the eyes, the lips, the "hillside smile," and the "seashore laughter" (lines 7–9) of the addressee in his mind to make life more bearable when he stands "alone" (line 11).

**57. (B)** Since a pause is a break in continuity, this option does not work.

**58. (E)** Strangely, this "I" *conspires* with the addressee's eyes to shake the speaker's soul, as if the "I" is doing something that his own soul would not be aware of. Perhaps this is a statement of reluctance or obstinacy: Some part of the speaker knows that a shaken soul is good, but the soul does not want to be shaken.

**59. (D)** The addressee's effect is profound because her smile and laughter are a part of, or encompass, large areas: the hillside and the seashore. Yet it is also an elusive effect, because her image has no guaranteed longevity. The speaker says that "If" he "could hold" her image with him, then he could face the loneliness of life better.

**60. (A)** If he can hold the addressee's image in his mind (stanza 2), then he can better handle being alone in the world and bearing "the pain/Of flesh" and "the time and space/And steel" alone.

**61. (E)** The hypothetical situation that the speaker begins in line 7 implies that the addressee's influence on him may not be permanent. The *but* of "but I am shaken," however, provides a contrast: He is saying that her image is affecting him now. In fact, he is referring to a previous idea in lines 4–6.

**62. (A)** The stone is "this stone": something the speaker has previously mentioned. He says that the addressee has "moved" it, and the most immediate movement in relation to this image is the speaker's being shaken. Furthermore, since the addressee has caused the movement in both images, (A) has more support.

**63. (C)** Several of the gaps occur in the last stanza, where the speaker describes himself as "alone." Since he has hinted that the addressee's influence on him may not be a lasting thing, he may still be concerned with his loneliness. Certainly, the gaps are appropriate for symbolizing loneliness, as they isolate the words from each other.

# Resources: **Authors and Works Used in the Practice Tests**

## Chapter 2

p. 11—Ralph Waldo Emerson: "The Rhodora"

p. 12—Benjamin Franklin: from "Rattle-Snakes for Felons"

p. 13—John Milton: from "On Time"

p. 13—Frederick Douglas: from *Narrative of the Life of Frederick Douglass, an American Slave*

p. 14—Percy Bysshe Shelley: from "Mutability"

p. 14—William Shakespeare: Sonnet #29

p. 15—Phillis Wheatley: from "On Imagination"

p. 15–16—Elizabeth Barrett Browning: from *Sonnets from the Portuguese*

p. 17—Percy Bysshe Shelley: "Ozymandias"

## Diagnostic Test

p. 31—Marge Piercy: "To Be of Use"

p. 33—Henry David Thoreau: from *Walden*

p. 35—Tim O'Brien: from *Ambush*

p. 37—John Dryden: from "All for Love"

p. 39—Emily Brontë: "Remembrance"

## Practice Test I

p. 125—Emily Dickinson: "Hope Is the Thing with Feathers"

p. 128—Francis Bacon: "On Revenge"

p. 131—John Keats: "Written in Answer to a Sonnet Ending Thus:—"

p. 133—Thomas Hardy: from *The Mayor of Casterbridge*

p. 136—Phillis Wheatley: from "On Imagination"

p. 140—Louis Simpson: "The Boarder"

pp. 142–143—Oliver Goldsmith: from *She Stoops to Conquer*

## Practice Test 2

## Practice Test 3

## Practice Test 4

## Practice Test 5

## Practice Test 6

p. 269—Edgar Allan Poe: from "To Helen"
p. 271—Olaudah Equiano: from *The Interesting Narrative of the Life of Olaudah Equiano*
p. 274—Lord Byron: from *Don Juan*
pp. 277–278—Anne Radcliffe: from *The Italian*
p. 281—Samuel Daniel: Sonnet 3 from *Beauty, Time, and Love*
p. 283—Percy B. Shelley: "Mutability"
p. 285—Peter Shaffer: from *Amadeus*

## Practice Test 7

p. 297—Edgar Allan Poe: "To One in Paradise"
p. 299—Thomas Hardy: from *Tess of the D'Urbervilles*
p. 301—John Milton: "On Time"
p. 303—Tobias Smollett: from *Humphrey Clinker*
pp. 305–306—Leigh Hunt: "The Fish, the Man, and the Spirit"
p. 309—Nadine Gordimer: from "The Train from Rhodesia"
p. 312—George M. Horton: "The Creditor to His Proud Debtor"

## Practice Test 8

pp. 323–324—Kate Chopin: from "A Pair of Silk Stockings"
p. 326—Lord Byron: "Stanzas Written on the Road Between Florence and Pisa"
p. 328—Bram Stoker: from *Dracula*
p. 331—Elizabeth Barrett Browning: Sonnet 12 from *Sonnets from the Portuguese*
p. 333—Samuel Richardson: from *Pamela*
p. 336—Thomas Hardy: from *Jude the Obscure*
p. 339—Etheridge Knight: "I and Your Eyes"

# NOTES

# NOTES

# NOTES

# NOTES

# NOTES

# NOTES

# NOTES

KAPLAN

# NOTES

# NOTES

# NOTES